UNSEEN LONDON

Written by Rachel Segal Hamilton

UNSEEN LONDON

The city through the eyes of contemporary photographers

HOXTON MINI PRESS

Rachel Segal Hamilton

Rachel Segal Hamilton is a London-based freelance journalist who has written extensively on photography for *The British Journal of Photography*, *VICE*, *The Telegraph*, *The Royal Photographic Society Journal*, *Professional Photography* and others. A champion of emerging talent, she has worked for the Barbican, Photoworks and IdeasTap to mentor and support young photographers. She was raised in North London but defected to the south of the city in 2012, where she now lives with her boyfriend and daughter. Her favourite hidden place in London is Myatt's Fields Park.

Hoxton Mini Press

Hoxton Mini Press is a small but award-winning independent publisher based in East London. We make collectable photography books about London, working with the best local photographers, either well known or emerging. We believe that books are precious objects and as the world goes online they need to be given a special place on neatly organised shelves. Hoxton Mini Press was started by Ann and Martin, and their two dogs, Moose and Bug. Thanks for supporting us.

Contents

Introduction

There's a feeling you get when you've been away from London. Maybe you've just nipped to the seaside for a few nights or maybe you've spent months on another continent, but when you step out onto those familiarly scuzzy pavements, you get this thrill. You're back. "London is every city that ever was and ever will be," journalist Stephen Graham wrote in his 1925 book, *London Nights*, and it really does feel like that, when you're in this endlessly eclectic 2000-year-old metropolis, home to nearly nine million people who speak 300 different languages. Not even the most dedicated Londoner can see everything that the city has to offer, but the sense that it's all out there somewhere within the confines of the M25 is intoxicating.

And yet so much of how we view this city comes not from tramping its streets but from looking at images of them. Certainly, earlier visual depictions of London – the unruly squalor of Hogarth's *Gin Lane* or Turner's dreamy Thames – feed in but it's since the birth of photography that our idea of London as a modern metropolis has truly taken shape. That London encompasses the tourist's tick list of Buckingham Palace and Tate Modern, red buses and black cabs, sights and symbols captured for posterity on postcards or holiday snaps. It's the London of Richard Curtis movies, in which everyone has clean, floppy hair and lives in smart Georgian houses. It's the London of art, high fashion and street style. But it's also a London where some are struggling, feeding their kids at food banks, taking the night bus at dawn to work. "Like a well-cut gem London has a thousand facets and in all of them is a picture", wrote E. O. Hoppé in *The Image of London* (1935).

This image has been centuries in the making. The oldest surviving photograph of London, taken in autumn 1839, shows a street near Trafalgar Square. London looks like a still, silent place. Back then exposure times were protracted and it was impossible to show people in motion with a daguerreotype, which captured images using mercury on a silvered copper plate. There's none of the energy that we now associate with London and will see some 150 years later in street photography. In fact, there aren't many photographs of early 19th century London because the daguerreotype (along with another process, the calotype, pioneered in Britain by William Henry Fox Talbot) was patented, and licences were expensive.

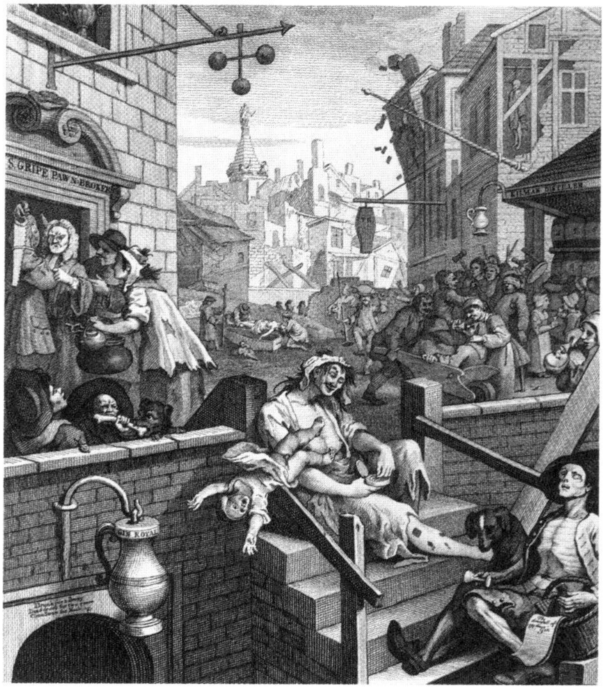

A drunk mother drops her child amid the gin-fuelled chaos of 18th-century London slums. William Hogarth, *Gin Lane*, 1751

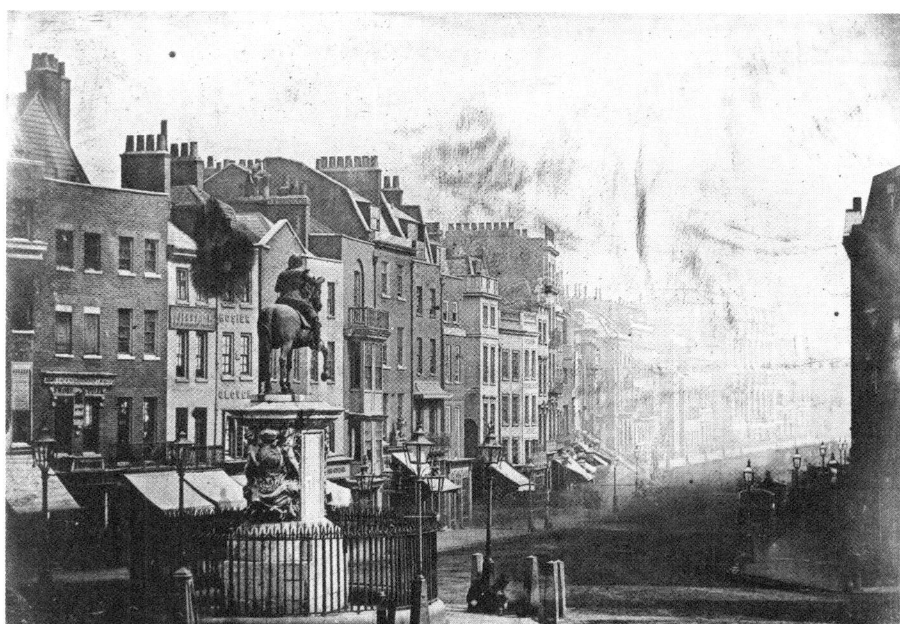

The earliest surviving photograph of London shows Whitehall, the road running from Trafalgar Square to Parliament. Monsieur de Sainte-Croix, 1839

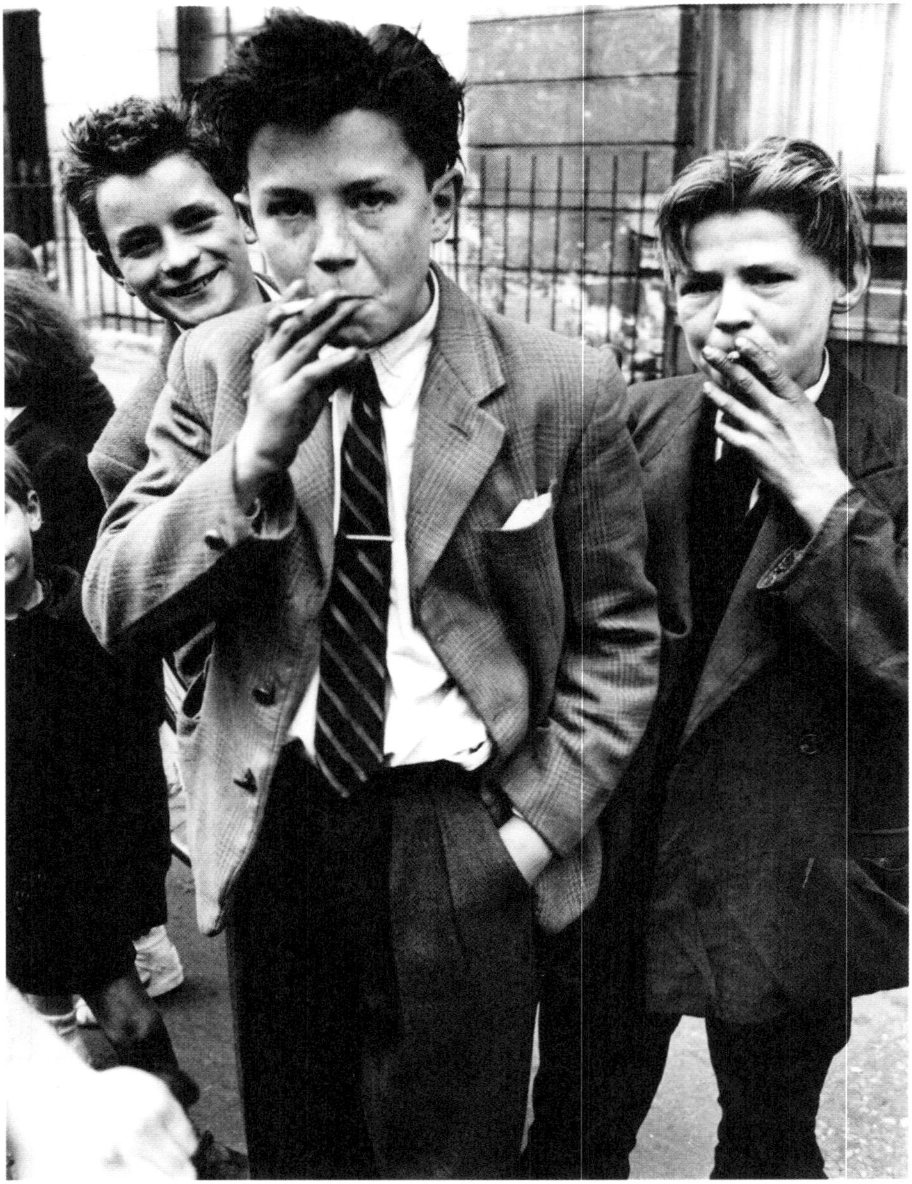

Teenage boys loiter on Portland Road smoking cigarettes in post-war North Kensington. Roger Mayne, 1956

As cheaper processes were developed, interest in photographing the city grew. By the 1860s, photographers could freeze movement and the London Stereoscopic Company did a roaring trade selling stereo views of the city which, when seen through special glasses, amounted to a sort of Victorian virtual reality. Meanwhile, well-to-do types took their families to photographic studios to stand stock-still for portraits. Alongside this explosion in popular photography among the wealthy, documentarians such as John Thomson used cameras to record the lives of ordinary folk, soldiers, river workers and market traders. The hand-held camera brought new possibilities. In the 1890s, Paul Martin became the first candid photographer as he wandered around some of the poorest areas of London with his camera disguised as a package, unnoticed by the street urchins and beggars immortalised in his pictures.

Over the 20th century, London changed dramatically. It was a period that saw two world wars and a huge influx of people: refugees from the former Austro-Hungarian empire and Nazi Germany, and, later, immigrants from ex-British colonies. Many of the most enduring representations of London life from this period are by photographers born abroad, including Wolfgang Suschitzky, Bill Brandt and

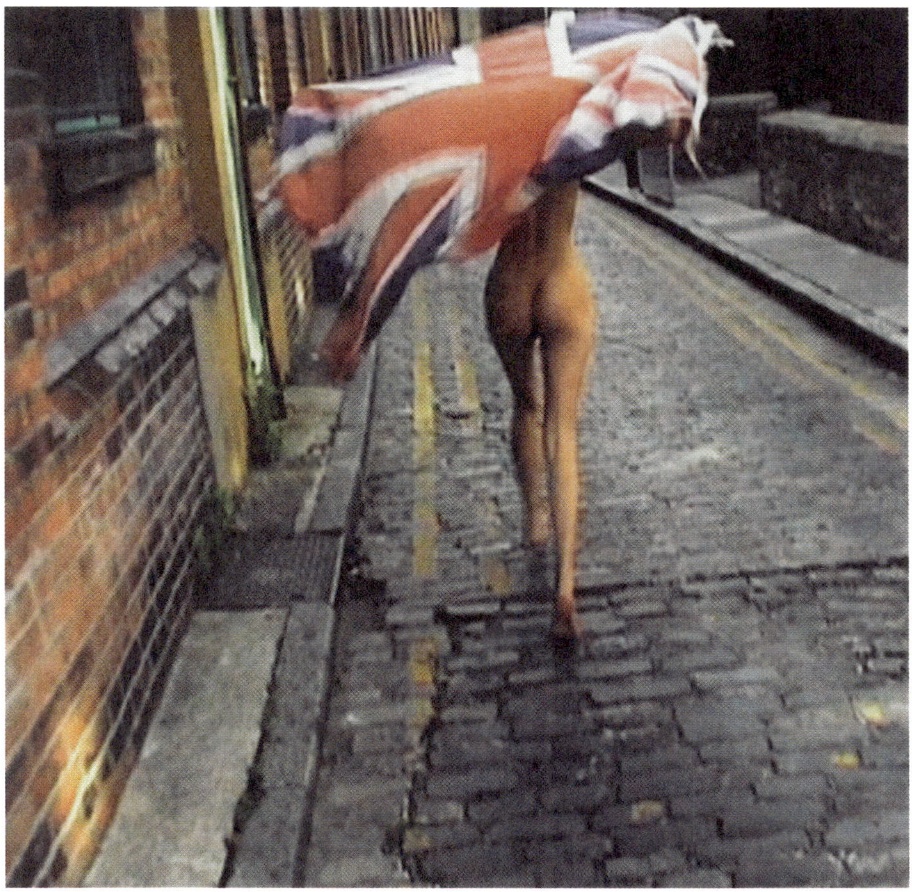

Young British Artist Tracey Emin races naked through the cobbled streets of East London (video still). Tracey Emin, *Running Naked*, 2000

Dennis Morris. Through their lenses, certain archetypal figures – workers at rush hour, bobbies on the beat, pearly kings, punks – came to the fore but they also shined a light on London as experienced by members of newly-arrived communities, whether from Europe or the Caribbean.

London arose from the Blitz bruised but hopeful. An intense programme of rebuilding followed, which broke down geographical barriers by constructing council housing in spaces left by bombs, interweaving social classes. The sparky resilience of the post-war city comes through in the work of humanist photographers like Roger Mayne, who documented lively street scenes in destitute slums, later replaced by modernist estates. In the 1960s, Swinging London emerged, a centre of fashion, music and celebrity. Carnaby Street rocked with hip, young baby boomers, all flowing locks and rainbow clothes, and iconic portraits from this time – of Twiggy, The Rolling Stones, Michael Caine, the Kray twins – have become synonymous with the city.

Since then, the visage London presents to the world has alternated between creative, tolerant, carefree optimism and something edgier, more discordant. London is police dancing goofily at the Notting Hill Carnival, and it's young people dragged through the streets during the 1981 Brixton riots. It's Tracey Emin running naked and jubilant down the East End's cobbled streets, a Union Jack flag billowing behind her like a cape, and it's the wreckage of the double decker bus blown up in the 7/7 bombings. There are more CCTV cameras than ever before but since those attacks it's been harder for photographers to work in the street, leading some to start a campaign under the banner "I'm a Photographer, Not a Terrorist". In a sense there are two Londons: an official, almost mythical London and another unsanctioned version that reflects the lived experience. Today that manifests in Instagrammed snaps of foxes, kebabs and secret raves in abandoned warehouses. When London's already-heaving photographic archive is coupled with a smartphone in the hand of virtually every inhabitant, every visitor, it can feel like there's nothing left to see.

But there is. And it's those hidden sides to the city that interest the photographers featured here. Shot between the 90s and the present day, the projects in this book are an alternative guided tour of the capital. Some give us privileged access to worlds that most can't enter: empty Olympic stadiums before the Games, the front rooms of fancy Barbican flats or backstage at grime gigs. Others draw attention to how the city appears at particular times of day or year: late at night or during the Jewish festival of Purim. Elsewhere, familiar subjects like skyscrapers, the Queen's Guard or Hampstead Heath are shown in new ways. We normally navigate the city at eye level but here we perceive it from unusual vantage points – looking into the top deck of buses, over the edge of tower blocks, straight down at the floor or miles beneath it. We're invited to observe things we might not normally consider worthy of our attention: litter, low-flying planes, even chewing gum.

Throughout, we're reminded of the power that photography has to make us pause and think. We're also reminded of the breathtaking variety of London, a place where by dint of location the lives of Harrods' shoppers, boho boaters, city suits

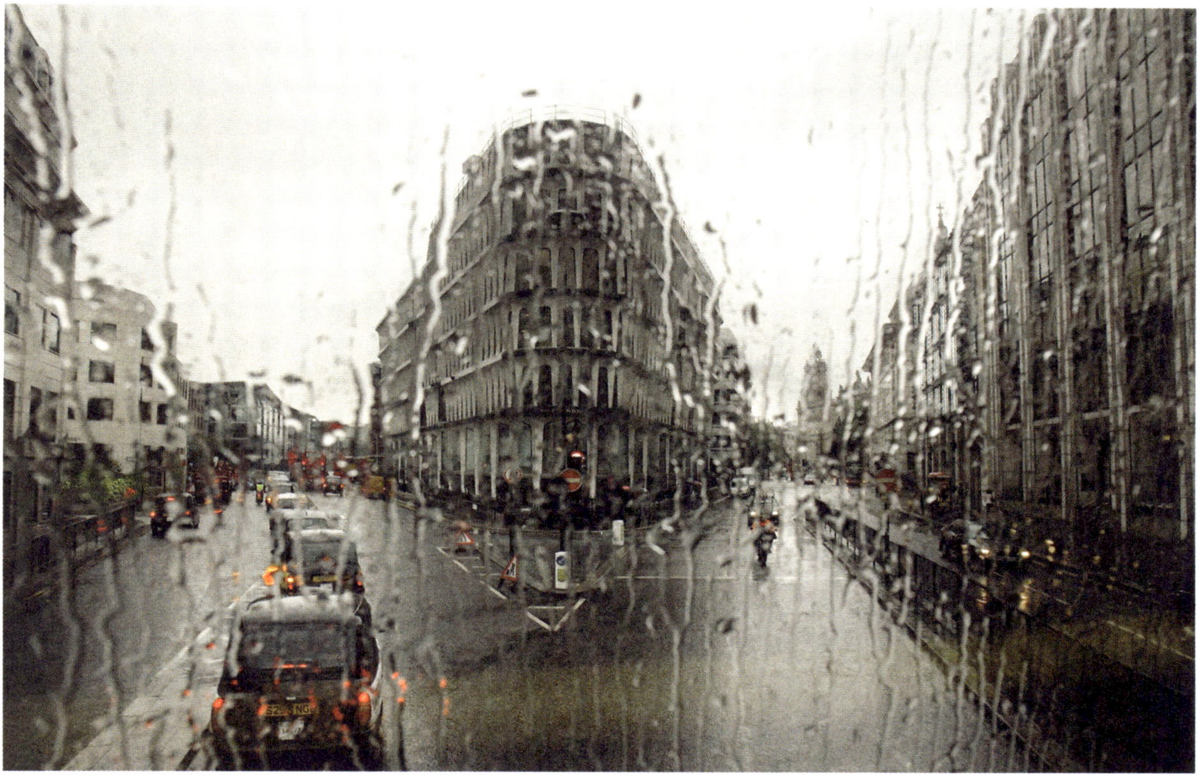

London black cabs viewed through the rain-spattered windows of a double decker bus. From the series *Last Stop* by George Georgiou

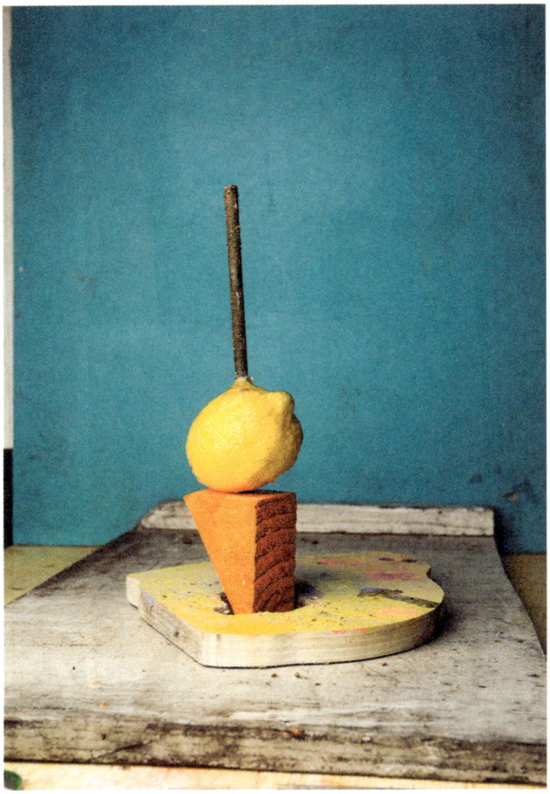

Market-bought fruit teeters on a chunk of salvaged wood in one of Lorenzo Vitturi's sculptures. From the series *Dalston Anatomy* by Lorenzo Vitturi

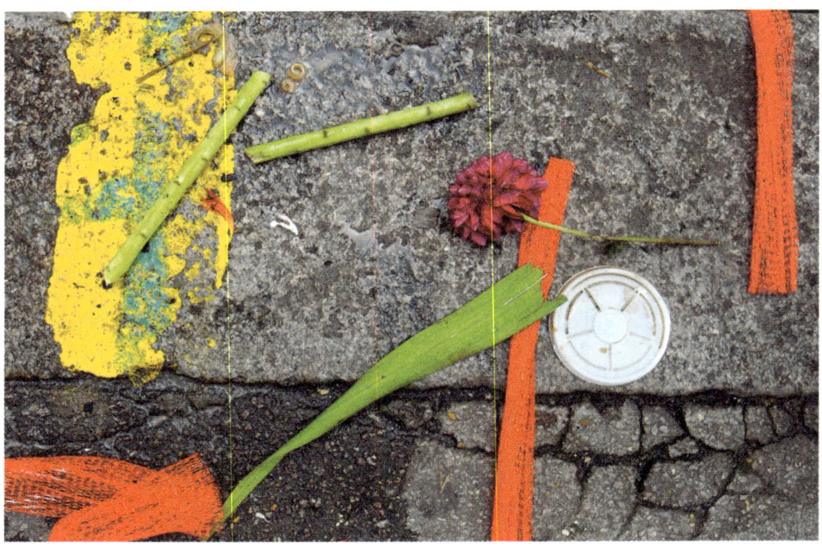

Plant stalks, a flower and plastic scraps scattered across the pavement of Columbia Road. From the series *Columbia Road* by Johanna Neurath

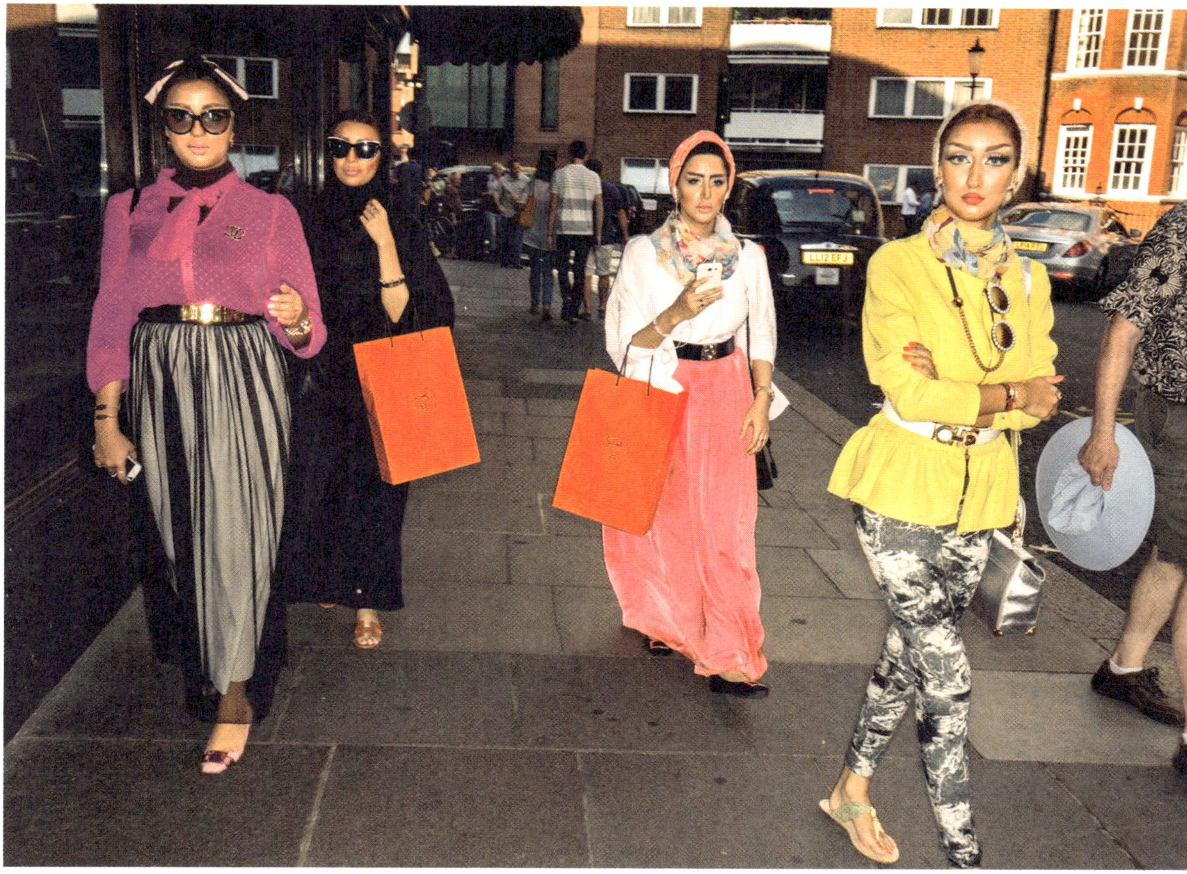

Wealthy shoppers stare suspiciously down the lens at photographer Dougie Wallace. From the series *Harrodsburg* by Dougie Wallace

and tracksuited youths converge, although they may never meet. Each area feels like its own village – and, indeed, some once were, swallowed up by the city's sprawl. "There is in London all that life can afford," goes the lesser-known second half of Samuel Johnson's famous quote. Hardly any of these photographers were born within earshot of Bow Bells. Several are among the 37% of London residents born outside the UK. When I was interviewing photographers for this book, many expressed concern that the exceptional diversity that's such a big part of London's character is under threat – a worry that plays out in their work. Lewis Bush explores how London's skyline has been altered by high rise developments, often sold overseas as investment flats, while Lorenzo Vitturi's work highlights how rapid gentrification is changing the face of Dalston. London is one of the most expensive cities in the world and a dire lack of social and affordable housing is pushing younger, poorer Londoners out to cheaper towns.

All of which has led some to talk pessimistically of the city's demise. Iain Sinclair calls it "endgame London". But when we scrape back London's layers, as Simon Norfolk does in *Under London*, we're reminded that this has always been a place of change, of destruction and renewal. The Plague, the Great Fire of London, the Blitz; London has emerged from each catastrophe to flourish anew. What might future London look like? Who can say? I prefer to think of London not as Hoppé's gem – well-crafted, glitzy – but in the terms that Andy Sewell describes it when discussing his series, *The Heath*: more like a forest – a wild, dense, opaque but strangely harmonious organism. "I wonder if anyone could succeed in photographing London?" asked photographer Bill Brandt in 1948, before concluding that, "London is something too complex to be caught within a set of views or by any one photographer." Perhaps that's because there is no single London but many – one for each pair of eyes that behold it. You'll never see them all, but this is a good place to start.

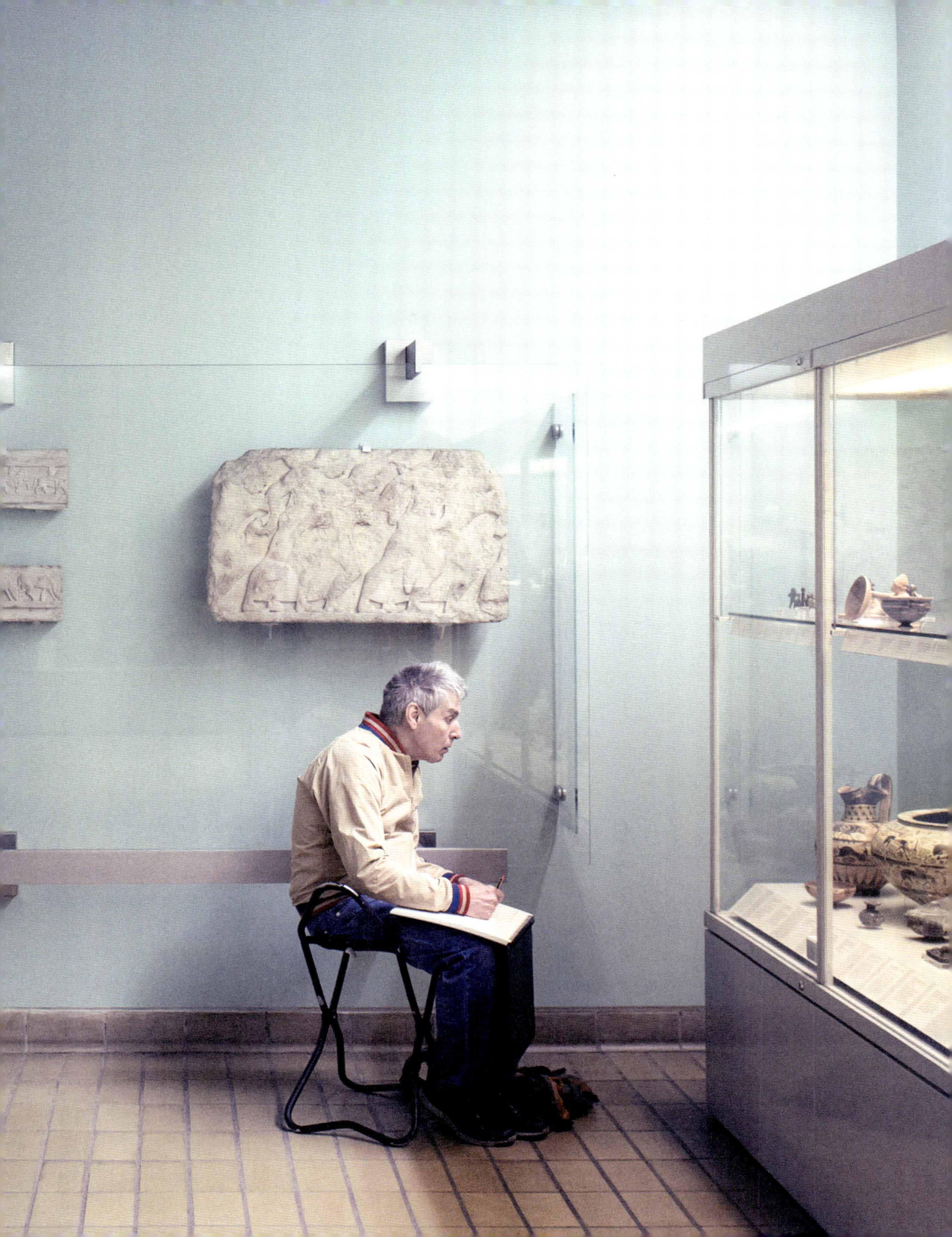

The Heath

Evocative shots of Hampstead Heath probe the paradoxical charm of a green space that's been manufactured to feel like wilderness.

Andy Sewell

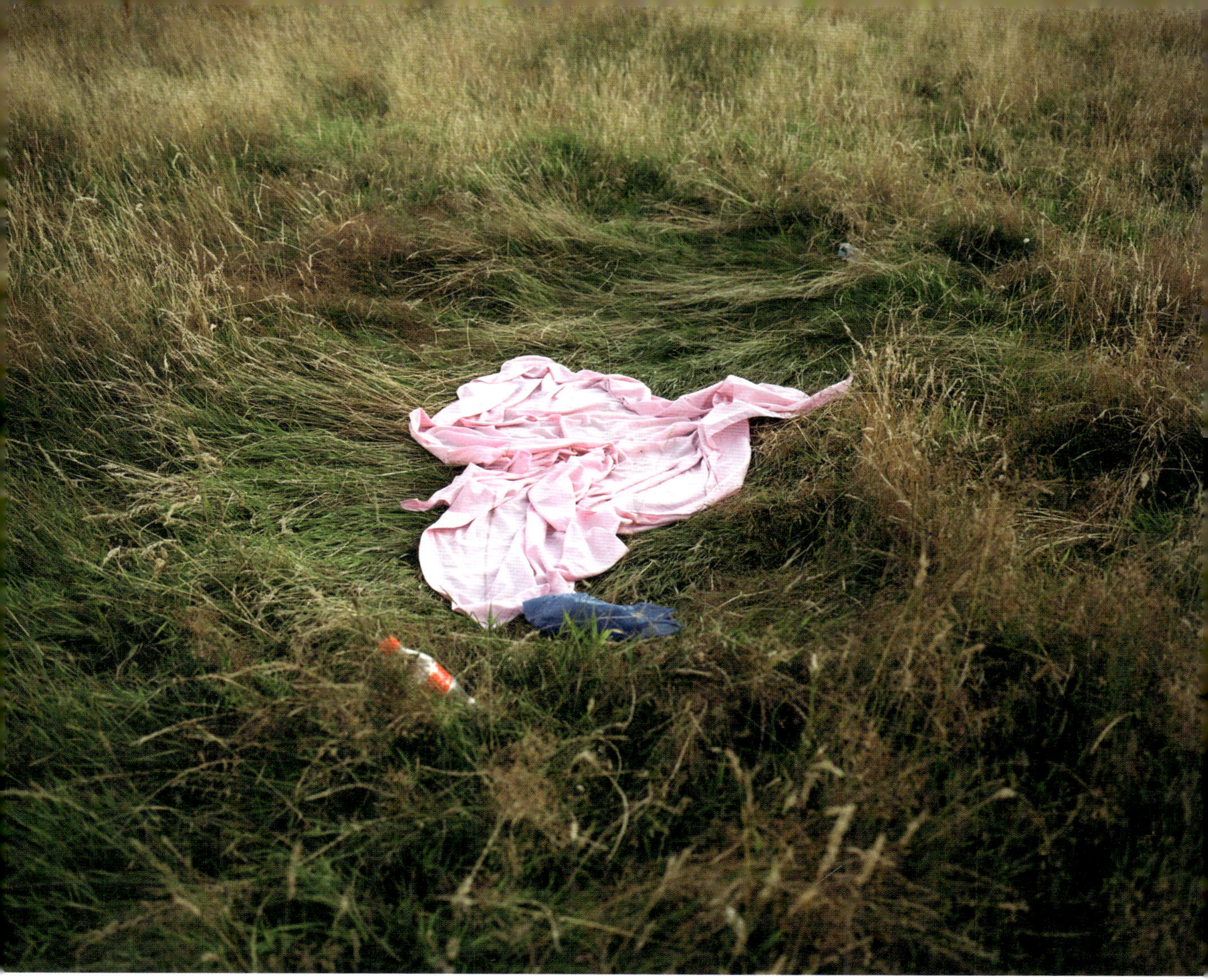

Ask a Londoner to name their favourite spot in the capital and they'll often choose somewhere that doesn't actually feel like it's in London. Hampstead Heath is a prime example. And yet the Heath's particular charm depends entirely on knowing that you *are* in the city. That once you trudge to the summit of that hill, you'll be rewarded with a panorama of London landmarks.

The Heath is "a paradox of managed wildness", says photographer Andy Sewell. "The look which we think of as being natural has to be laboriously maintained otherwise it would become overrun with scrub." We see nature and culture as opposing categories but in most cases they "bleed into each other", Sewell adds, and nowhere more so than on the Heath. Pathways through the thicket, benches, long grass where tangled lovers hide, "everywhere you look there are signs of the way this landscape has been created to facilitate a certain idea of what we're looking for".

It was in the 19th century that Hampstead Heath first captured the imagination of artists and thinkers. In *Ode to a Nightingale*, Romantic poet John Keats praised, "The grass, the thicket, and the fruit-tree wild", while painter John Constable rendered its sweeping landscapes and swirling clouds in lush oils. Today's Heath may be a very different place – the grazing cattle have been replaced by lawnmowers – but still that bucolic fantasy persists.

In a similar vein, conventional landscape photography presents nature as an escape, humbling in its majesty and scale. Contemporary urban photography, meanwhile, often finds magic in banal, non-spaces like car parks. Sewell's pictures work both with and against the idealised vision of the Heath, delicately teasing out evidence of cultivation.

Five years in the making, *The Heath* was Sewell's first major personal project, followed by *Something Like a Nest*, which also explores the constructed quality of rural life, this time looking at the English countryside. For Sewell, photography is about "trying to hold together things which can't be reconciled", he says. "The more you look at the world, the more you realise that there are things that don't make sense, where two things are both true and yet contradictory." These are the moments that Sewell tries to capture, moments where you suddenly have "a sense of heightened lucidity but at the same time a sense of heightened mystery".

Ultimately Sewell concluded that just as Hampstead Heath isn't as natural as we might think, London as a city is more so. "There are so many different layers of life happening in the same place, interrelating with each other, existing alongside and working against each other." Here, when the "murmurous haunt of flies", as Keats put it, briefly drowns out the roar of the traffic, you appreciate how the city teems with vitality.

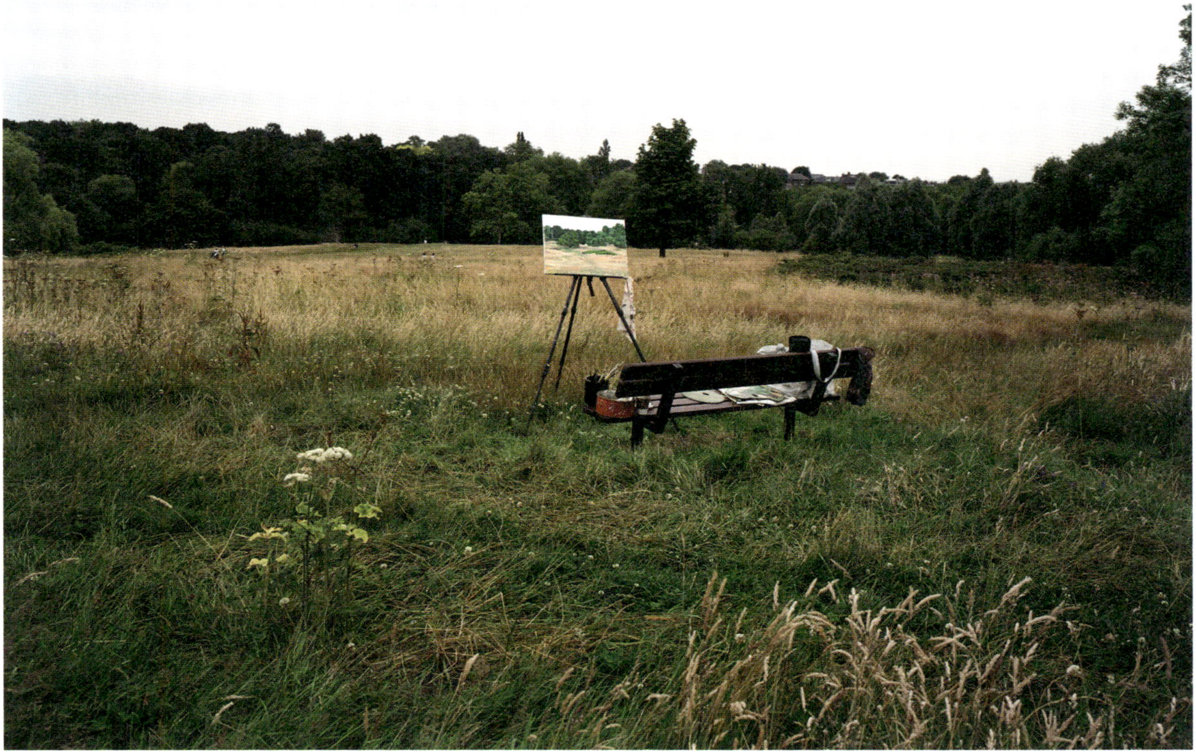

Previous: Untitled 34, Hampstead Heath, 2007
Above: Untitled 33, Hampstead Heath, 2007

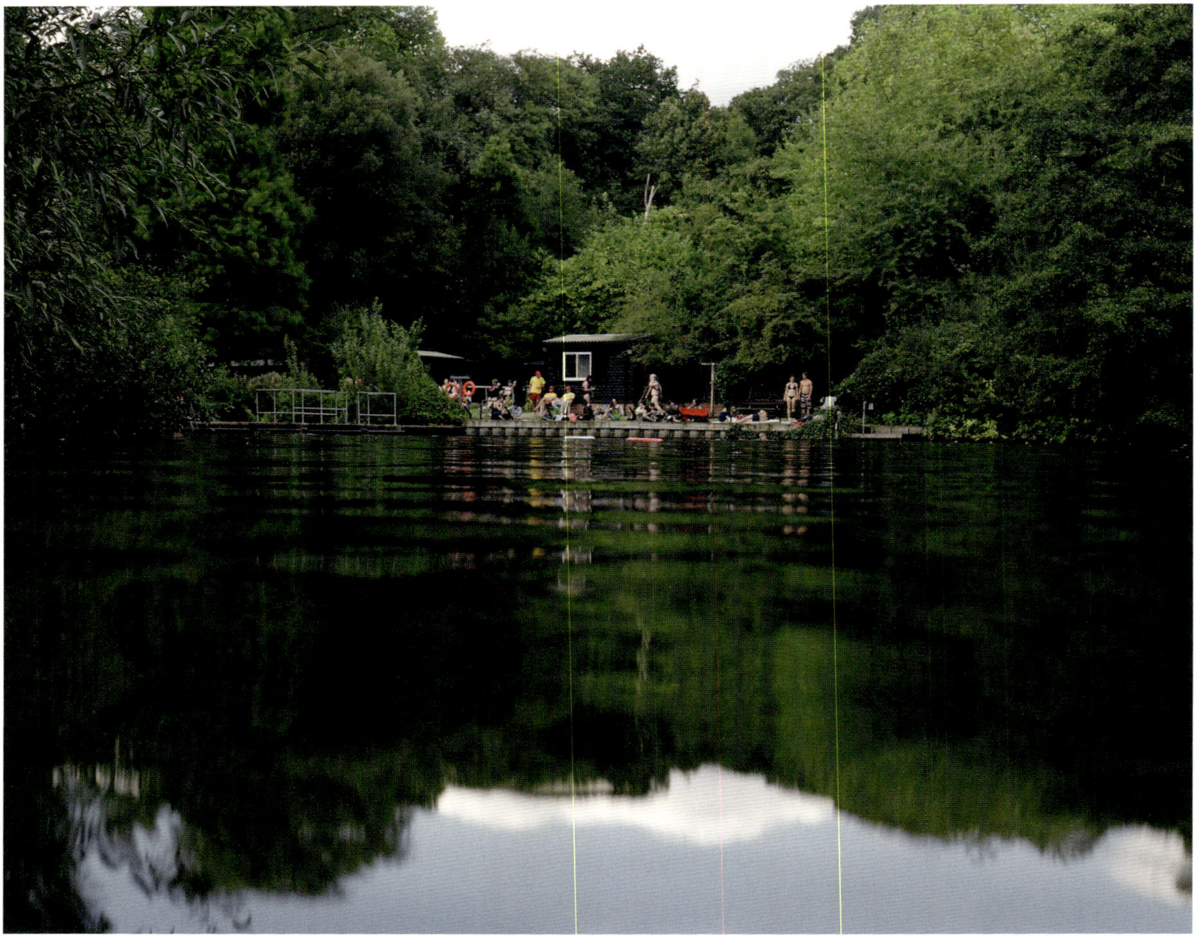

Untitled 26, Hampstead Heath, 2009

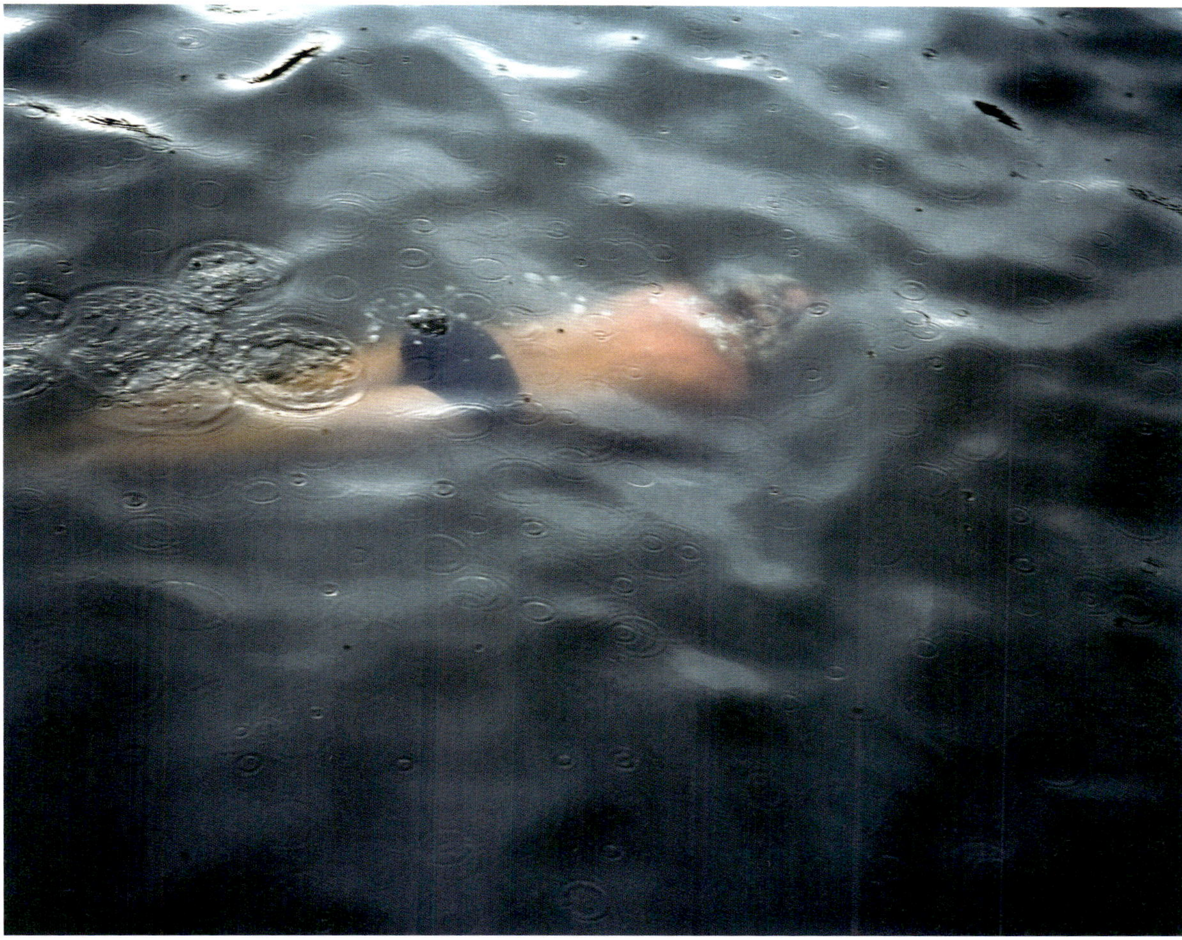

 Untitled 12, Hampstead Heath, 2009 Andy Sewell

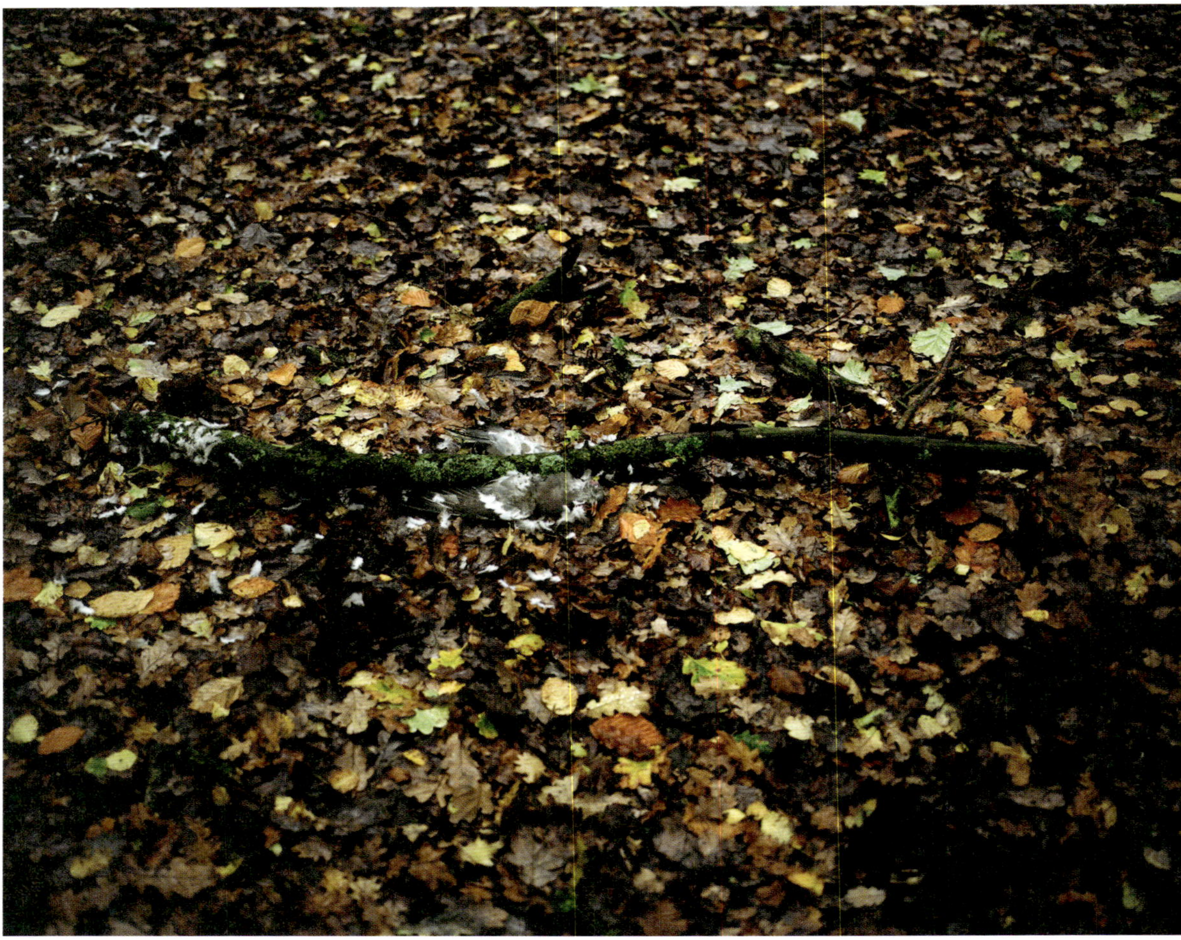

Untitled 14, Hampstead Heath, 2009

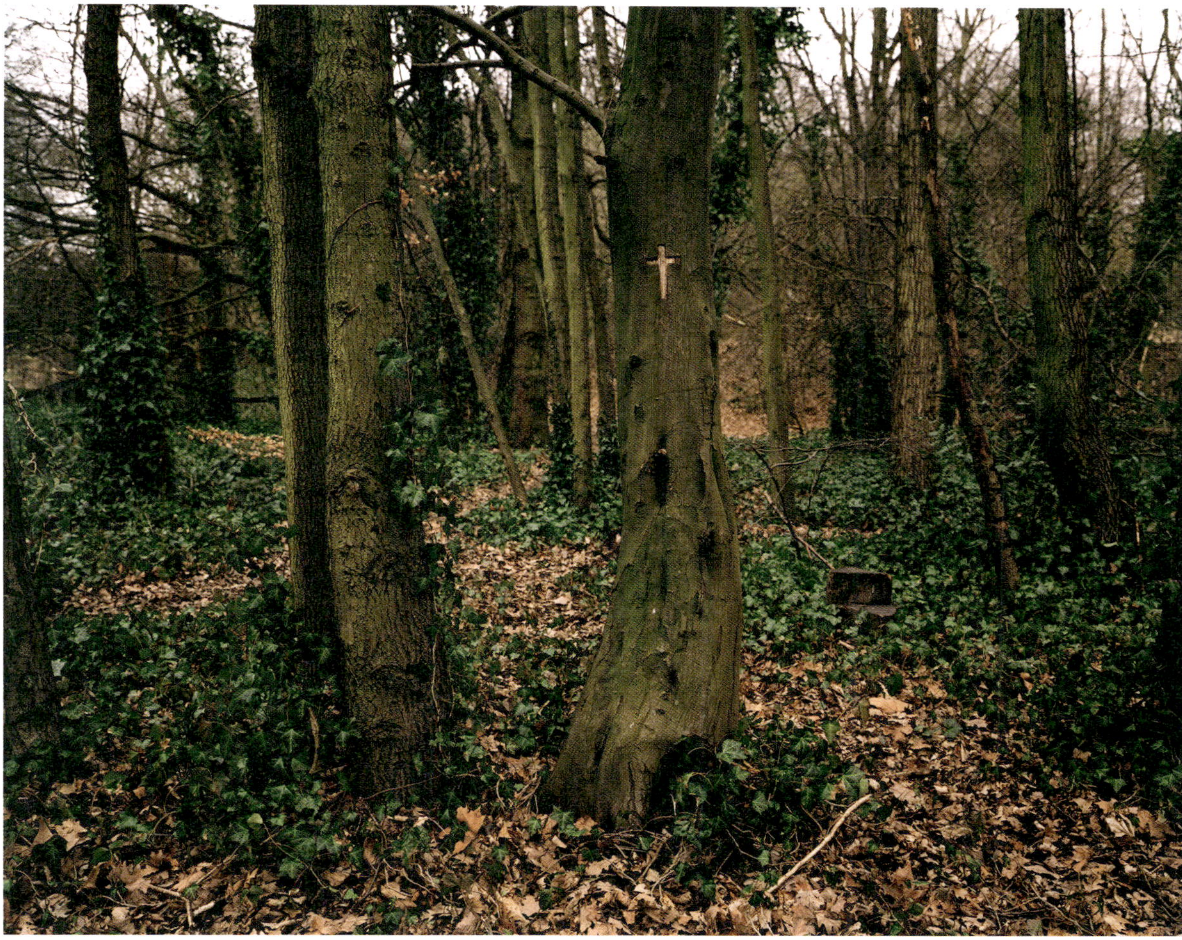

Untitled 19, Hampstead Heath, 2009

Overleaf: Untitled 39, Hampstead Heath, 2009

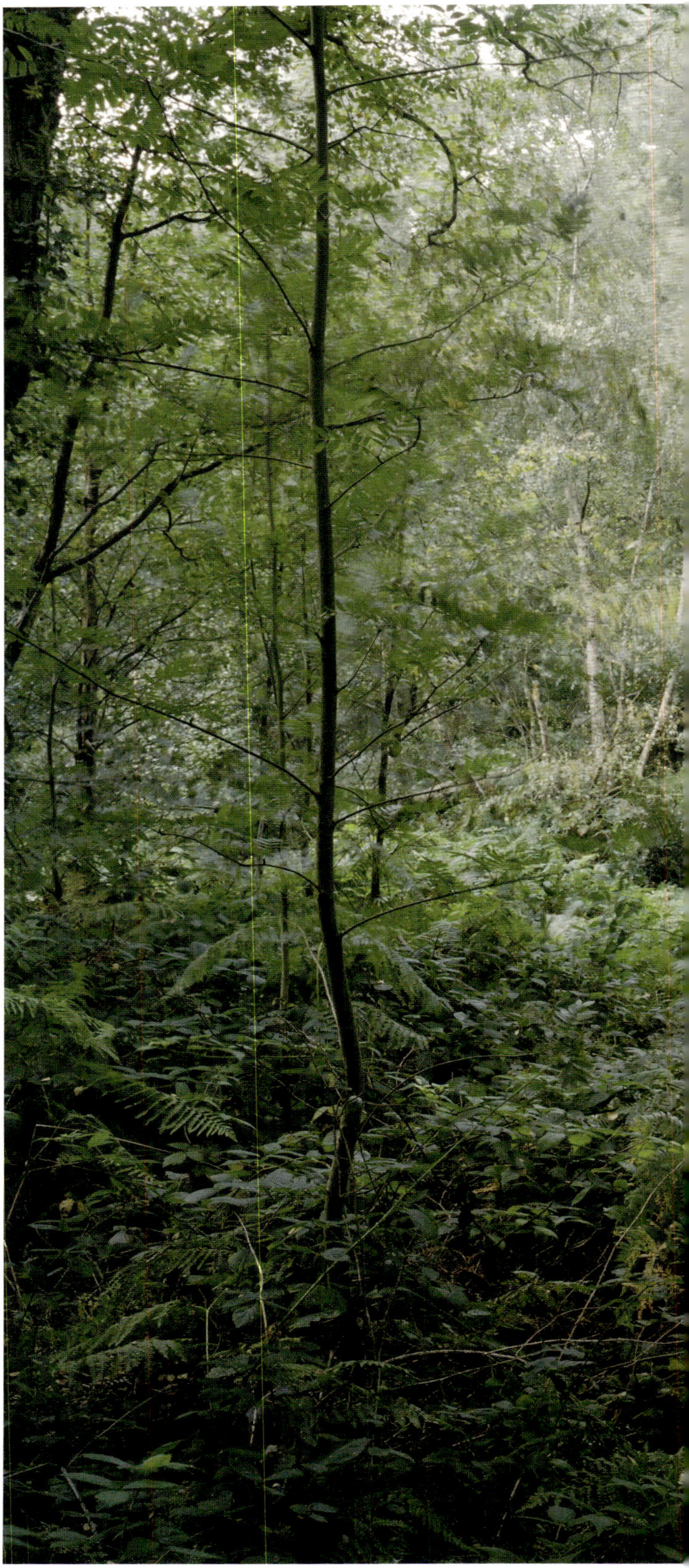

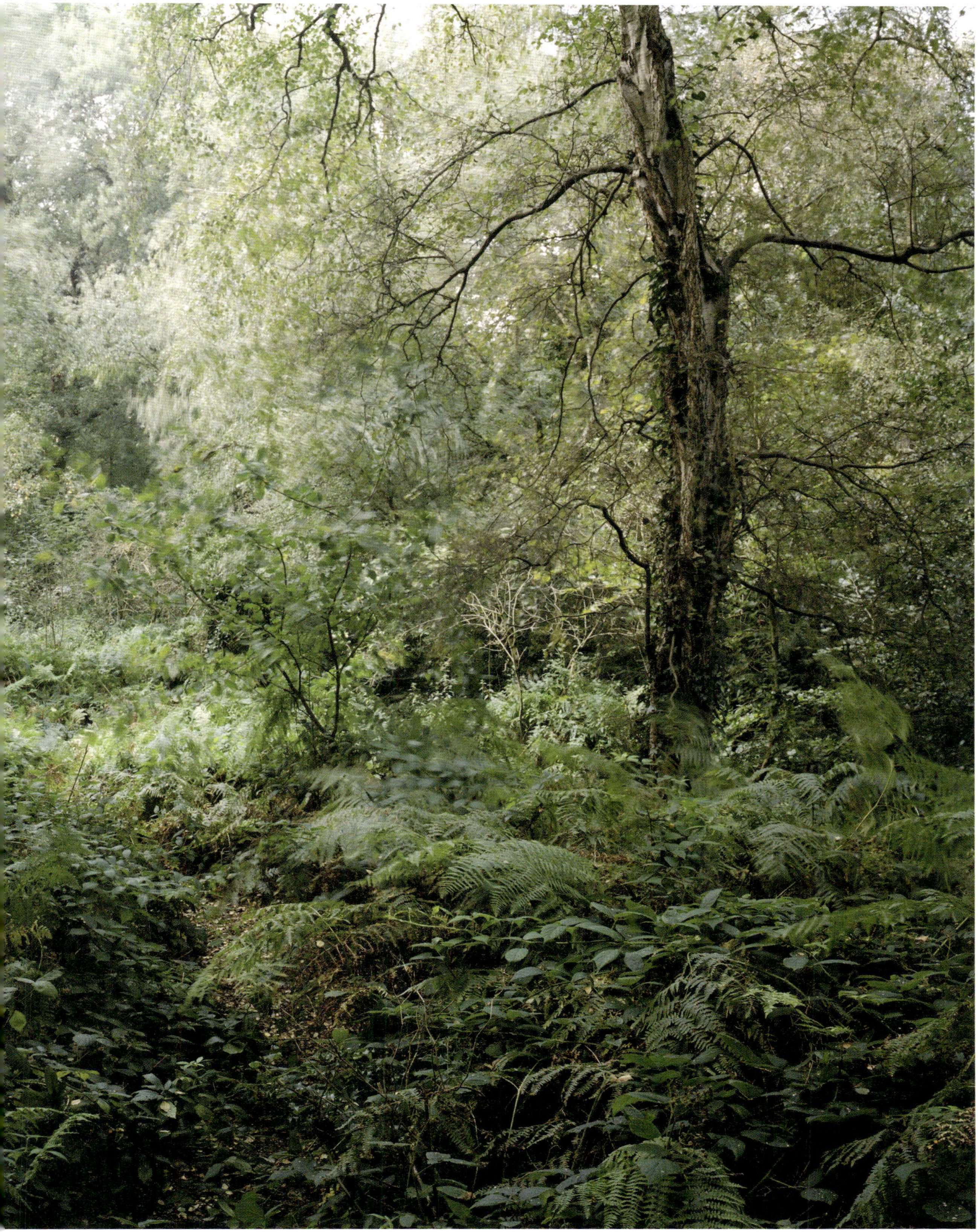

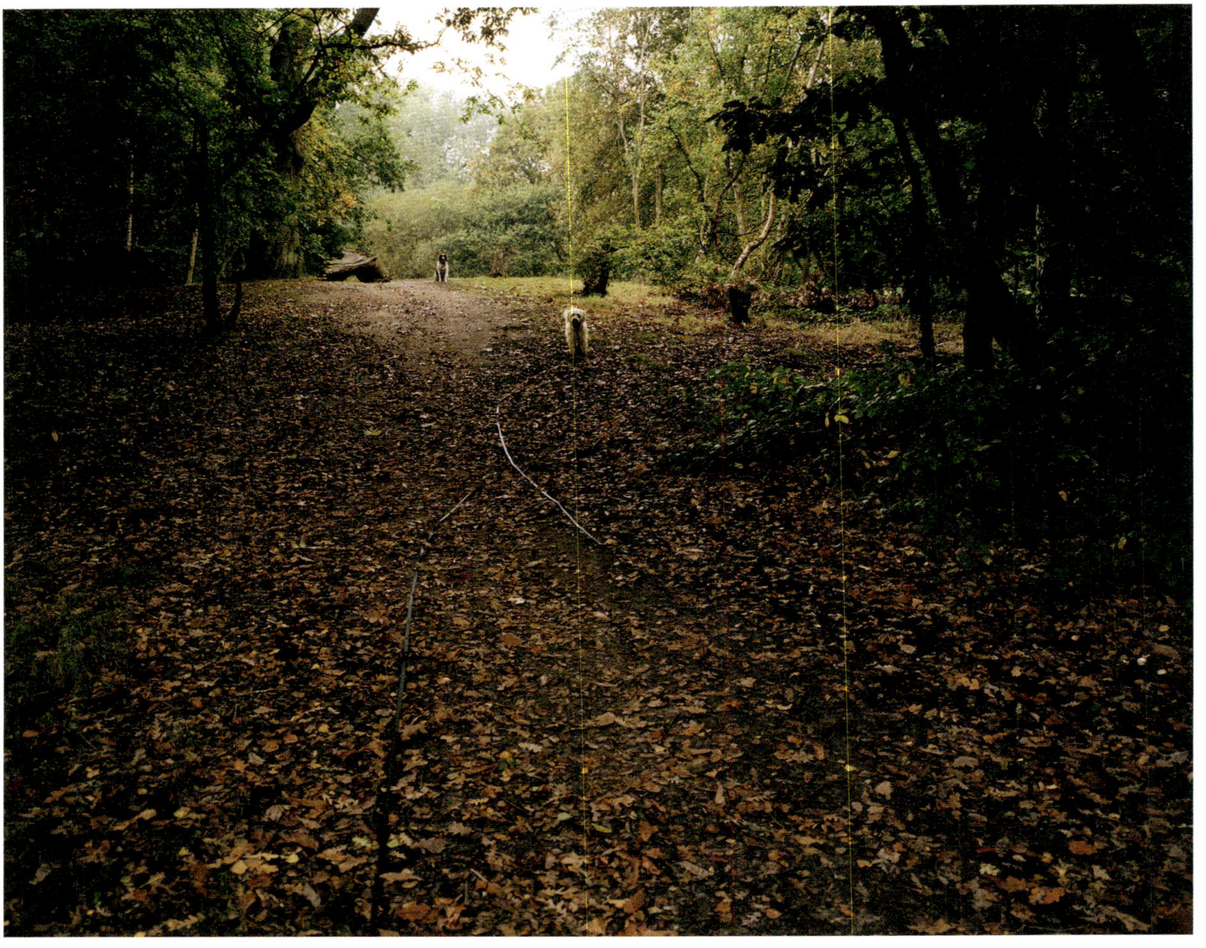

Untitled 05, Hampstead Heath, 2009

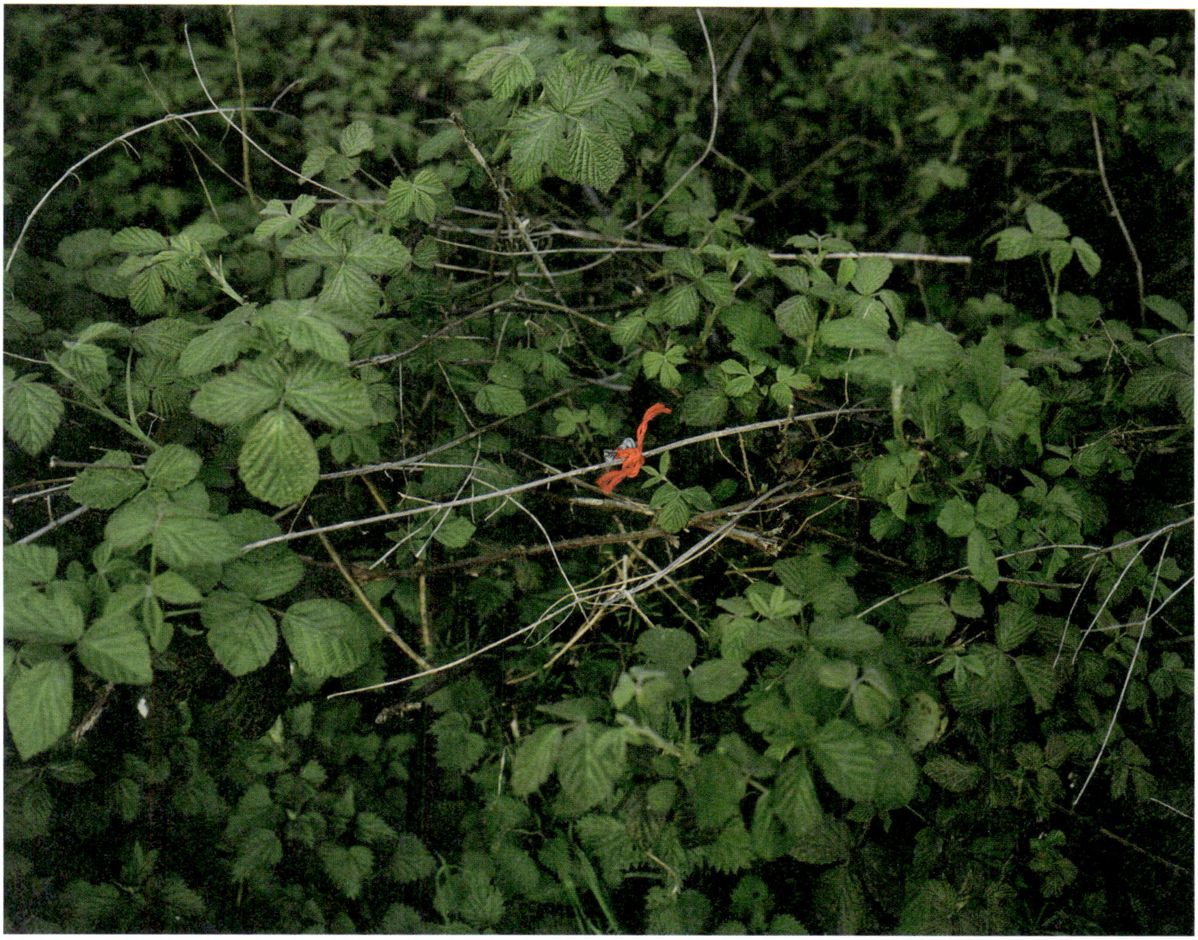

 Untitled 28, Hampstead Heath, 2009 Andy Sewell

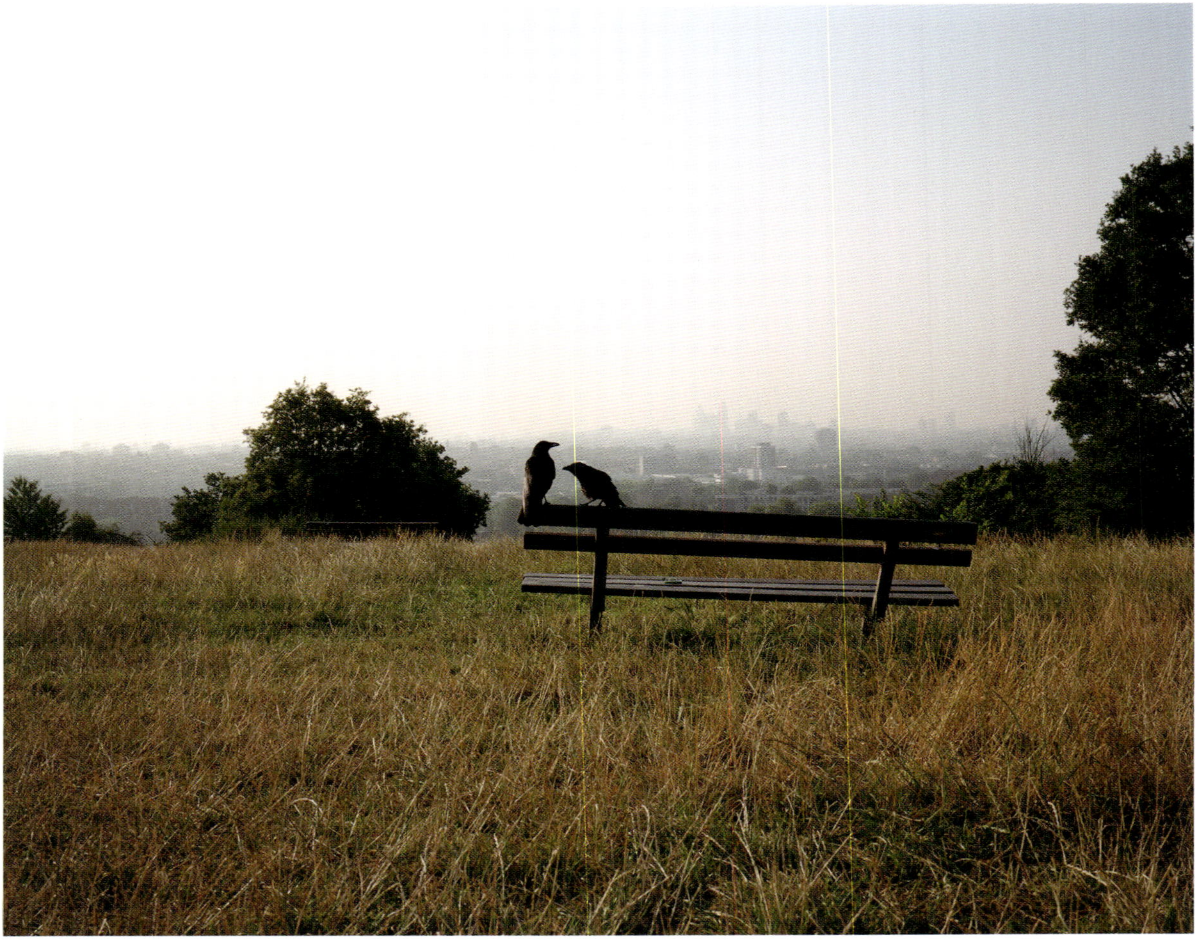

Untitled 31, Hampstead Heath, 2009

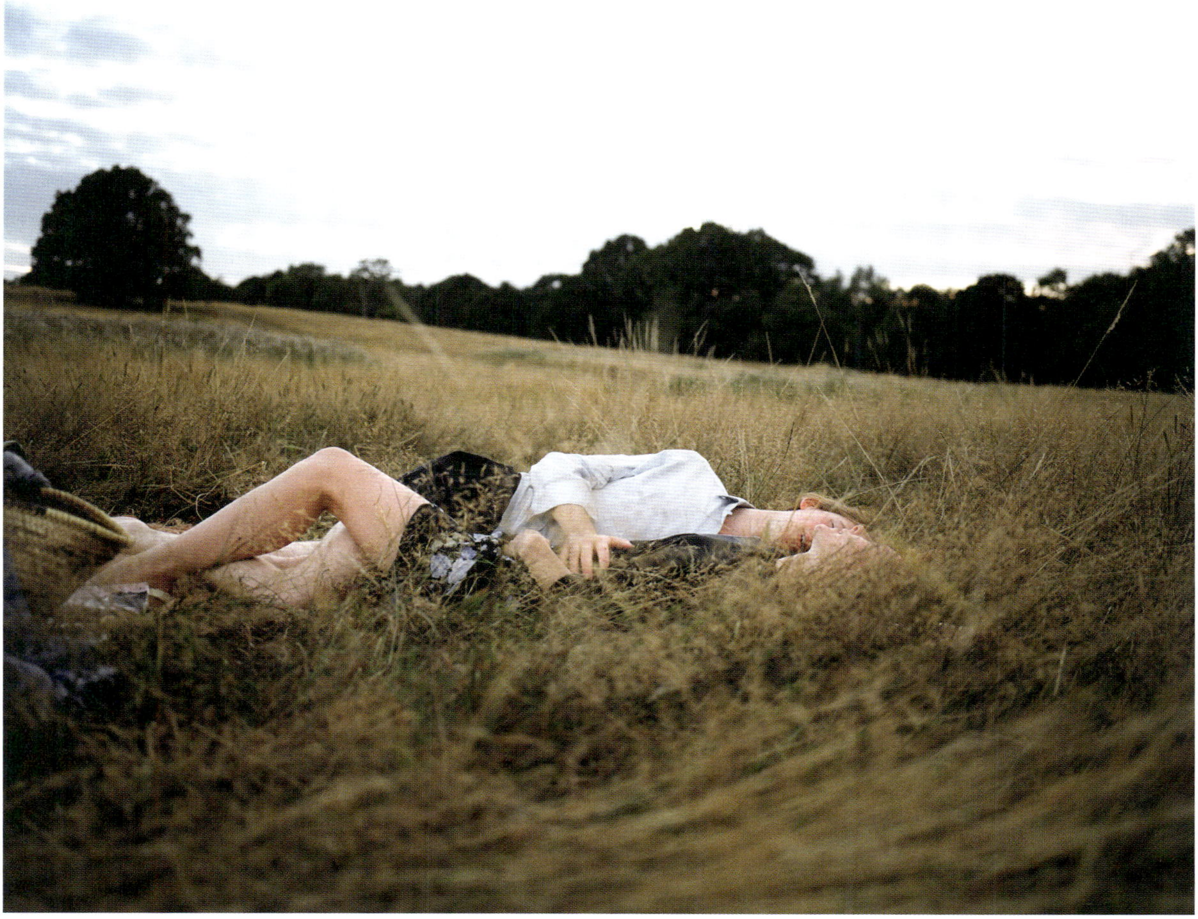

 Untitled 09, Hampstead Heath, 2009 Andy Sewell

Andover & Six Acres

A sensitive, graceful study of two Islington housing estates once stigmatised in the press for their criminal associations.

Cian Oba-Smith

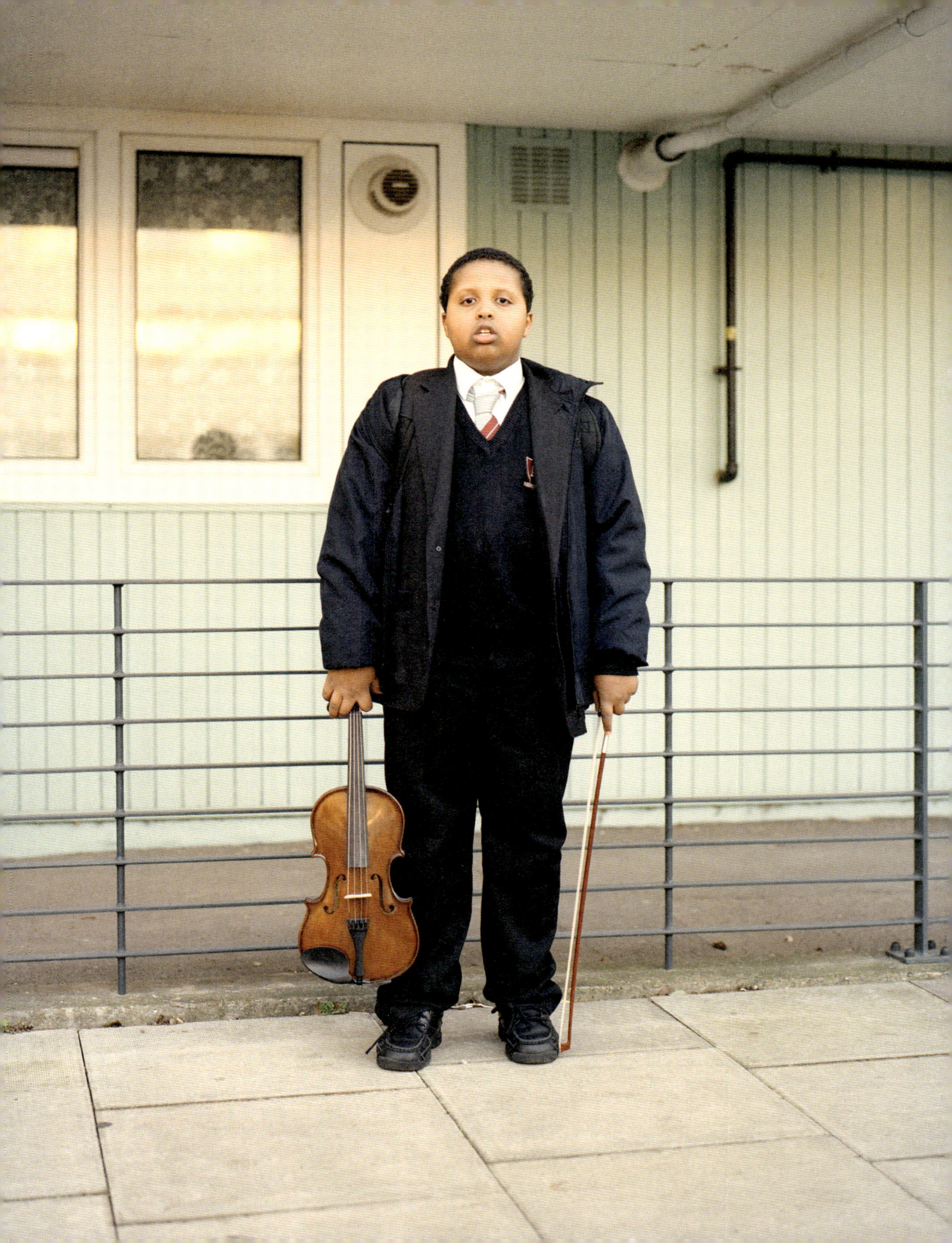

"There are parts of Britain where yobs rule... where hoodies run riot." Ann Widdecombe's 2007 TV documentary about Islington's Andover estate began with a voiceover that sounds like it could have come straight from an episode of 90s TV satire show *Brass Eye*. The then Tory MP went on to describe Andover, notorious in the 1980s and 90s for associations with crime and drugs, as "a dump", "nasty", "threatening" and filled with "dark corners". But this couldn't be further from Cian Oba-Smith's experience of the place.

"It's very quiet there during the day," he remembers. "Everyone I met was nice to me, no one was rude or aggressive. My experience over the course of a year was that it was a real community." Oba-Smith grew up not far from Andover and neighbouring Six Acres, which also features in his series. He remembers driving past the estates as a kid but it was only in 2014 when he returned to London after three years studying in Bristol that he ventured inside. Shot slowly, using a big medium-format film camera and a tripod, the resulting photographs present a nuanced, almost romantic view of the estate.

Through Oba-Smith's eyes we see everything that Widdicombe couldn't – or wouldn't – see. Instead of dark corners, his pictures reveal how the estate is designed to allow the gorgeous late afternoon light to flood through the glass walls or flare pink and golden across the metal interior of a lift. Instead of dismissing the residents as one homogenous faceless mob of "hoodies", his portraits of men and boys who live there have a softness, a candour and a clarity that dignifies them as individuals with their own dreams.

Many photographers have felt compelled to document working class neighbourhoods. In the 1950s, Roger Mayne's pioneering pictures captured the impromptu drama and desperate squalor of a North Kensington slum earmarked for redevelopment as a housing estate. Dana Lixenberg's 2017 Deutsche Börse Photography Foundation Prize-winning *Imperial Courts* is a long-term study of a single housing project in Los Angeles, radical in its quietly respectful portrayal of subjects otherwise ignored or misunderstood by the media. Although the visual aesthetic is different from Lixenberg's, Oba-Smith was also conscious of how estates, and Andover in particular, had been represented in the press, not least by Ann Widdecombe. "I didn't want to feed into the stereotype of knives and drugs," he says. "Those things do happen, but it's a very small part of what living there is like."

This dedication to challenging misconceptions and teasing out the mundane beauty in everyday life has set the tone for his subsequent work. Whether photographing African American horsemen in Philadelphia, a community on a tiny island off the coast of Donegal, Ireland, suburban dirt bikers or the residents of Woolwich in South London, Oba-Smith brings a welcome authenticity and empathy. "I want to make images that look nice because I want people to spend time looking at them," he explains. "If you make really ugly and horrible images people might be shocked but they're not affected by it in the same way."

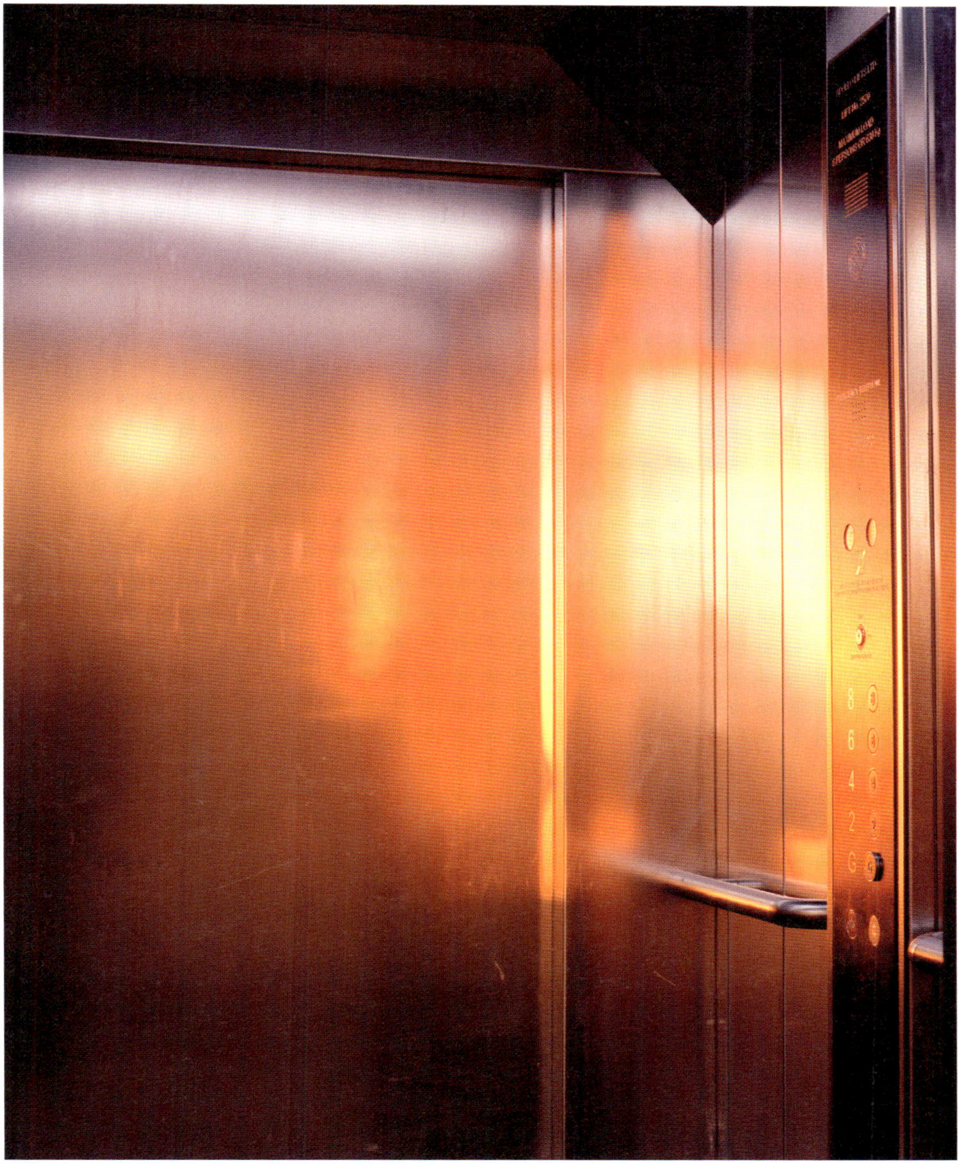

Previous: Abdullahi with his viola on the Andover Estate, 2016
Above: The sun sets in a lift on the Andover Estate, 2015

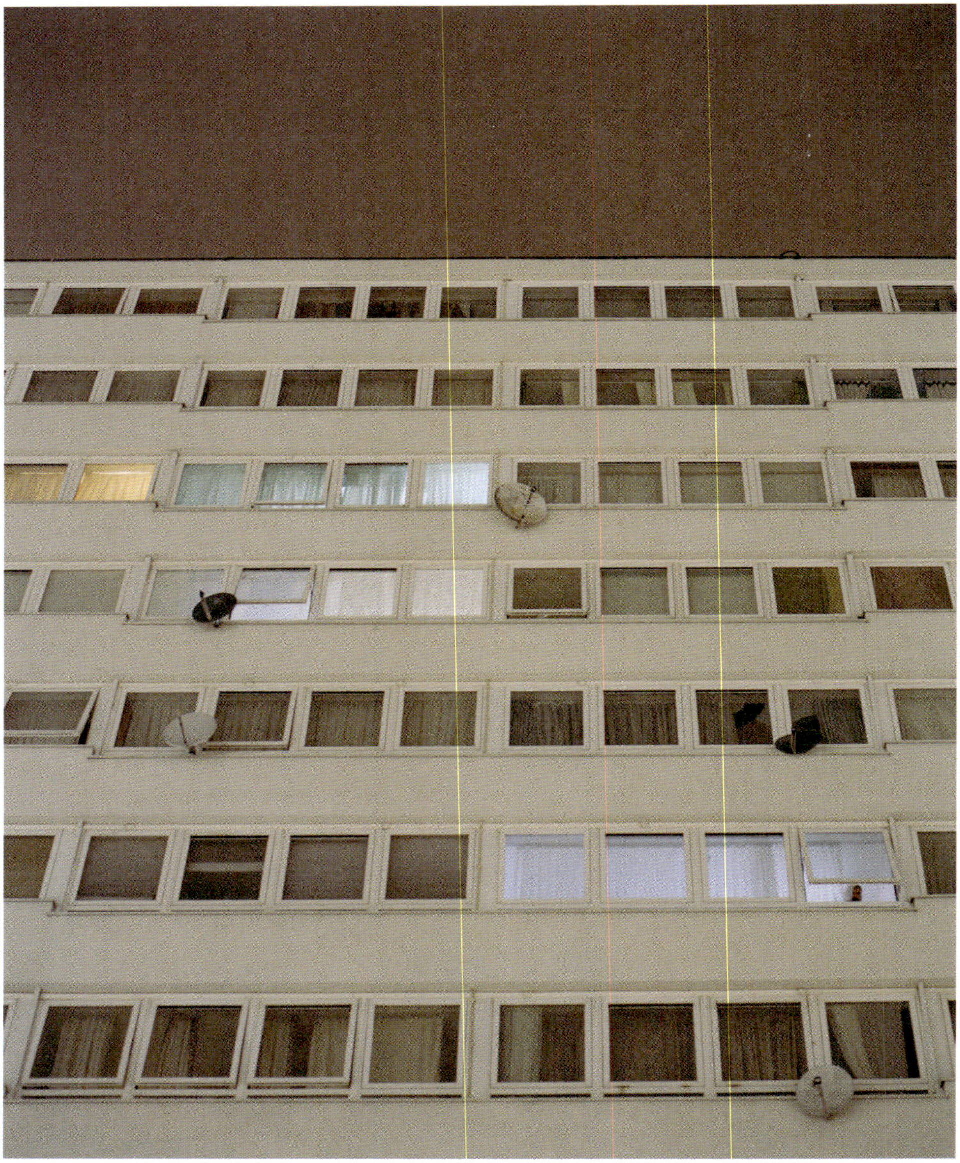

A man watches from a window on the Six Acres Estate, 2015

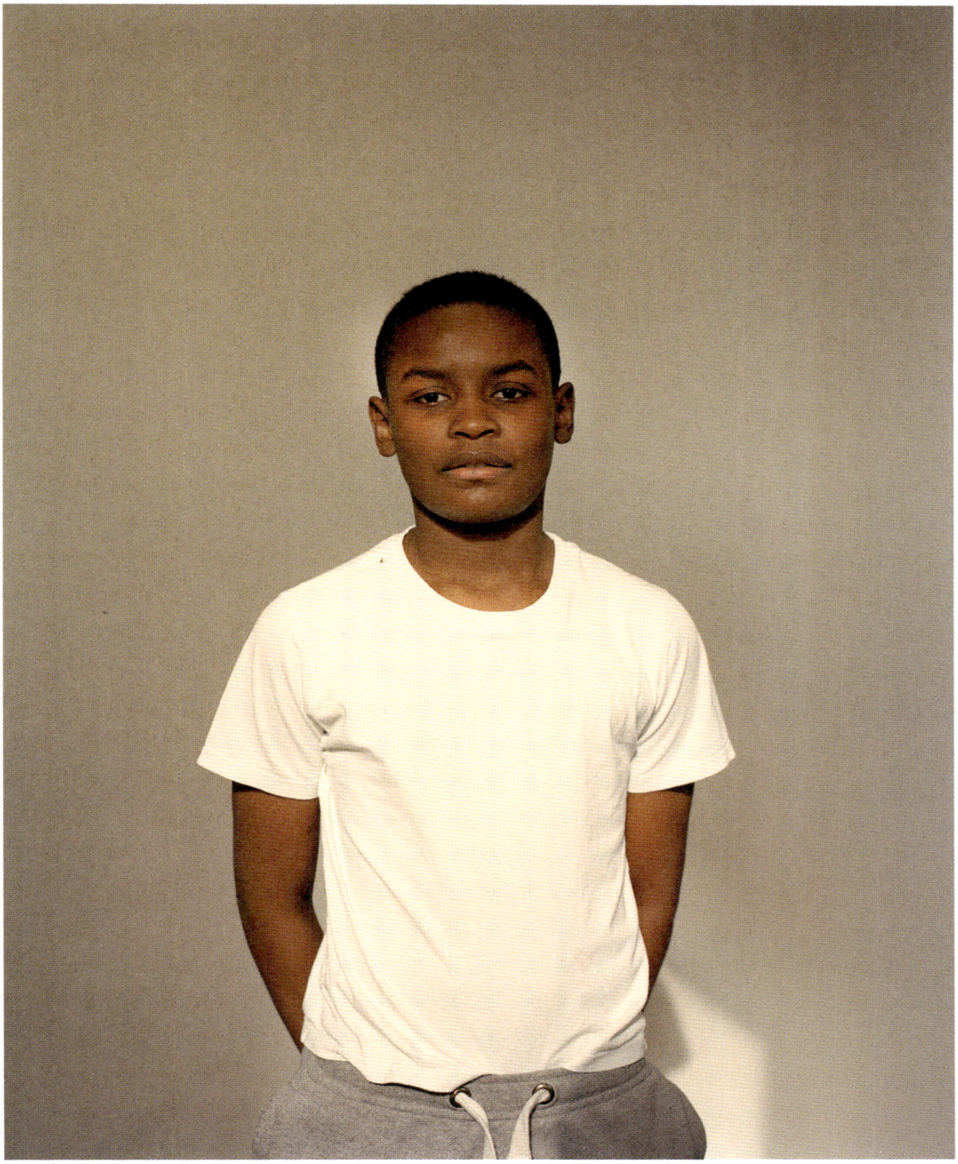

A young boy poses for a portrait on the Six Acres Estate, 2015

Cian Oba-Smith

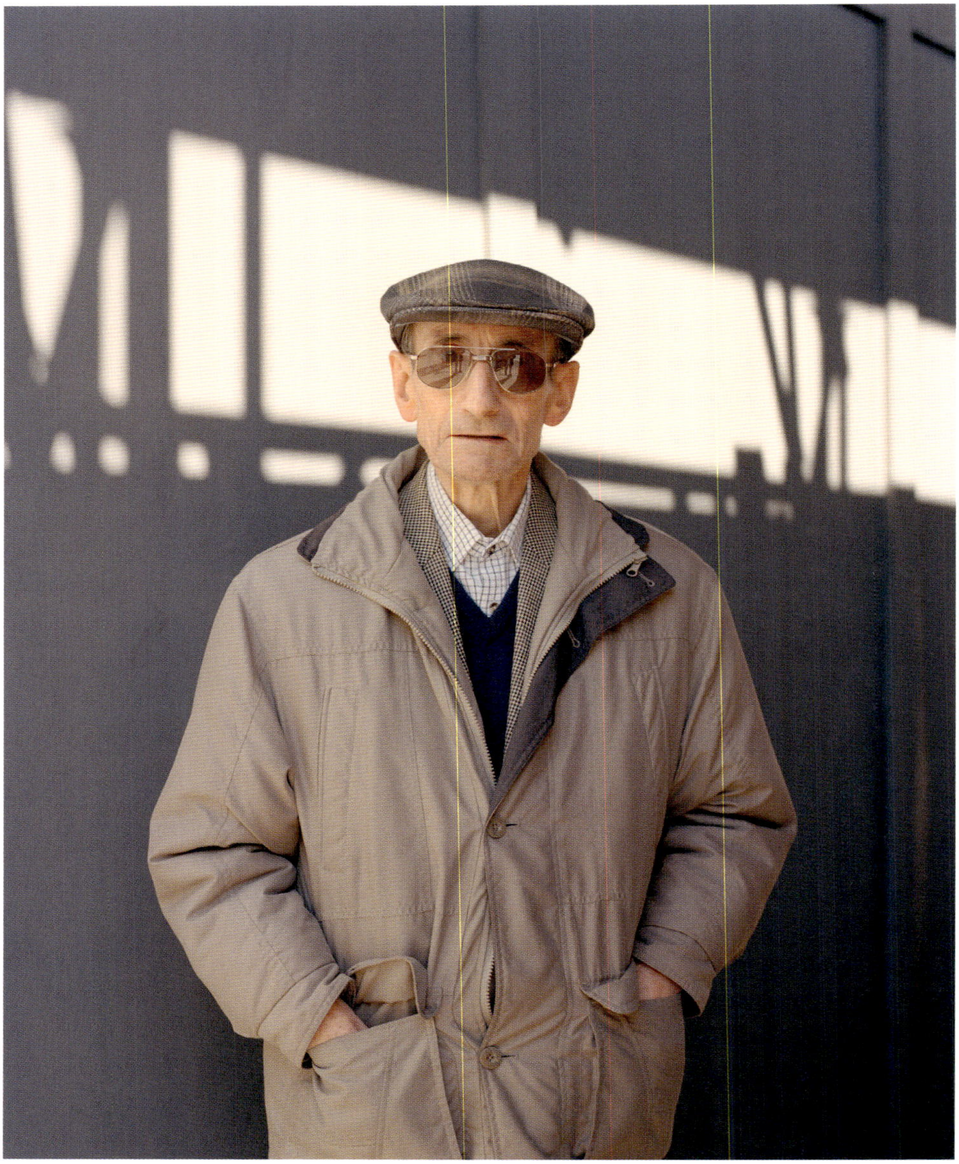

An old man poses for a portrait on the Andover Estate, 2015

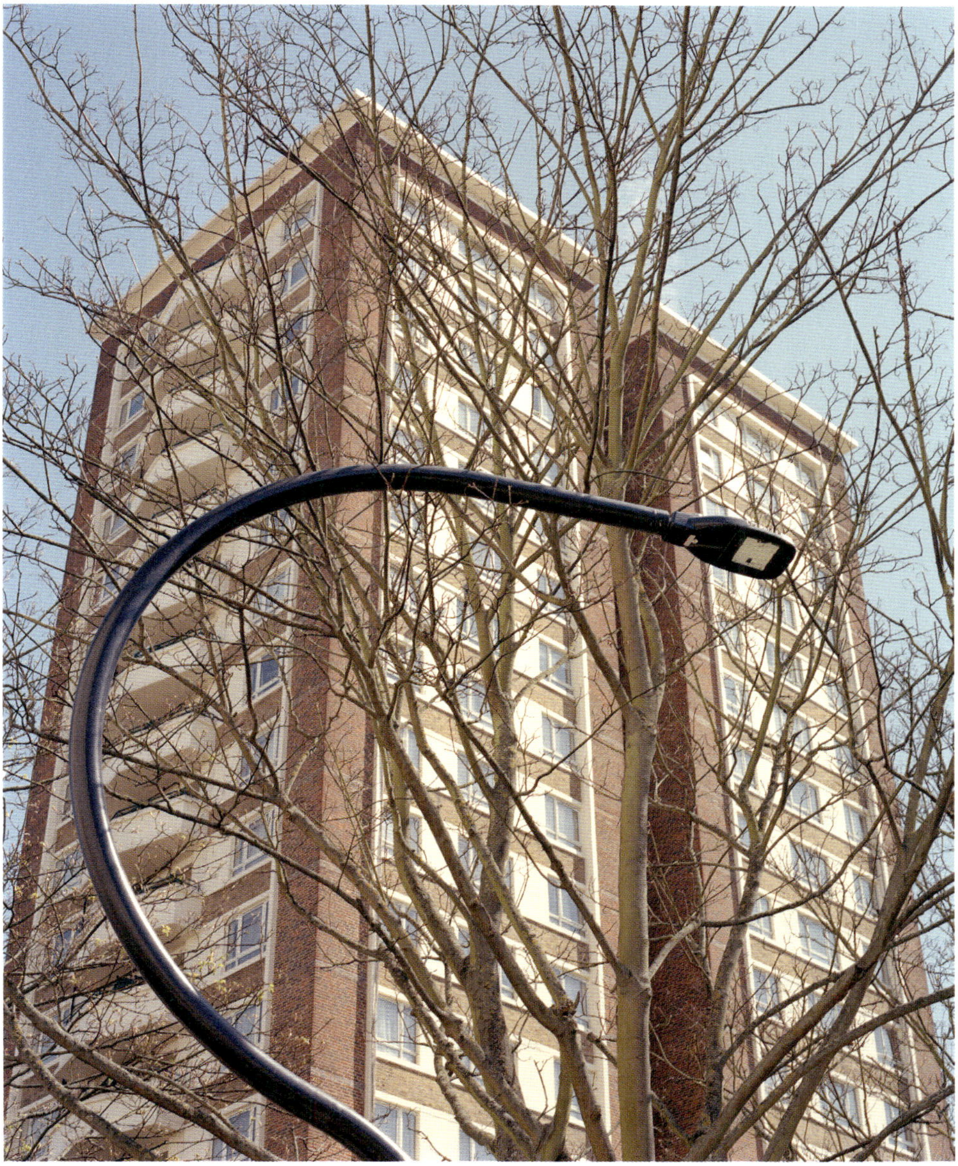

 A tower block on the Six Acres Estate, 2015 Cian Oba-Smith

A patch of light moves through the
architecture of the Six Acres Estate, 2015

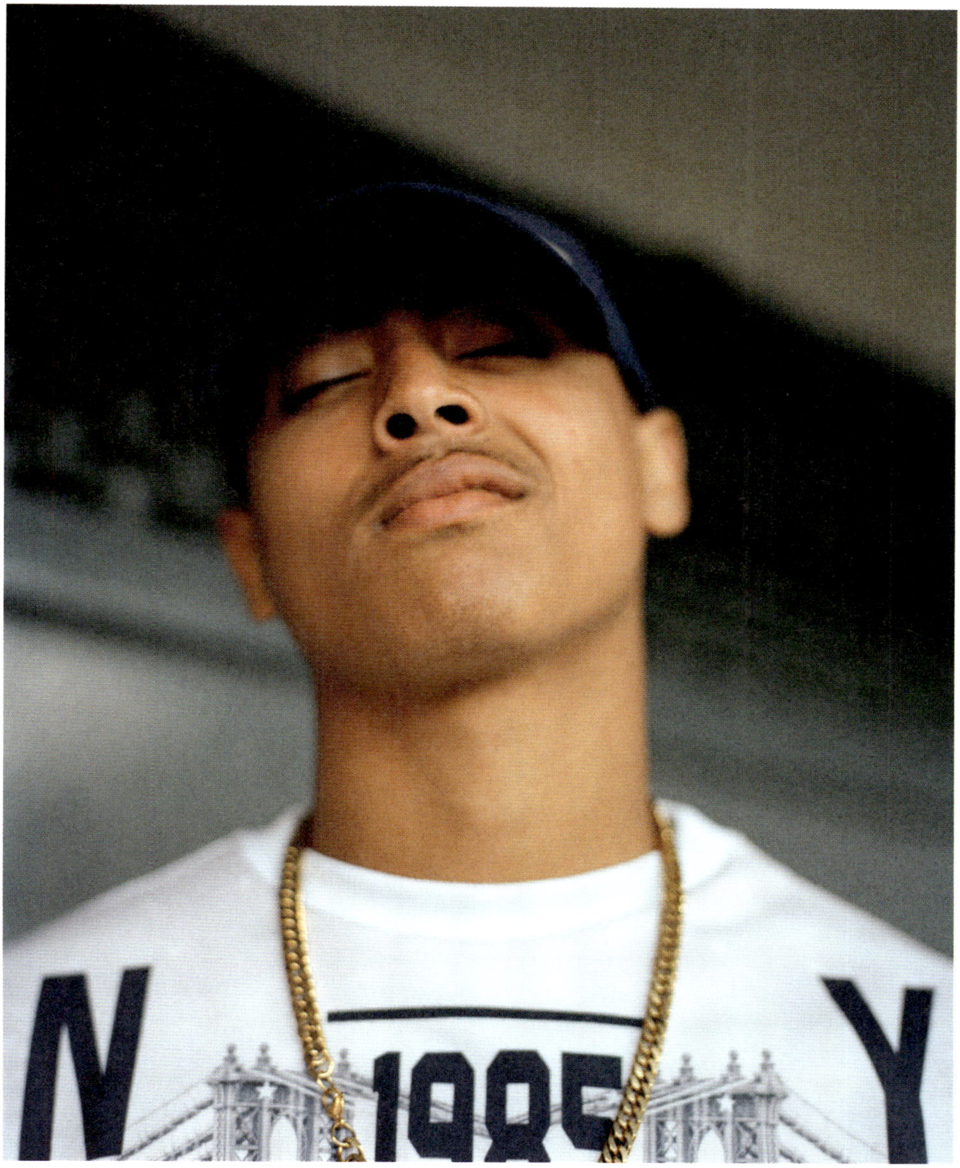

 Ricardo poses for a portrait on the Andover Estate, 2015

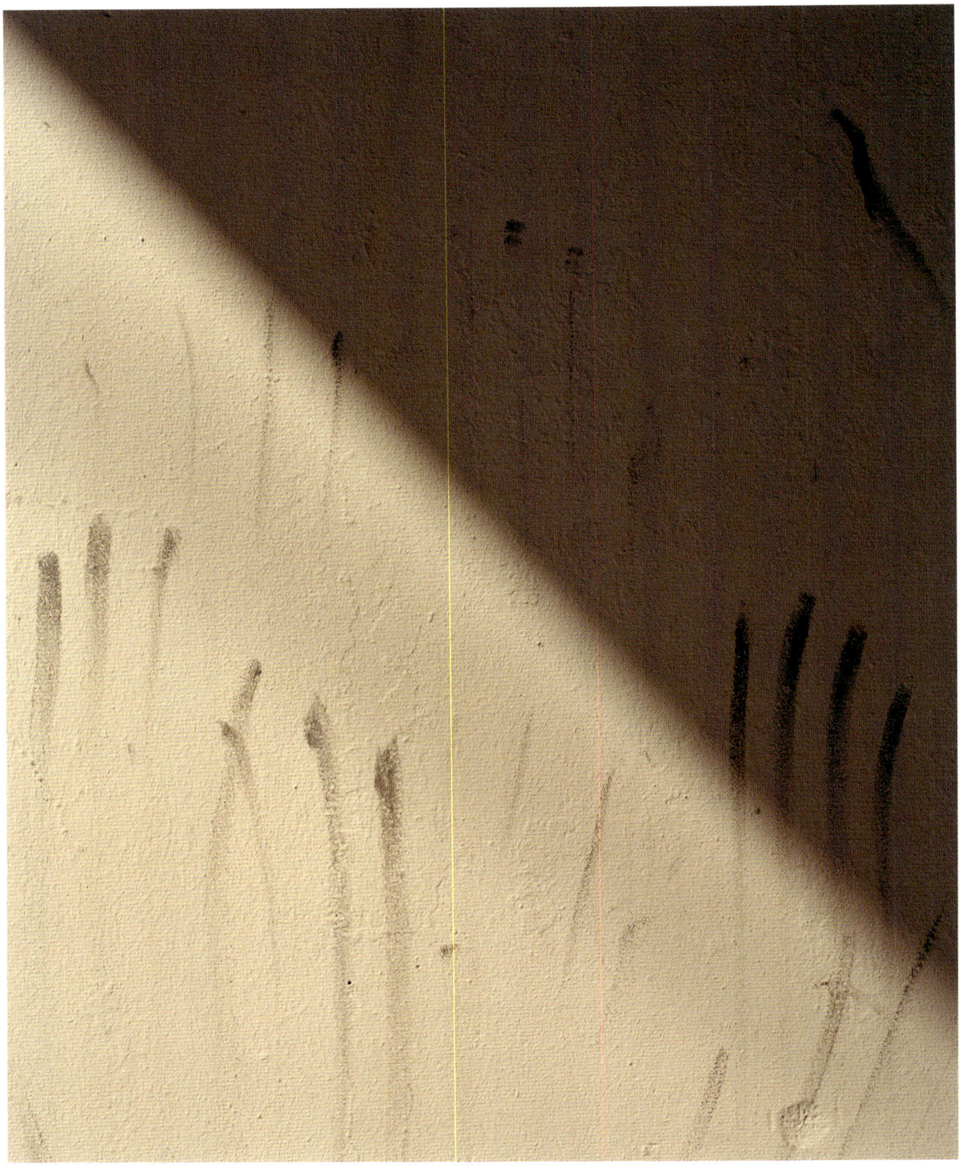

 Hand prints on the Andover Estate, 2015

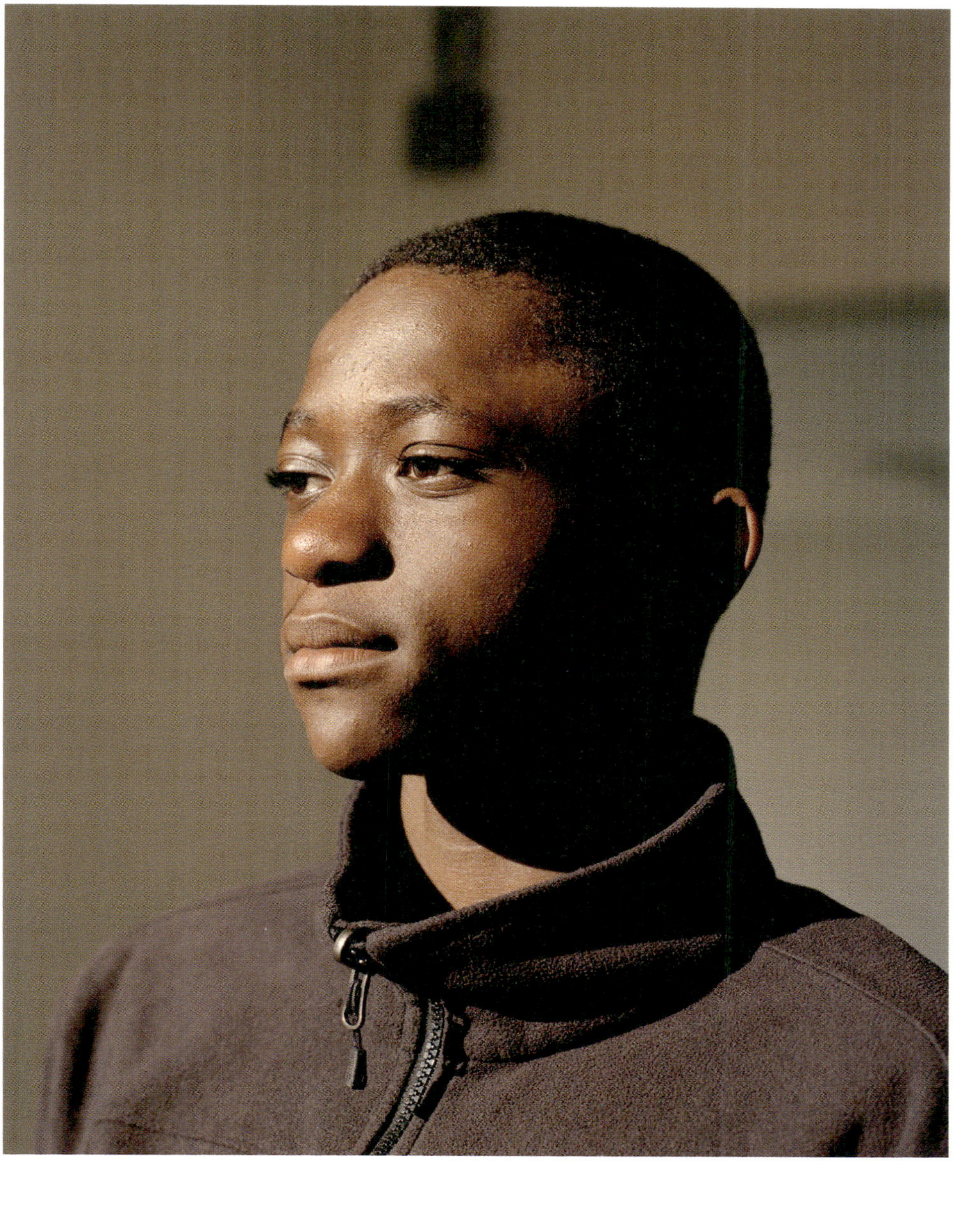

A young boy poses for a portrait on the Six Acres Estate, 2015

Cian Oba-Smith

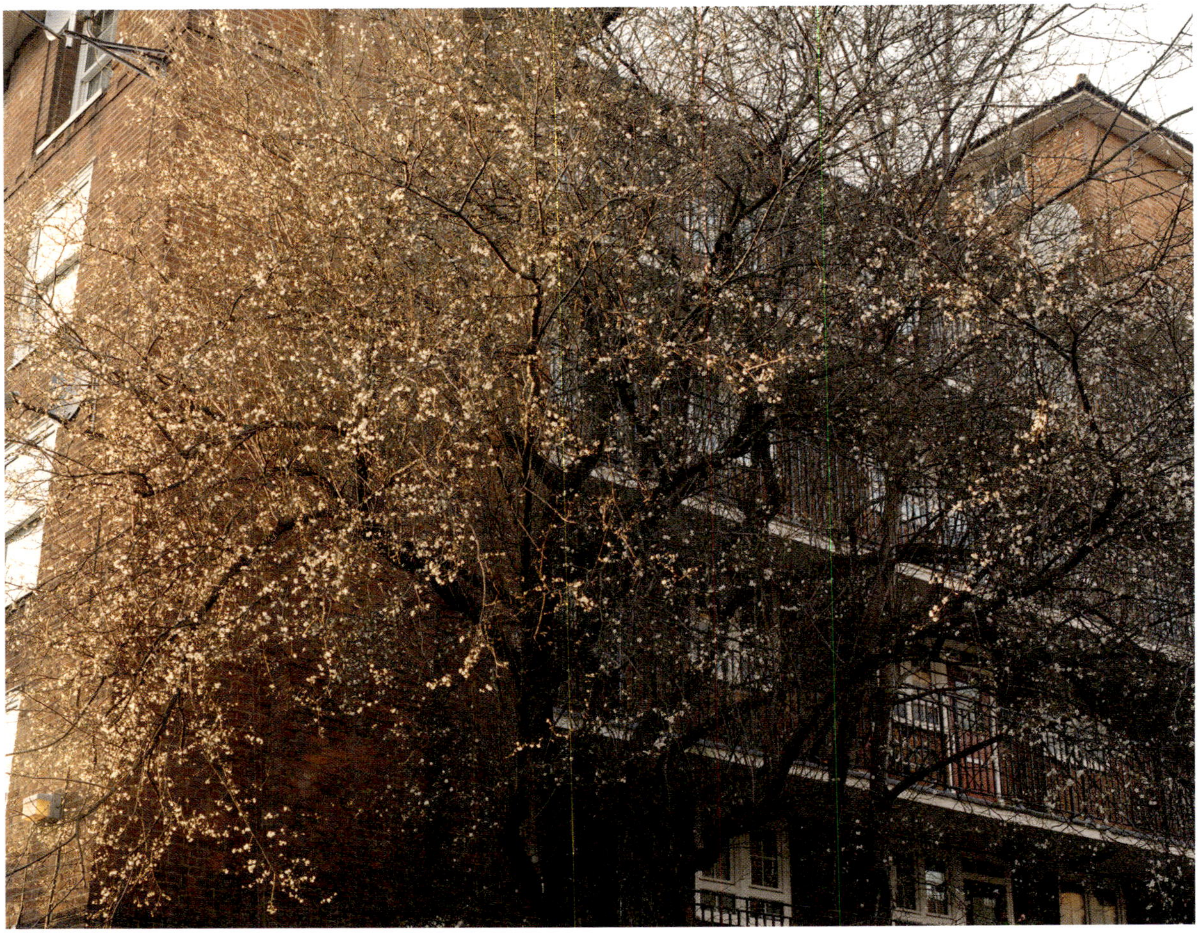

A tree explodes into bloom on the Andover Estate, 2016

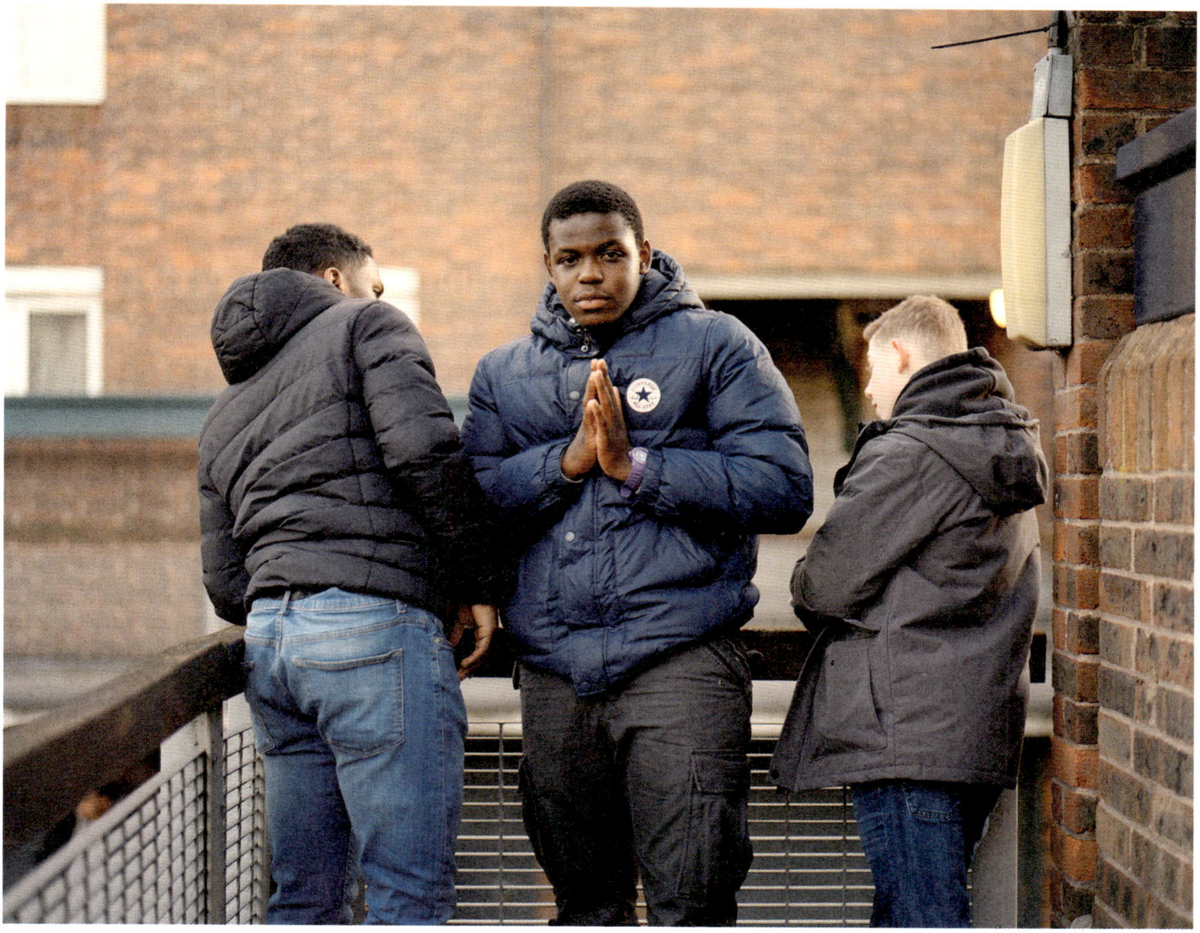

A group of residents on the Andover Estate watch from a balcony as two of their friends are searched by the police, 2016

Cian Oba-Smith

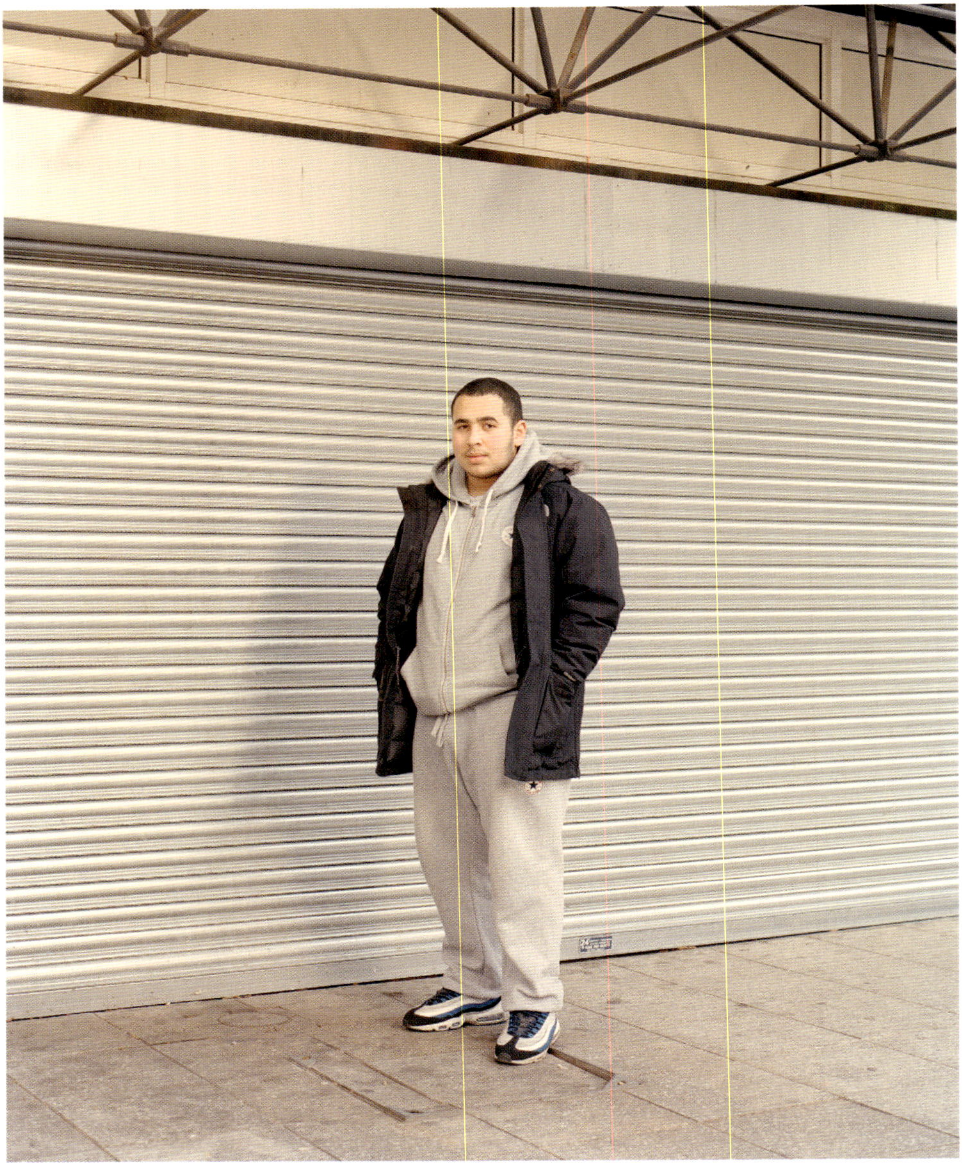

Daniel poses for a portrait in front of
a closed shop on the Andover Estate, 2016

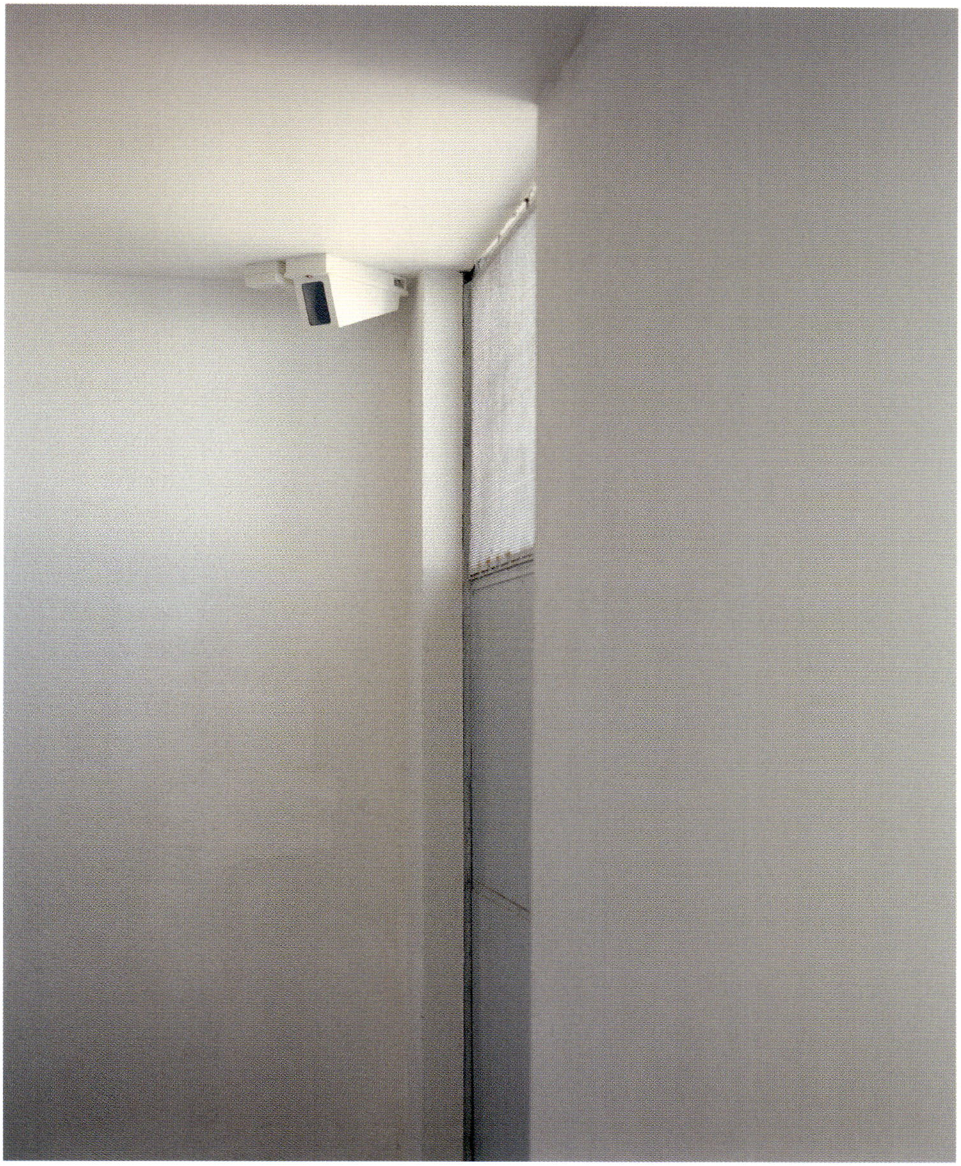

A CCTV camera watches over a lift on the Six Acres Estate, 2015
Cian Oba-Smith

Missing Buildings

Exploring the effects of the Blitz through the ghostly remnants of London's bombed-out buildings.

Thom and Beth Atkinson

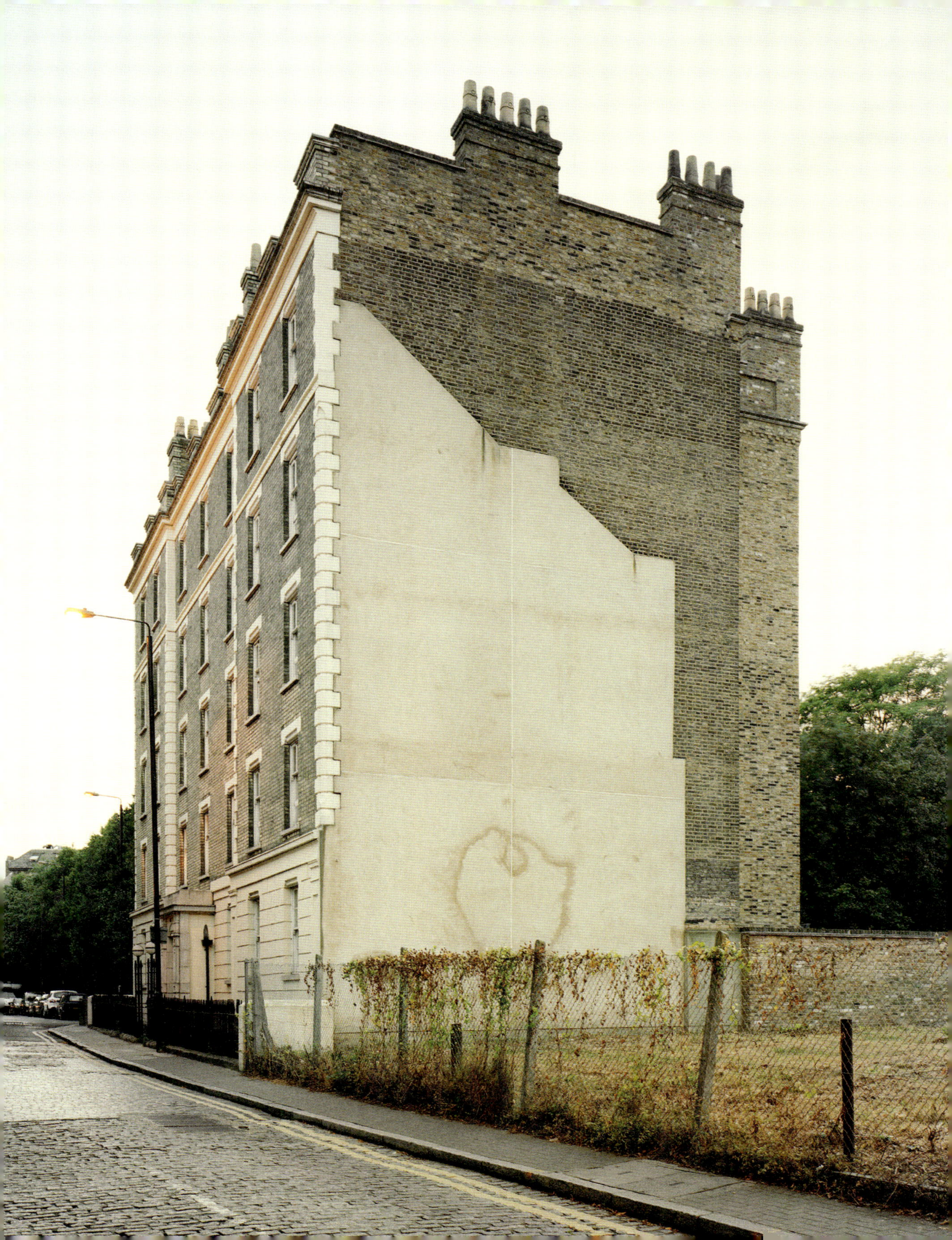

The Blitz may have struck London decades before Thom and Beth Atkinson were born but images from that era are imprinted on their minds. It's the same for most of us who studied it in school. Although we didn't experience the events ourselves, we share in the cultural memory through photographs, newsreels and movies. Kids play with dolls and teddies amid the wreckage, milkmen wade through broken bricks to make their morning deliveries and hairnet-clad housewives huddle together, sipping cups of tea and chatting. London's streets may have been reduced to rubble but, the narrative goes, her defiant spirit remains intact.

"It's such an integral part of British culture, that concept of stoicism, survival. It reappears everywhere," says Thom Atkinson who, along with sister Beth, spent six years photographing spaces left by the city's bombed-out buildings. "We'd almost be sad to lose it from our history because we wouldn't know who we were anymore. Despite how horrible it was, we've owned it."

The siblings grew up in Leicestershire and moved to London within a few years of one another. Their grandfather Norman had been an air raid warden in Balham, South London, during the Second World War, tasked with mapping bomb damage. Inspired by him, they decided to team up and do something similar. Cue Sunday mornings spent traipsing around London with their large-format camera, keeping an eye out for odd gaps in the architecture instead of consulting archives beforehand. "Some were real bomb sites, others weren't, but it was more about that sense of how the landscape represented that story rather than a straight documentary approach," says Beth.

It was a true collaboration, continues Thom, "less about taking the photographs, more about finding the photographs." They saw themselves less as photographers, more as art directors – and in many cases they can't even remember who pressed the shutter. As they walked, they talked and reflected. "Our grandparents were in the war, our parents grew up eating rations and playing on bombsites but our relation with conflict is so removed," notes Beth. "We're interested in the stories told about that time, how they influence your feelings about where you live."

There's a quiet contemplation to these pictures that couldn't be further from the heightened drama and emotion of Blitz imagery shot both by press at the time and in the years that followed. In the 1950s, before he made his name as a conflict photographer, Don McCullin was driven by a documentary impulse to record the devastation wrought on his Finsbury Park neighbourhood. *Missing Buildings* is a kind of war photography, too. The Atkinsons were influenced by An-My Lê, a Vietnamese-born photographer evacuated to the US at 15, who brings that ambiguous identity to photographs of her homeland. Like Lê's book *Small Wars*, *Missing Buildings* fits into a new genre – highlighted in Tate Modern's 2014 exhibition *Conflict, Time, Photography* – that explores how the effects of war continue to reverberate long after the fighting stops.

As the last of the generation of men and women that survived it pass away, the Blitz will no longer be in living memory. "In London there are lots of memorials commemorating the institutional and military losses but there's not much about the homes that were lost," says Beth. "We were really aware of that," adds Thom. As London is redeveloped, many of these ghostly reminders of houses that once stood will no longer be preserved physically, "but by doing this, we thought, maybe we could make our own memorial to it." And what a fitting memorial it is.

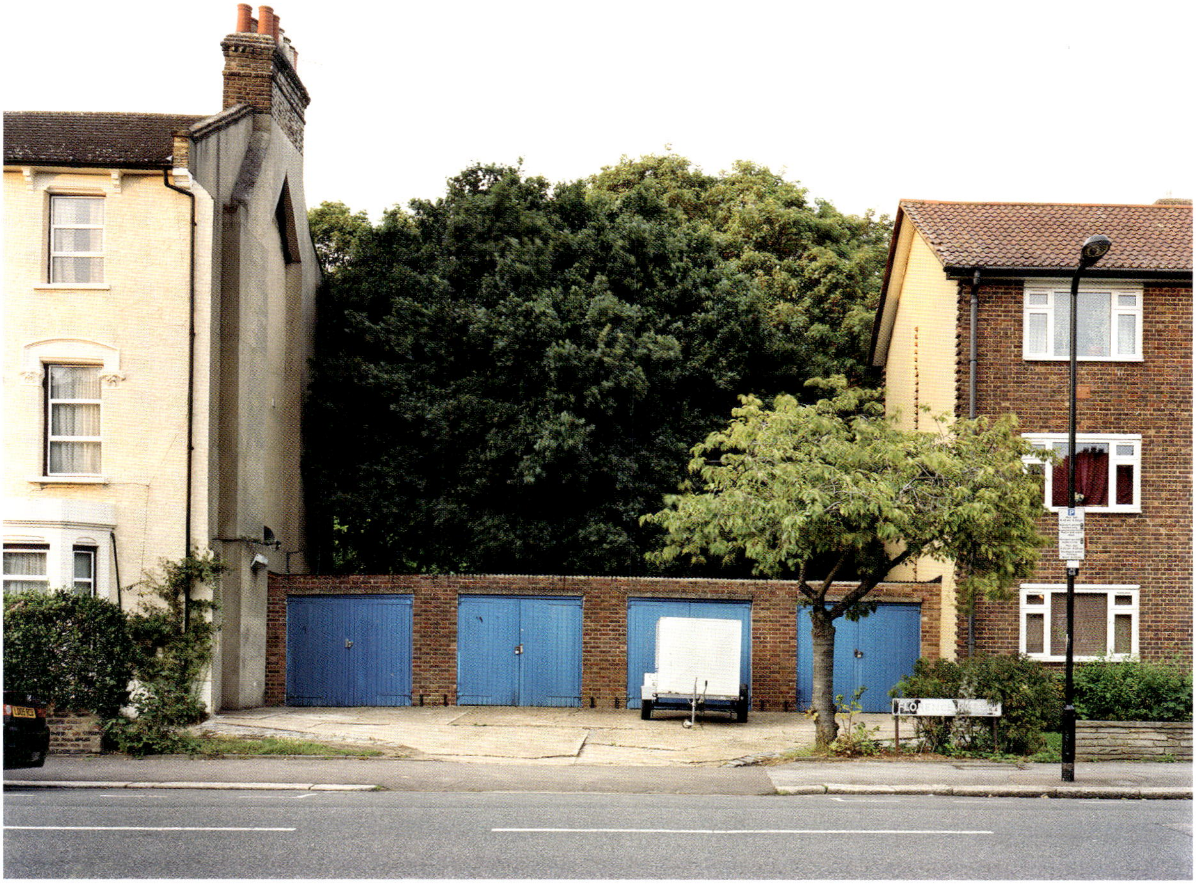

Previous: Wapping High Street, Wapping, 2015

Above: Florence Road, Stroud Green, 2015

Thom and Beth Atkinson

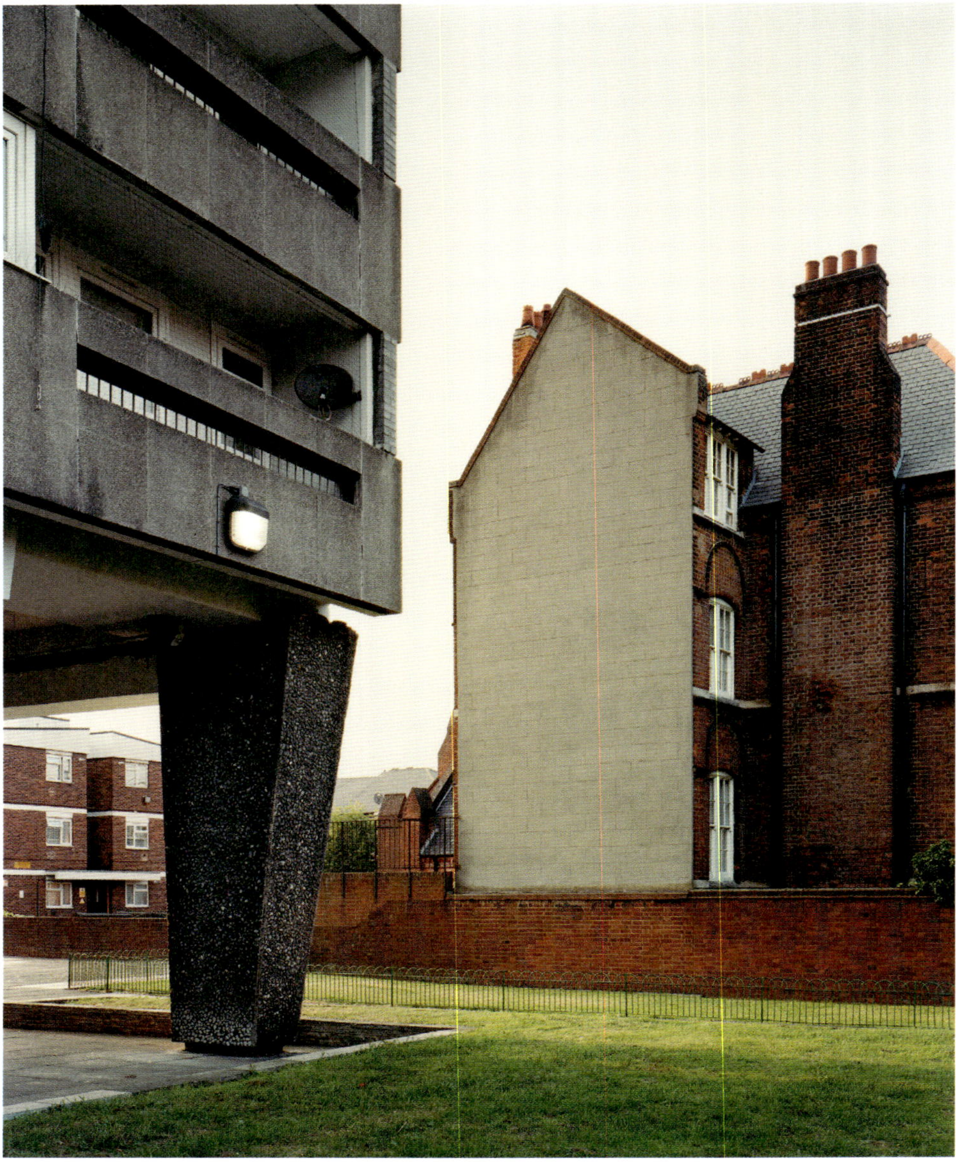

Fellows Court, Shoreditch, 2015

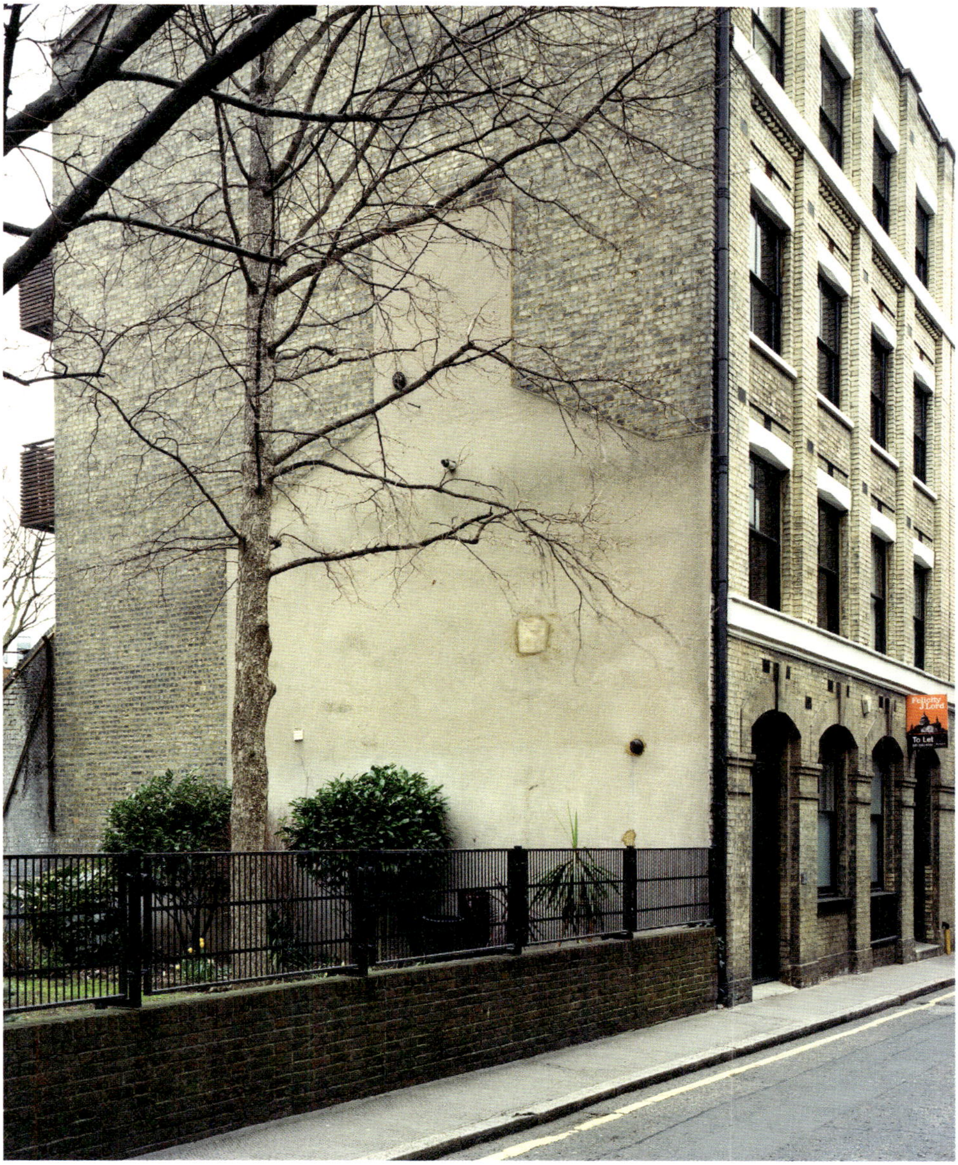

 Dingley Place, Finsbury, 2015 Thom and Beth Atkinson

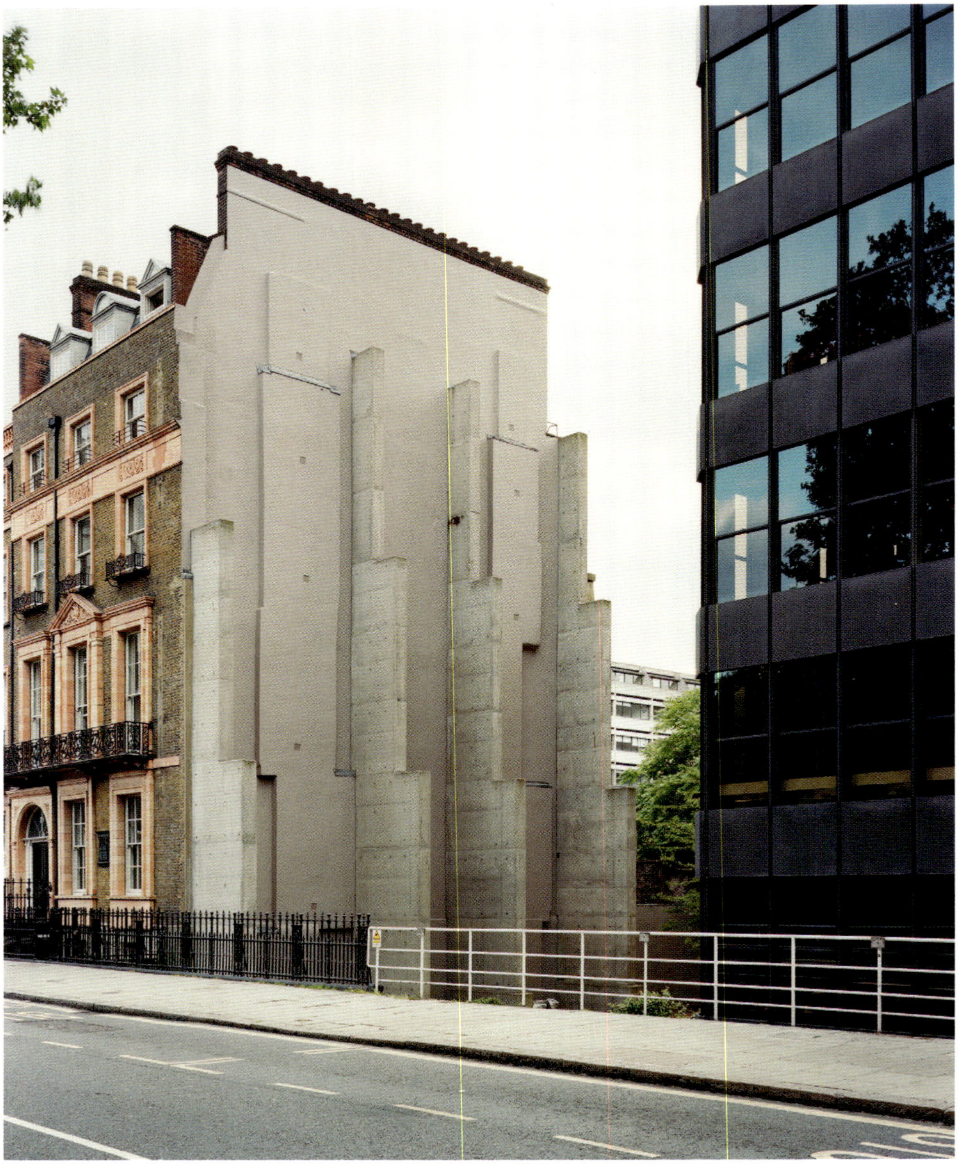

Russell Square, Bloomsbury, 2015

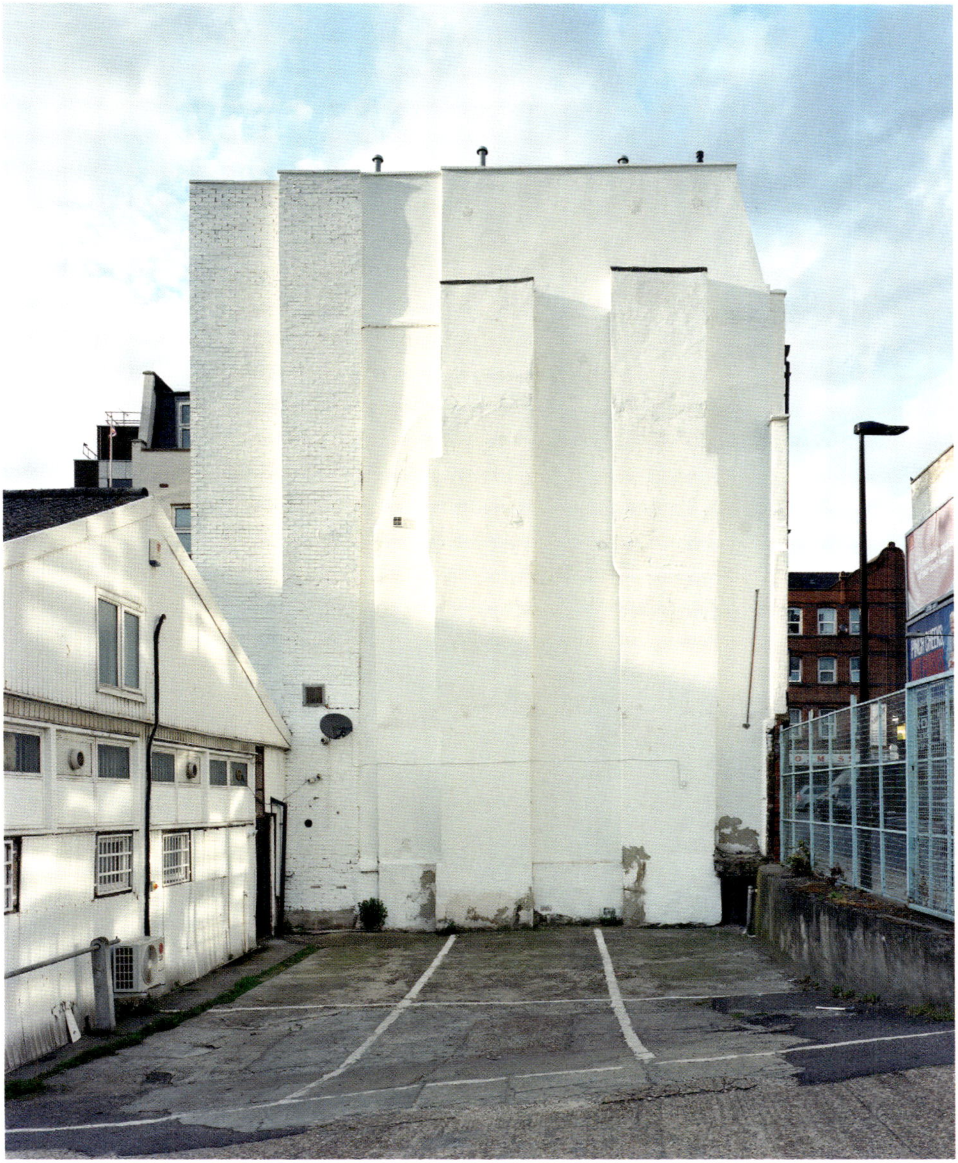

 Christian Street, Whitechapel, 2015 Thom and Beth Atkinson

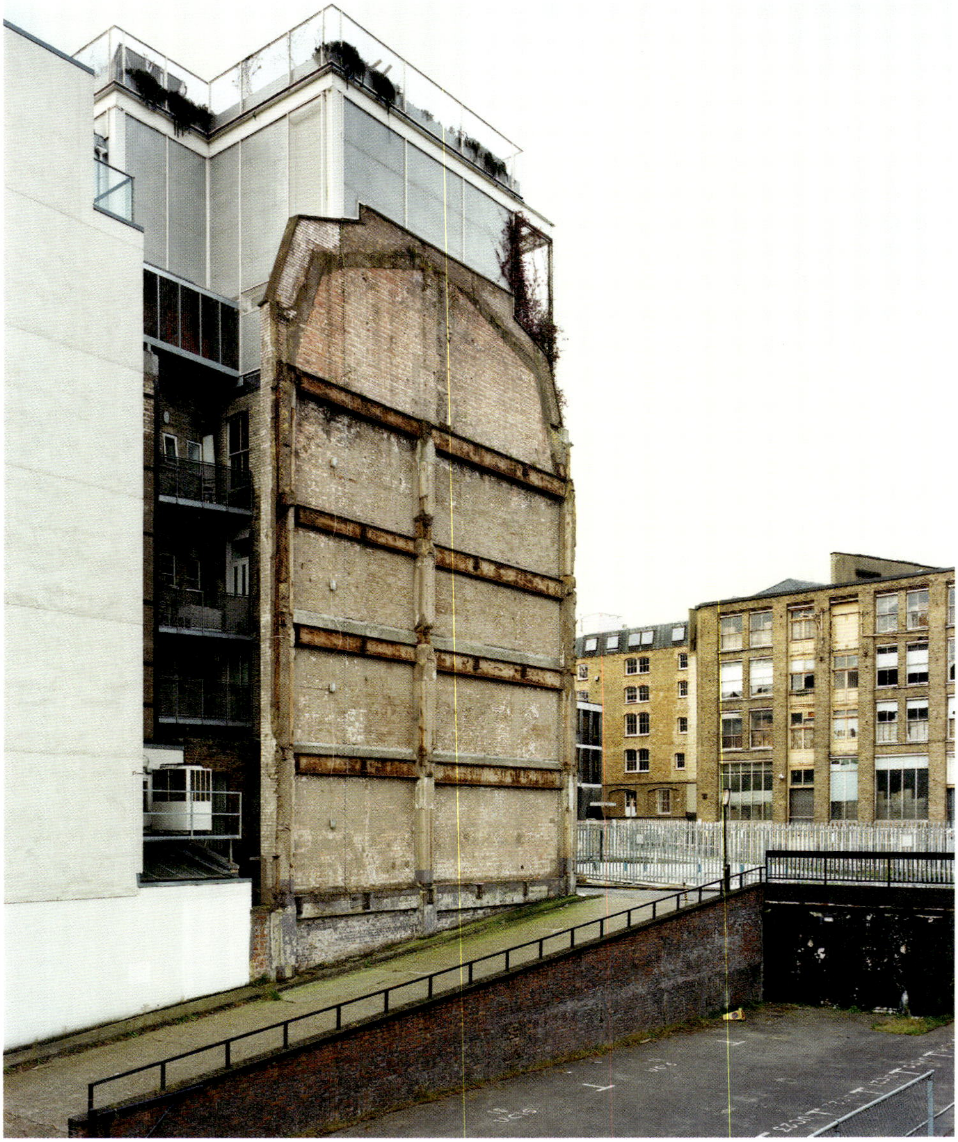

Kiffen Street, Shoreditch, 2015

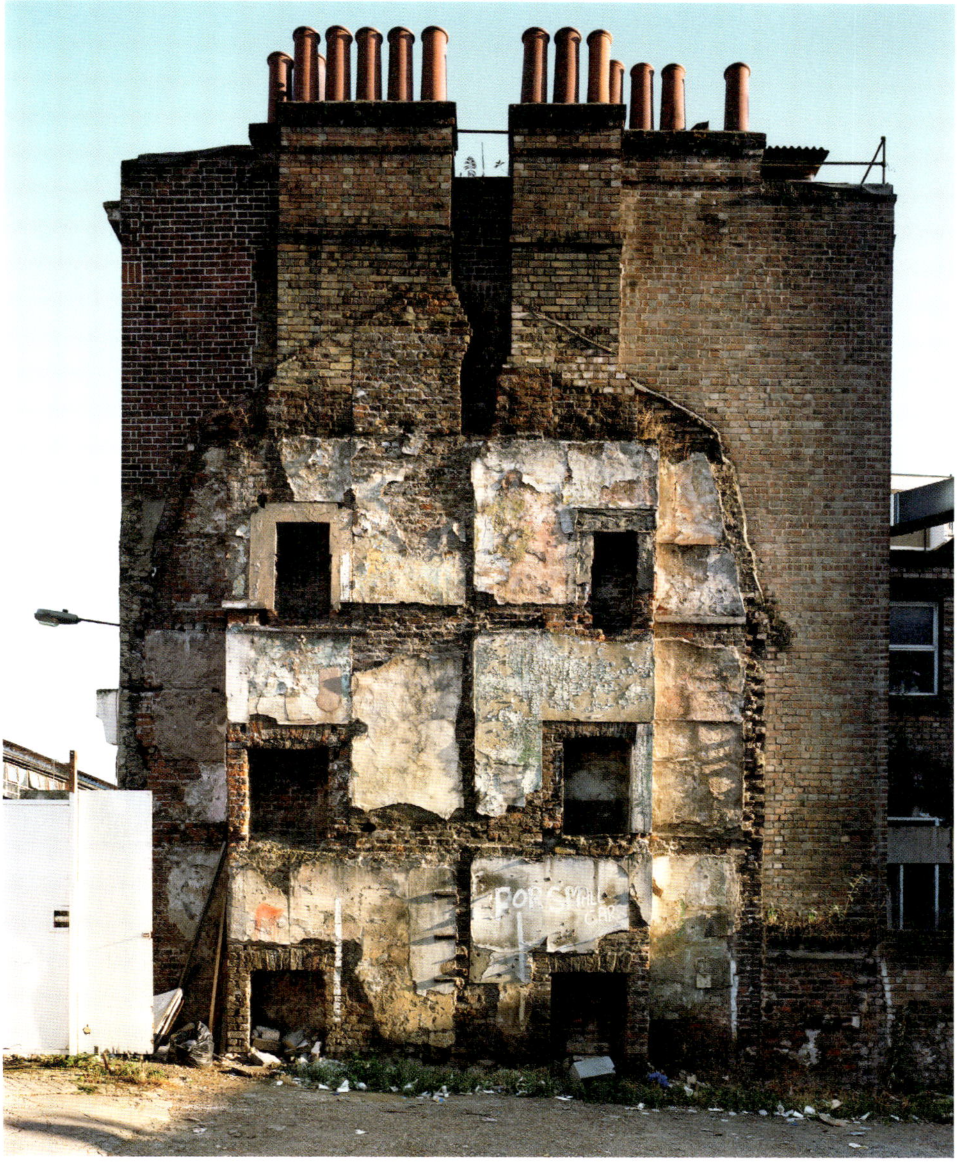

Hessel Street, Whitechapel, 2015

Thom and Beth Atkinson

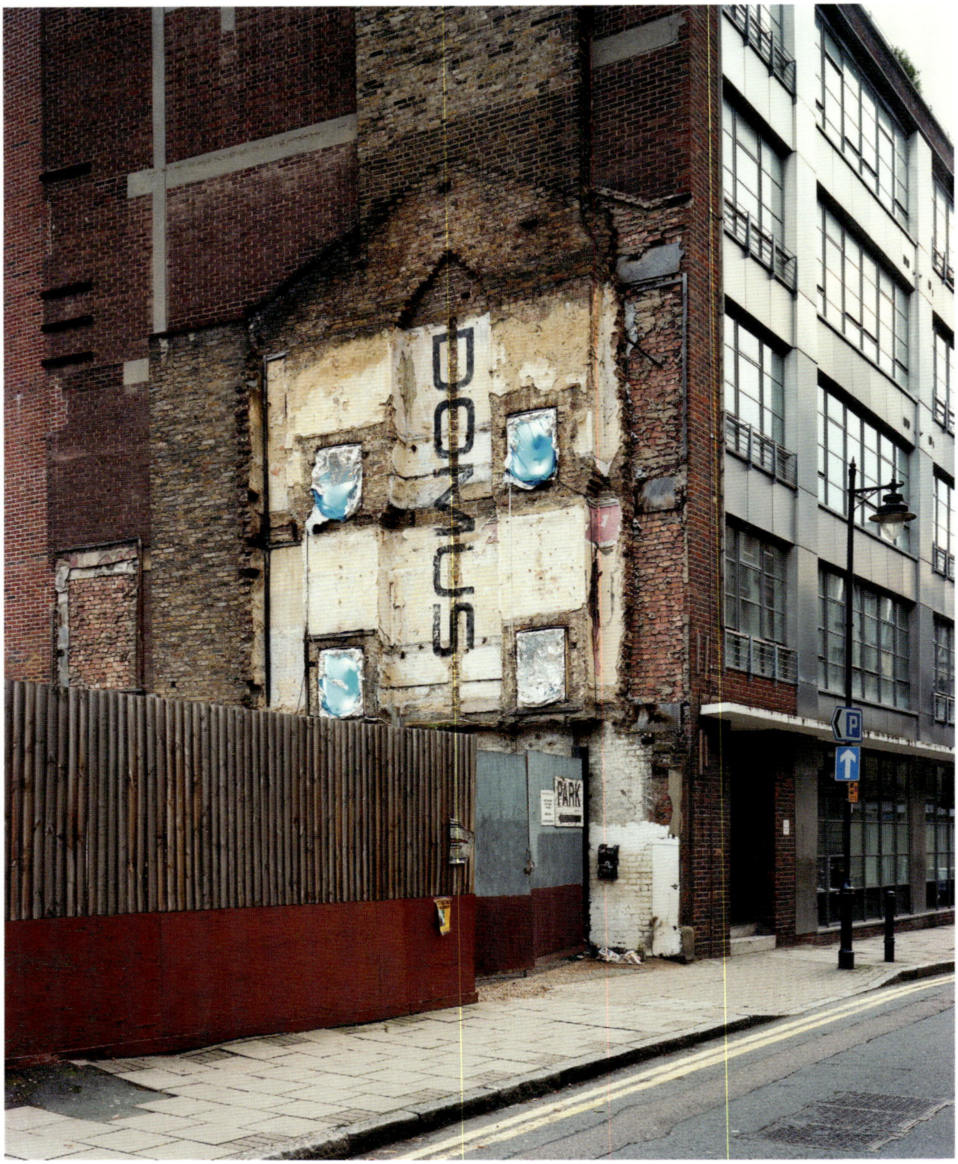

 Great Sutton Street, Clerkenwell, 2015

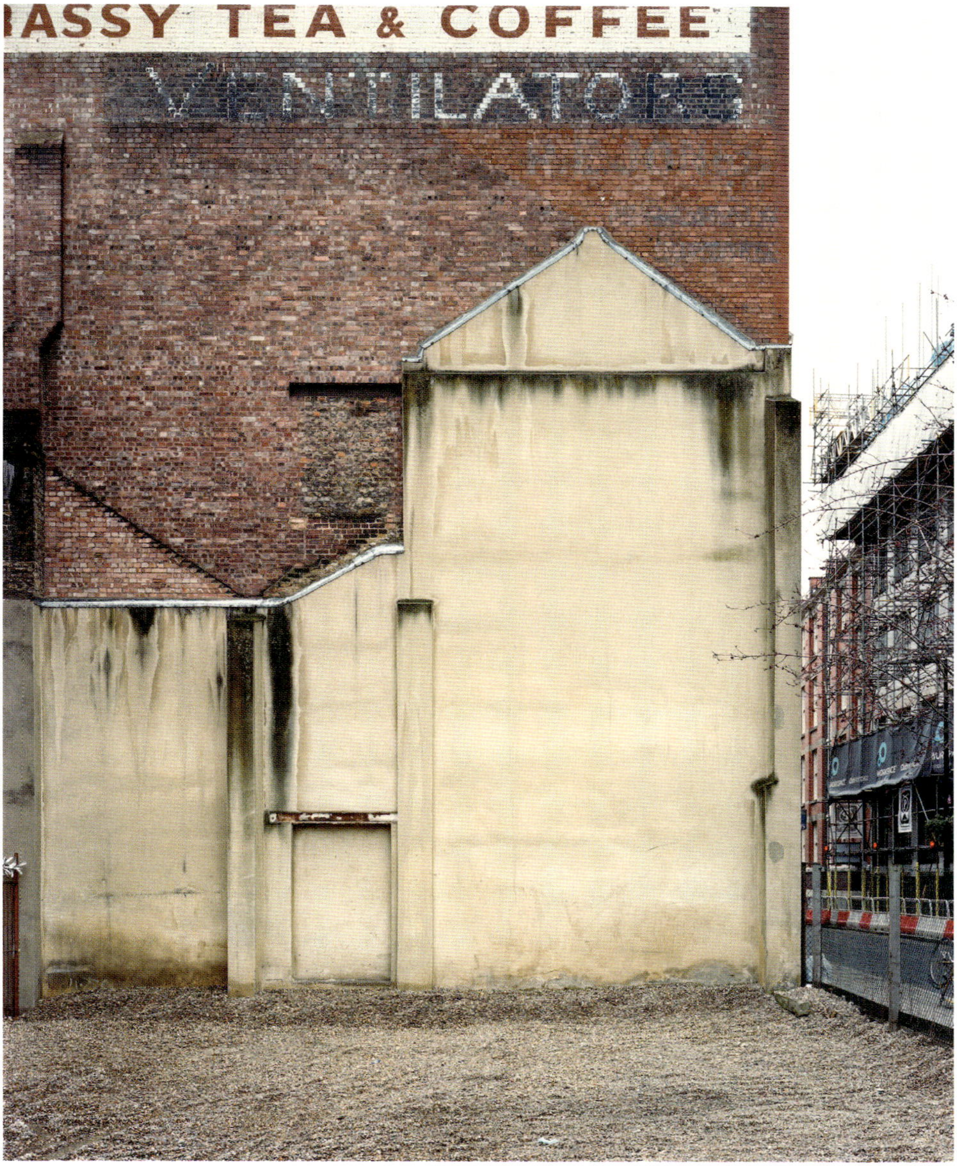

Union Street, Southwark, 2015

Thom and Beth Atkinson

London Mosques

An architect observes how the spaces where Muslim Londoners go to pray have developed in resourceful and imaginative ways.

Shahed Saleem

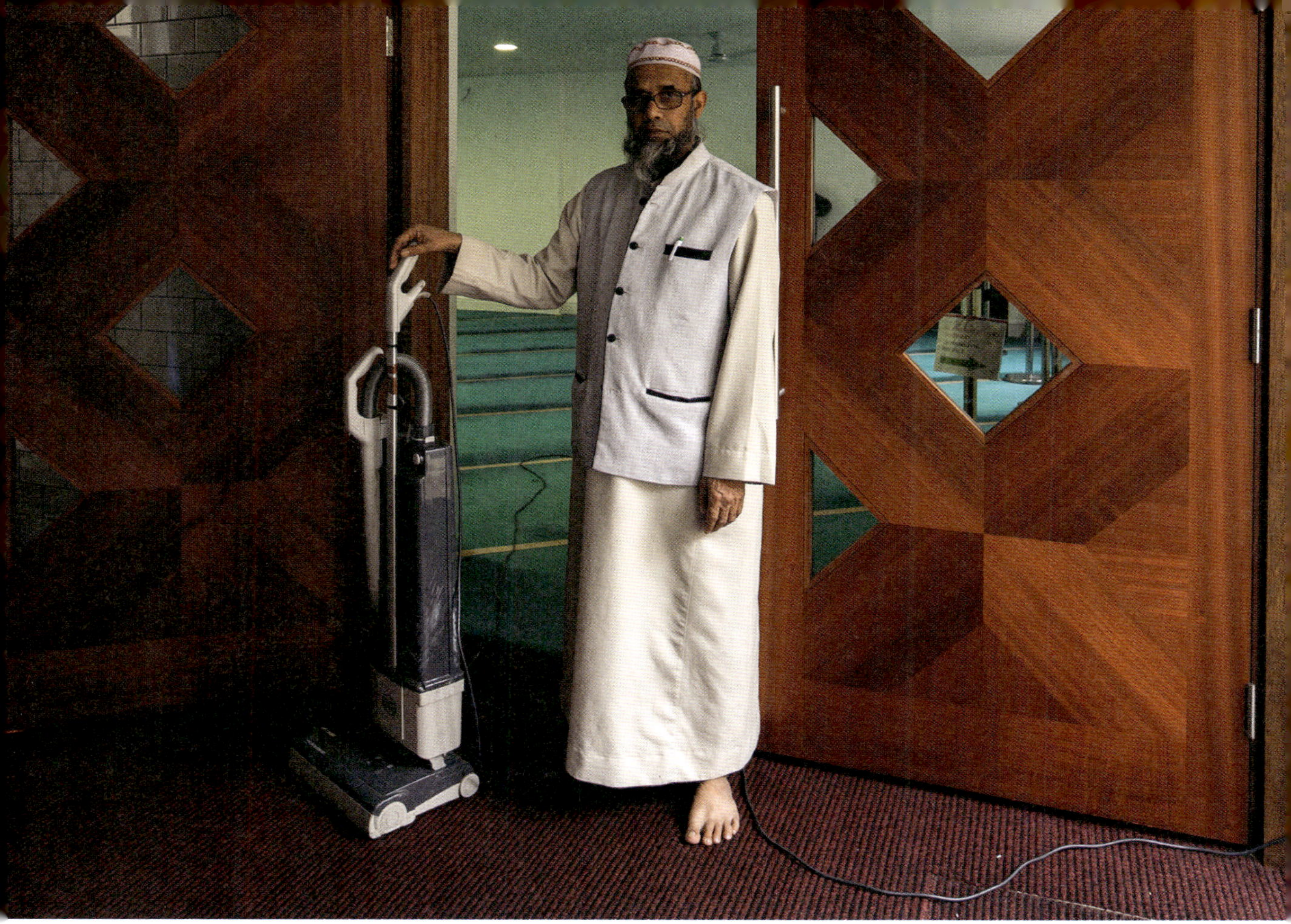

The red carpeted floors, bay window and white net curtains suggest we're looking at a front room. Just two clues indicate that it is something more: a speaker and an extractor fan. In fact, this is not someone's home but a mosque, Brixton Mosque, converted from a house in the mid-1990s. The speaker broadcasts the service in the main hall upstairs to worshippers down here, and the fan has been installed to relieve the heat produced when lots of people are packed in together to pray.

The "improvisational" way that Brixton Mosque has been adapted is typical of the mosques that feature in Shahed Saleem's photographs. A practising architect who has designed mosques himself, mostly in London, Saleem began the series in 2013 while researching a weighty book on the history of mosque architecture in Britain. Many of the examples he visited across across the country had, he discovered, been funded, designed and sometimes even built by members of the community, with improvements added incrementally over the years.

Saleem admired these self-taught designers. With no formal training, they created "in some cases quite significant civic buildings that have changed the landscape of towns, cities and neighbourhoods," he says. "In architecture you don't often get such a direct connection between a community and a building." It's a spirit that he strives to keep in mind himself. Instead of replicating the domes and minarets of the traditional 14th century mosque, Saleem's designs are in dialogue with their surroundings, "taking into account the history of communities, the layering of generations".

This ad hoc reuse of space produces unanticipated architectural juxtapositions, he says. "I'm interested in capturing that shift in meaning." In one picture, we see a man kneeling in what looks like it could be an office. During the week, that's exactly what it is. This building, adjacent to Whitechapel Mosque, is used for study and work – but on Fridays when the mosque is busy, carpets are rolled out and they are transformed into spaces of worship. In his focus on "the everyday, the incidental", Saleem is influenced by the New Topographics movement of the 1960s, which saw Robert Adams, Lewis Baltz and others present "an anti-heroic image of towns and places". It was an approach that revolutionised photography.

What comes across in Saleem's photographs is how culturally adaptable Islam is. Anyone can set up a mosque, all you need is to pray in the direction of Mecca. In the Süleymaniye Mosque on Kingsland Road, the far wall is at an unusual angle. It's an internal wall constructed to ensure that the orientation of prayer is correct. But that phenomenon of modifying existing environments is not unique to any one religion. Another picture shows a foundation stone with Hebrew writing on the wall of a mosque that used to be a synagogue, and before that a church. Since the Roman settlement of Londinium was born nearly 2000 years ago, new communities have always found ways to flourish here, making London the uniquely diverse and remarkable city that it is today.

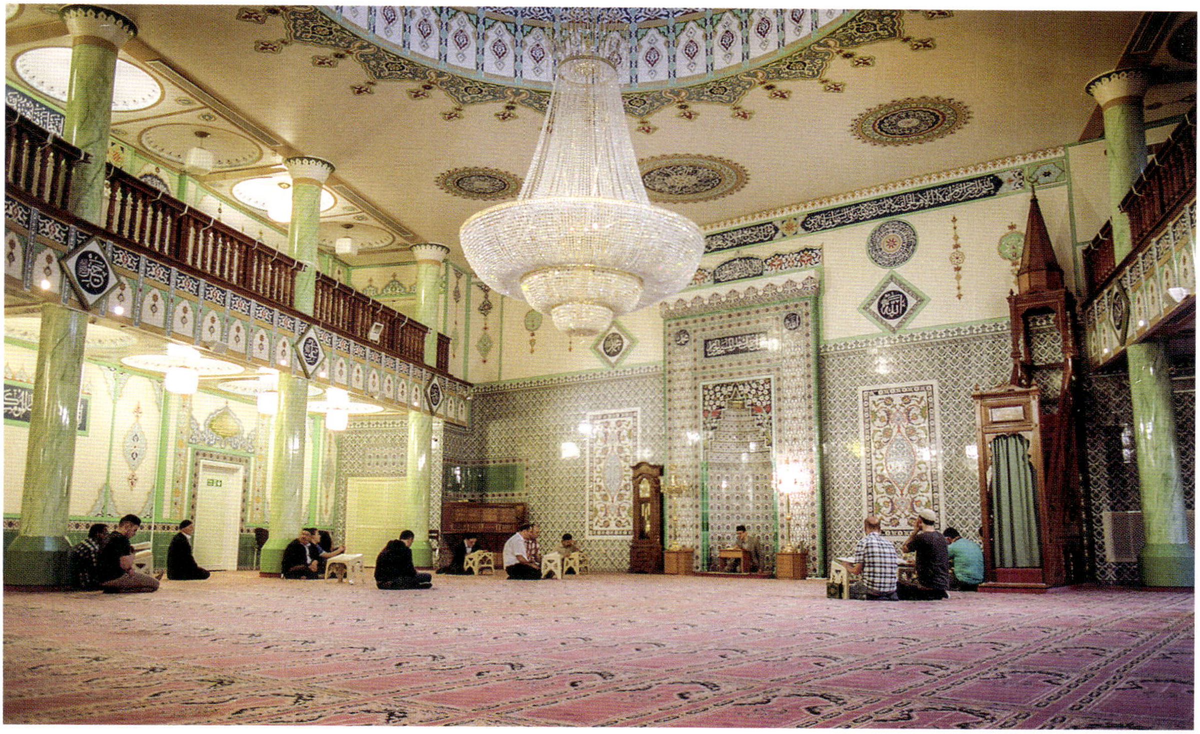

Previous: The caretaker, Bethnal Green, 2015
Above: Men's prayer hall, Dalston, 2016

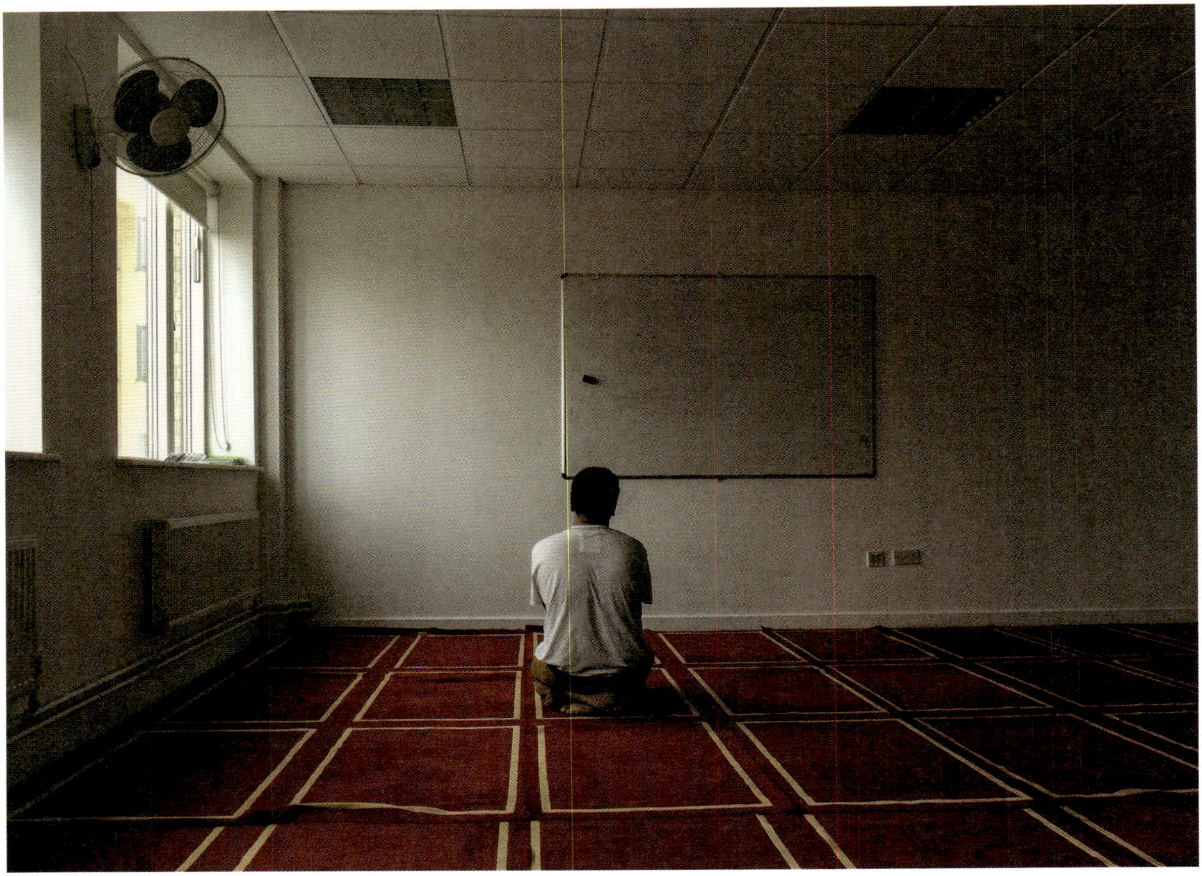

At the end of the Friday prayer, Whitechapel, 2016

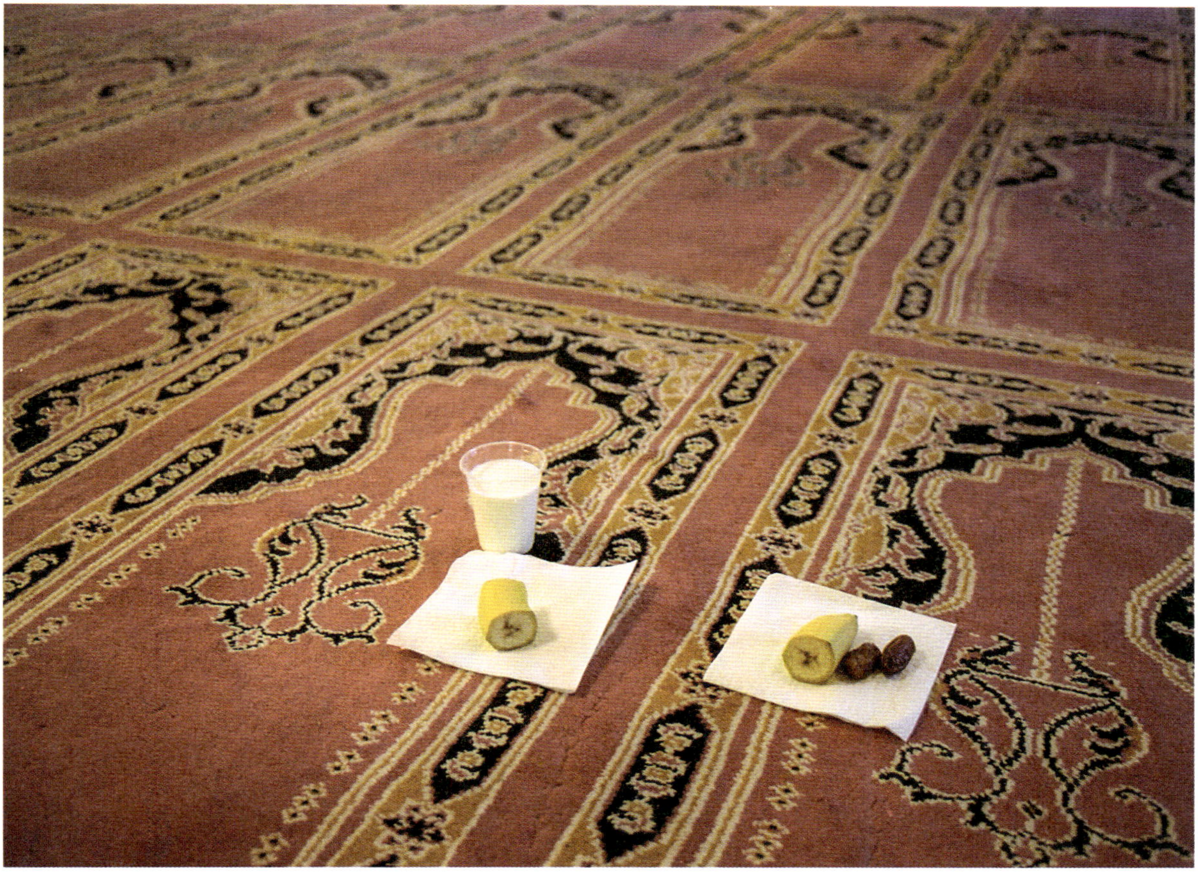

Breaking the fast, Dalston, 2015

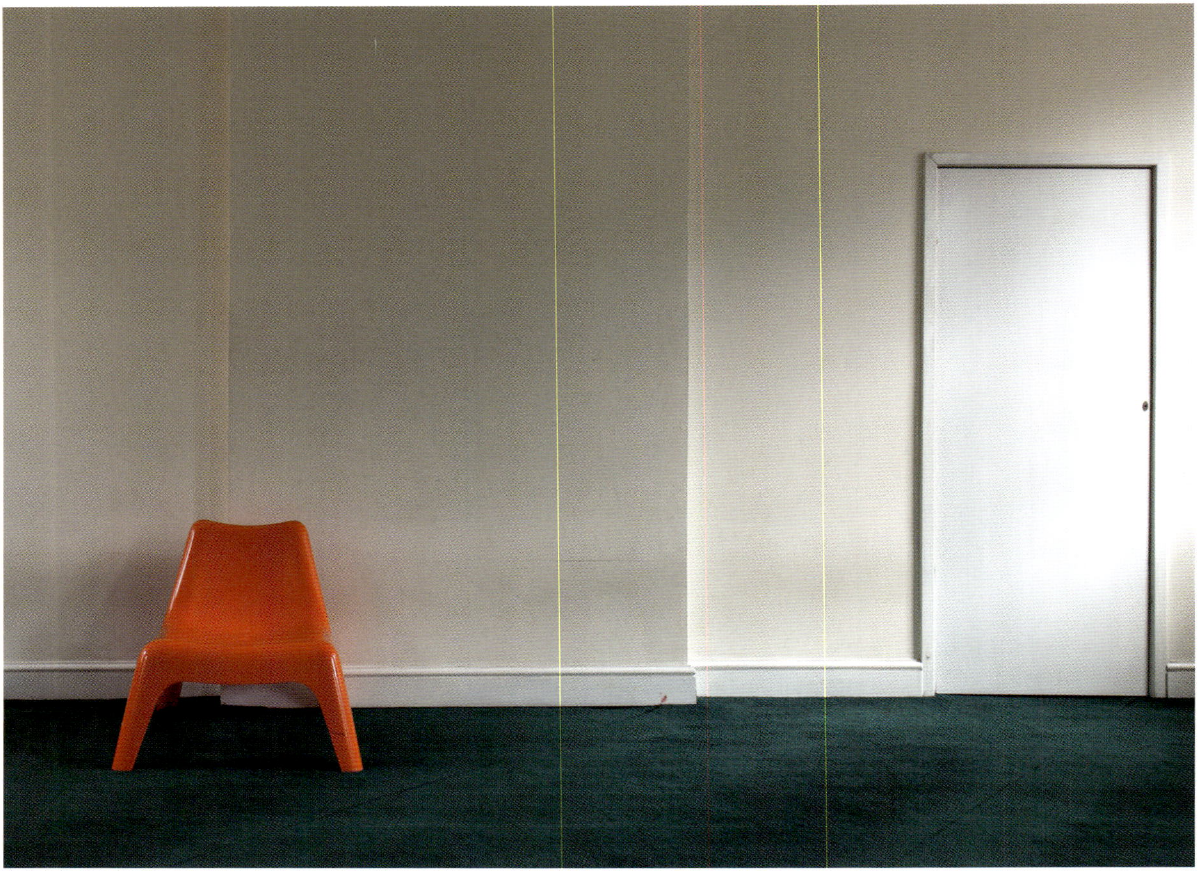

 Upper floor prayer hall, Spitalfields, 2014

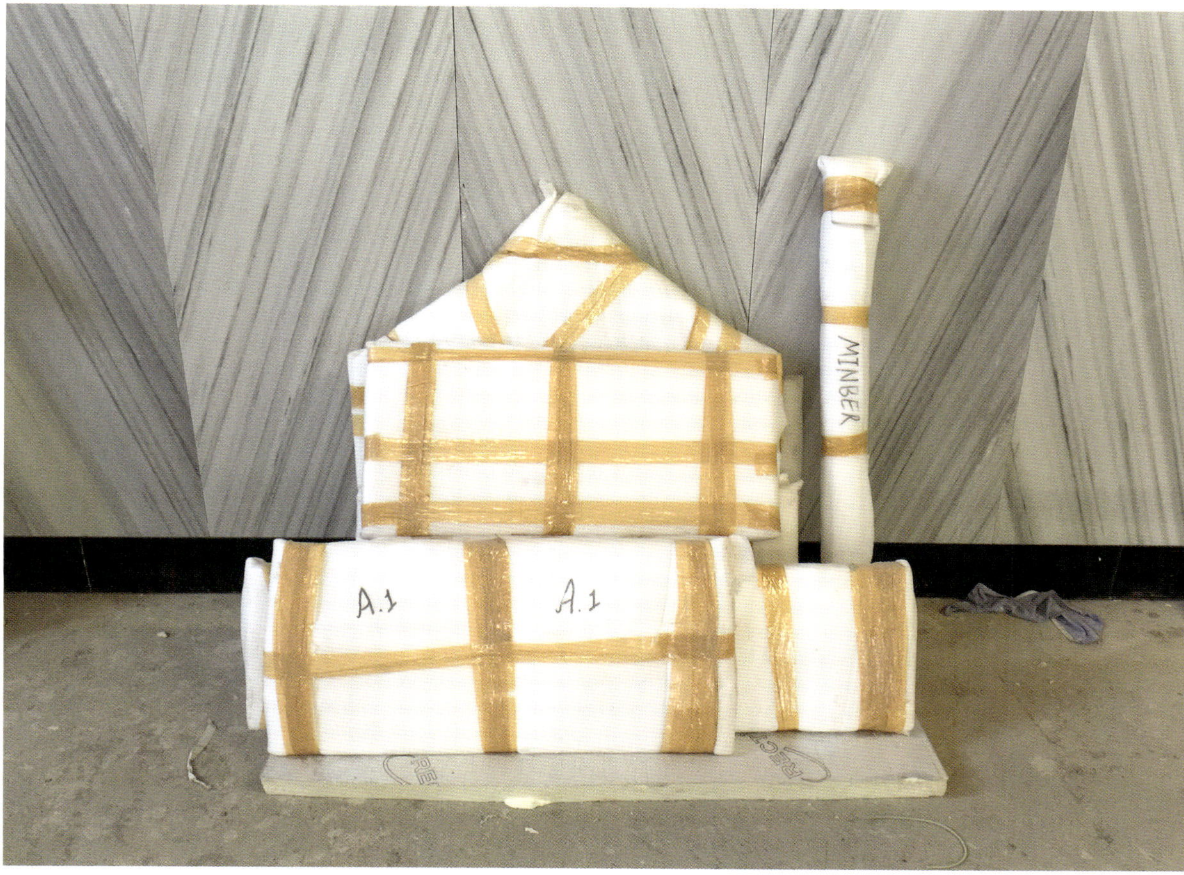

Delivery of marble to make the prayer niche, Bethnal Green, 2017

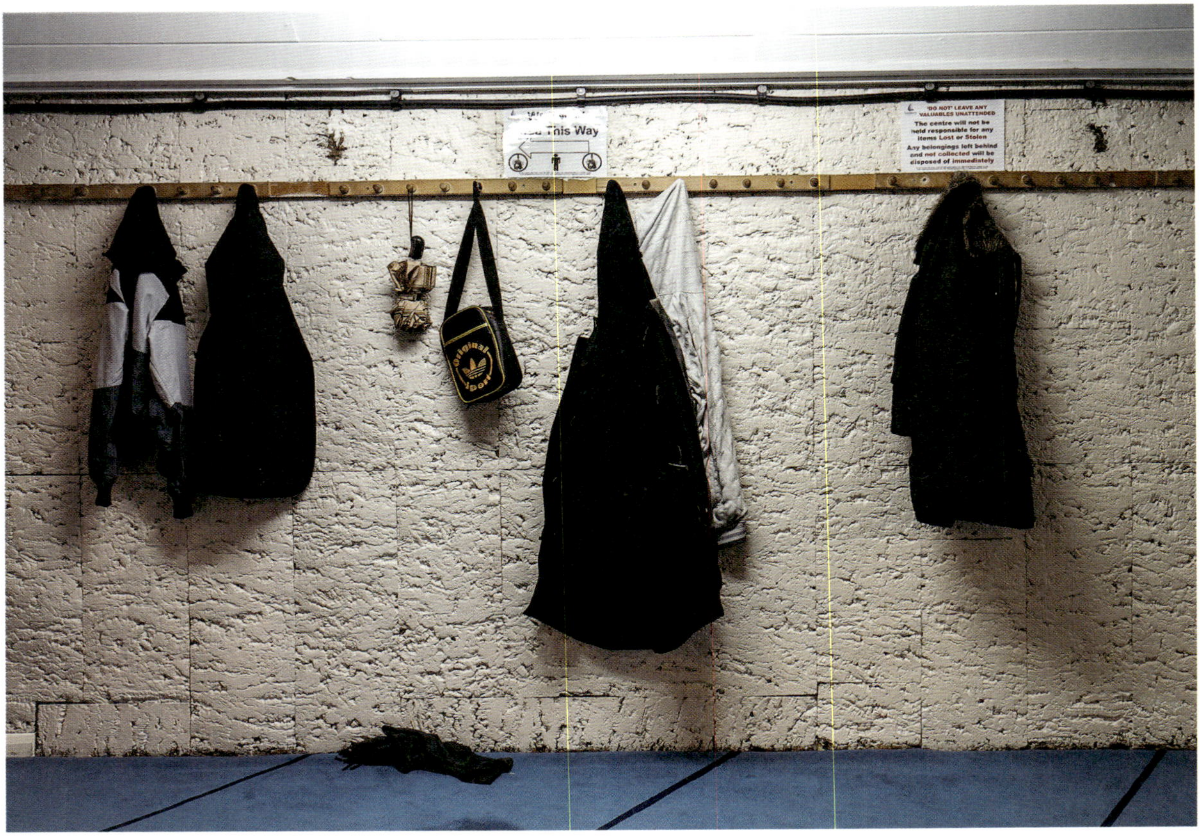

Coat racks outside the ablution room, Lewisham, 2014

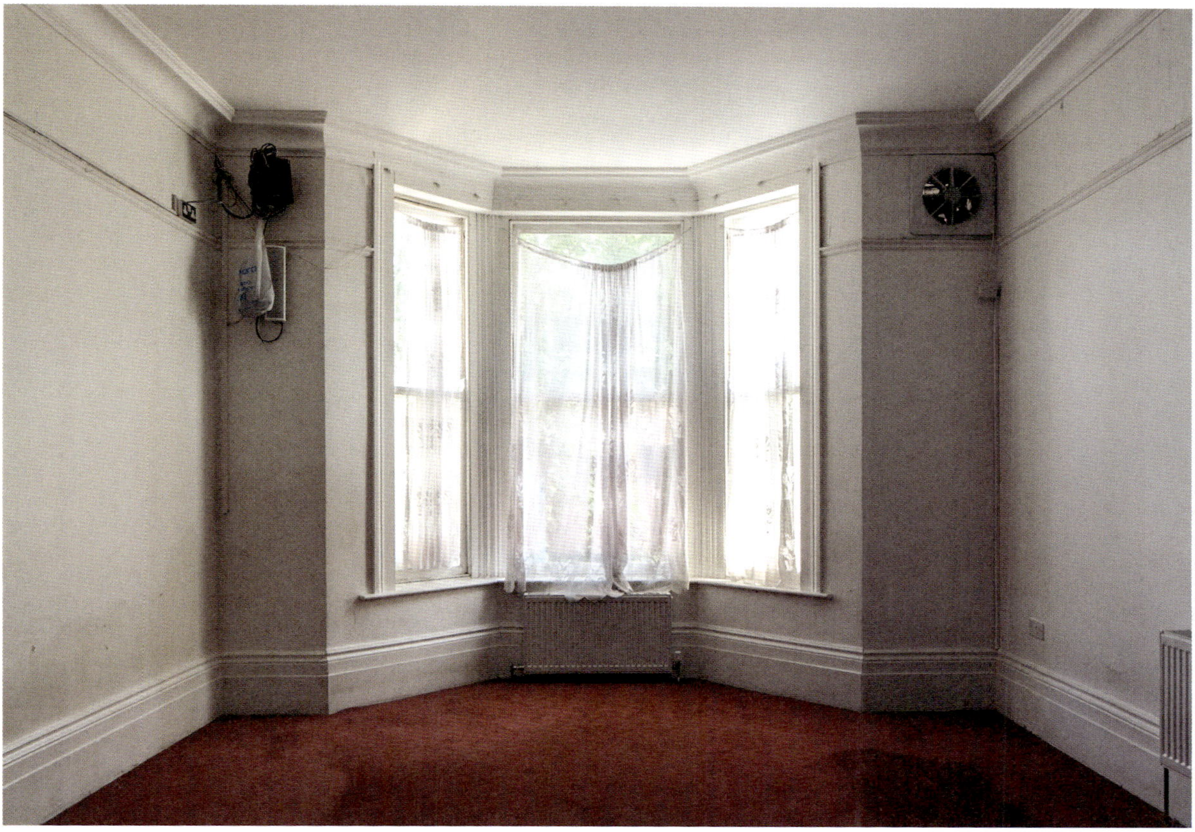

 Ground floor prayer hall, Brixton, 2015

Columbia Road

After the traders pack up for the day, scraps of petals and rubbish from an East London flower market form harmonious still lifes.

Johanna Neurath

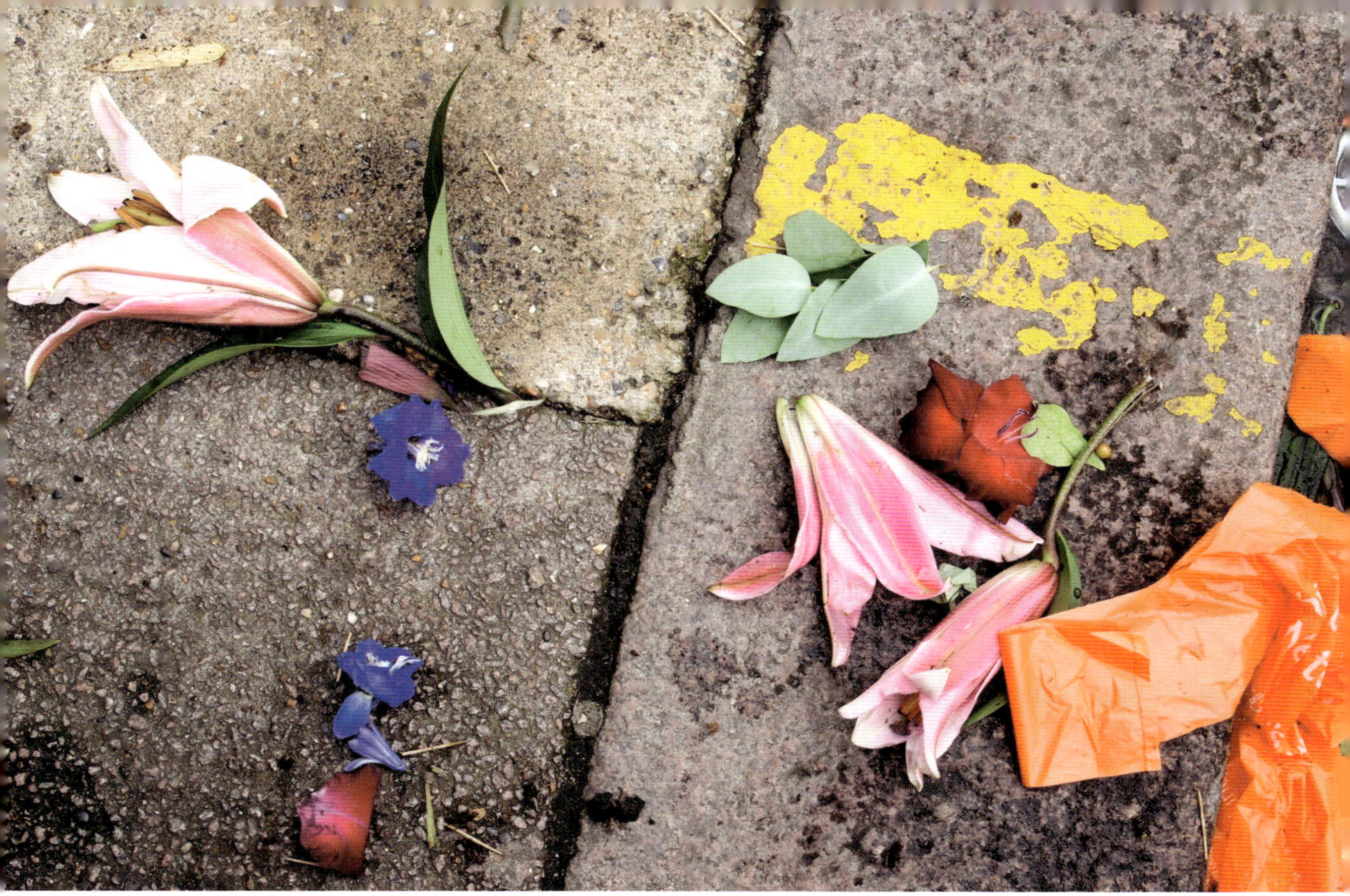

“Every photographer is a collector and I collect dead flowers,” says Johanna Neurath. After a decade of photographing Columbia Road, her collection numbers thousands. On Sundays, London’s famous flower market is awash with floral specimens, potted and cut. Neurath’s lens wasn’t trained on the stalls, however, but on the end-of-day debris scattered around them. At 3pm, as the traders pack away their wares, tatty petals, torn leaves, sodden scraps of plastic and discarded coffee cup lids litter the rough tarmac streets. Their chance configurations reveal a bright and sudden splendour, colours and textures glinting in the light.

Neurath has worked in illustrated publishing for 30 years and is currently Design Director at Thames & Hudson. Originally this project was a method to glean inspiration for book cover designs. “When I started, I was shooting with a graphic designer’s eye,” she remembers. “It was about the colour, the composition.” But over time it became something more. “What interested me was the fine line between whether something is ugly or beautiful, between whether it’s chaos or has a pattern.”

At first the stallholders weren’t sure what to make of this “crazy lady who photographed the rubbish” but soon she became a fixture. Neurath is the latest in a long tradition of urban photographers drawn to flower markets, starting with early black-and-white masters such as Eugène Atget and André Kertész who, in the late 19th and early 20th century documented the flower sellers and flea markets of Paris. The appeal is clear. If everyday urban life is your subject, a market offers untold pickings: piles of eye-catching produce, characterful traders, wiley shoppers and curious tourists all jostling about unpredictably in your viewfinder.

It’s not the obvious drama of the market on display in these pictures but something more elusive. In her day job Neurath was working on a big street photography anthology while shooting *Columbia Road*. “I had quite a strong reaction to that macho idea that it’s only a good picture if it’s really hard to get,” she says. “It’s a good photograph if it gives you pleasure to look at it.” And her pictures certainly do that; in a way, they’re more like still lifes than street photography, recalling in tone 16th century vanitas paintings in which flowers are carefully arranged alongside skulls and fruit. In the 20th century, American photographers Irving Penn and Robert Mapplethorpe, in their different ways, also shot flowers isolated against plain backdrops to highlight the elegance of their form.

But Neurath’s flowers are inseparable from their grimy environment. Beyond her choice of framing, there’s no intervention at play here. When she first published the pictures online, some overseas viewers expressed surprise that they were shot in the capital. “It’s so colourful, I thought London was grey,” came one comment. The sky might have been the dullest grey imaginable, but that’s not where we’re looking. These flowers may have been jettisoned, forgotten, trodden underfoot but they’re extraordinary nonetheless.

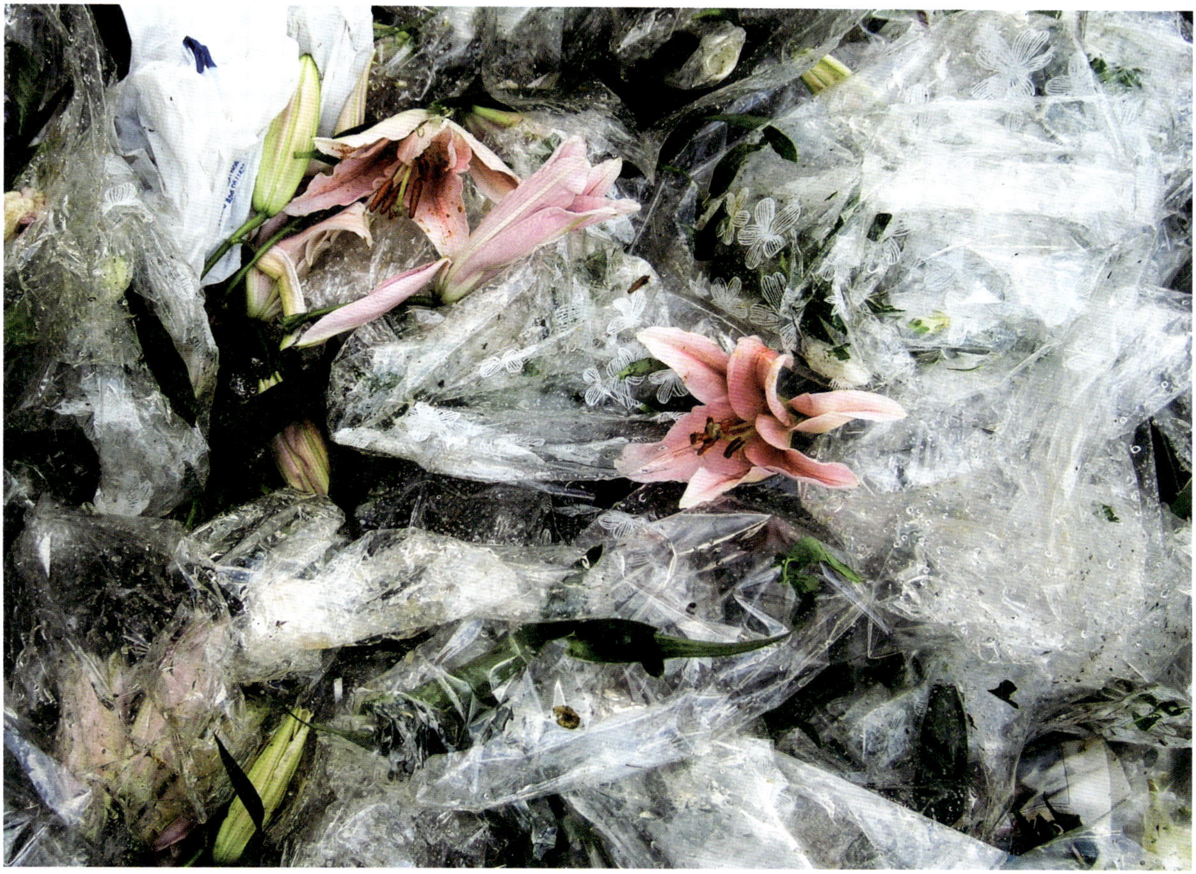

Previous: Columbia Road, London E2, 2009
Above: Sea of plastic and lilies, London E2, 2006

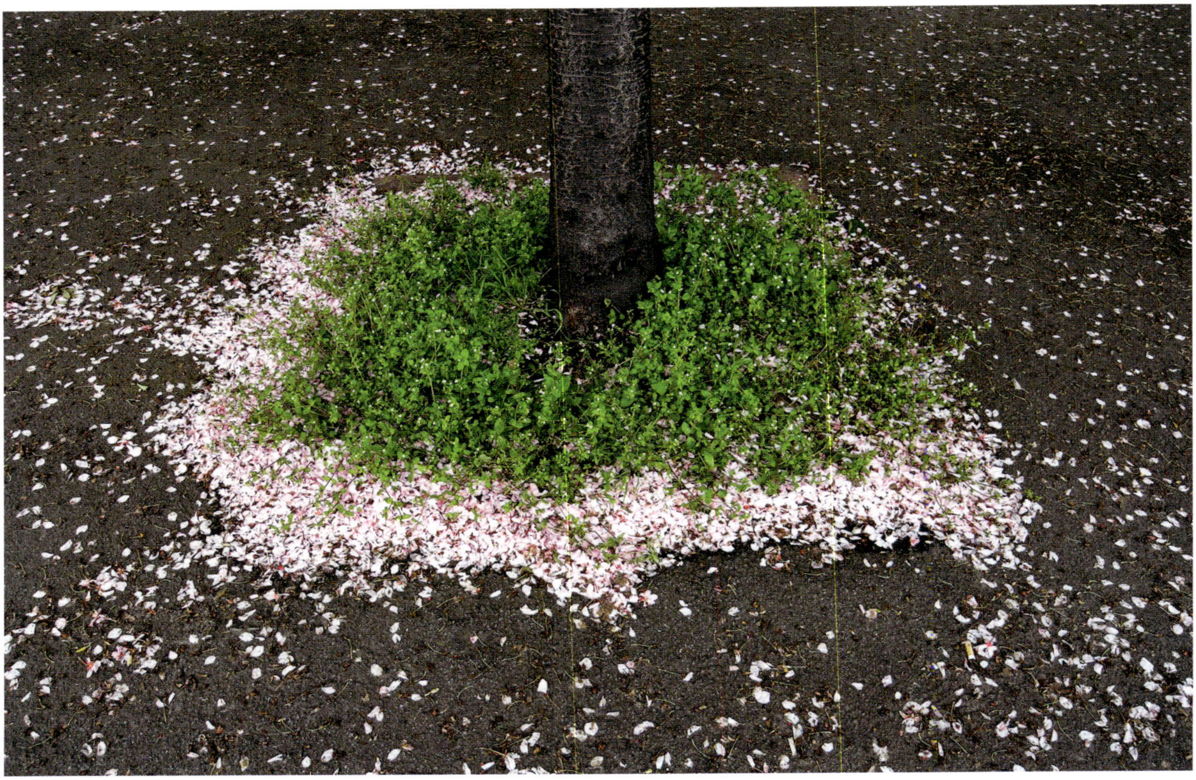

May day green and pink, London E2, 2008

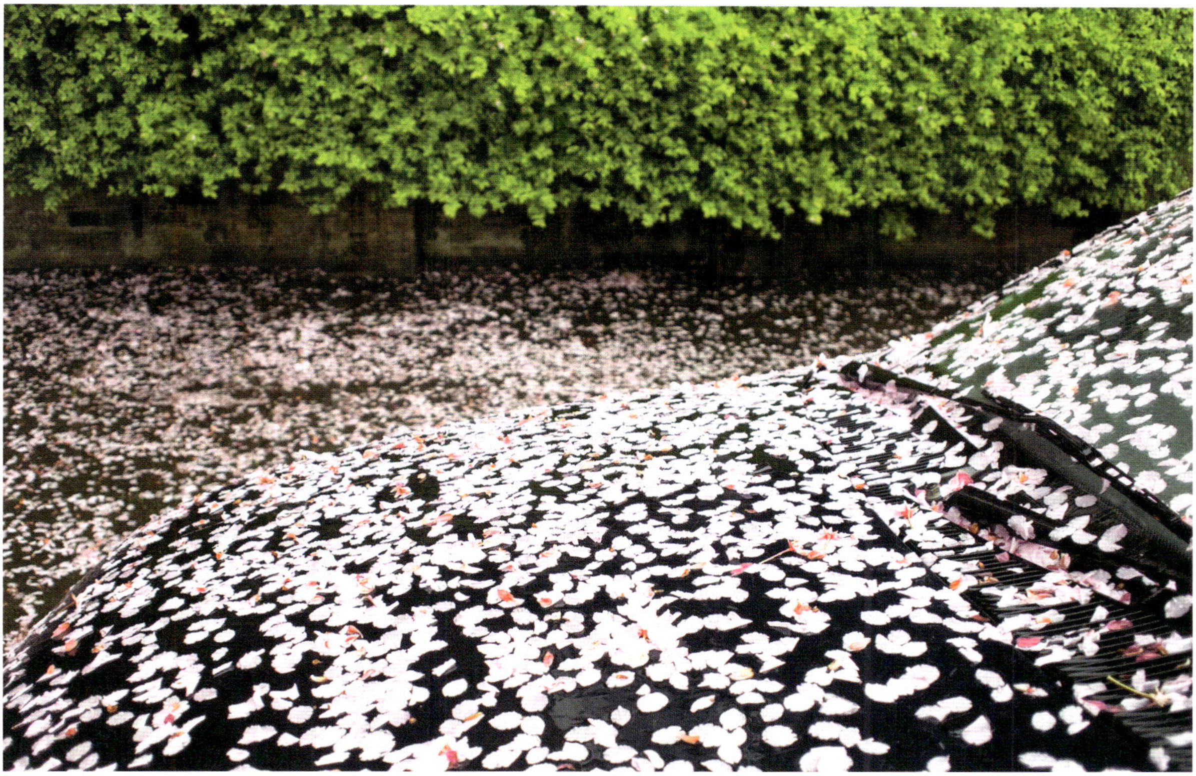

Pink camouflage, London E2, 2010

Overleaf: The gutter (under an orange awning), London E2, 2006

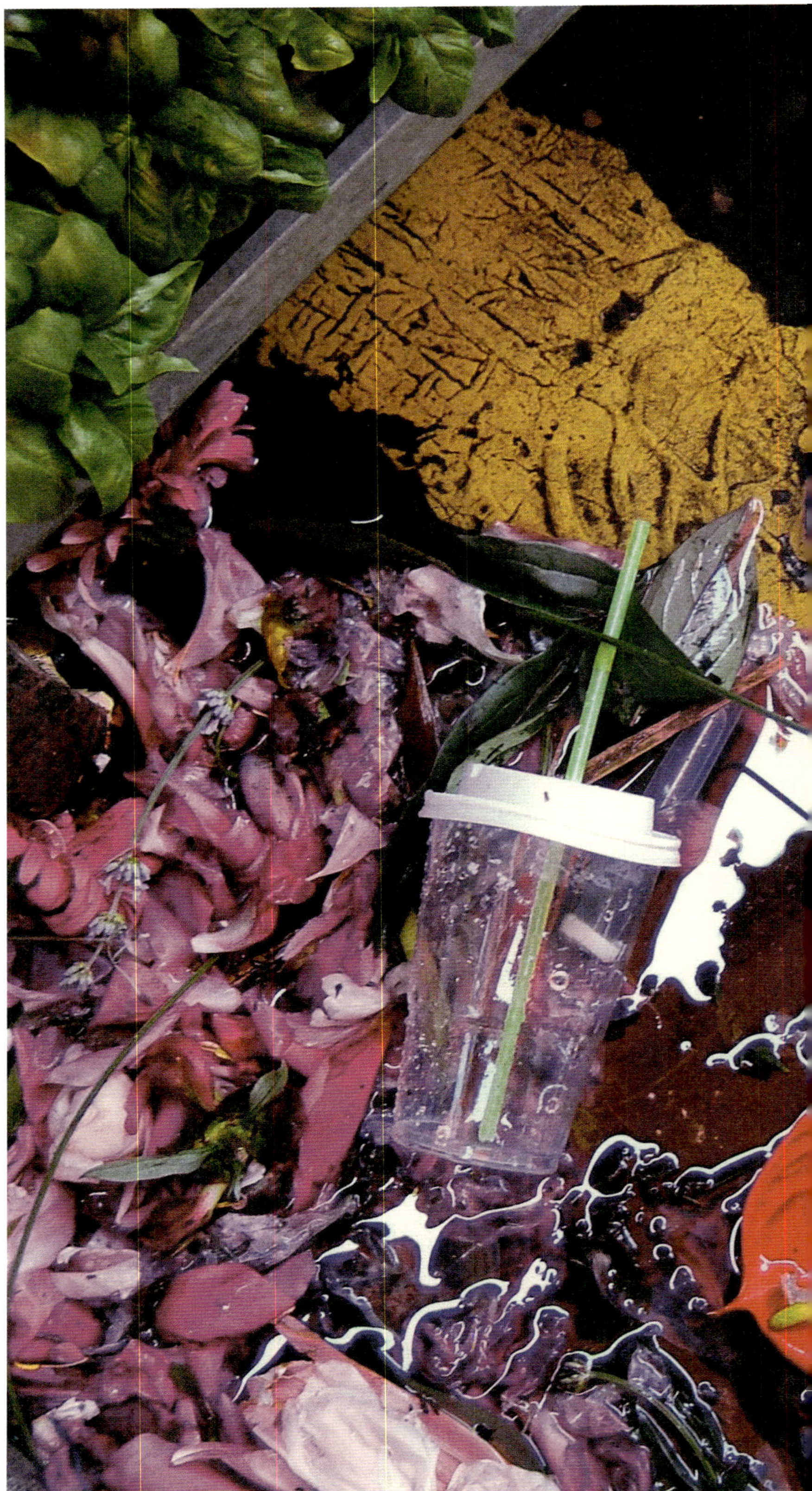

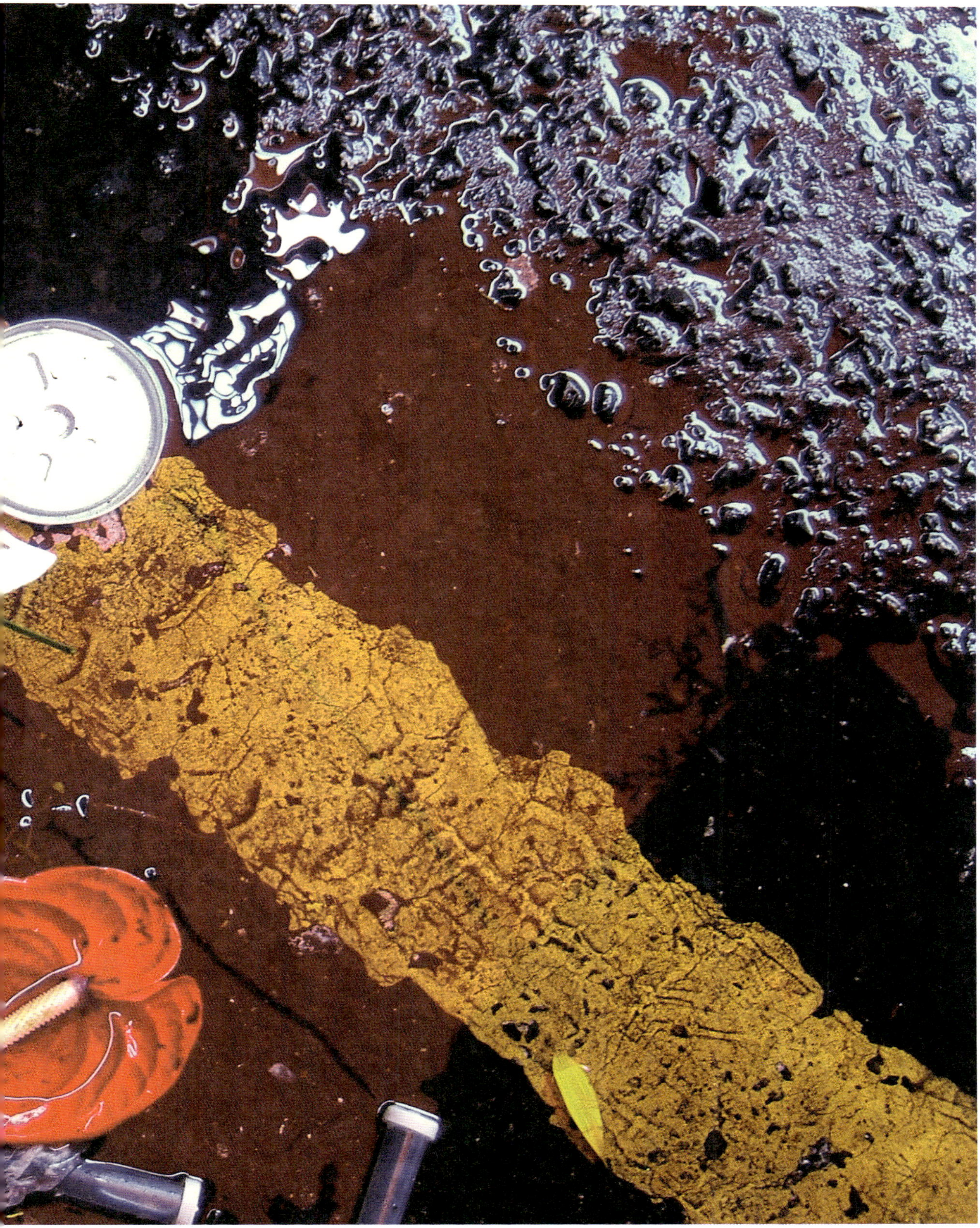

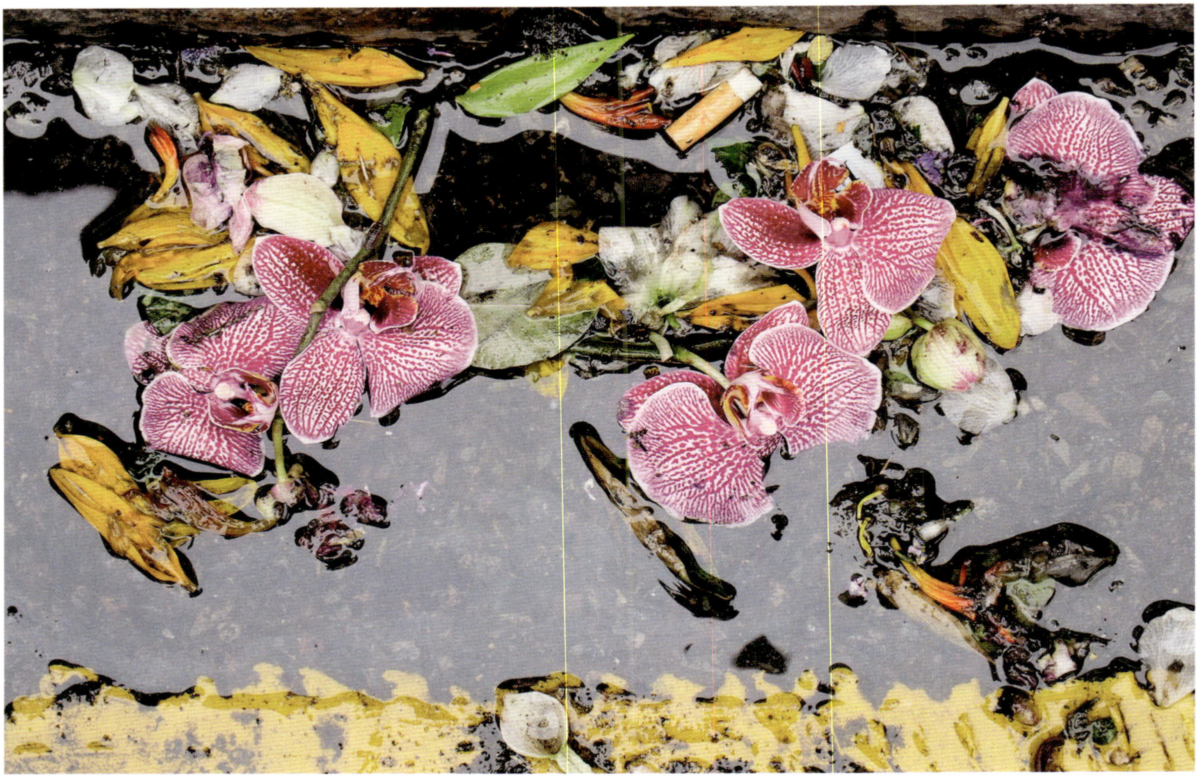

Orchids and a fag butt, London E2, 2009

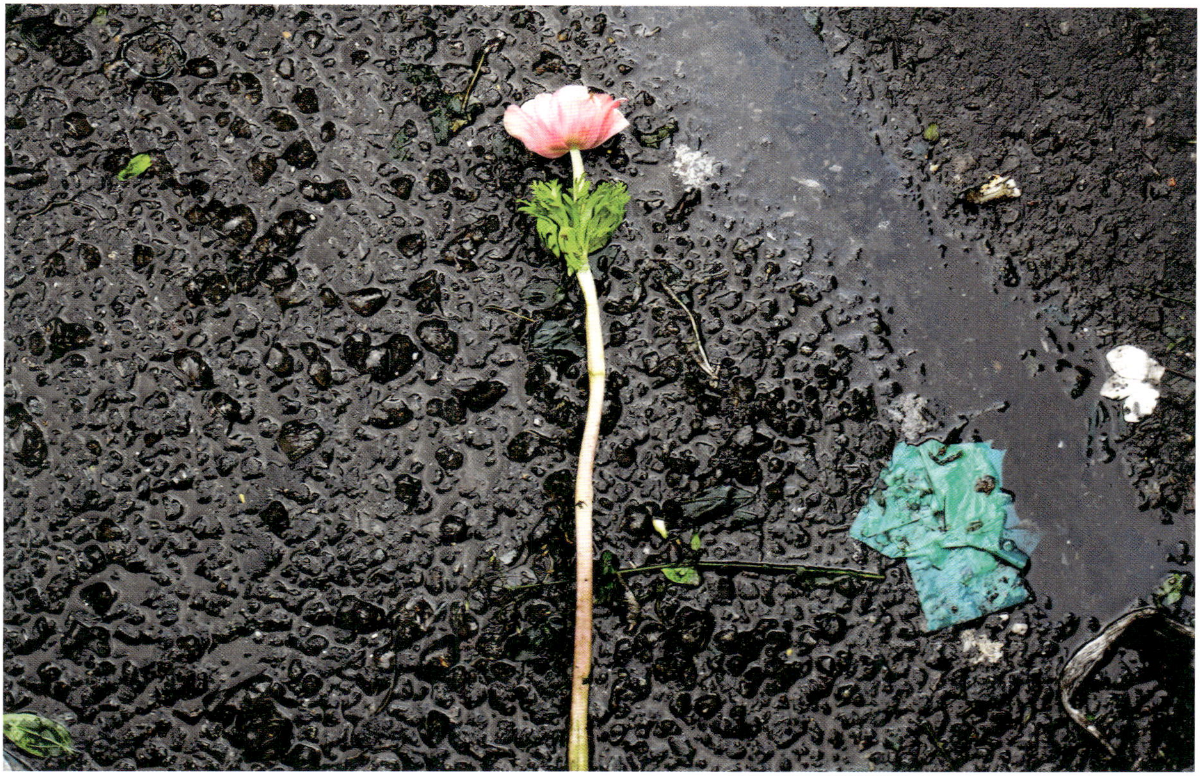

Lonely anemone, London E2, 2008

Overleaf: Peppers (again), London E2, 2006

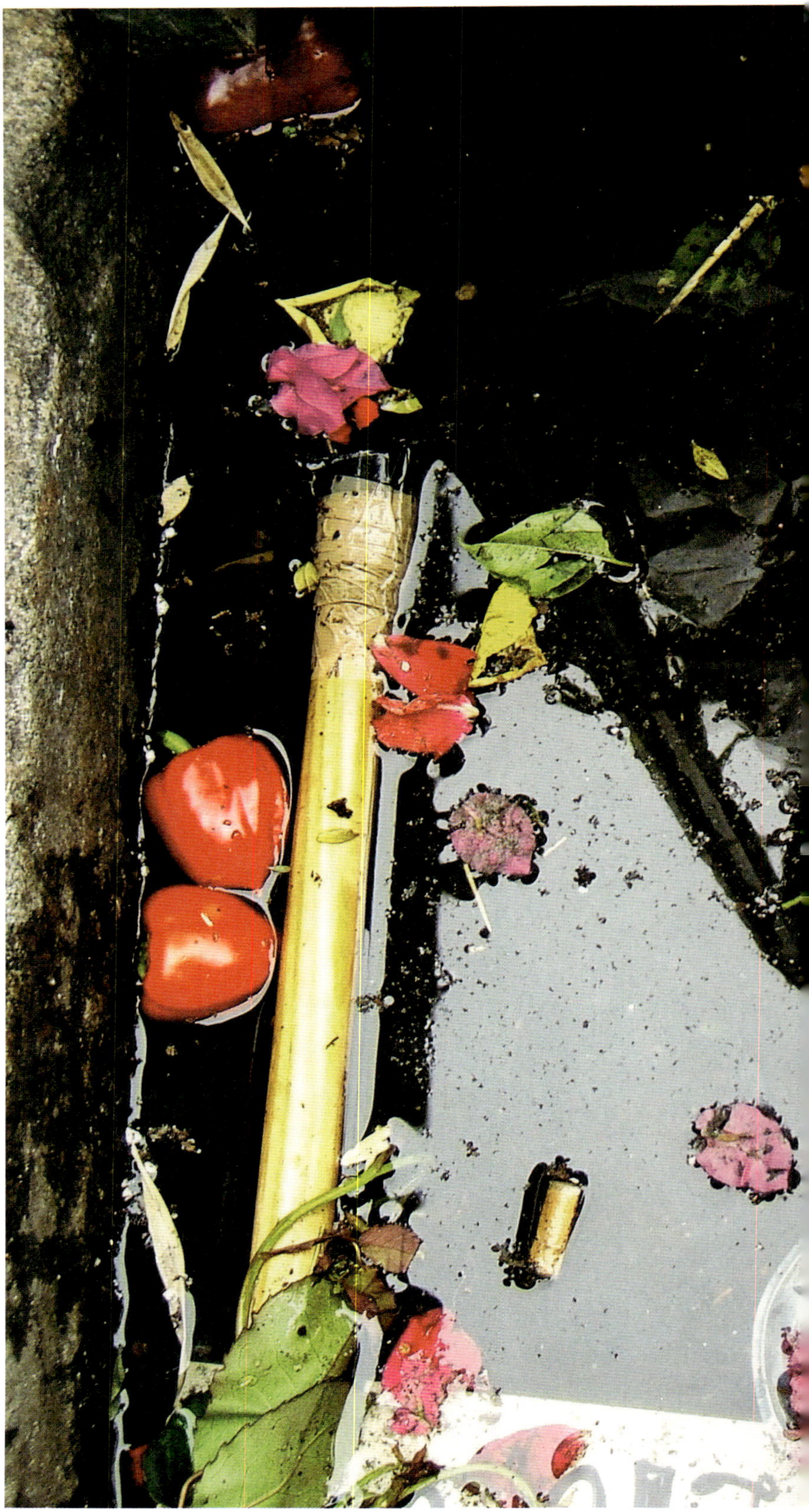

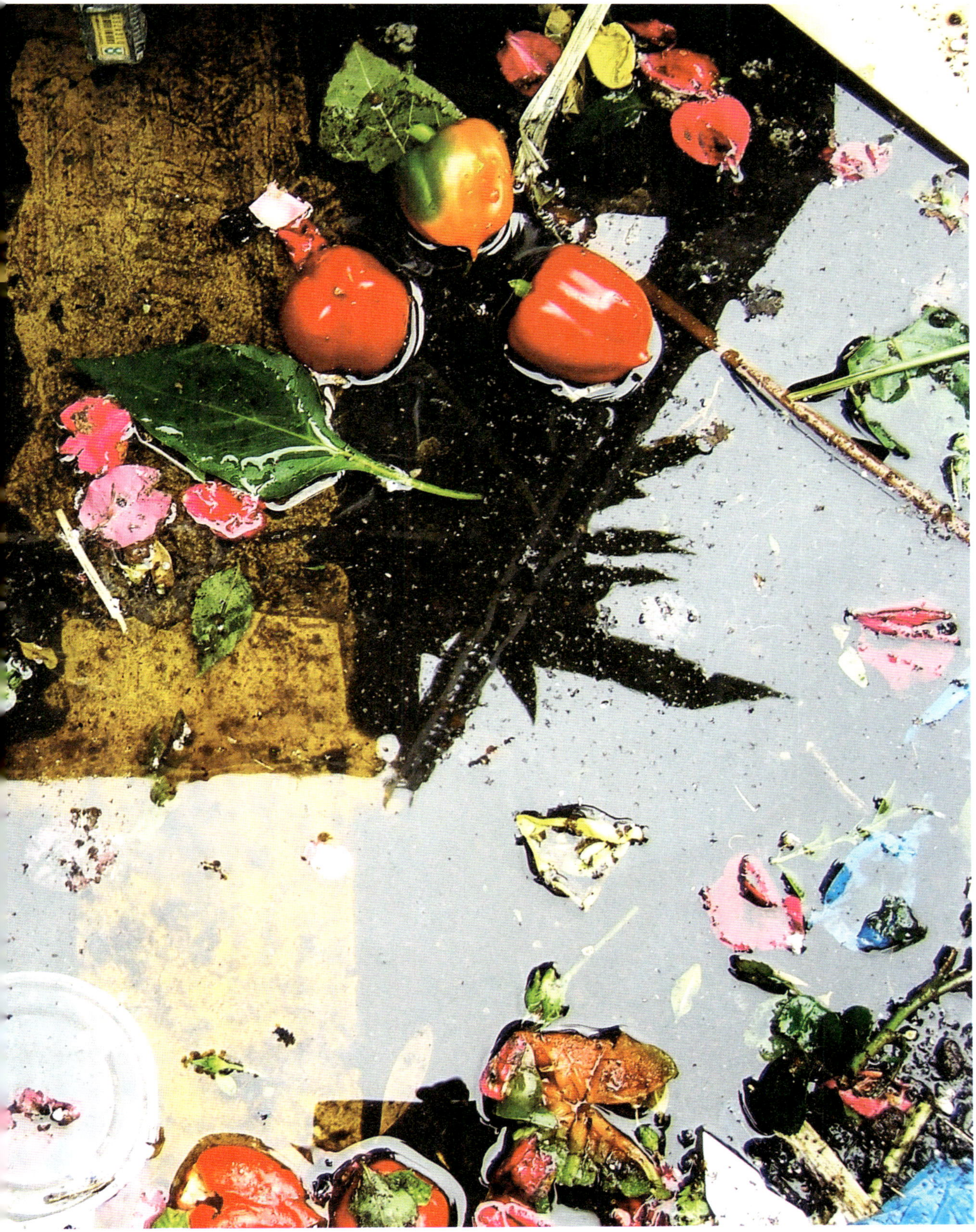

Microcosms

Mapping the city through chewed-up gum found on pavements produces pictures that resemble moonscapes.

Effie Paleologou

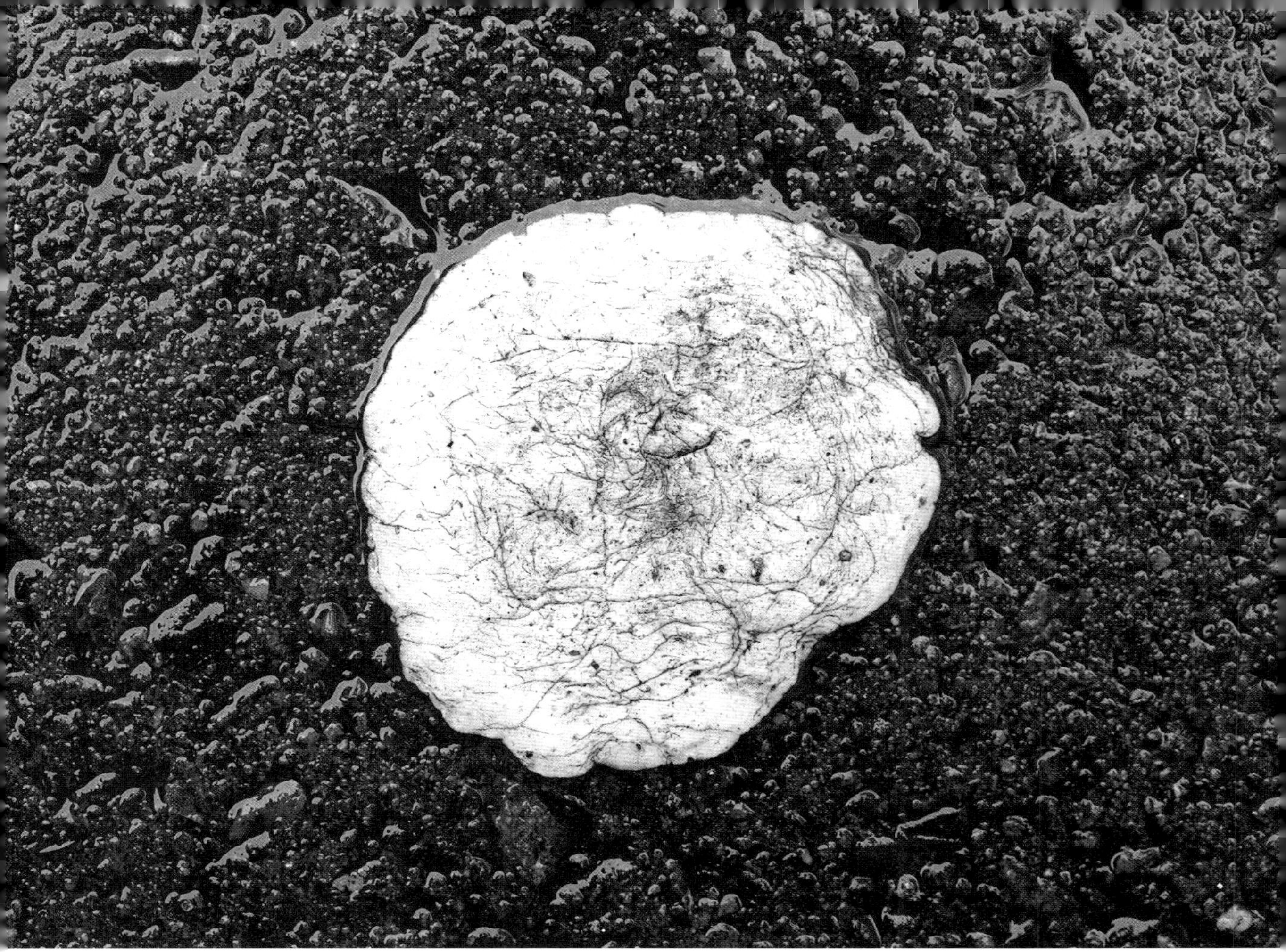

There's something exceptionally revolting about chewing gum. Perhaps because we see it littering the streets, knowing it doesn't biodegrade – but also because of the yuk factor: it once mingled with someone else's bodily fluids. "It gives pleasure, but has no nutritional value," Effie Paleologou points out, "And it's something to be discarded afterwards." Spitting your gum is generally seen as deviant, and carries heavily penalties in some cities. But as anthropologist Mary Douglas wrote, dirt is just "matter out of place" and in Paleologou's studies of the encrusted chewing gum on London's pavements, it appears rather lovely.

Paleologou shot the pictures from close-up, using a large-format camera and macro lens. The subject remains ambiguous despite every corner of the frame being in pin-sharp focus. She likens her pictures to "aerial photography" and it's true that these strange structures look more like vast geological, even celestial, formations than small gob-soaked blobs of flavoured synthetic rubber. "I call them collaborative landscapes because the city is in constant flux," says Paleologou. "One person spits it out, many others step on it, then the weather changes it – some become almost one with the background."

Microcosms is the result of many walks around a triangle of London that connects Old Street, Bethnal Green and Liverpool Street stations, locations selected as much for the varying textures of their ground surfaces as their distance from the photographer's studio. Paleologou is fascinated not just by London but by cities in general. Both *Microcosms* and Paleologou's previous work in London, Paris and New York, *Mean Streets*, is inspired by literature about the modern metropolis. The 19th century French poet Baudelaire wandering among the urban crowds was an influence, says Paleologou, as was the 20th century German cultural theorist Walter Benjamin's descriptions of these wanderings in his essay *The Flâneur*.

As well as an artist and observer Paleologou is also a kind of detective, mapping the city through fossilised traces of human saliva. The abandoned gum is both anonymous and identifying, she hypothesised, if it carries a trace of DNA. When *Microcosms* was first exhibited at the Science Gallery in Guy's Hospital, it was this idea that came to the fore. It turned out that there had been no research into whether chewing gum does contain DNA, so Paleologou collaborated with scientists from King's College London to find out. The result: there is some DNA but not in sufficient amounts to test it with today's technology.

And so, out of disgust comes something enlightening, something enchanting. *Microcosms* is a visually pleasurable experience, maybe even more so once you know what you're looking at. "It's about the act of looking and finding," adds Paleologou, before quoting Oscar Wilde. "We are all in the gutter, but some of us are looking at the stars." In *Microcosms*, though, it's only by looking into the gutter that we find stars.

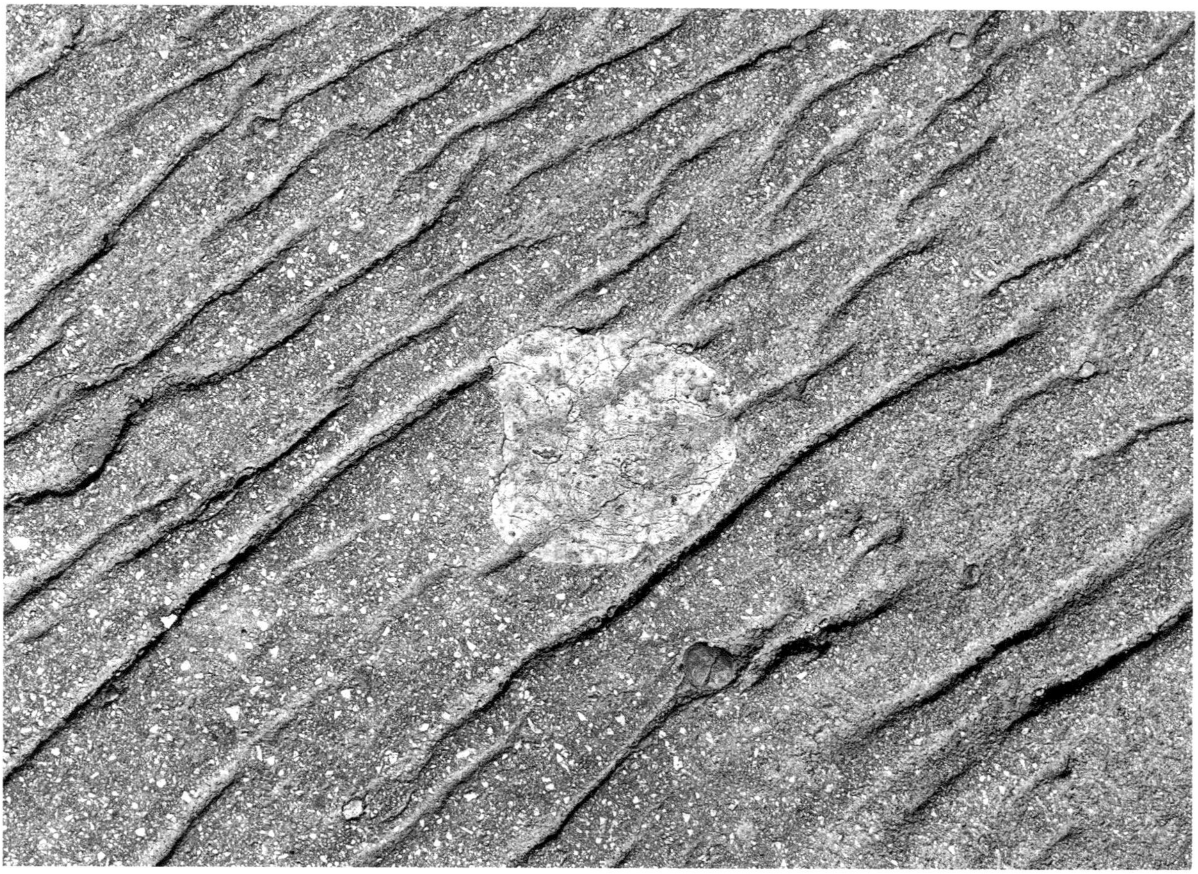

Previous: Aerial View No.3, 2013–17
Above: Aerial View No.7, 2013–17

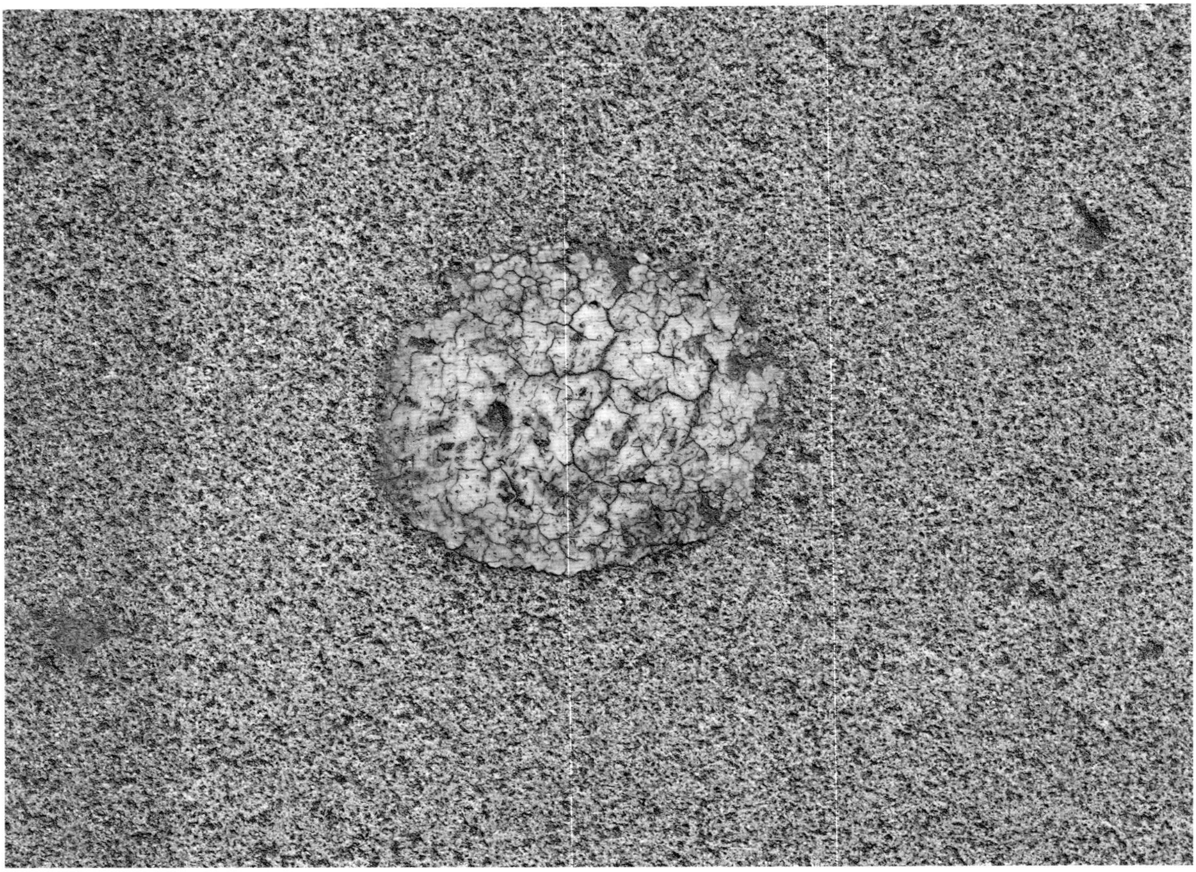

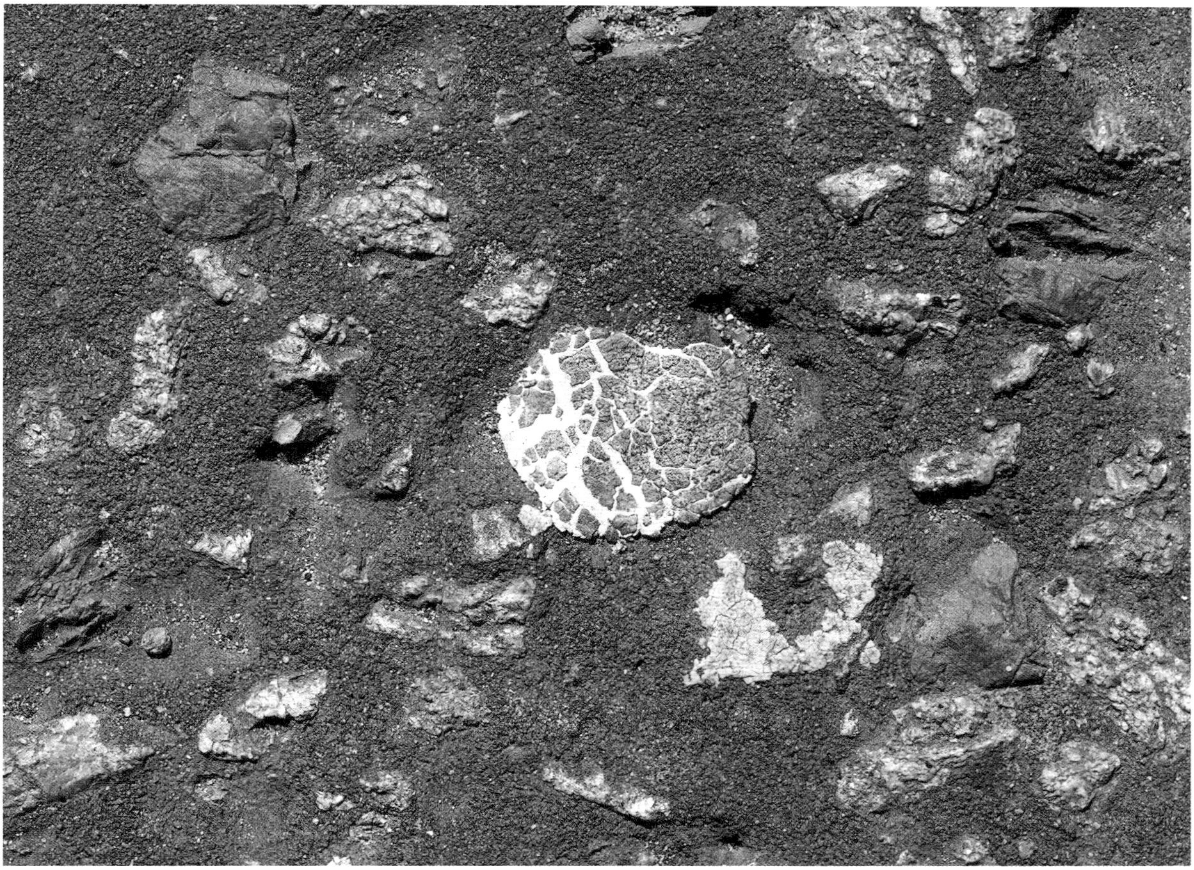

Aerial View No.6, 2013–17

Overleaf: Aerial View No.9, 2013–17

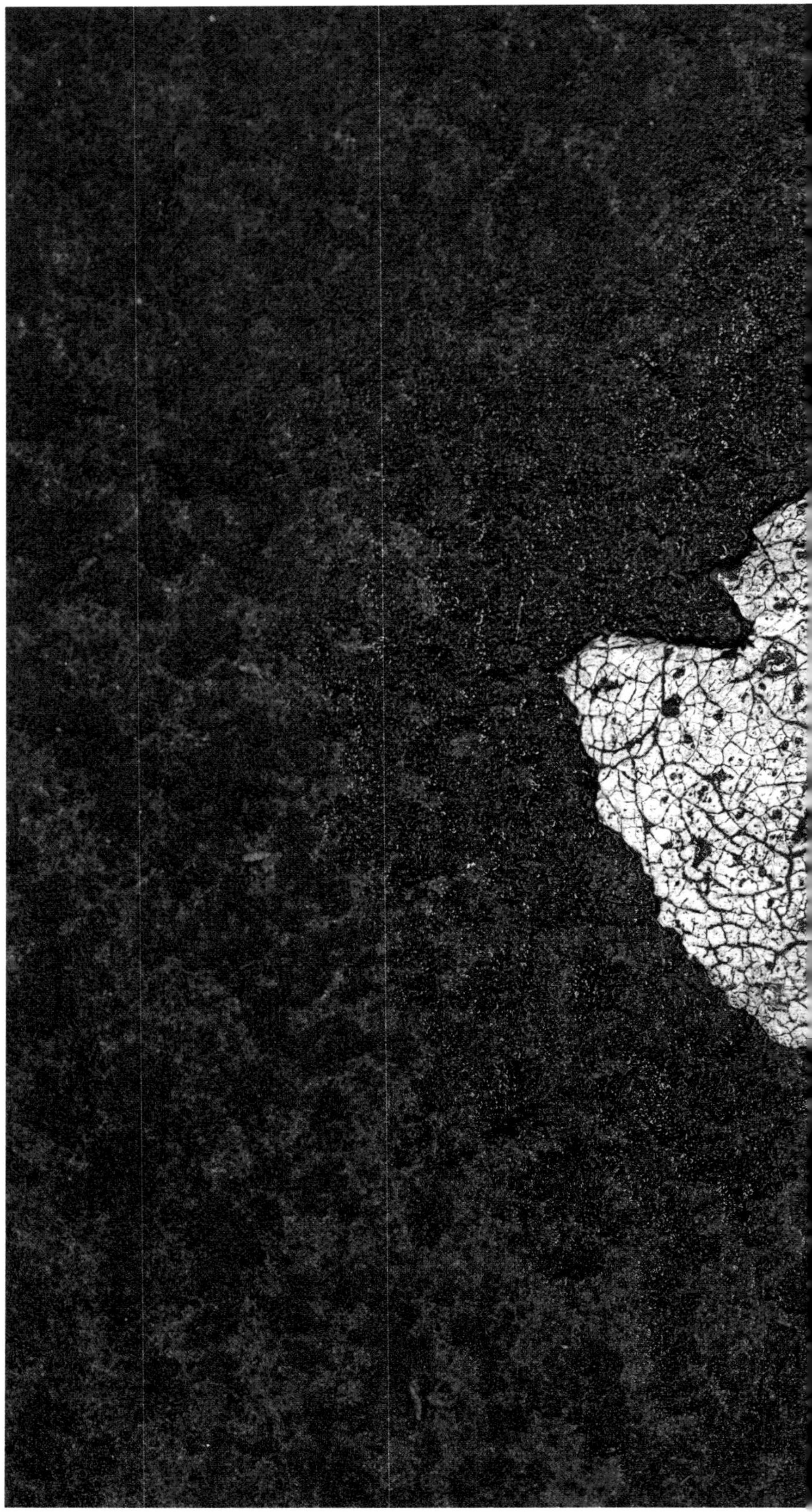

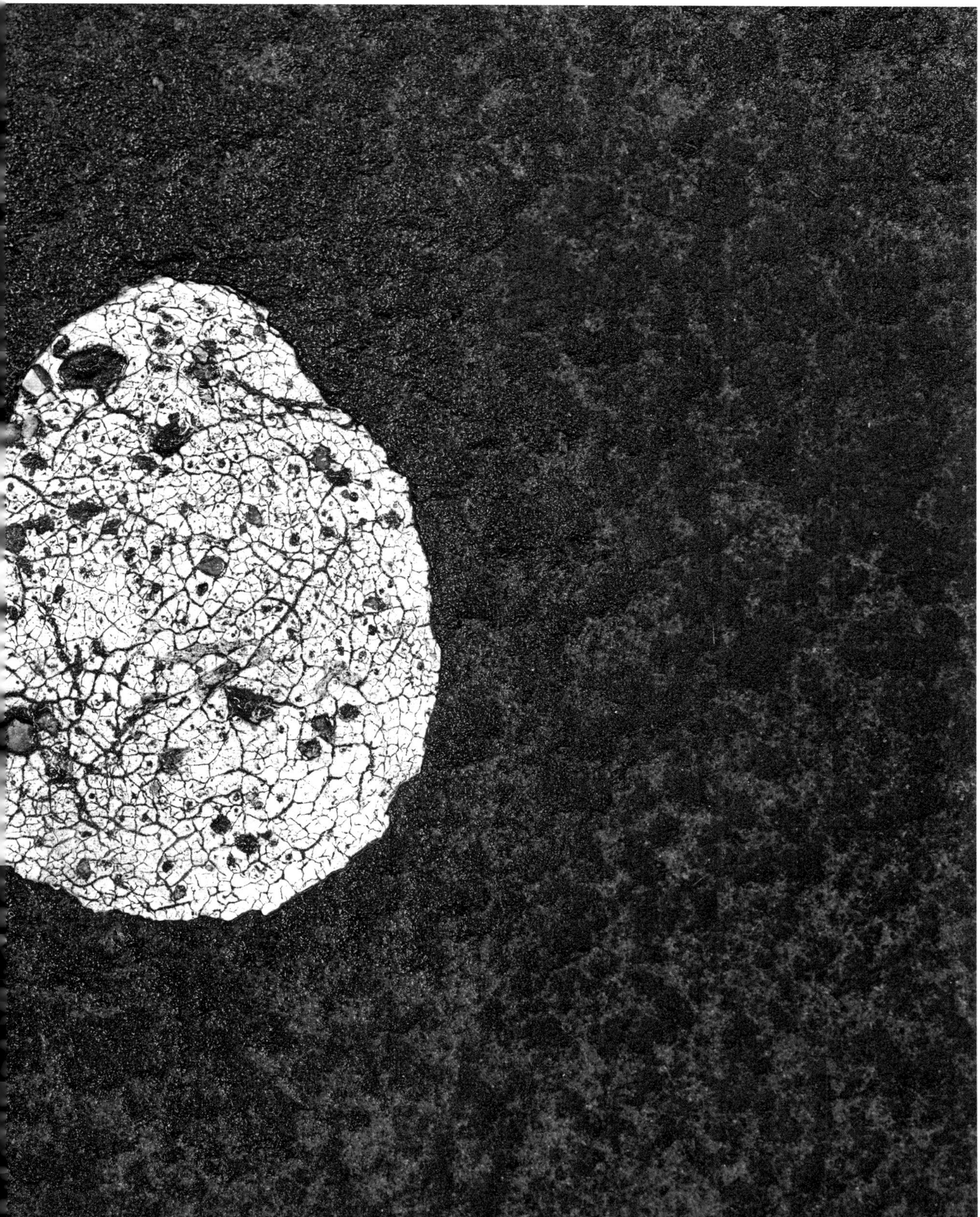

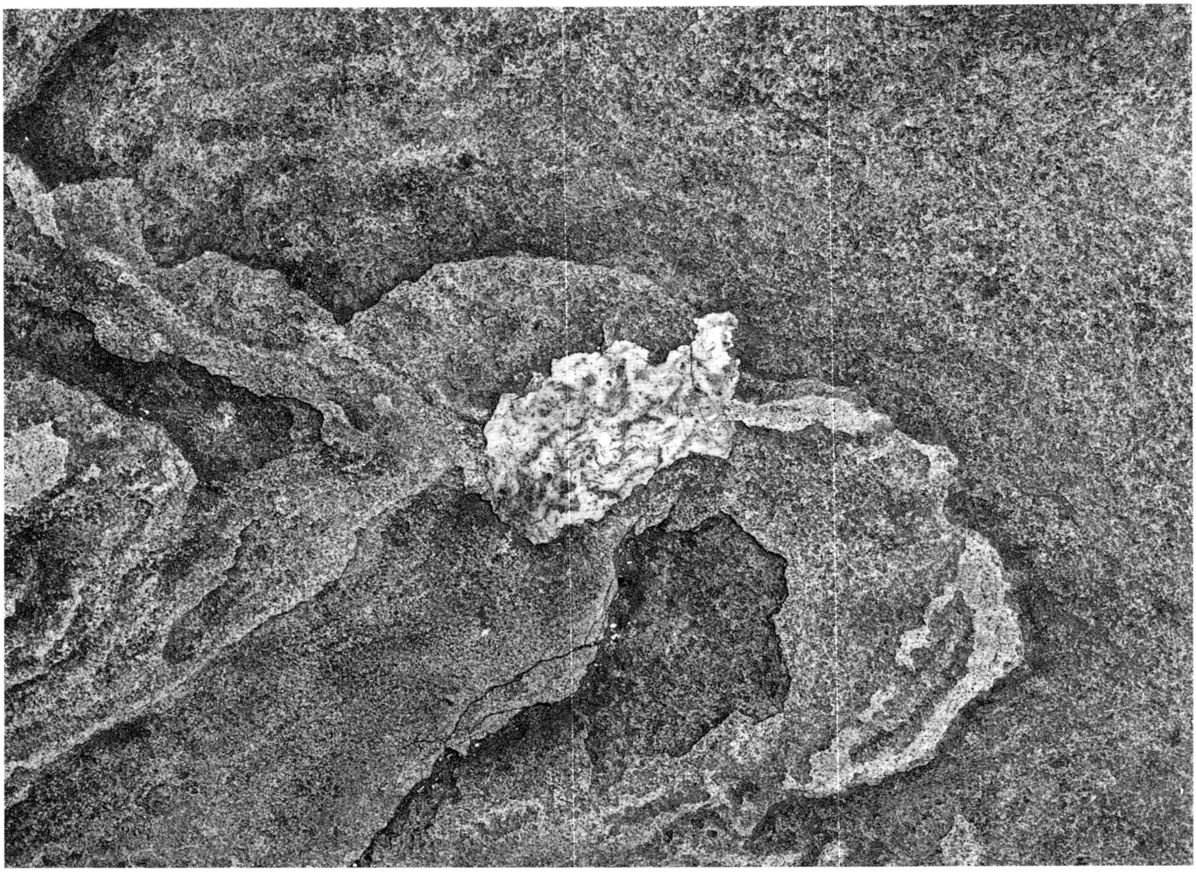

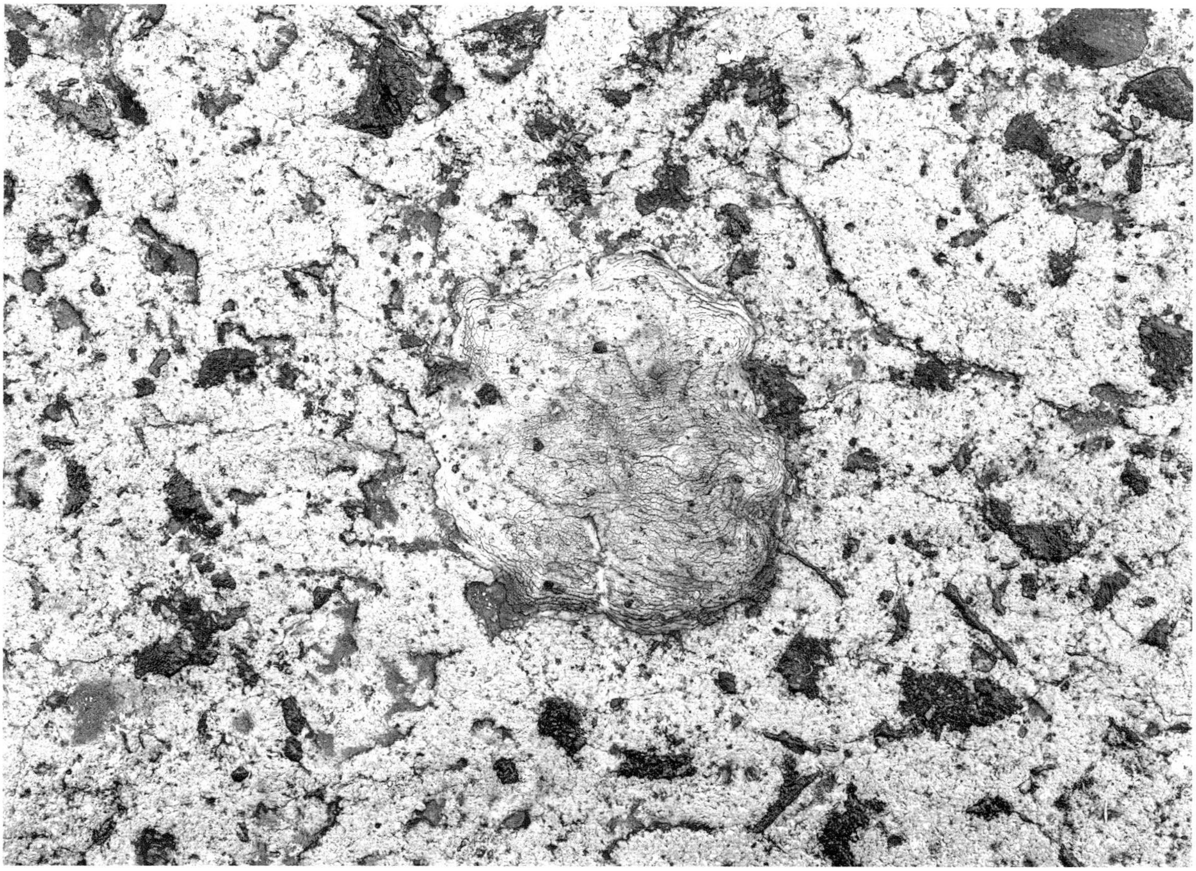

Aerial View No.5, 2013–17

Effie Paleologou

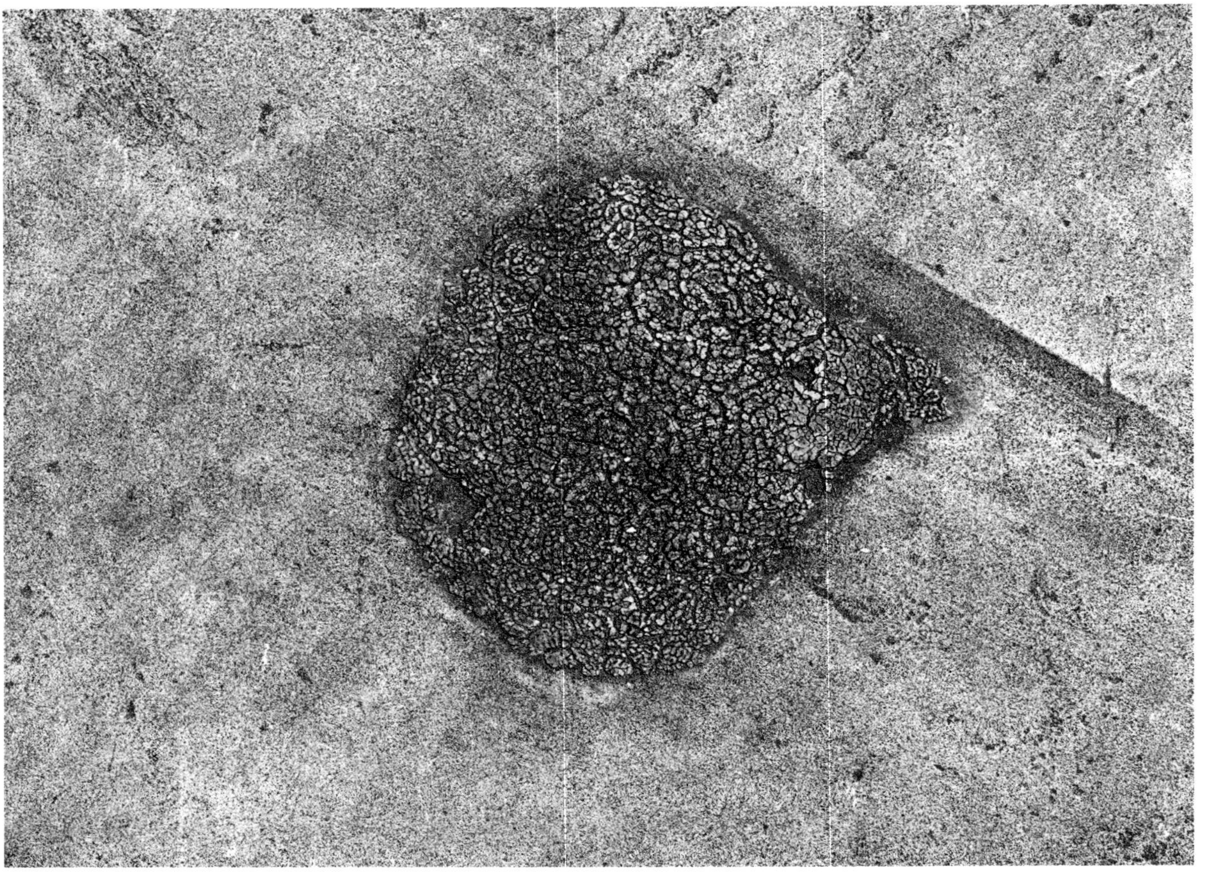

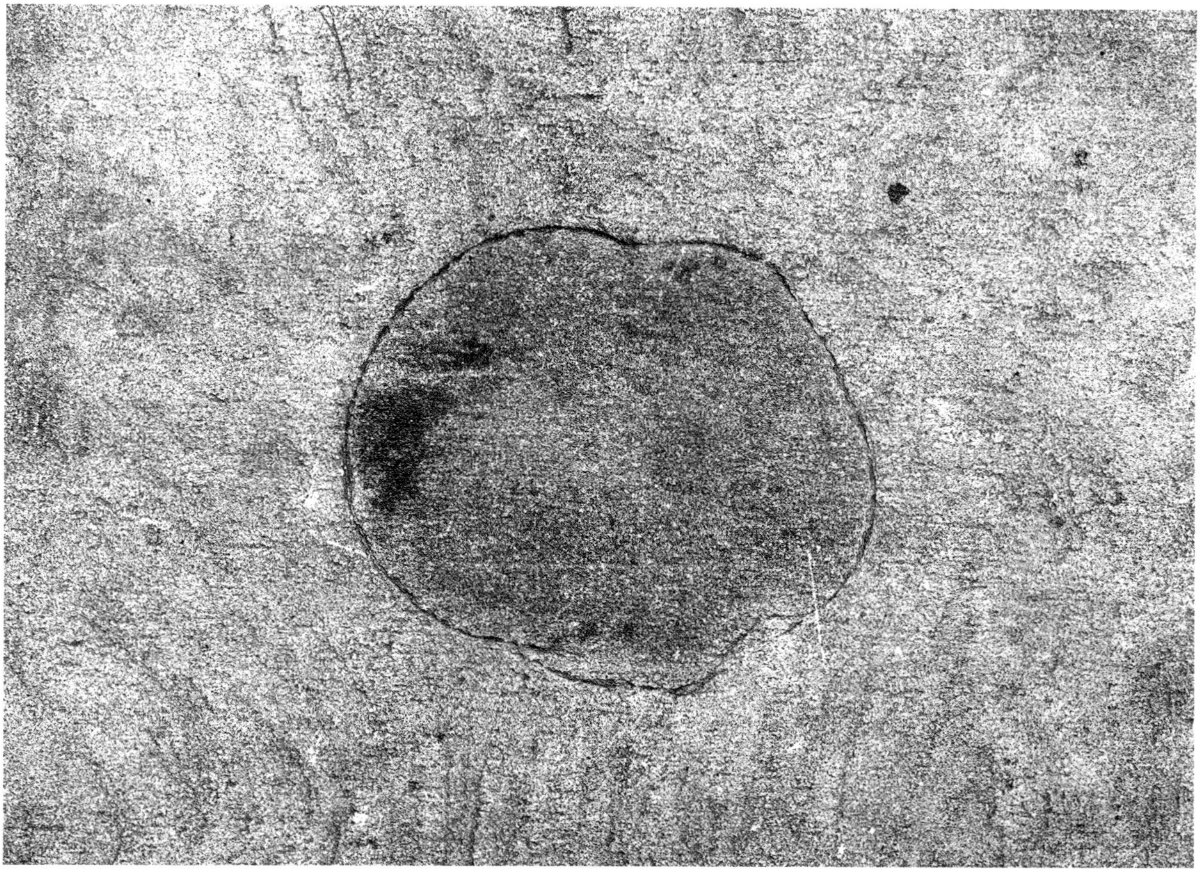

Aerial View No.13, 2013–17

Effie Paleologou

All That Life Can Afford

Freezing the urban surge for a second reveals surreal moments, some witty, some wistful, others downright odd.

Matt Stuart

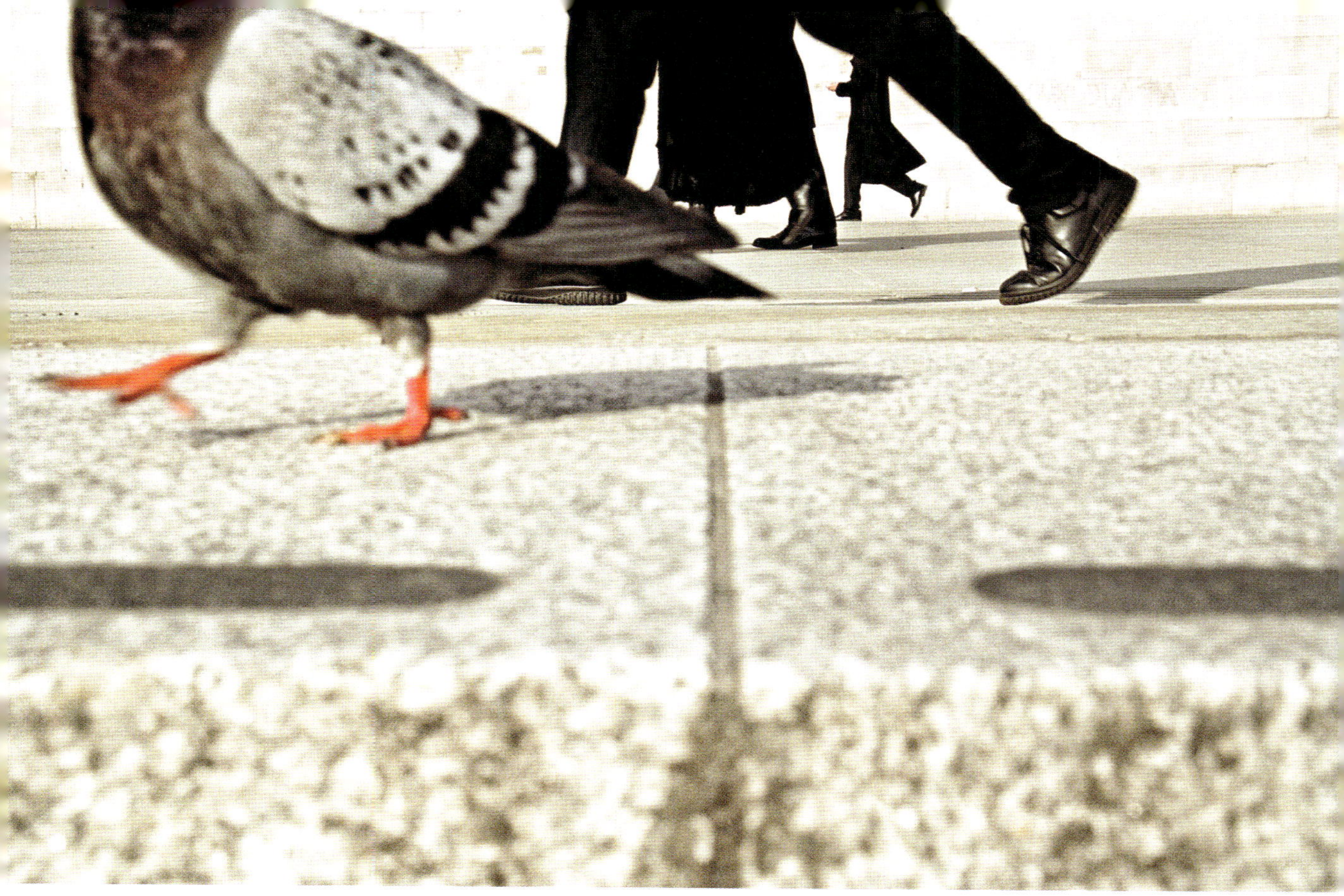

A dog peers nonchalantly out from the front seat of a convertible as though at the wheel. A man pulls off a gravity-defying flip in front of a London gallery. The moments captured in *All That Life Can Afford* feel like half-remembered dreams but, bizarre though they are, things like this happen in London all the time – it's just that in the split second they occur, most of us are so wrapped up in our own thoughts or glued to our phones that we miss them. Matt Stuart doesn't, though. The seasoned street photographer has learnt to be invisible, to melt into his surroundings. He's flat on his belly, ready, when a pigeon strolls across the frame, perfectly in step with the pedestrians behind.

Stuart's always been a nifty navigator of the city. Before he was a photographer, he was a skateboarder. Throughout his teens, he spent most days on four wheels, obsessively scouring the capital for the best hills and kerbs to hone his tricks. Aged 20 he picked up a camera and more than 20 years on he's still shooting. *All That Life Can Afford* brings together pictures taken in London between 2004 and 2016. The work is about the speed of the city, "how quickly we make our way through life in this crazy town," he says. "I'm not sneering at anyone but I am standing back and going, 'Aren't we strange?' There's a degree of tragicomedy about them."

When shooting, Stuart's standard route loops from Oxford Street to New Bond Street, Piccadilly Circus and Soho and then back again, taking in a busy bunch of tourists, shoppers and theatregoers along the way. His approach is street photography in its purist form – discreet and observational – and over the years he's come to recognise the rhythm of the city. "Monday is delivery day, Tuesday is the most normal day of the week, Wednesday is matinee day, Thursday is the new Friday, Friday is when the tourists arrive, Saturday is a shopping frenzy and Sunday is the day of rest," he explains. So in tune is he now with the flow of West End street life that at times he can predict precisely how a scene will play out.

"I find the process really meditative, going out with no agenda. Without sounding like a hippy, it's good for your soul," he says. Stuart's work is about hitting the pause button and appreciating the oddity that the urban crush provides, especially London with its unmatched mix of characters. But even after two decades this isn't easy. "Street photography is so difficult – there's no story, there's nothing, you just go and try to be in the best place for weird and wonderful things to happen. You have to be extremely positive because if you think it's going to be hard work, it will be." Not so different from skateboarding, then, which is also about risk and hope, about throwing yourself open to what the city has to offer. Street photography, like skating, is about patience and, more often than not, about failure. But in both cases, he adds, "You're completely free."

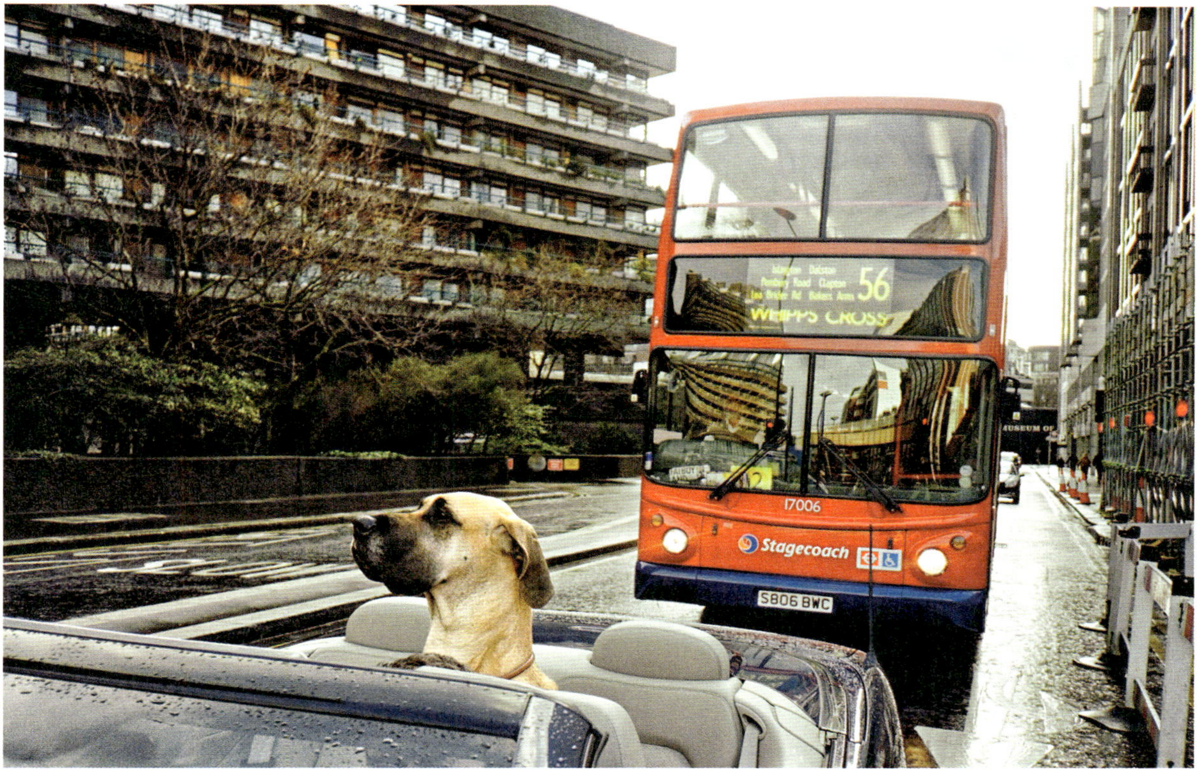

Previous: Trafalgar Square, 2004–16
Above: Aldersgate Street, 2004–16

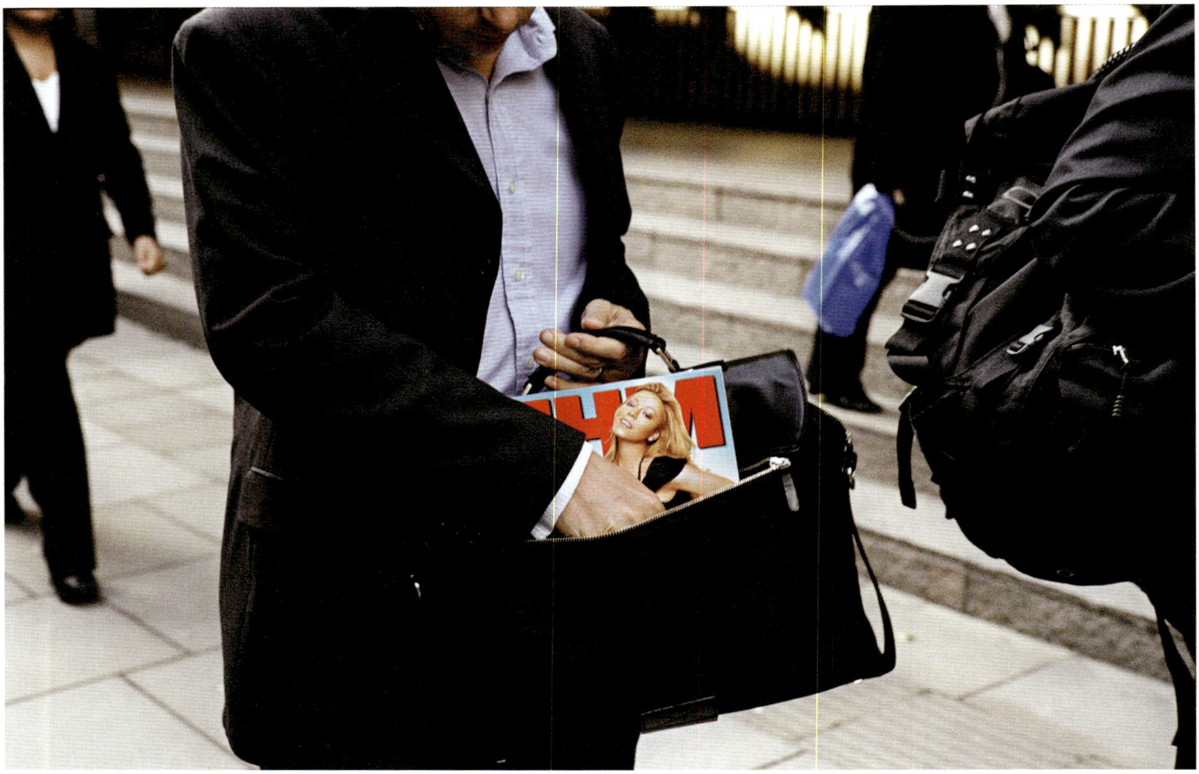

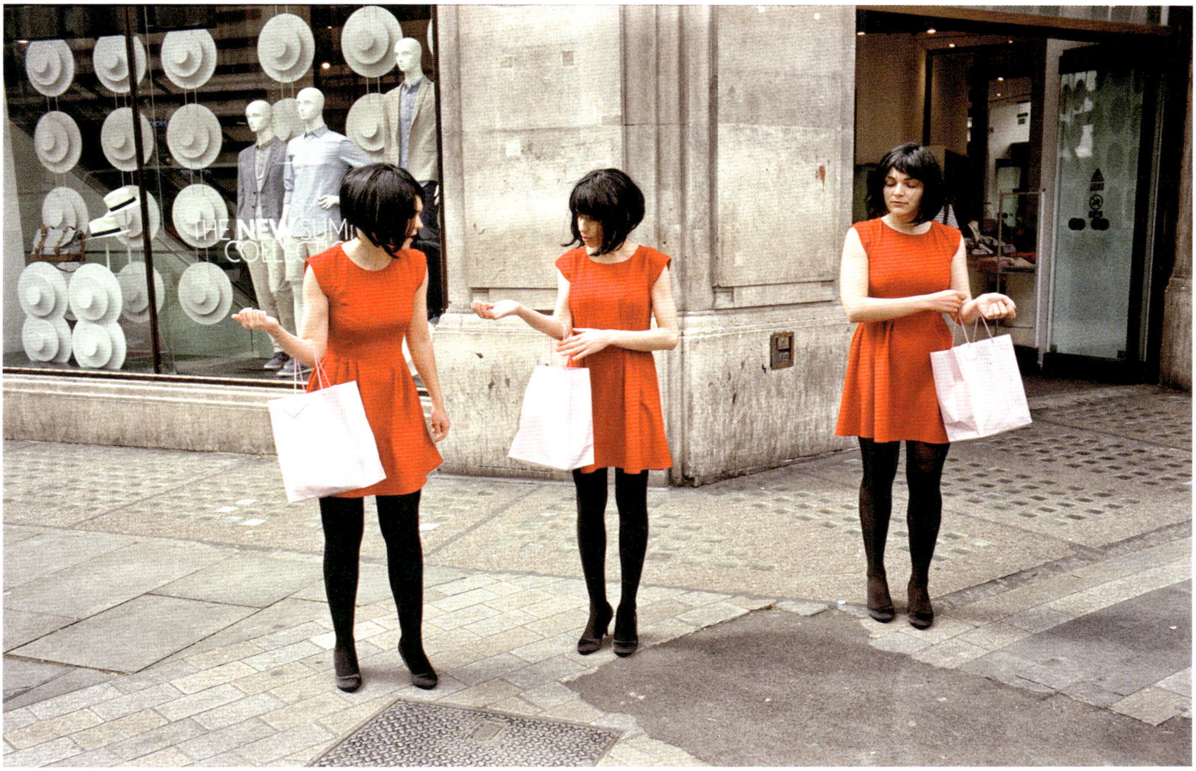

Regent Street, 2004–16

Overleaf: Needham Road, 2004–16

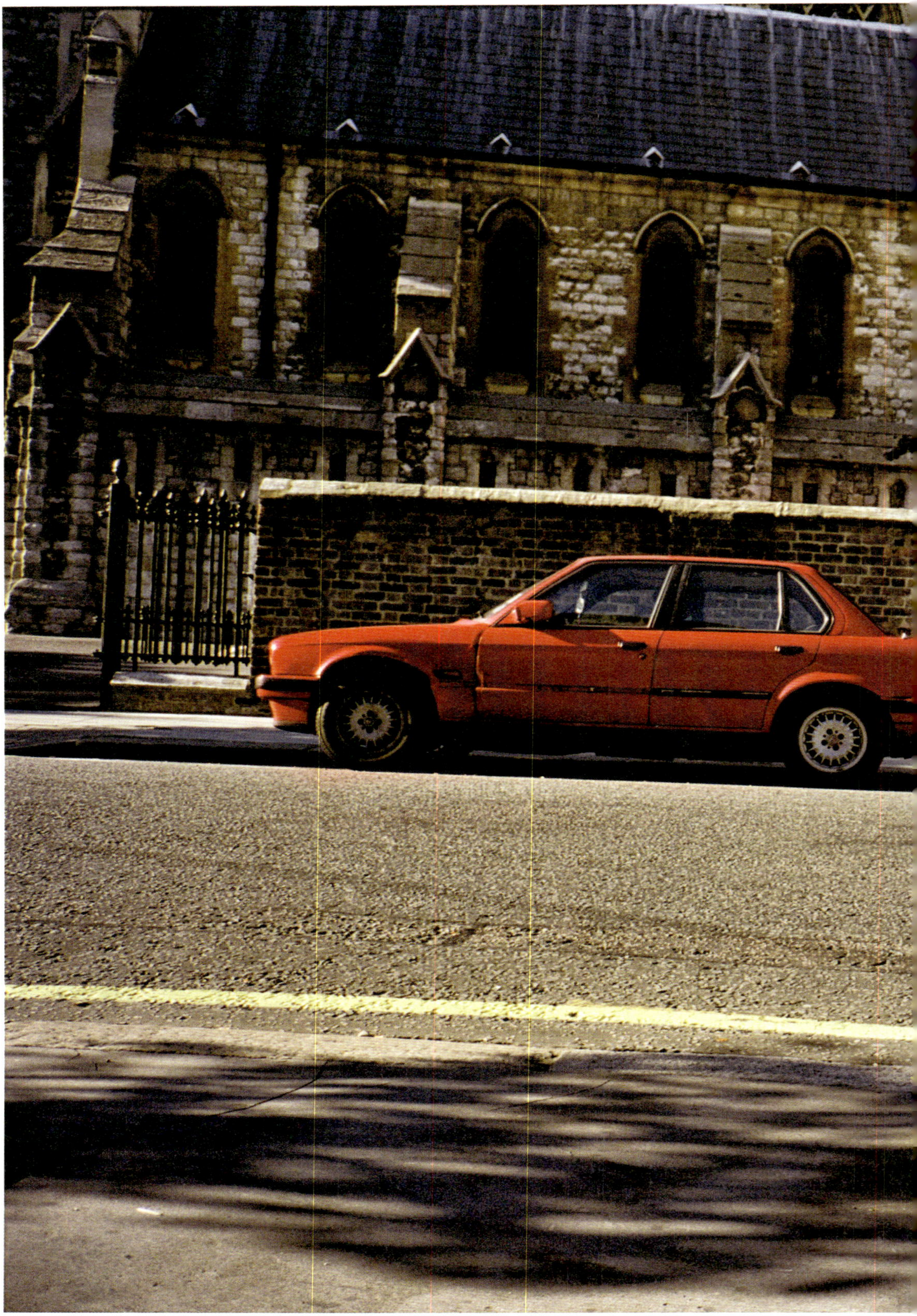

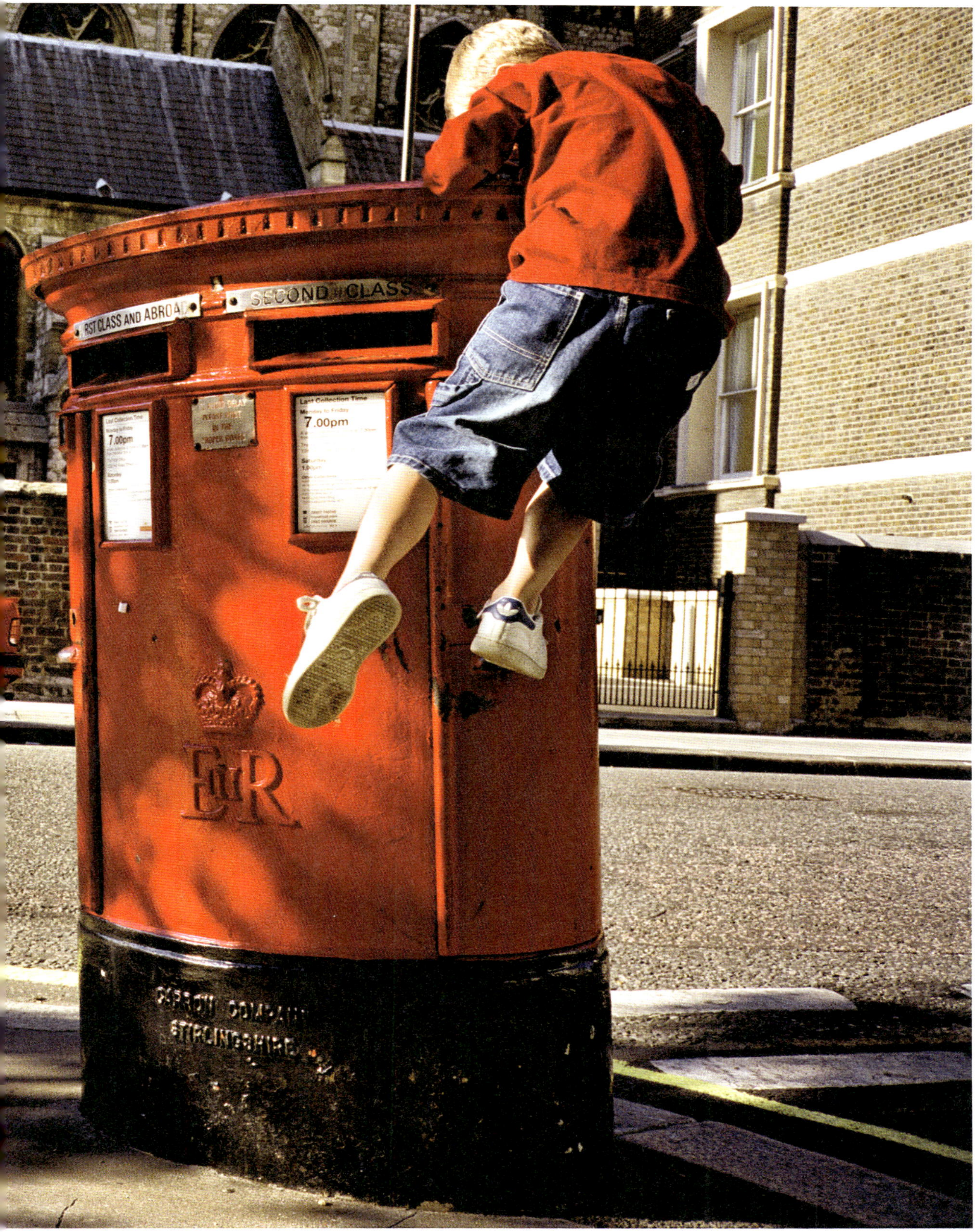
SECOND CLASS
Last Collection Time
Monday to Friday
7.00pm
STIRLINGSHIRE

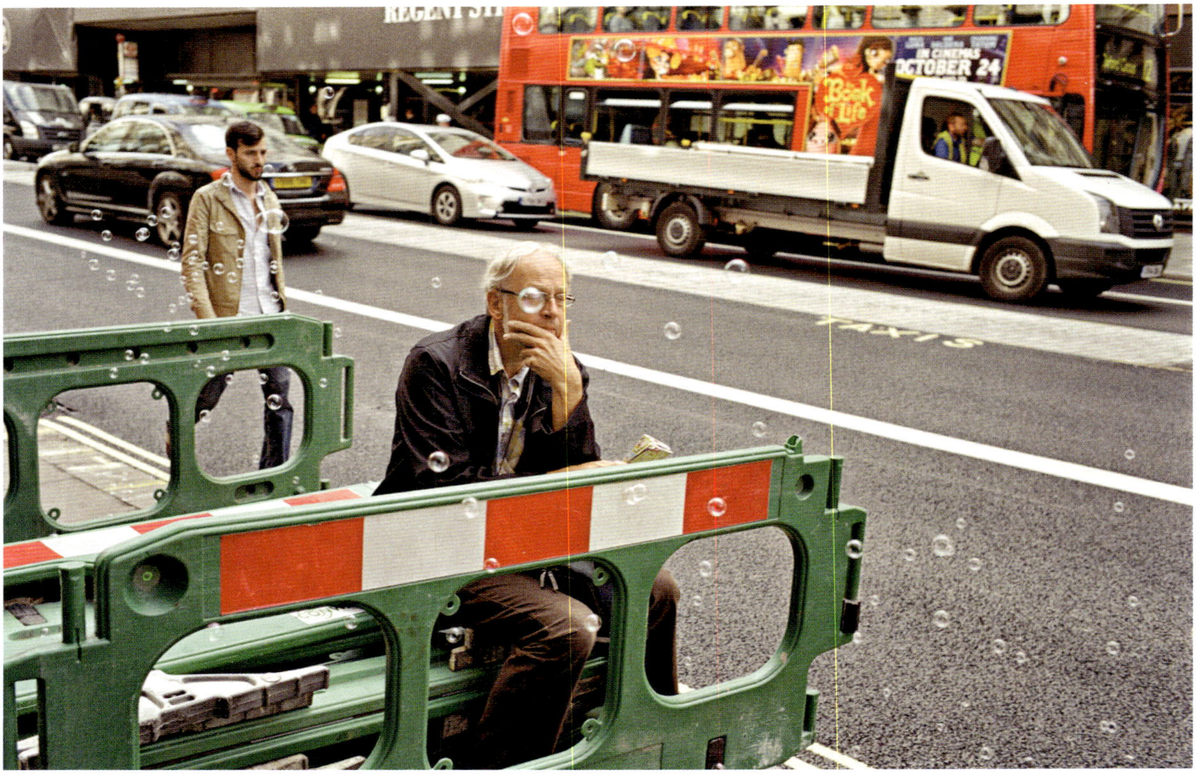
IN CINEMAS
OCTOBER 24
TAXIS

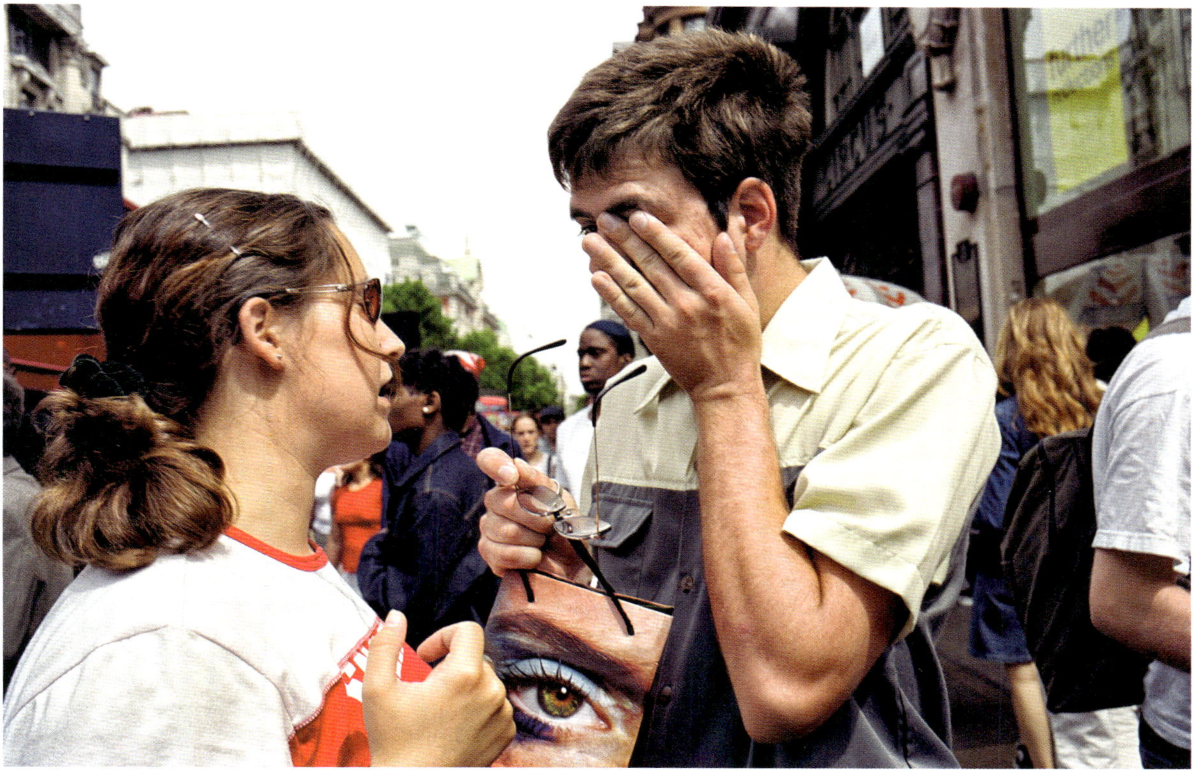

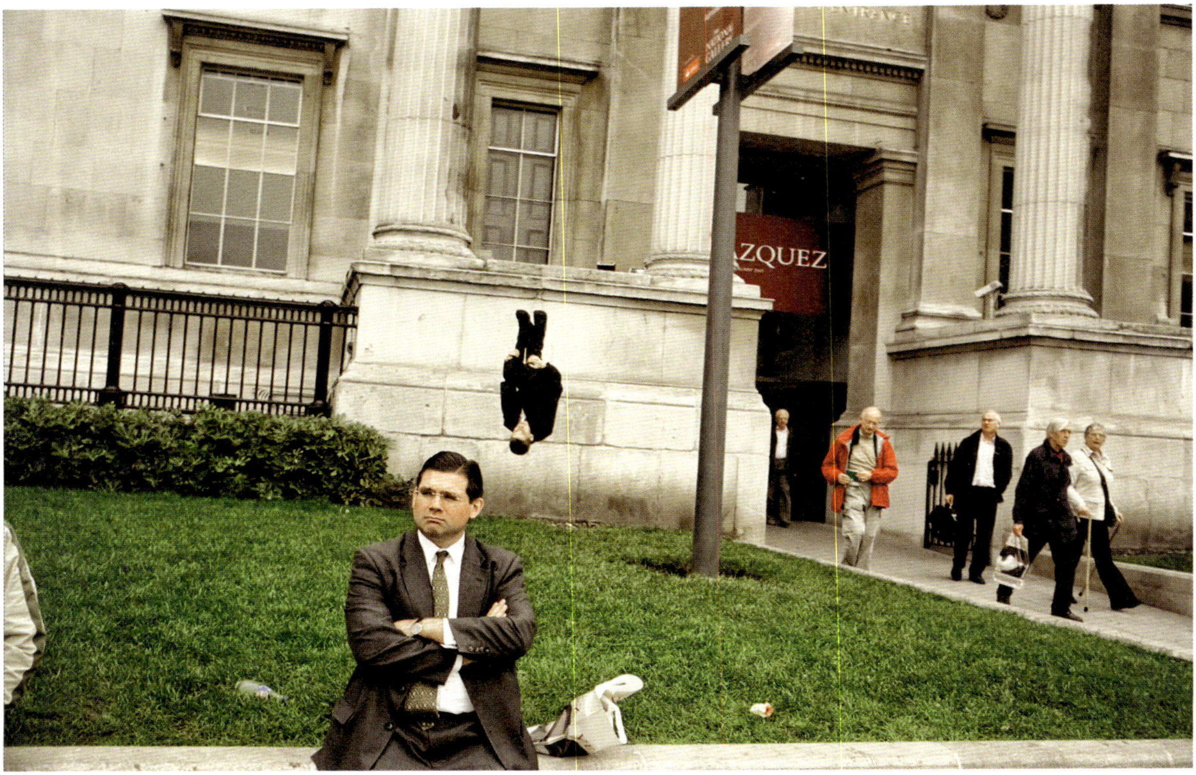
AZQUEZ

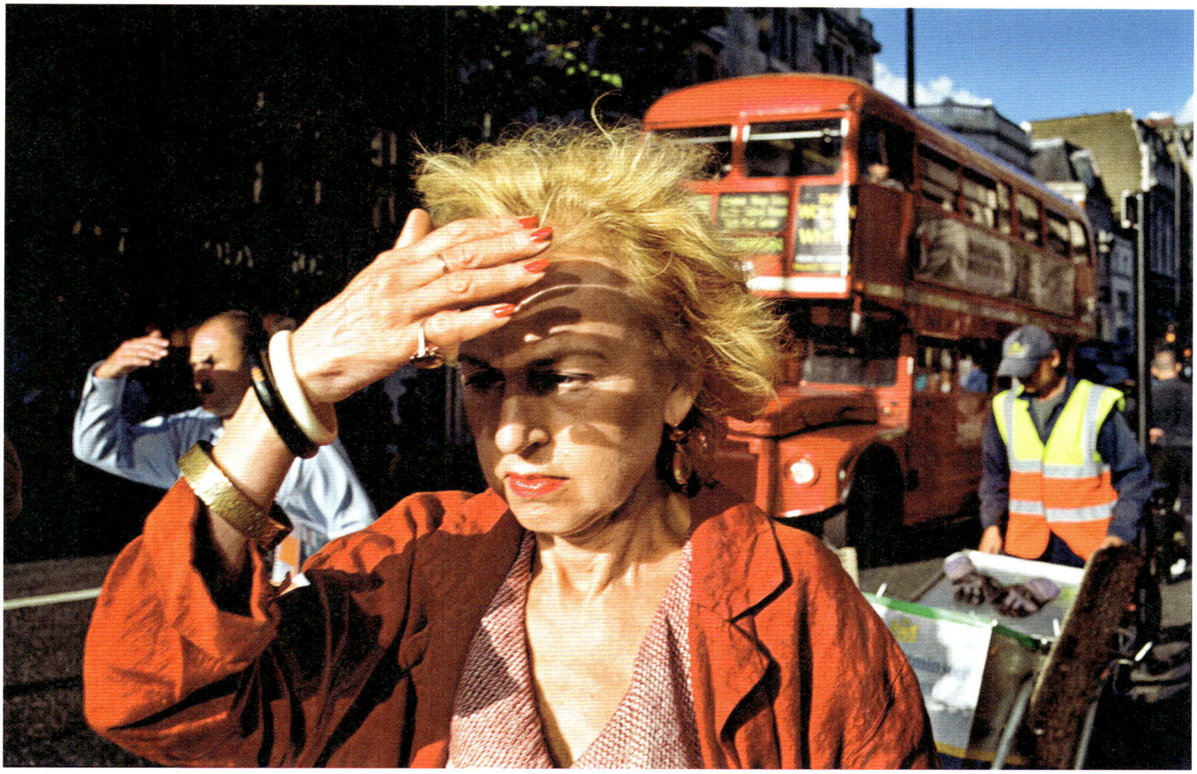

The Queen's Guard

Portraits highlighting the quirky individuality of the famous fur-hatted soldiers who stand to attention outside Buckingham Palace.

James O'Jenkins

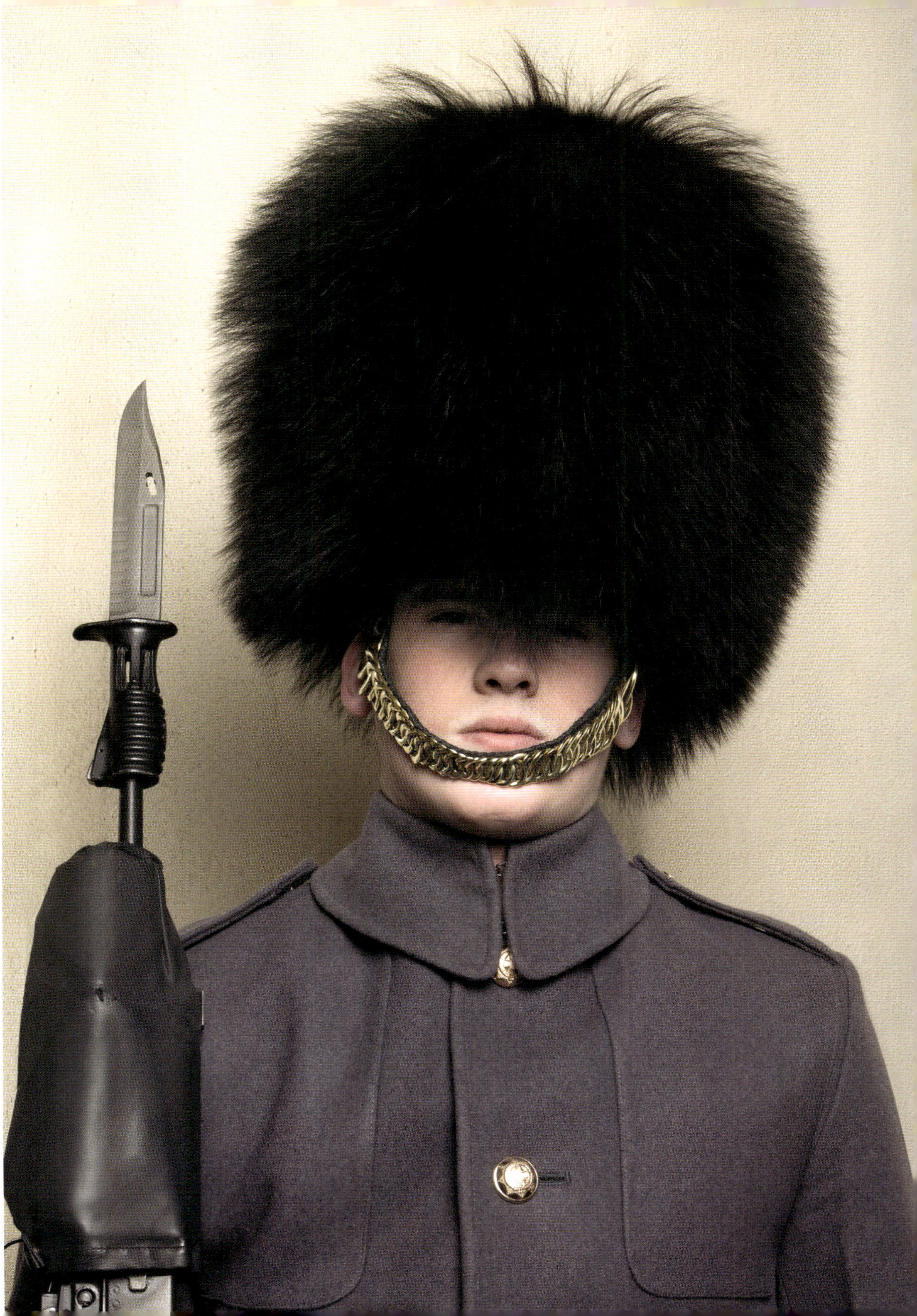

Like black cabs and red phone boxes, Tower Bridge and Big Ben, the Queen's Guard – known for their towering black fur hats – are a feature of London that's easy to write off as cliché. Tourists from all over the world march over to take selfies with the Guard as they stand outside Buckingham Palace. Unfathomably still and straight-faced, they are not so different from the human statues you find in Covent Garden. A much-photographed phenomenon, it's rare to see them from close up as you do in James O'Jenkins' portraits – and the results are surprising, witty and warm.

It was while on a commission for an army charity at Wellington Barracks that the Welsh-born photographer first had occasion to photograph the Queen's Guard. He'd just finished *United Kingdom*, a large-scale study of the flamboyantly kitted out participants in annual customs across Britain, everything from the World Conker Championships to the Eton College Wall Game. Several years earlier he'd photographed every one of the 100 people who occupied the fourth plinth in Trafalgar Square, as part of artist Antony Gormley's *One & Other*.

This wasn't the first time he'd come across the Queen's Guard. "I have a picture of me standing next to one when I was three at St James's Palace. I thought they were massive," says the photographer, whose other London-related work includes commissions for the Mayor of London, pictures of Margaret Thatcher's funeral and a series on Soho's cycle couriers. "What struck me this time is that they're so young, they look like teenagers. A few of them had just arrived in the city and I got the sense that they'd been told, you're going to go to London! And then ended up stuck outside Buckingham Palace all day, bored out of their minds, holding loaded guns."

Being a soldier – and they are active soldiers, their role isn't merely ceremonial – is about giving up your individuality. "I wanted them to be uniform, like a pack of cards," says O'Jenkins, who shot each Guard against a matching background – an approach he'd used previously in both *United Kingdom* and *One & Other*. There was something a bit obsessive about the process. "I wanted to collect the whole set," he says. Here, though, we're invited to peer right into their eyes, barely discernable below their elaborate head gear, and consider what's unique about their faces: the particular way their nostrils flare, the curl of a lip, the hint of a frown, the pink pimples on the end of their noses.

The Falling Soldier, an iconic photograph taken in 1936 by war photographer Robert Capa of a Spanish Civil War fighter at the moment of death, epitomises the classic representation of soldiers in photography. His chest thrust forward, gun slipping from his hand, he is tragic but heroic. This is neither. Instead, plucked from their posts, we see the Queen's Guard, with their extraordinary hats and their ordinary faces, in the context of the *United Kingdom* and *One & Other*: curious specimens of an ever so British, ever so London brand of eccentricity.

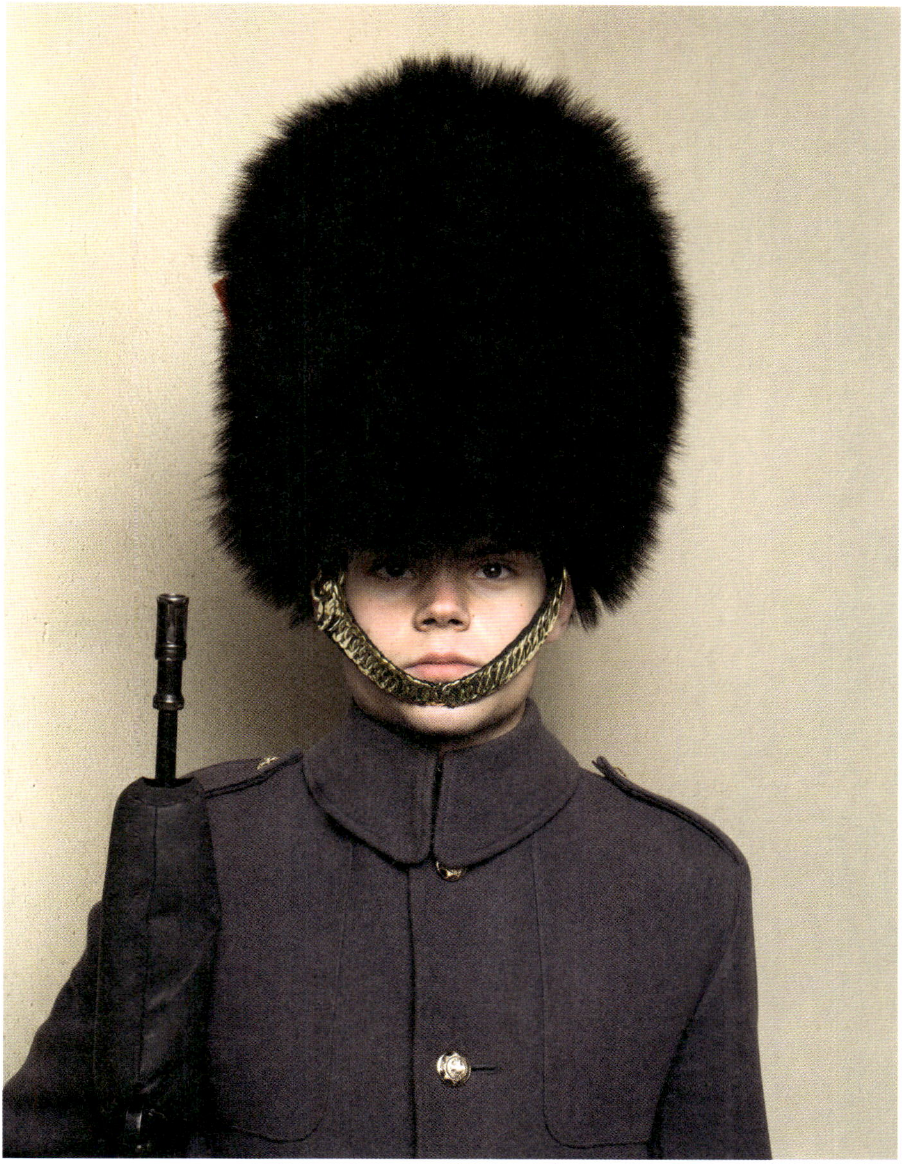

 Previous and above: The Queen's Guard, Wellington Barracks, 2008

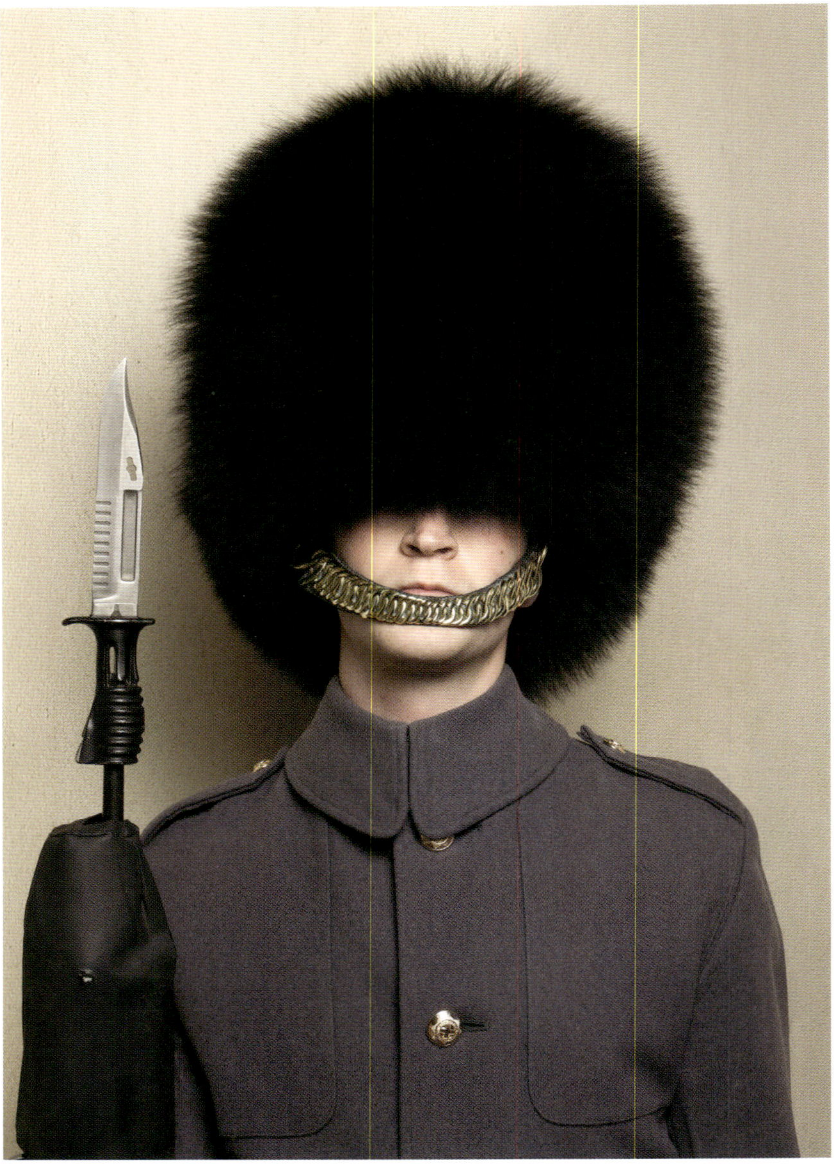

The Queen's Guard, Wellington Barracks, 2008

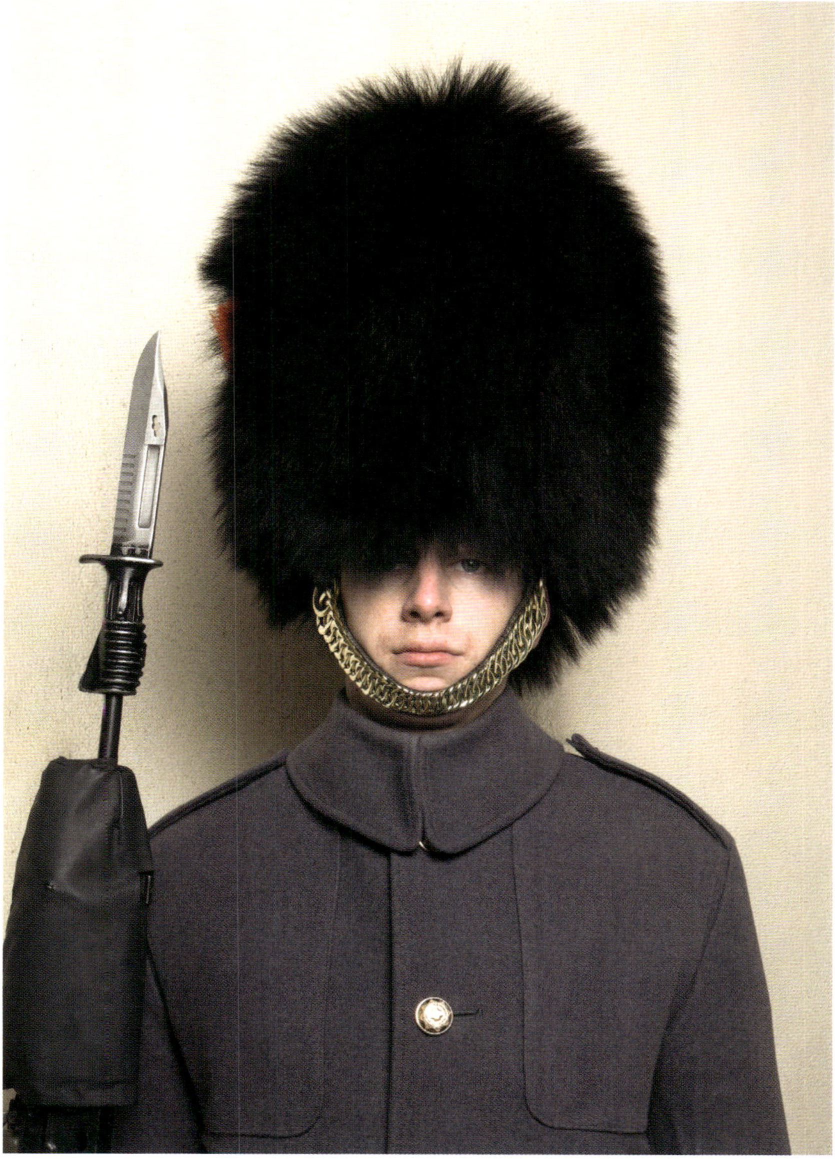

 The Queen's Guard, Wellington Barracks, 2008 James O'Jenkins

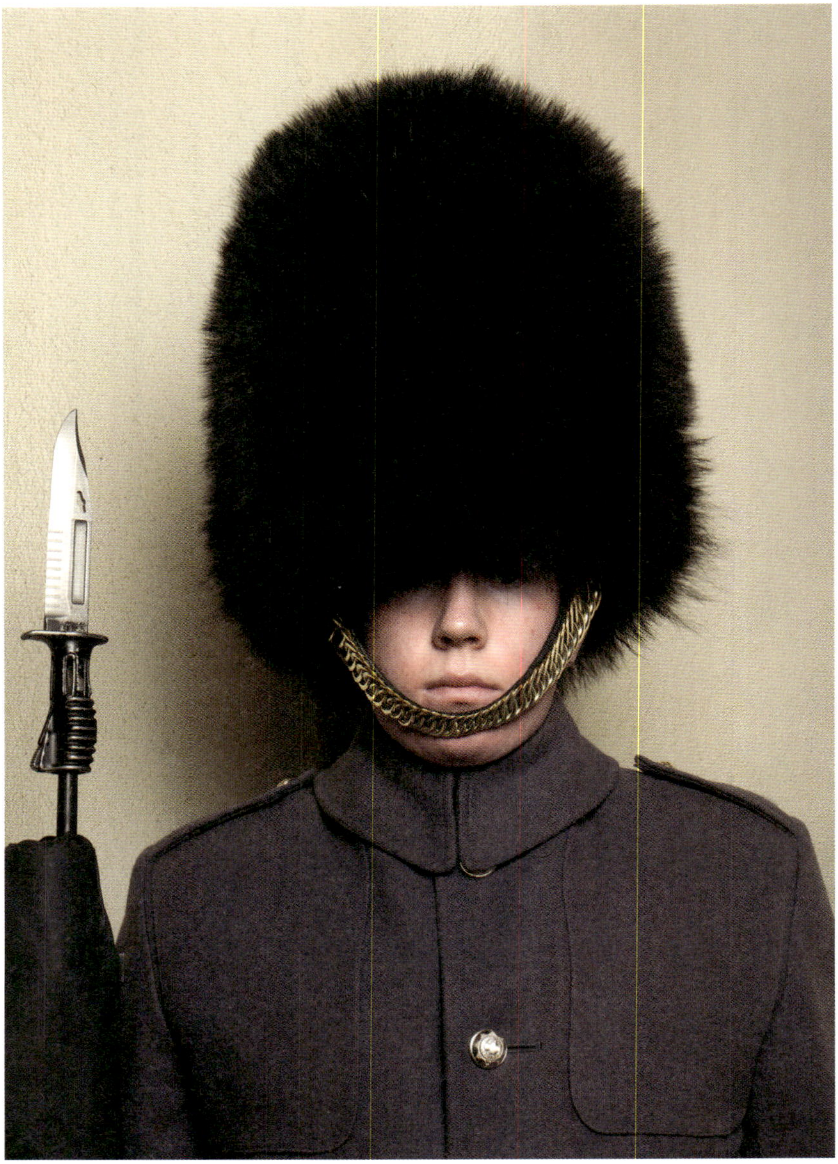

The Queen's Guard, Wellington Barracks, 2008

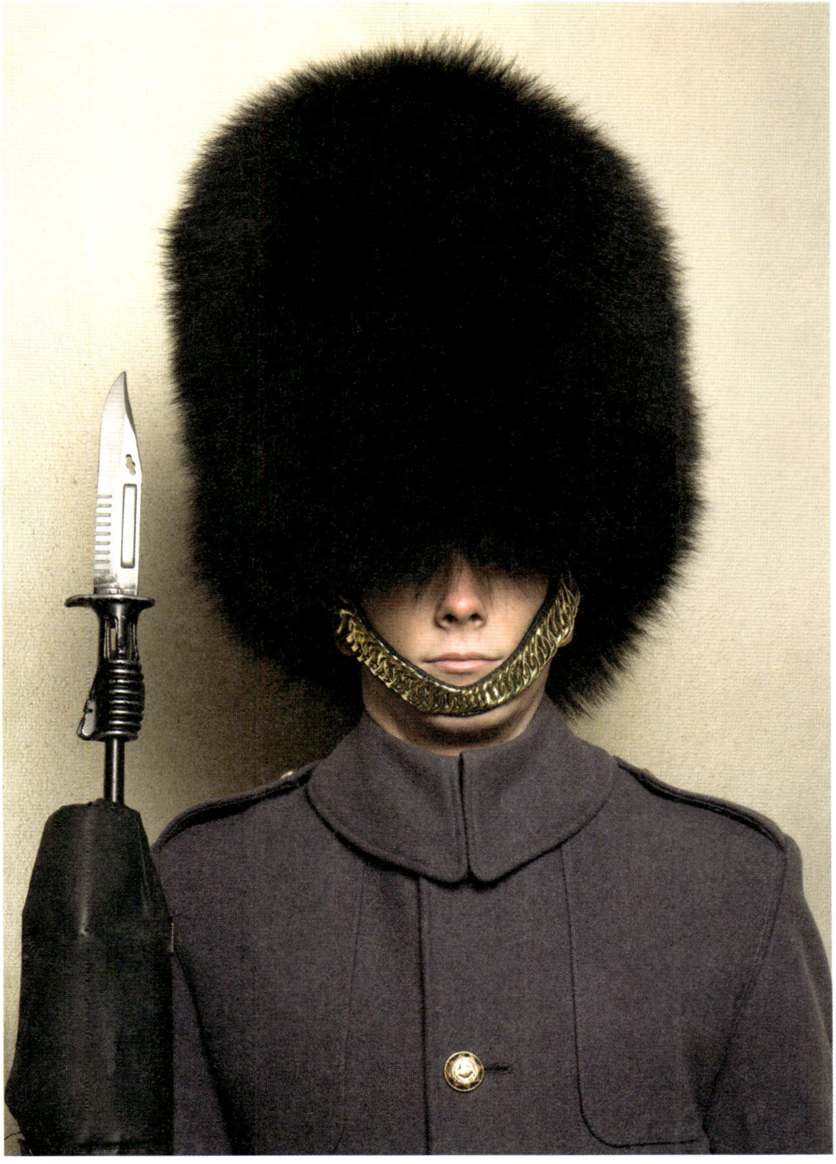

 The Queen's Guard, Wellington Barracks, 2008 James O'Jenkins

London Grime

An insider documents the key players of the most charged subculture to emerge from London since punk.

Vicky Grout

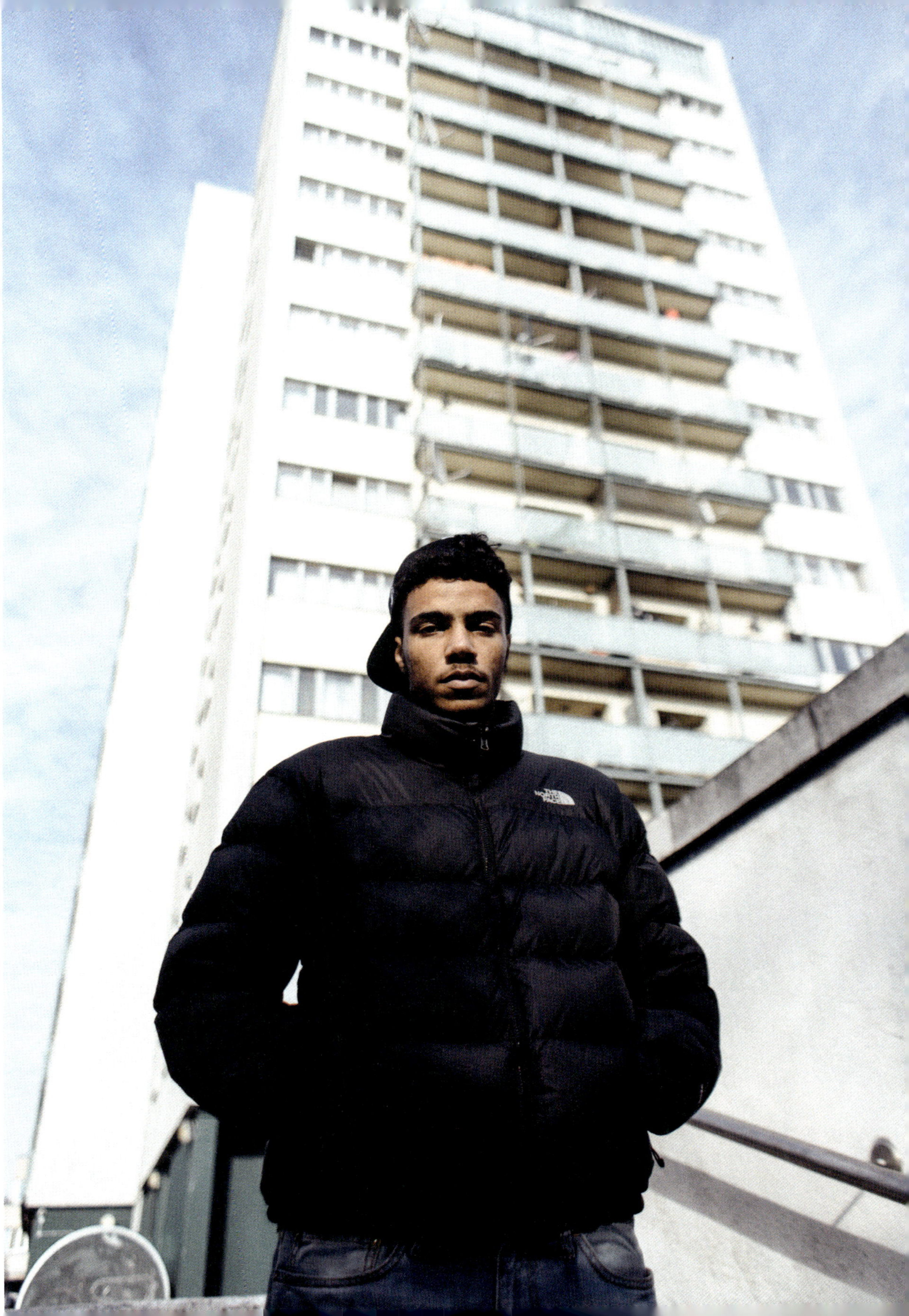

Not since punk has a music genre captured the raw dynamism of London quite like grime. It started underground in sweaty East London basements and swept through the city skies from the pirate radio antennas of high rises before emerging into the charts. Dizzee Rascal, Wiley and Kano led the first charge in the early noughties, followed a few years later by the likes of Jme, Skepta and Stormzy. Influences from garage, hip hop and jungle are clear in its skittish beats and rapid-fire lyrics, but the sound is startlingly original.

Born in Poland, Vicky Grout has lived here since she was four, "a true Londoner", she says with pride. At 17, she was stunned by "the pure energy" of her first grime gig and soon became a regular at raves, always snapping away as she's done since finding an old film camera in her dad's drawer at the tender age of 10. "I wasn't even trying to document grime, I was just shooting for me and people happened to like it," she says, well aware that she isn't the first photographer to document the scene.

Ewen Spencer, dedicated chronicler of UK dance music subcultures, was capturing the spirited posturing of its young pioneers before the burgeoning genre yet had a name, and Simon Wheatley's 2011 photobook *Don't Call Me Urban!* panned out to grime's social context – run-down estates, gun crime, police brutality. But because 20-year-old Grout grew up in the scene she sees it in a way that other photographers cannot. Grout's reputation soon spread and now she has photographed grime's biggest names. But these guys aren't just her subjects, they're her peers. "Other people would go in as strangers and try to take photographs of them but because they'd met me before, they felt more comfortable in front of the camera."

That intimacy is palpable in the pictures. They throw us right into the throng, into the rowdy crowds surrounding the MCs, faces scrunched, teeth clenched in concentration, mics in hand. We see the style – the bright white tracksuits, hoods, bandanas – and we see London, with its scruffy pavements and modernist estates, a constant presence. But through Grout's work we also see another, lighter side to grime. Artists off-duty, relaxed, smiling, hanging out behind the scenes at a video shoot or casually eating a bag of chips in the street. The refreshingly unguarded feel of the pictures is partly down to the way Grout shoots, with minimal direction and maximum chat. "I like to capture natural moments. I don't always want a hard image. I think it's nice to see a softer side to people. A lot of people's attitudes towards grime and most black music is that it's aggressive, angry, violent, and that's not true at all."

Despite being a digital native, she prefers to shoot film. "I think it looks so much better, there's something so personal about going and getting it processed and then seeing the results, not really knowing what you're going to get," she says, although it's not always feasible now that she's a professional photographer limited by time constraints and client budgets. Increasingly in demand, on the rare occasions Grout makes it to a club, she avoids commissions. Sometimes she doesn't even take her camera – putting her love of grime ahead of her love of photography, at least for that evening. "I want to keep it as authentic and enjoyable as possible. I wouldn't photograph a show I wouldn't go to anyway," she says. "I don't want to kill it, I want to keep it fun."

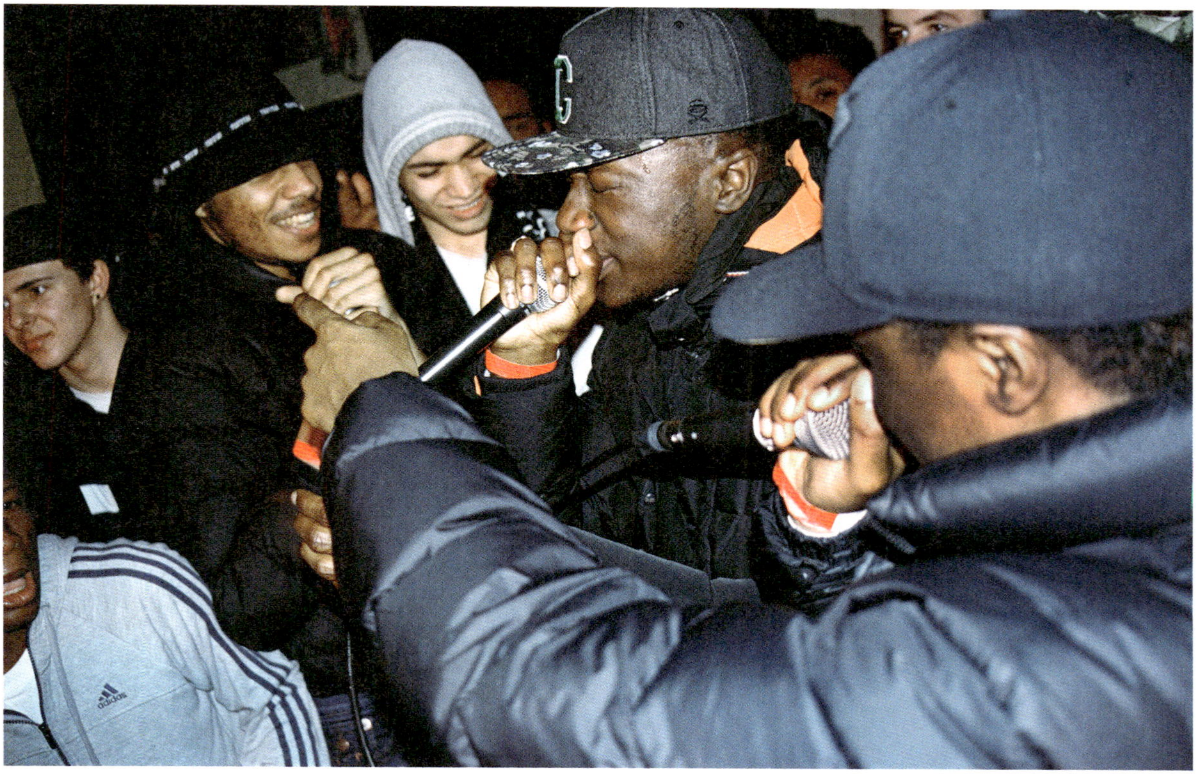

Previous: AJ Tracey in West London, 2015
Above: AJ Tracey, ETS, Saint & PK at Ace Hotel, 2015

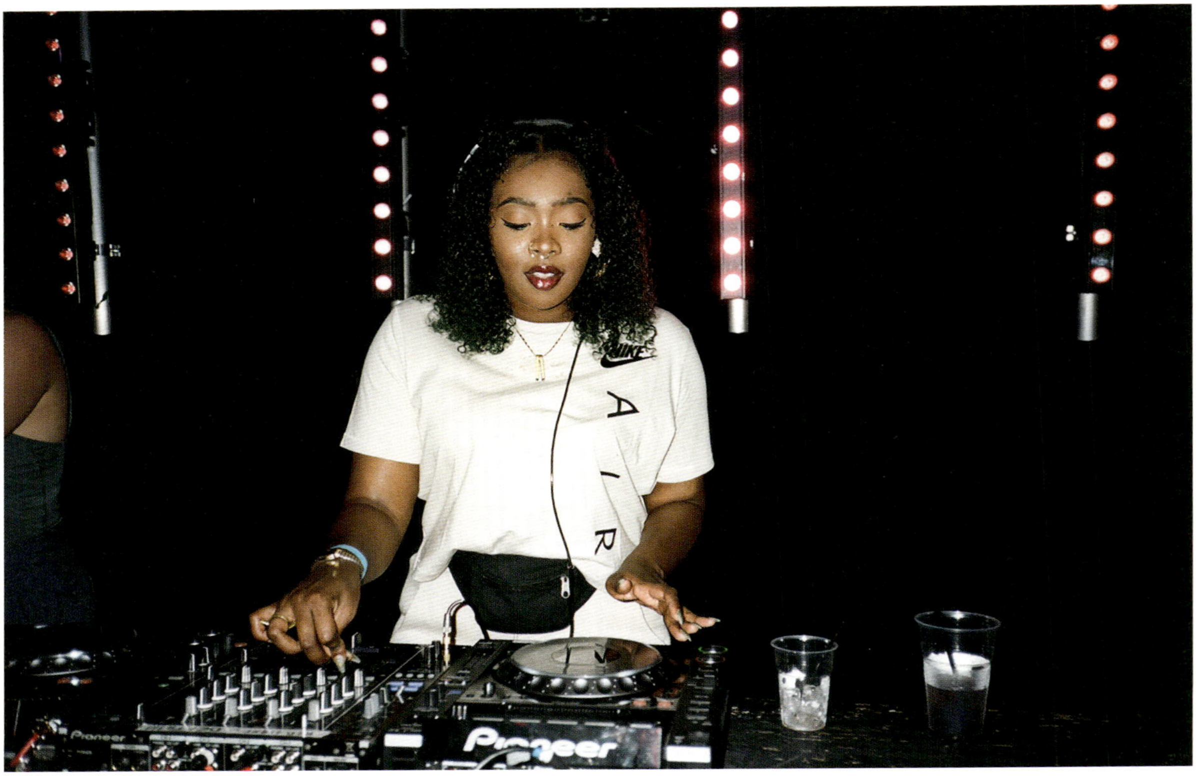

A.G at Kamio, 2017

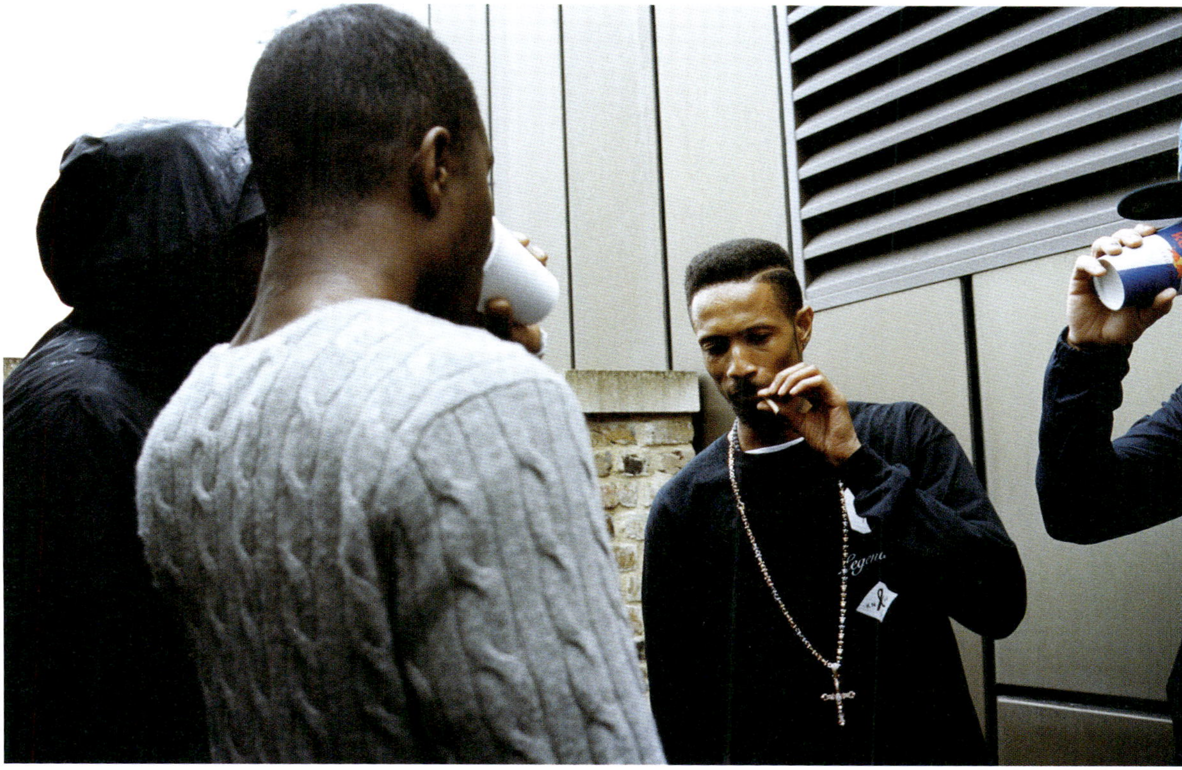

D Double E, 2015

Overleaf: Spooky, Novelist & The Square at The Alibi, 2014

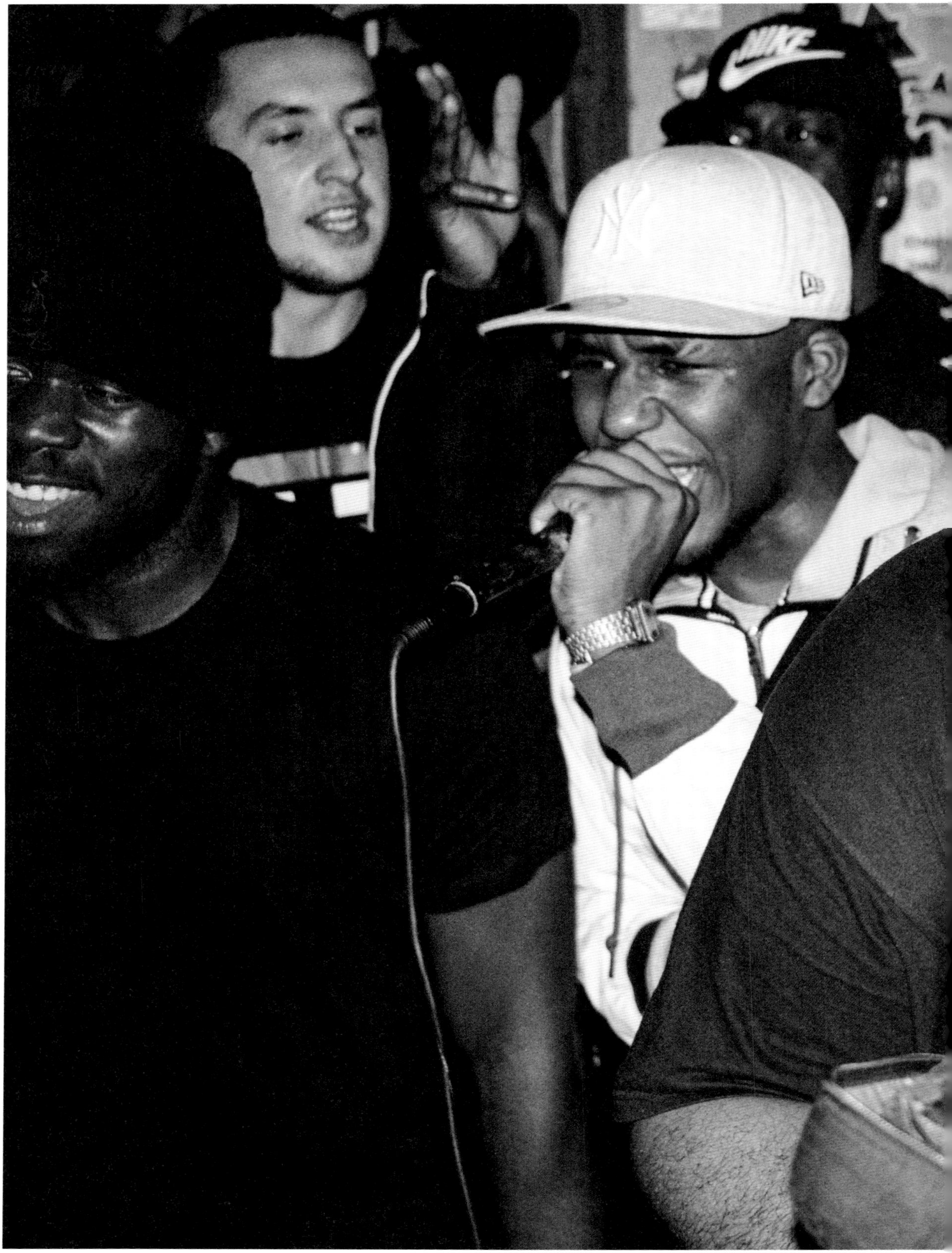
NIKE

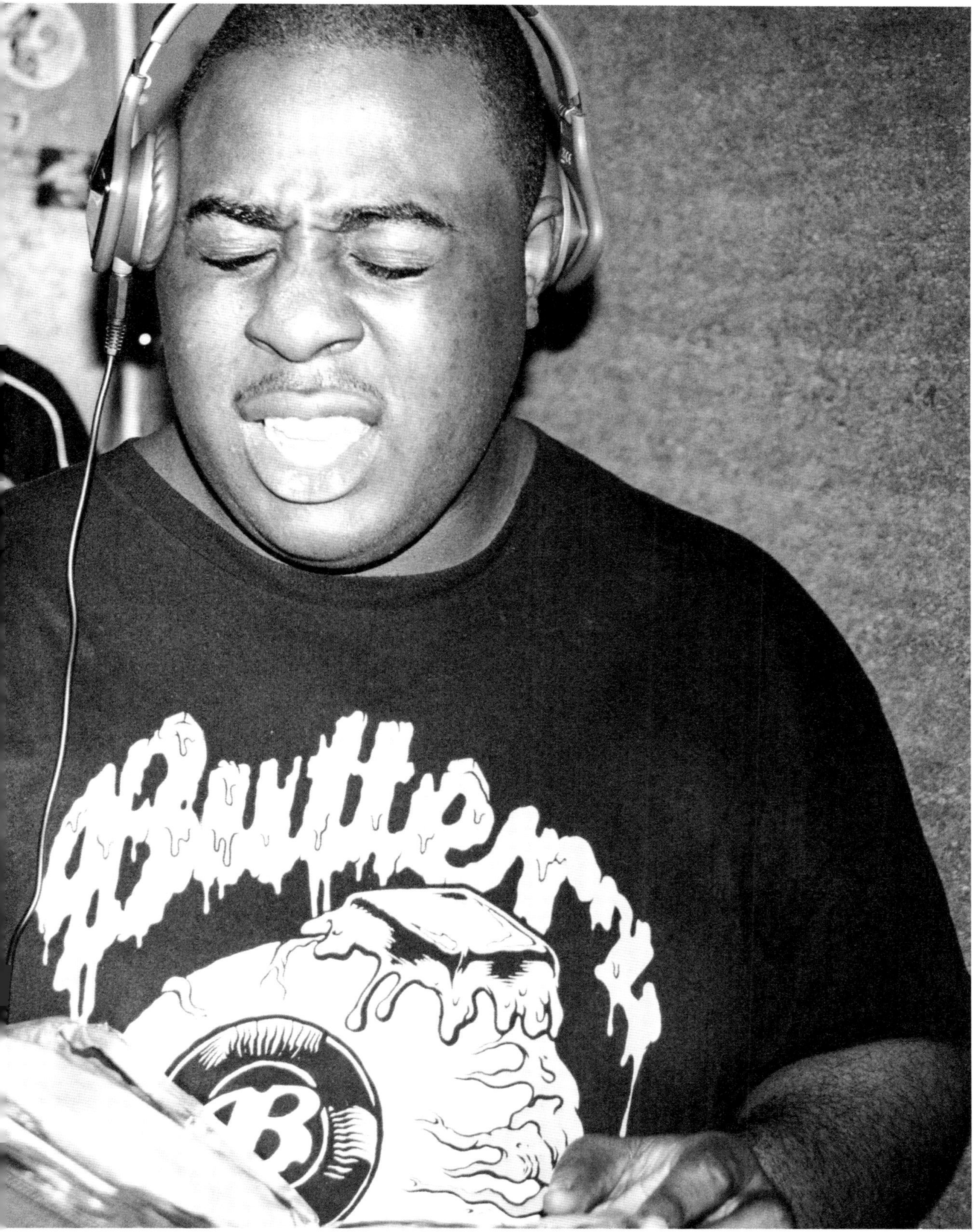
Butter

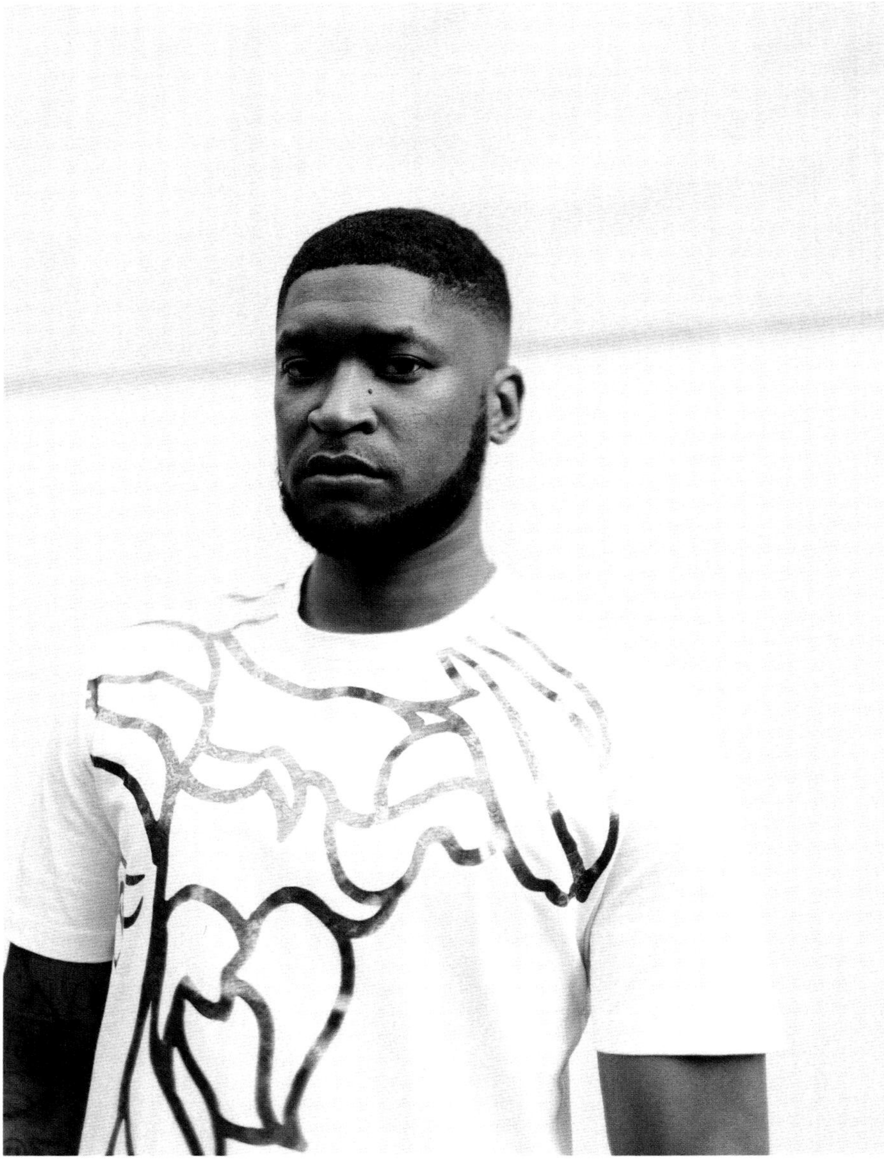

Frisco in East London, 2016

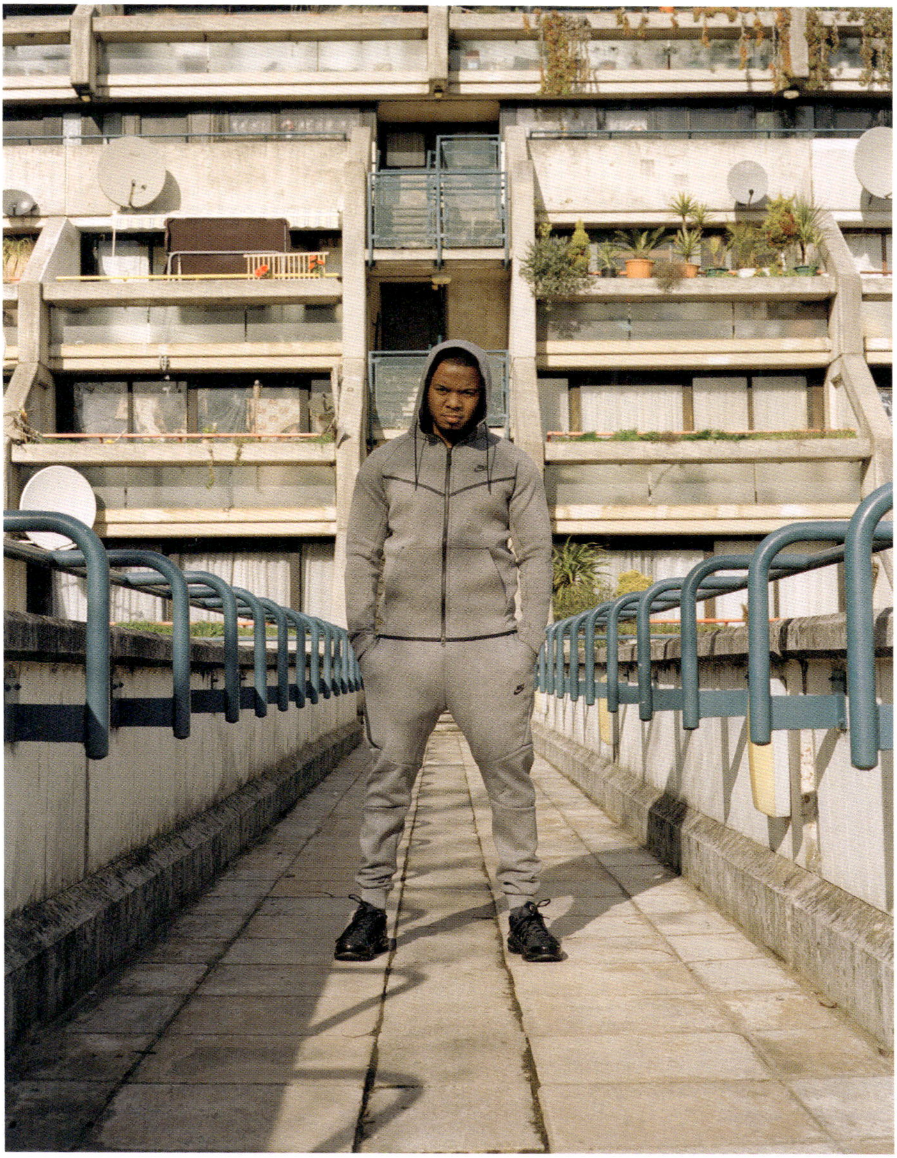

 Bossman Birdie at Rowley Way Estate, 2017 Vicky Grout

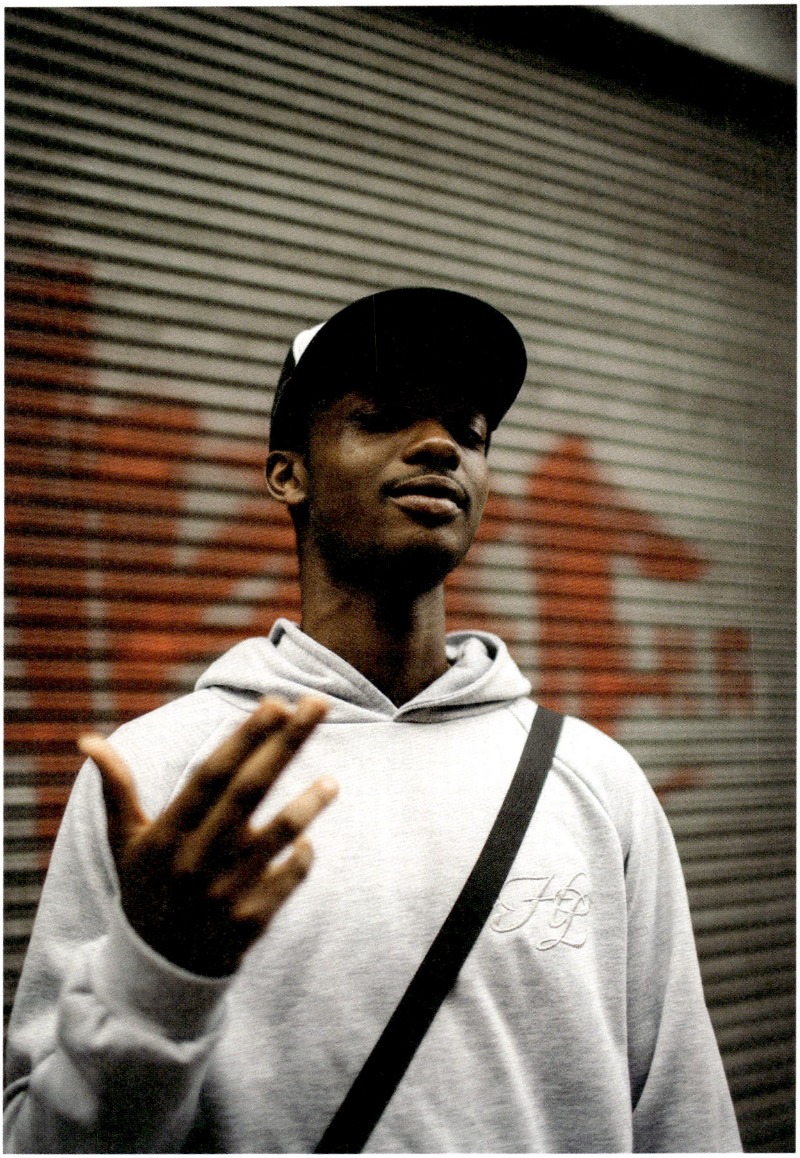

Mez in East London, 2016

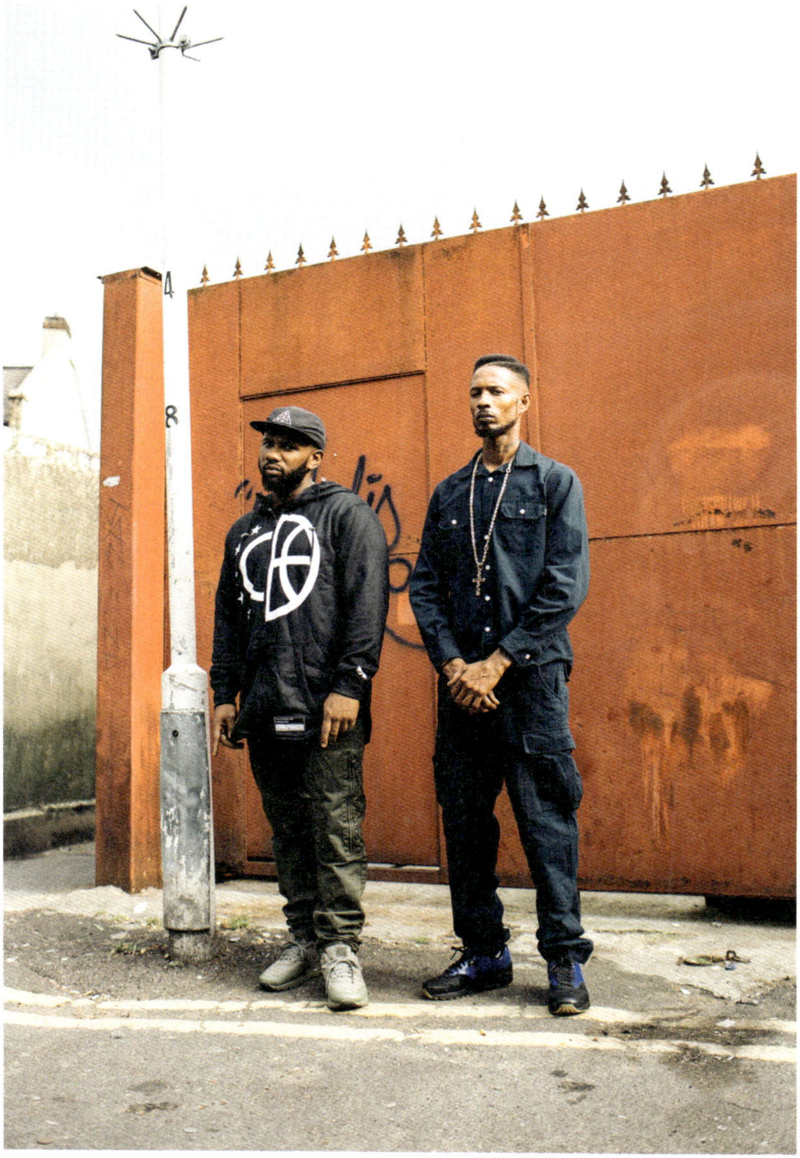

Newham Generals in Newham, 2016

Vicky Grout

Sketch

Tucked away in London's iconic museums we find a dedicated tribe of artists on a mission to commit the capital's curios to paper.

David Vintiner

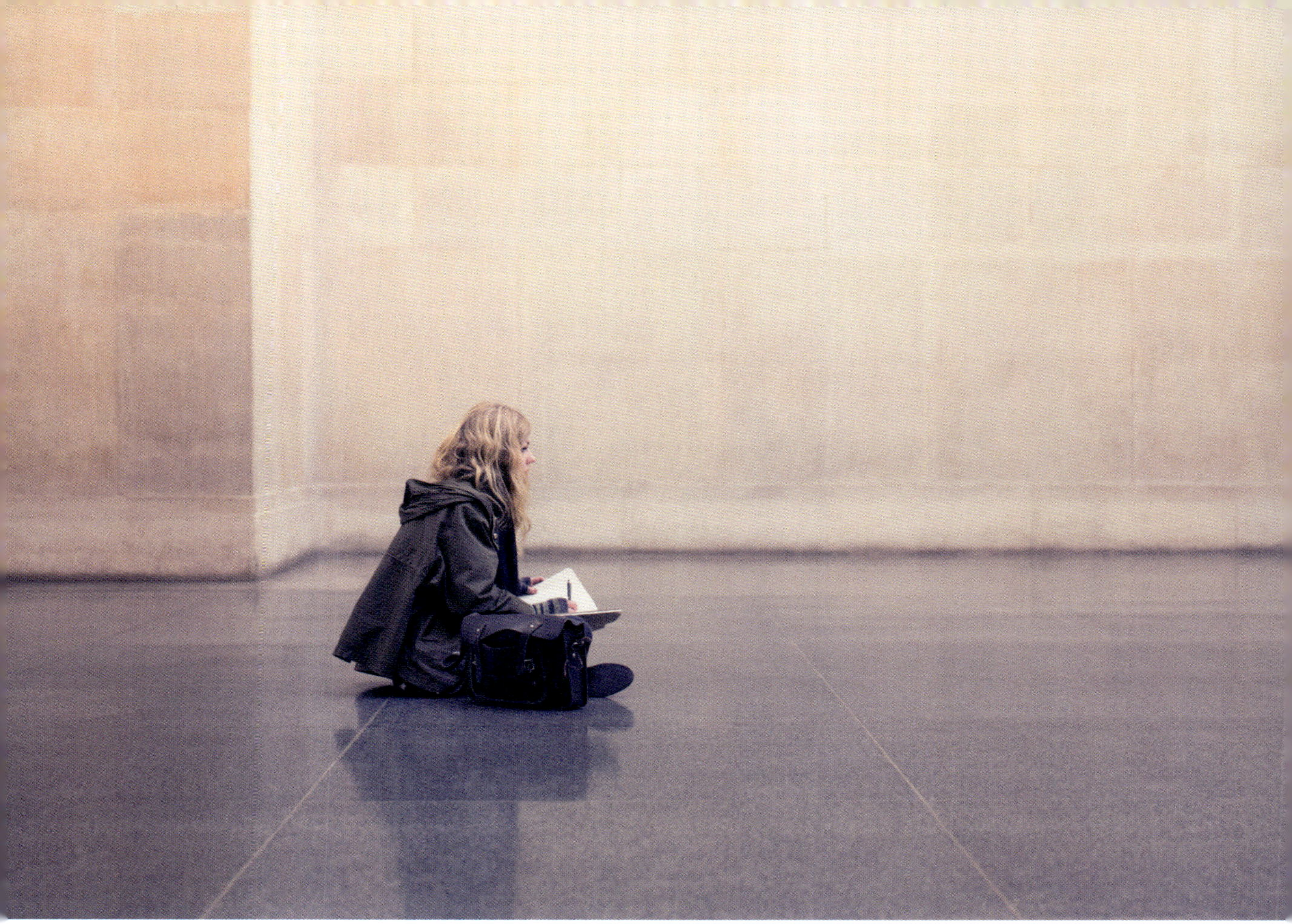

David Vintiner is not a sketcher himself. "I realised I was crap at drawing when I was at art college – that's why I reached for a camera," says the London-based photographer, who shoots portraits for *The Sunday Times*, *The Guardian* and *Esquire*. Nonetheless, on his regular visits to the capital's galleries and museums with a faithful Fuji x10 – his own digital "sketchbook" – around his neck, Vintiner found himself drawn to the figures he saw silently scribbling away.

Sketch started with a couple of casual shots at the Hendon RAF Museum and evolved into an ongoing series that has taken Vintiner to Tate Modern, Tate Britain, The British Museum and The National Gallery. These vast, symbolic London museums, free to visit and brimming with intriguing objects and beautiful artworks, are perfect fodder for sketchers of all ages and stages. "Because of the scale you get school trips or art classes on days out there, or individuals, and it's quite anonymous," he explains. "You can always find a quiet corner."

Back in the late 80s and 90s, German photographer Thomas Struth's *Museum Photographs* examined how groups of people behave when looking at art, shot in museums in Paris, Rome and Chicago. Struth, working with a hefty large-format camera, would have been an obvious presence within the space. All but one of Vintiner's sketchers were oblivious to his camera, immersed in their drawing. Some perch on chairs, materials spread out around their feet. Others stand at easels or sit on the floor, cross-legged, like children at storytime. One young man lays down on his front, bag slung down to the side, as though floating.

To the photographer, their indifference to anything going on around them represents a corrective "to the instant world we live in with social media, news, everything expected at the touch of a button". The sketchers' immersion in the moment is a sharp contrast with the museum selfie craze which reached its zenith when Beyoncé and Jay-Z visited the Louvre and posed in front of the Mona Lisa, the art an amusing backdrop to their famous pouts.

An air of calm seeps out from Vintiner's serene pictures. Glimmering with lilacs, mint greens, dusty blues and pastel pinks, the deliberately desaturated colour palette reflects "the slow, gentle act" pictured, as much as the individual character of each institution. "In Tate Britain the colour is warm, whereas with Tate Modern it's bright and white. The British Museum is darker and moodier," explains Vintiner. "The colour was important in terms of the feelings you get in those spaces – whether you're looking at a Jackson Pollock or some Egyptology."

Though he might not share their drawing skills, Vintiner has other things in common with the sketchers: their curiosity and their embrace of London's museums as monumental, almost magical places where you can get delightfully lost. "I like the far flung corners of these establishments. At The National Gallery, if you just keep going up and up and up and out the back you get to this room where I've never ever seen anyone else there. I like to find those parts of museums where you've got it to yourself." Until the sketchers catch on, that is.

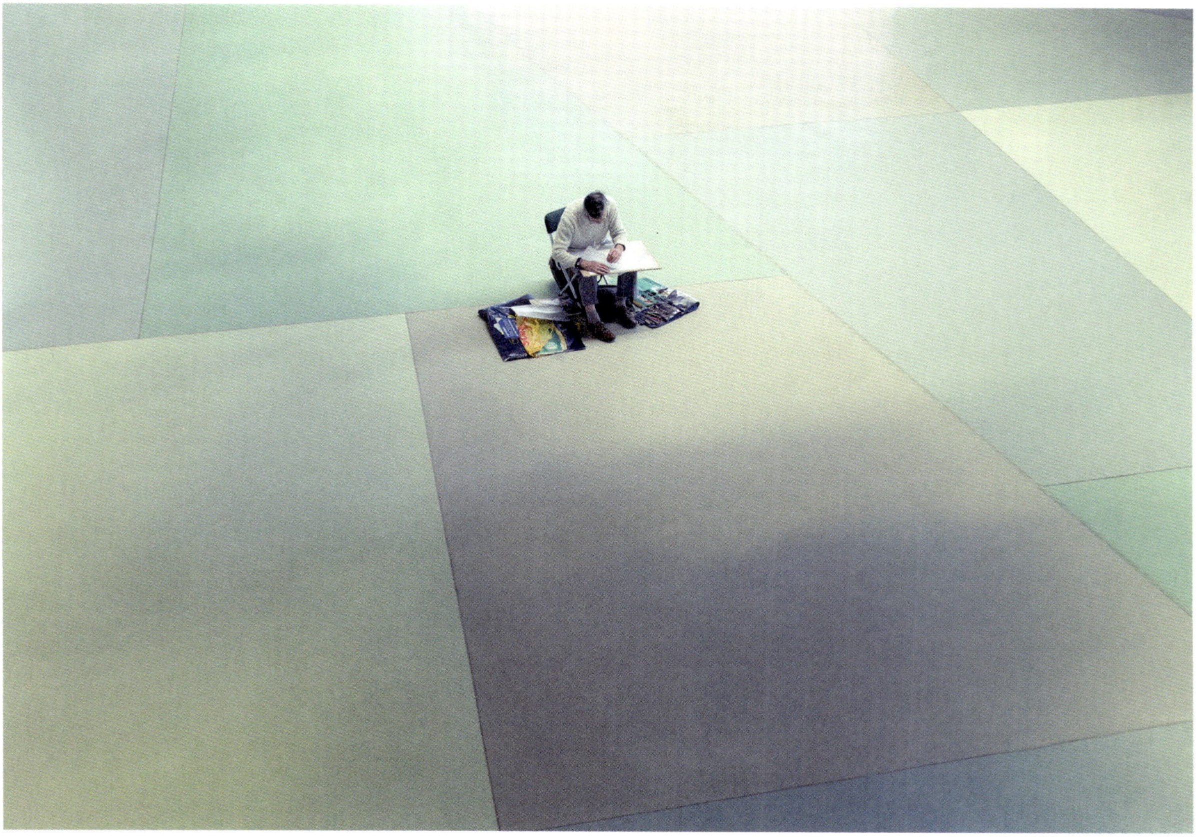

Previous: Untitled, Tate Britain, 03.12.2015
Above: Untitled, RAF Museum Hendon, 05.05.2012

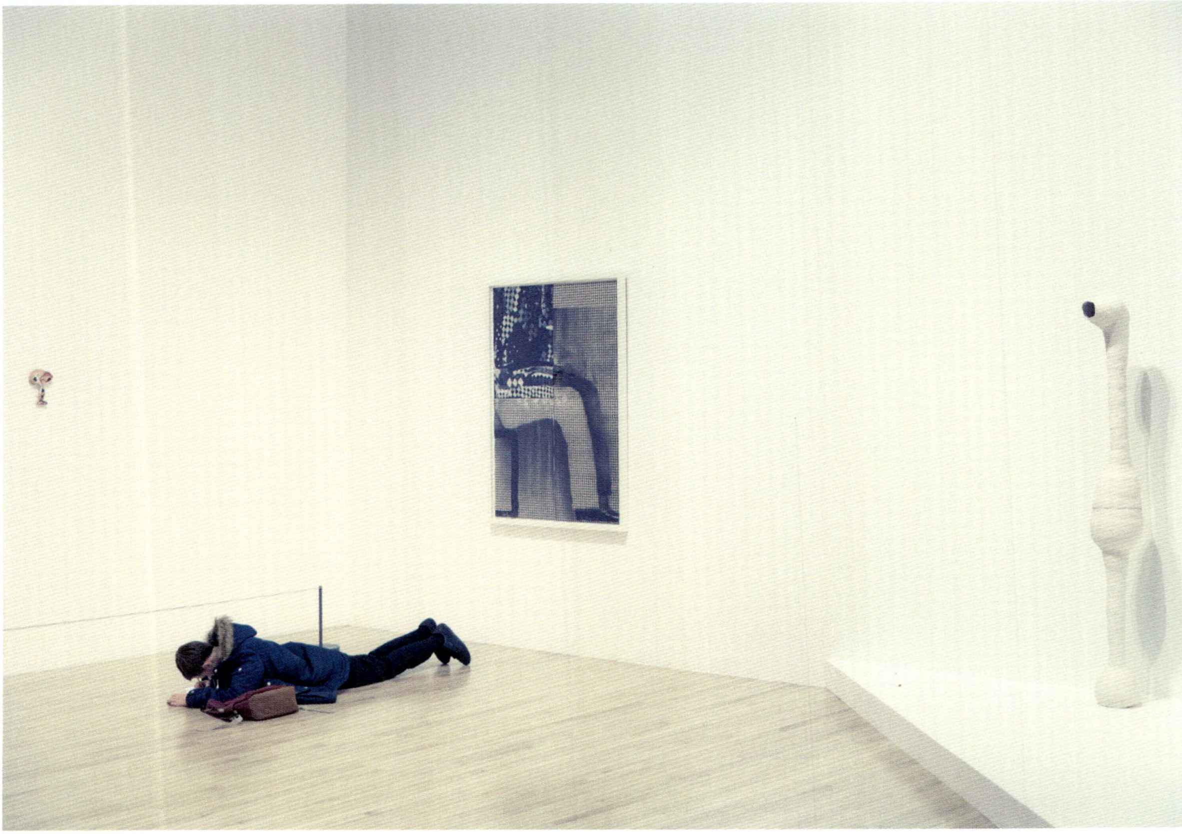

Untitled, Tate Modern, 03.12.2015

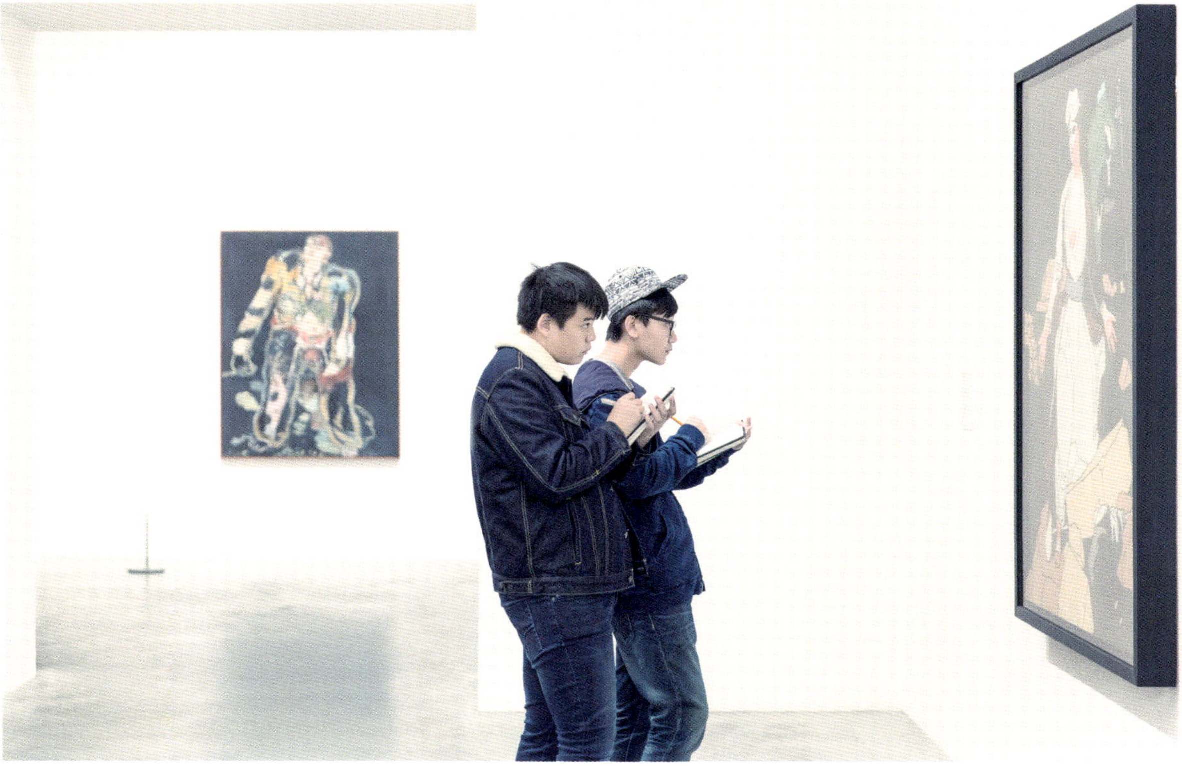

 Untitled, Tate Modern, 03.12.2015 David Vintiner

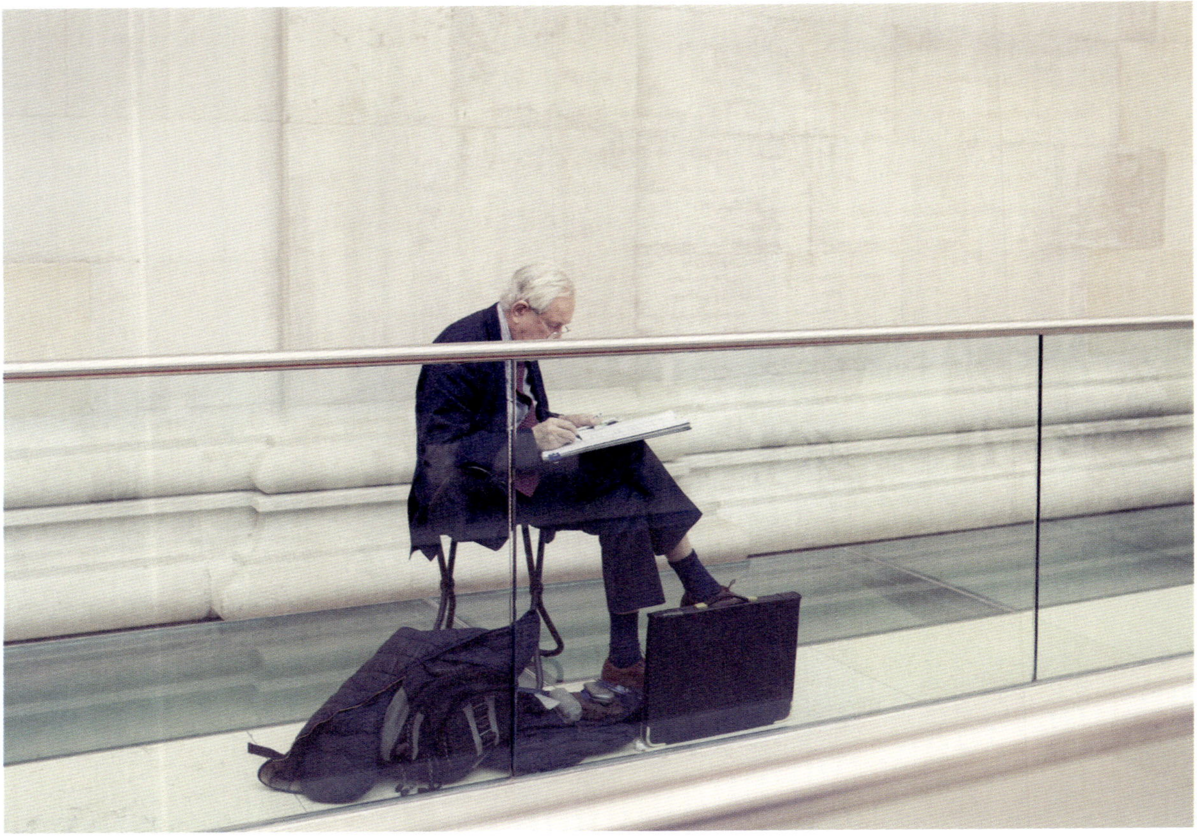

Untitled, British Museum, 13.02.2013

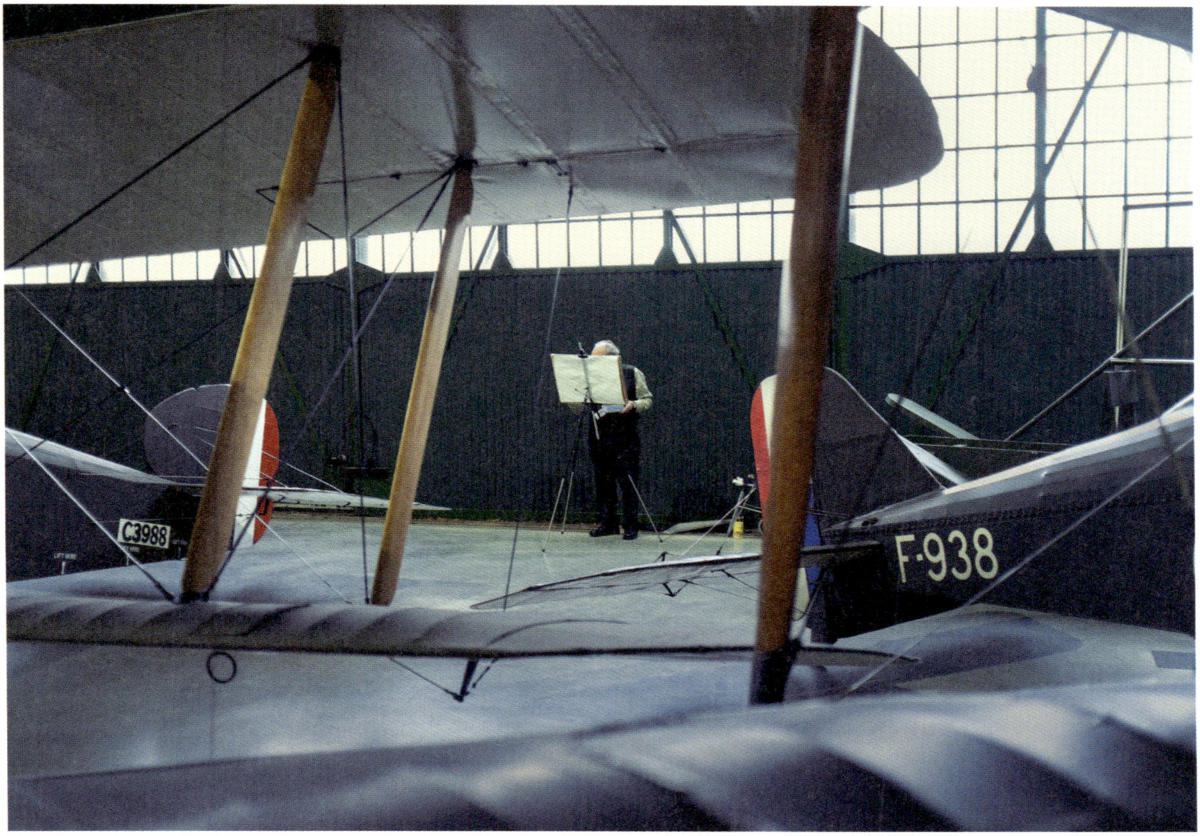

 Untitled, RAF Museum Hendon, 05.05.2012 David Vintiner

Flightpath

Life in West London suburbs closest to Heathrow Airport, where planes fly low overhead every two minutes.

Ben West

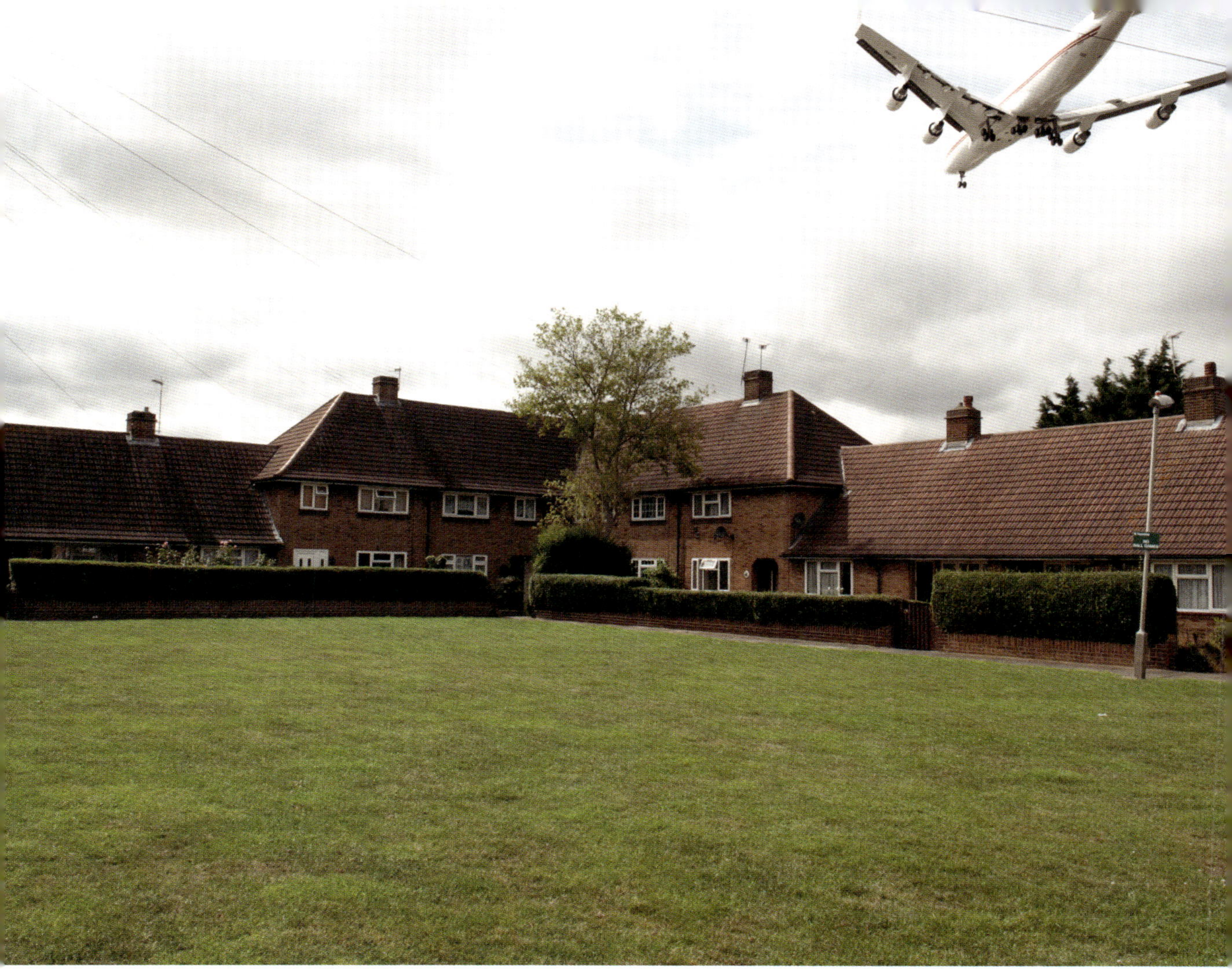

It's an ordinary scene. A row of 1940s houses, plastic white-framed windows and satellite dishes, tarmac driveways, the odd bit of foliage – just another street under the grey skies of suburban London. And then you spy it: the tail of an Air Canada Boeing 747 creeping stealthily between two roofs. If you were there you'd have noticed it immediately, of course. "You get these monstrous metal shapes coming in from about 5am," says photographer Ben West. "They cause spiralling turbulence over the houses. The noise is intense – even if you have two or three-layered glass windows, you still feel it." For the residents of Hatton and Cranford in West London that ugly sight, that roaring din *is* ordinary – it happens every two minutes when you live directly under the Heathrow flightpath.

Most major airports are deliberately located away from big cities to avoid precisely this issue but Heathrow was never intended to be a major airport. Built in 1929, its first incarnation was as a tiny grass airfield off a country lane, used for light aircraft displays. Following the Second World War, during which it was commandeered by the RAF for long-distance flights, it grew into the two-runway, five-terminal beast of a civil airport that it is today. For the past decade a potential third runway has been hotly debated – it has yet to get the nod. It was this angle that interested West. Blending in with the planespotters he meandered around the airport perimeter fence at first before shifting focus to the communities below the flightpath.

One of the most striking things about these pictures is how eerily desolate the landscapes are. Where have all the people gone? "They have two runways, north and south, and at some point they switch them round so one part of the community gets the problem in the morning and one in the afternoon," West explains. "As soon as you get the runway shift you start to see people come out."

There's a sense of playfulness as you try to spot the plane, but it comes with a sense of foreboding. West deliberately alludes to our ambiguous relationship with flight – at once a terrifying and astonishing prospect. "I have this strange fascination with aircraft," he says. "I hate flying but when you see these big objects in the air, you think, how is that possible?"

"My photographic practice is about habitats being changed and destroyed," he continues. His wider work encompasses a multidisciplinary approach that includes photomontage, collage, digital scanning and sound recording with the more traditional documentary photographic approach we see in *Flightpath*. "Just before I started this I spent some time in North Vietnam where they were building a huge dam and they were going to move 10,000 people whether they liked it or not. I'm interested in how environments are changed by human developments."

Heathrow's third runway is still awaiting approval. If it goes ahead as many, West included, suspect it will, people living in the houses we see in these pictures won't be forced to move but they will face an increase in the number of planes flying over their homes. Whatever happens, people will continue to live there – because it's cheap, perhaps, or because that's where their family lives – just as they do around the Westway, the vast motorway that slices through West London and is the subject of the photographer's next project. "Something's been built against everyone's wishes and yet there are stables, little farms, art spaces, bars," he explains. "People have managed to take something so negative and domineering through their communities and turn it into something they can work with."

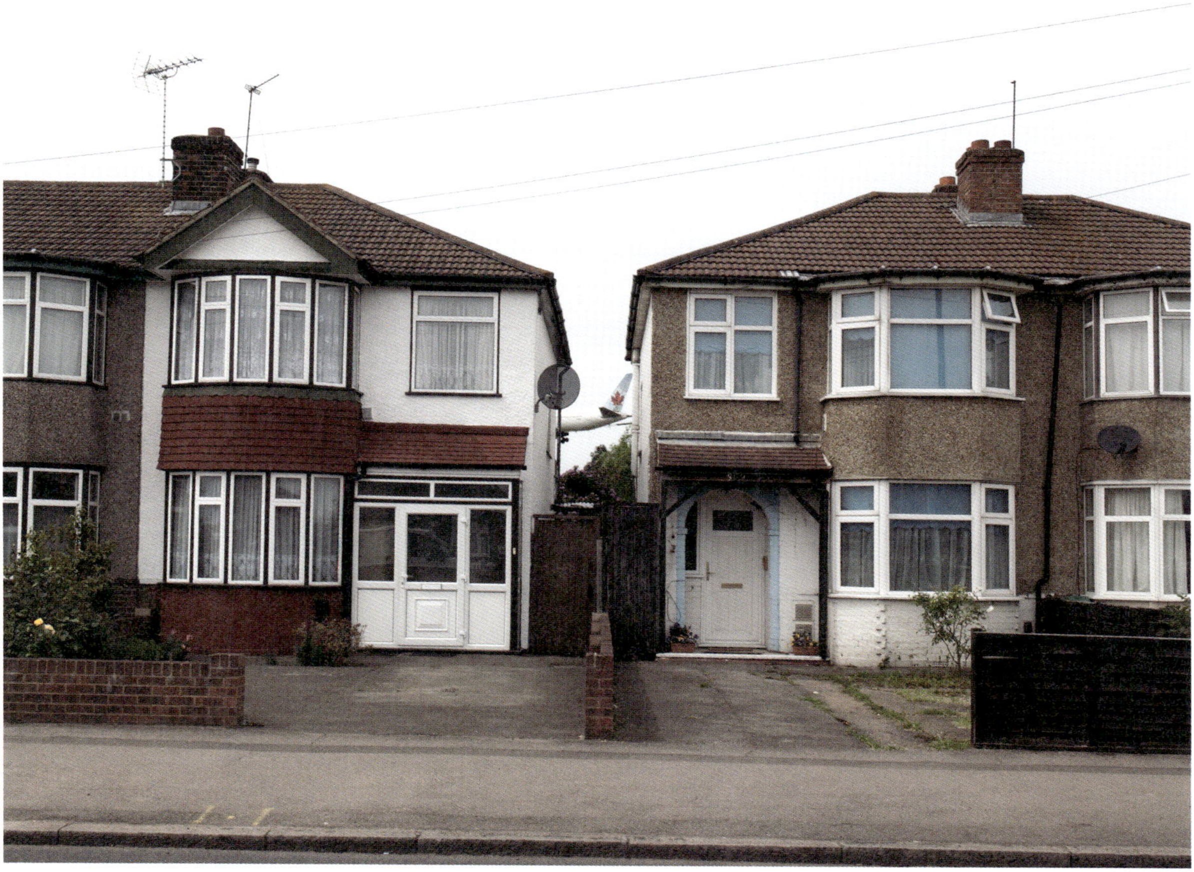

Previous: Untitled, Cranford, 15.08.2009
Above: Untitled, North Feltham, 23.05.2009

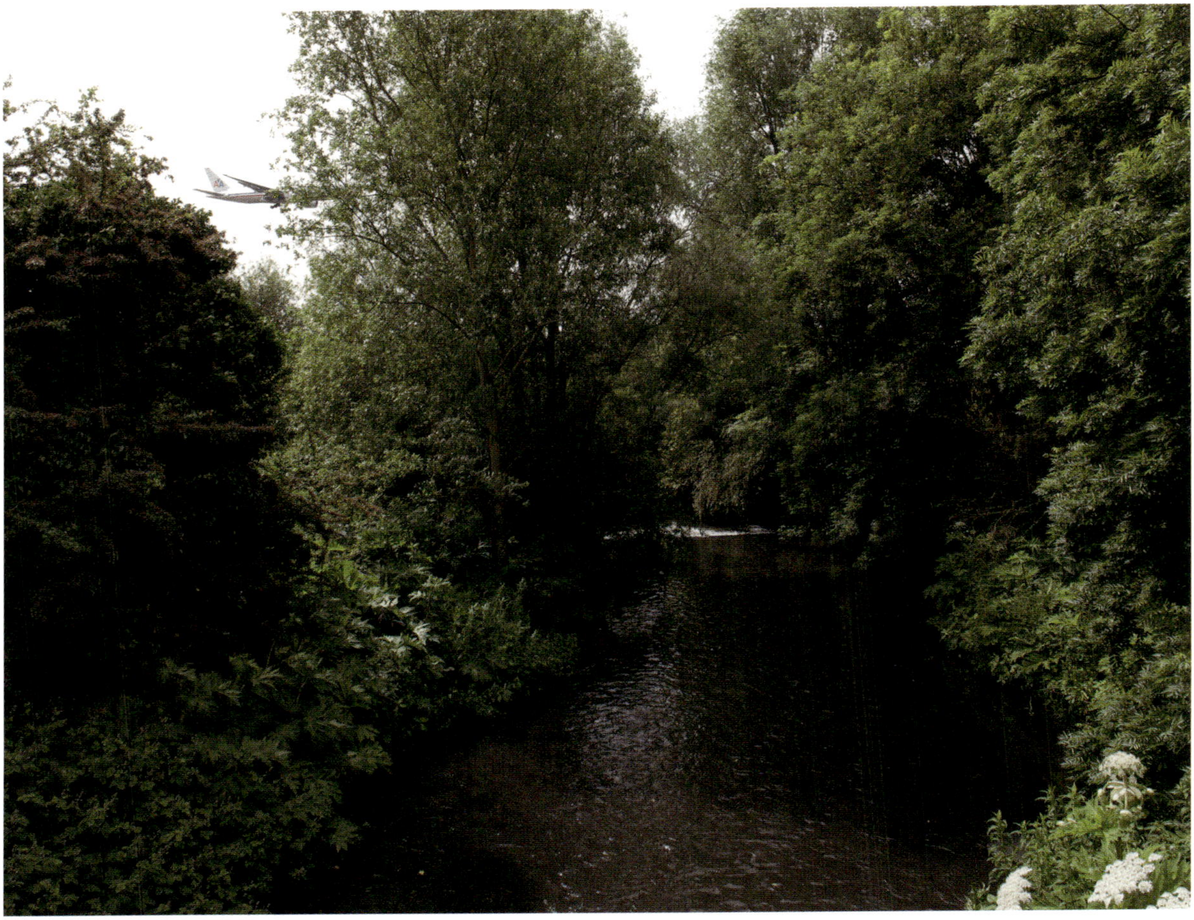

Untitled, Cranford Park, 26.05.2009

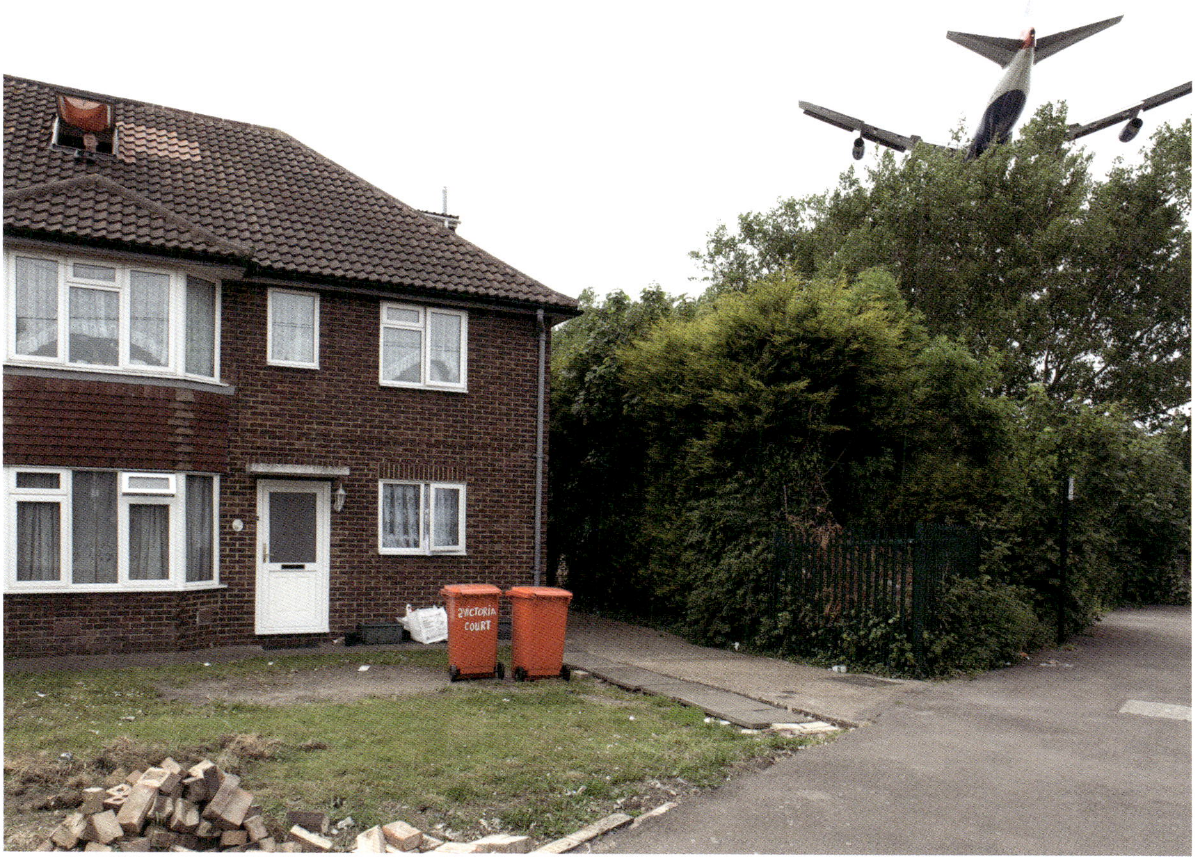

Untitled, Cranford, 23.05.2009

Overleaf: Untitled, Hounslow Urban Farm, North Feltham, 09.05.2009

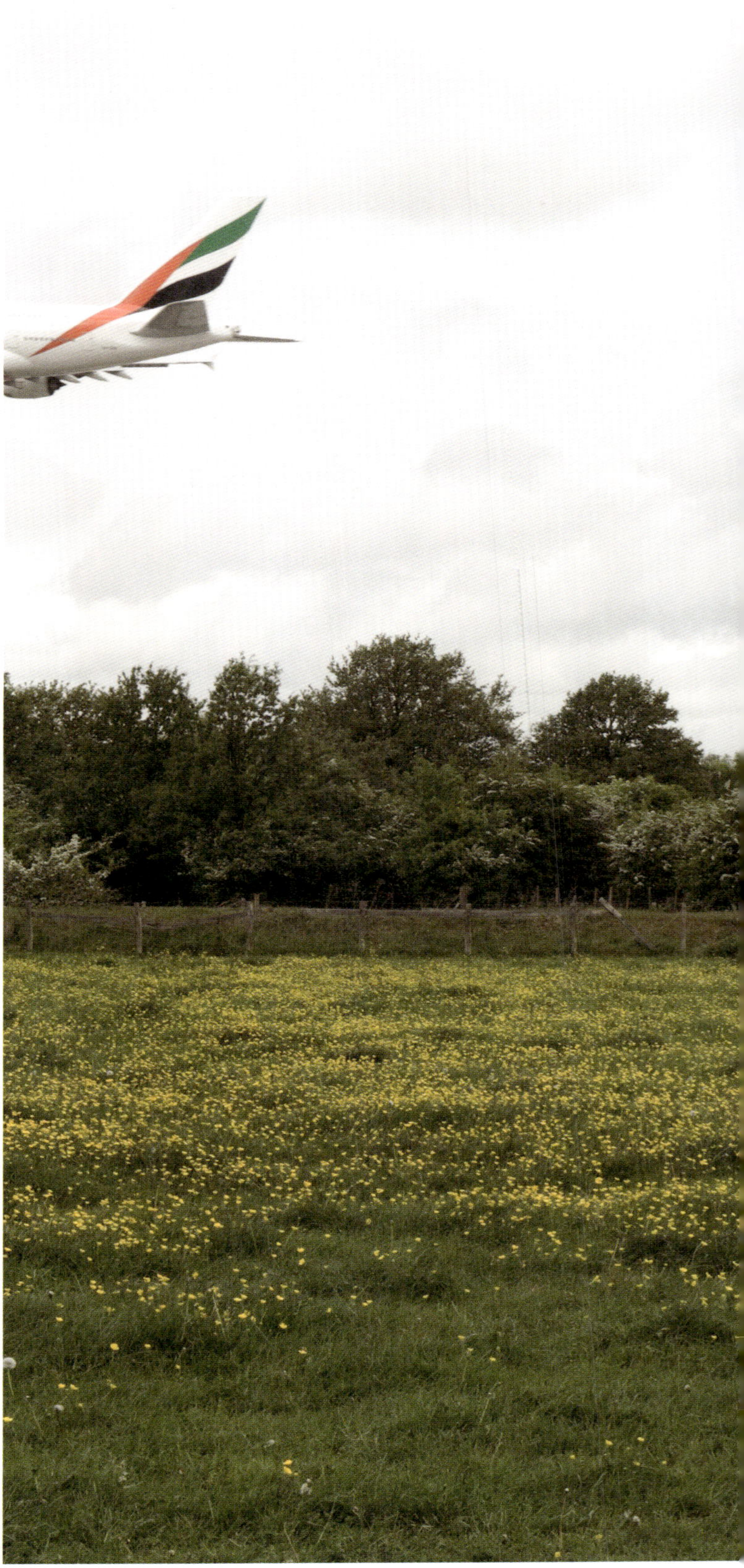

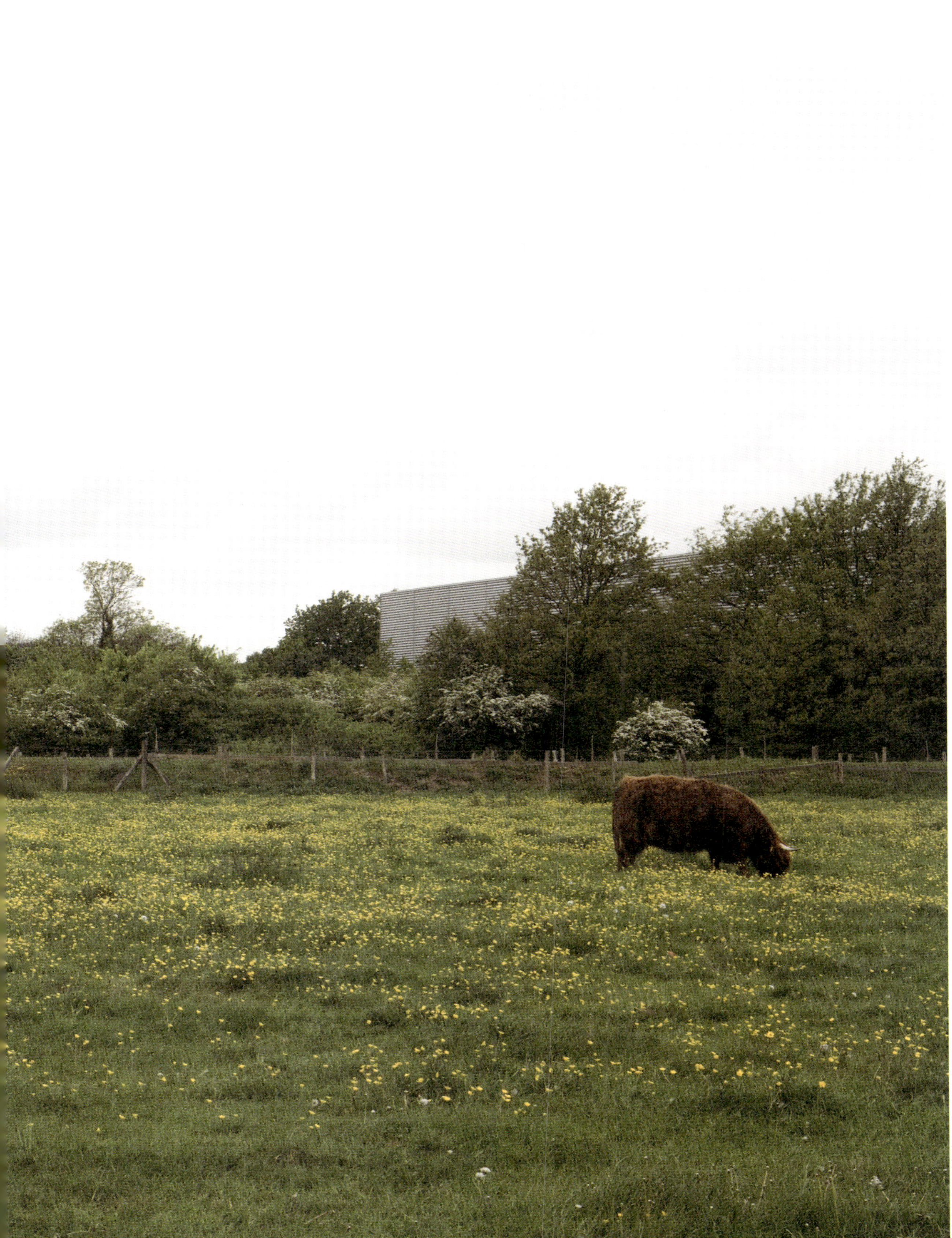

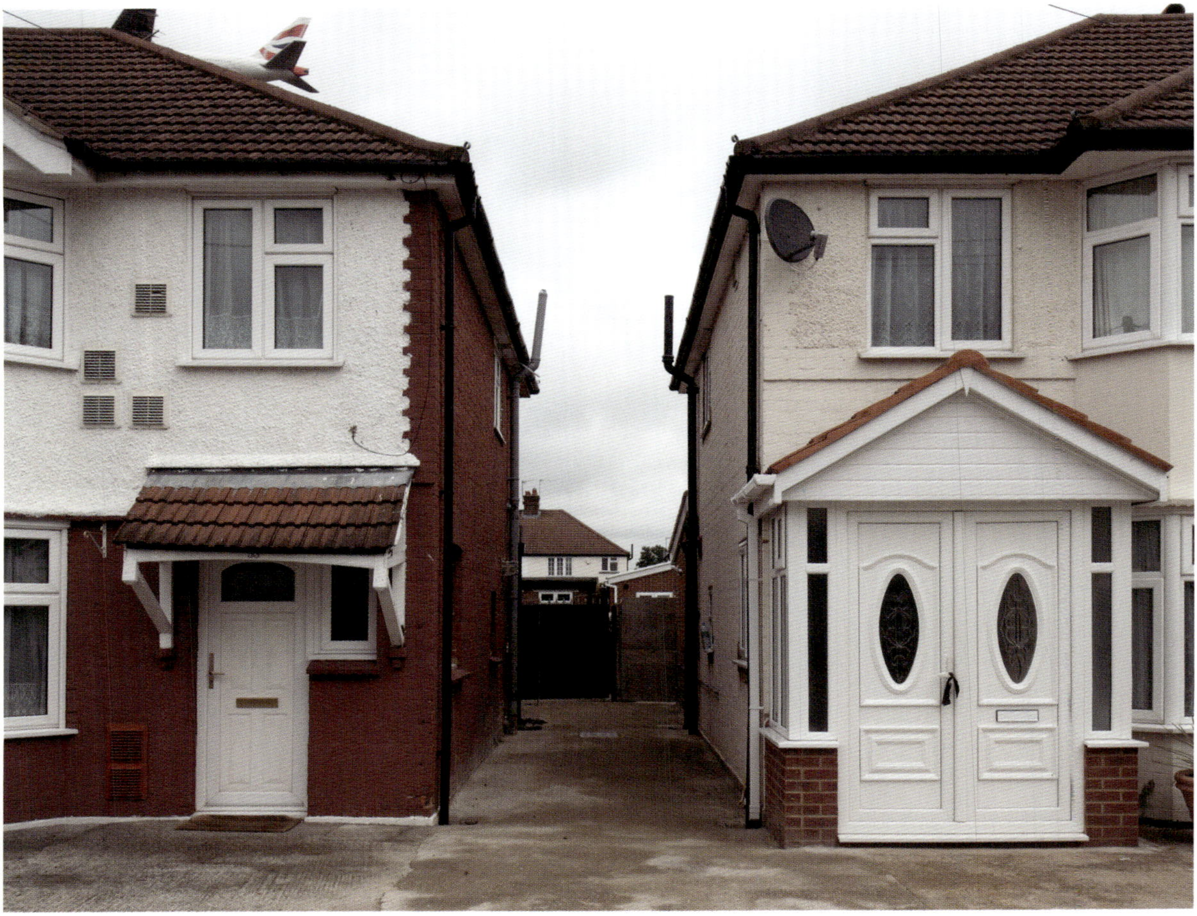

Untitled, North Feltham, 08.07.2009

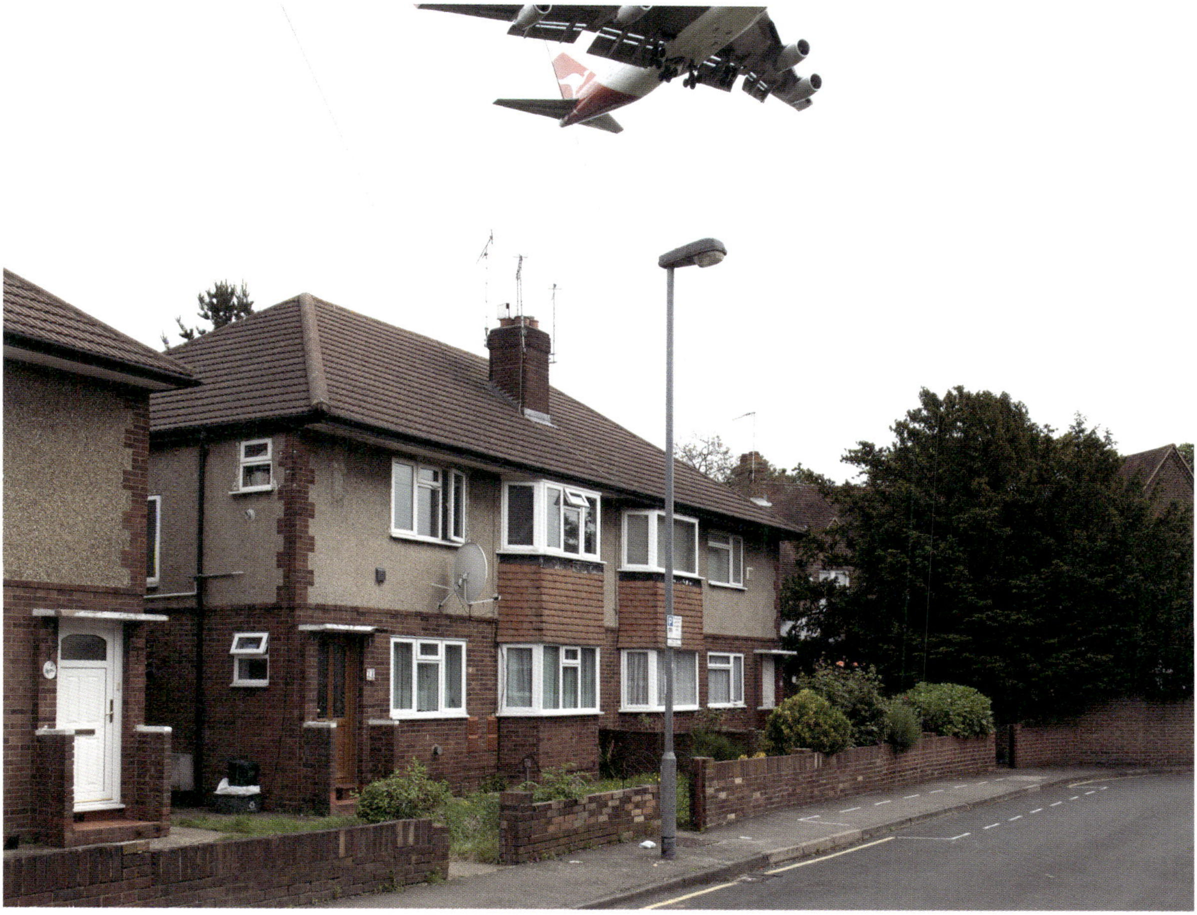

Untitled, Cranford, 23.05.2009

Ben West

Boaters

Photographing the bohemians who've escaped the stress of London renting for a slower, more basic existence on the canals.

Carl Bigmore

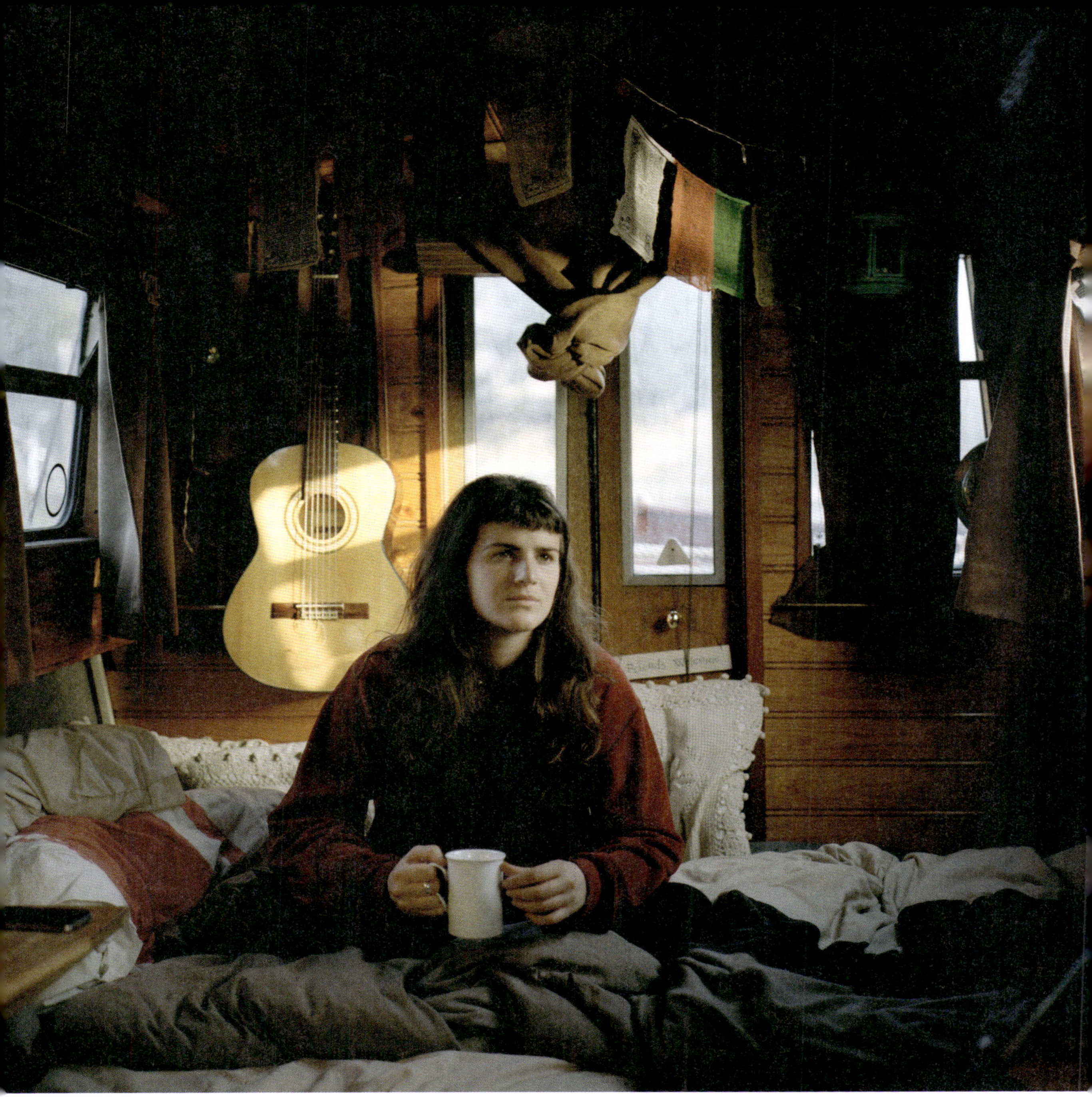

What could be more idyllic than living on a boat? Waking up to ducks quacking, the stench of a broken toilet, your neighbour metres away drunkenly stumbling home in the early hours... Boat life isn't for everyone, as Carl Bigmore discovered when making his series about the residents of East London's canals. "A lot of people don't last when they realise what they've signed up for," he says, "but those people that do last love it. They love the lifestyle, doing all the repairs, all the challenges that come with it."

London-based for 10 years, Bigmore had just moved to Bethnal Green when he shot *Boaters*. Initially his approach was reportage. He shot the exteriors of canal boats, often beautifully decorated in a similar style to traditional Romani wagons, and views across the water. However, after one friendly, ginger-bearded boater invited him in for a coffee, he started to hop aboard and knock on doors. Awaiting him was a world of artists, students and dreamers, drawn to a slower, simpler existence. "In the canal there's still people hanging on to an alternative way of living, rallying against the gentrification of everything." Bigmore photographed them bathed in the magical light that spills in through the boat windows, in interiors dotted with tatty books, Tibetan prayer flags, animal skulls and other neo-hippy totems.

In some ways, *Boaters* continues photography's long-held fascination with unconventional, itinerant groups. In the 1960s, Diane Arbus took unsettling pictures of circus performers, and was accused of exploiting her subjects' otherness. Tom Hunter's 1990s portraits of squatter friends, by contrast, are imbued with a familiarity that's down to his insider's perspective. *Boaters* sits in between, not of the world depicted, but not wholly removed either. For Bigmore, whose work includes a poetic series about the impact of climate change on California's waterways, and life in the free-spirited Pacific Northwest of America, the idea was to "capture an atmosphere rather than to just tell a story. To convey a sense of what it feels like to live on boats."

"I love the way you can drop down onto the canal path and you feel slightly removed from the city," says Bigmore. Like many Londoners, he was aware of the canals that crisscross through the city – from The Grand Junction in the west, up north to Regent's Canal, out east to the Lee Navigation – but hadn't explored them at length. The bulk of London's waterways don't run alongside the road – you have to make a point of seeking them out. And that was exactly what Bigmore did, cycling along the paths, pausing now and then to take pictures as he went.

The number of boaters has shot up in recent years, fuelled by the capital's housing crisis. Along its more central stretches the canals are heaving. For all the die-hard veterans, there are now others living there by necessity, not choice, barely scraping by in one of the world's most expensive cities. "One guy had to leave his flat because he couldn't afford rent anymore. He was living with his girlfriend and his dog in a tiny boat, there was a bed and that's it." But the canal's days as a cheap alternative may be numbered. Recently Bigmore was walking through Broadway Market when something caught his eye: "An estate agent was selling a canal boat in the window. Now *that* tells you how much East London has changed."

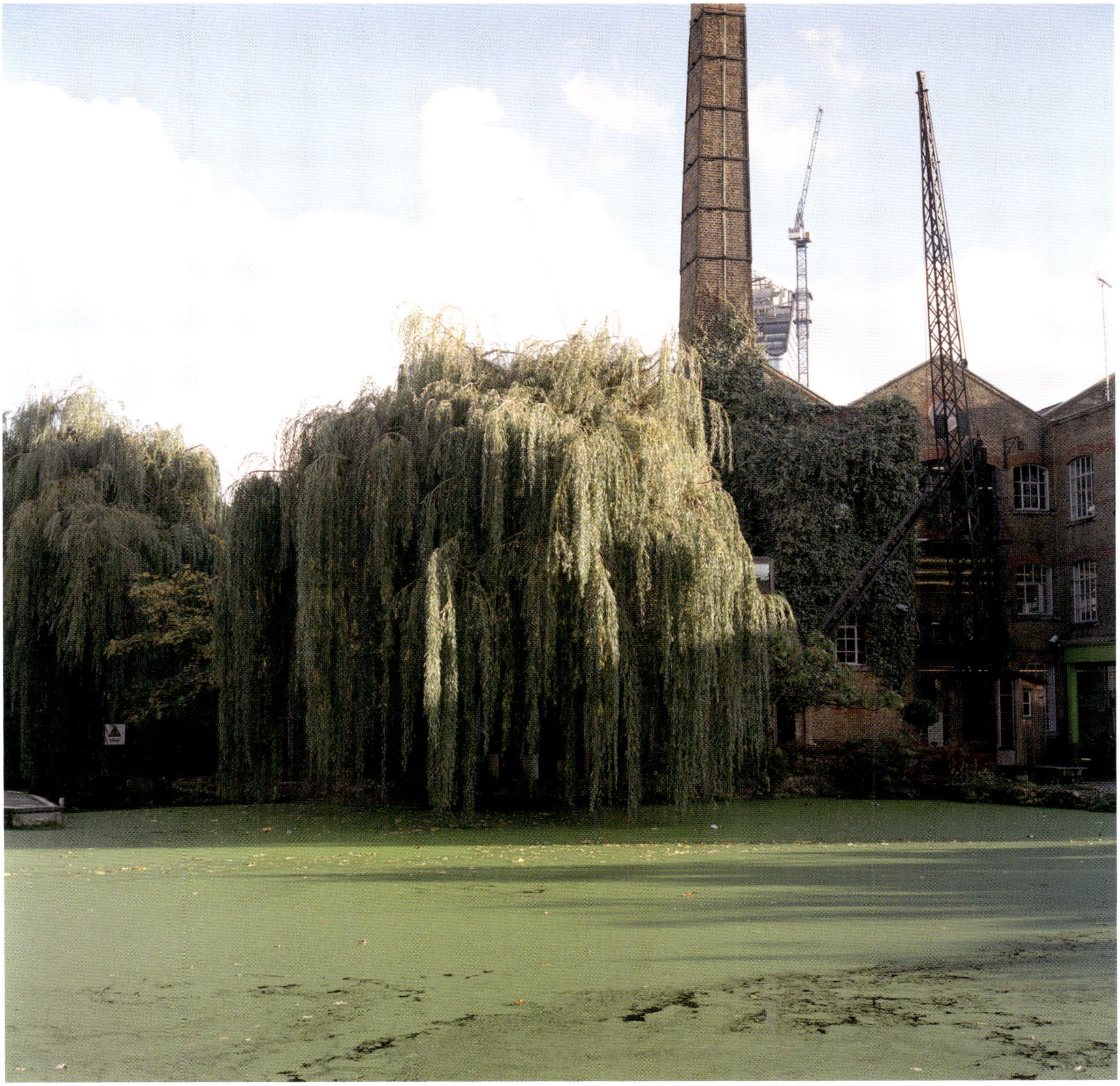

Previous: Elena, Regent's Canal, March 2014
Above: Regent's Canal, Islington, November 2015

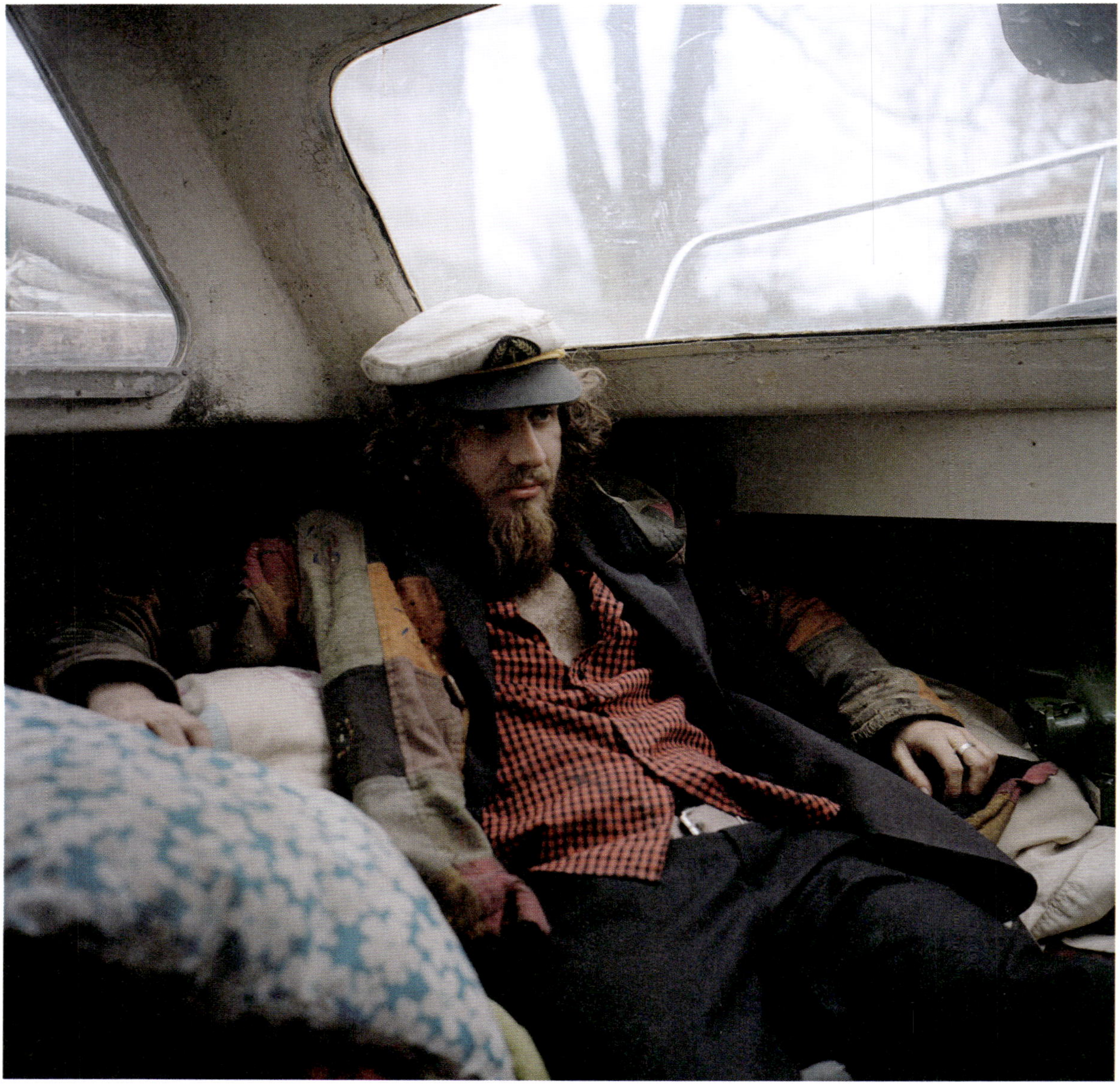

Preston, Regent's Canal, March 2014

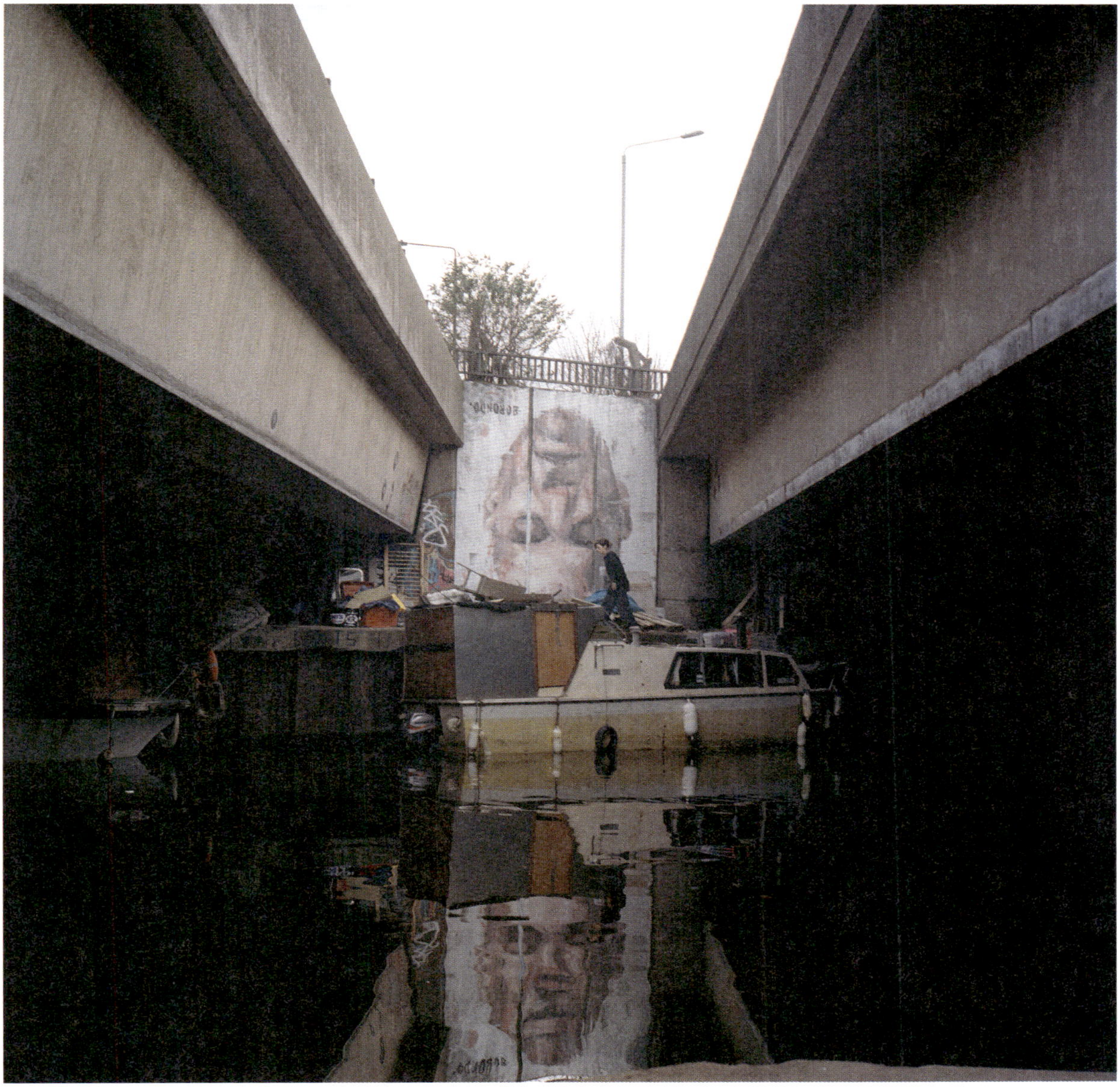

 Hertford Union Canal, March 2014 Carl Bigmore

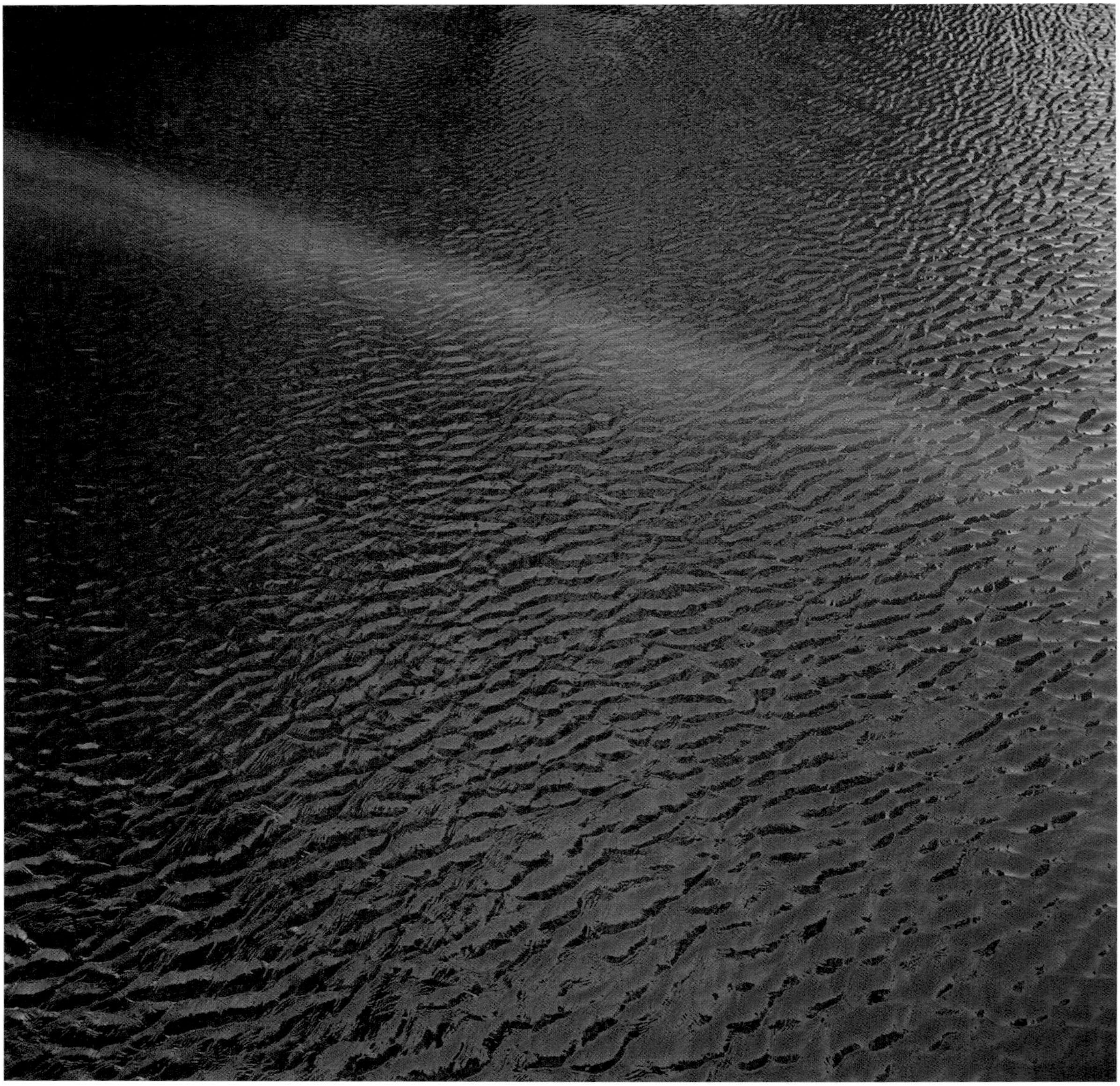

 Regent's Canal, Mile End, April 2014

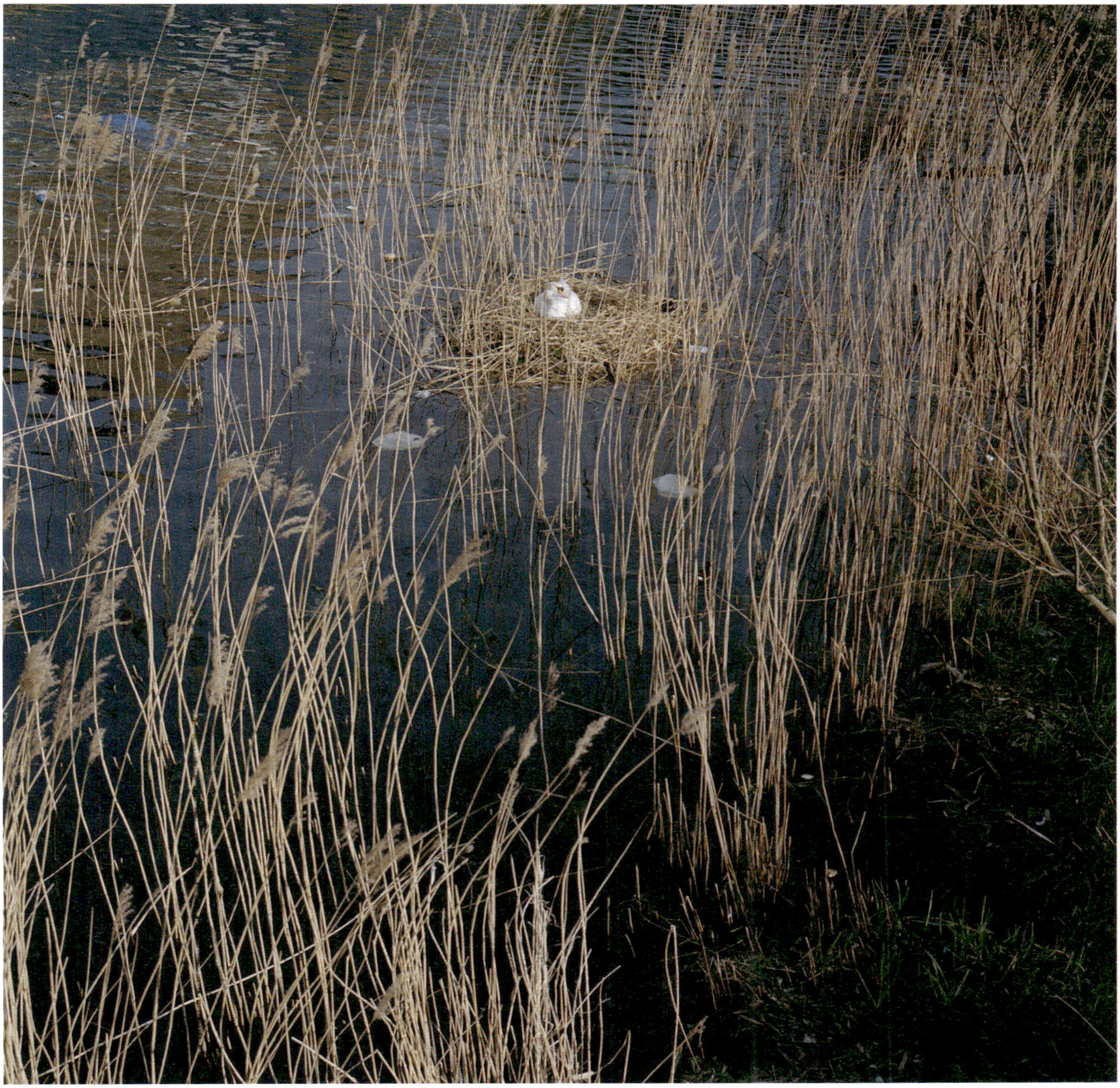

Regent's Canal, Mile End, April 2014

Carl Bigmore

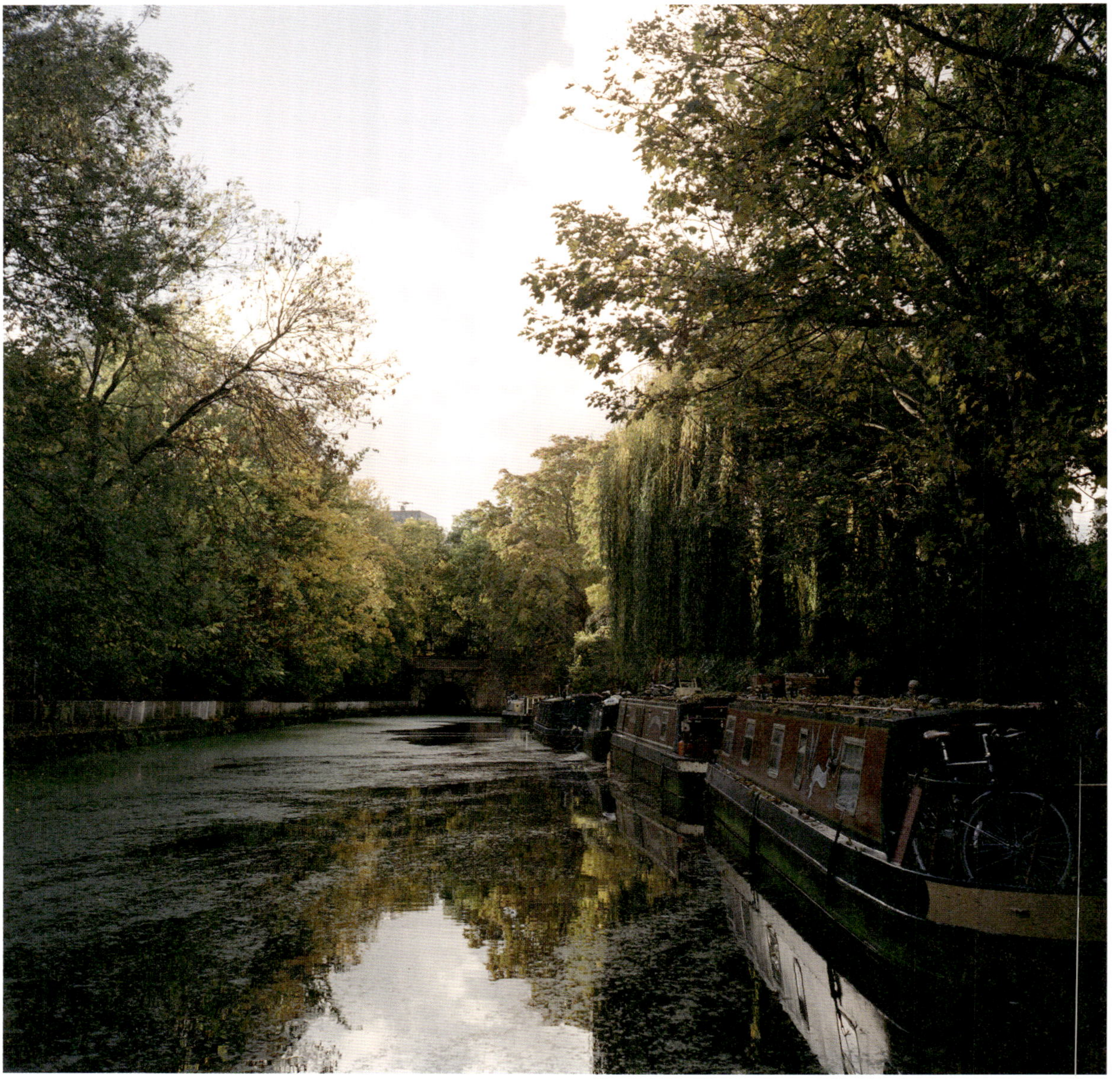

Regent's Canal, Islington, November 2015

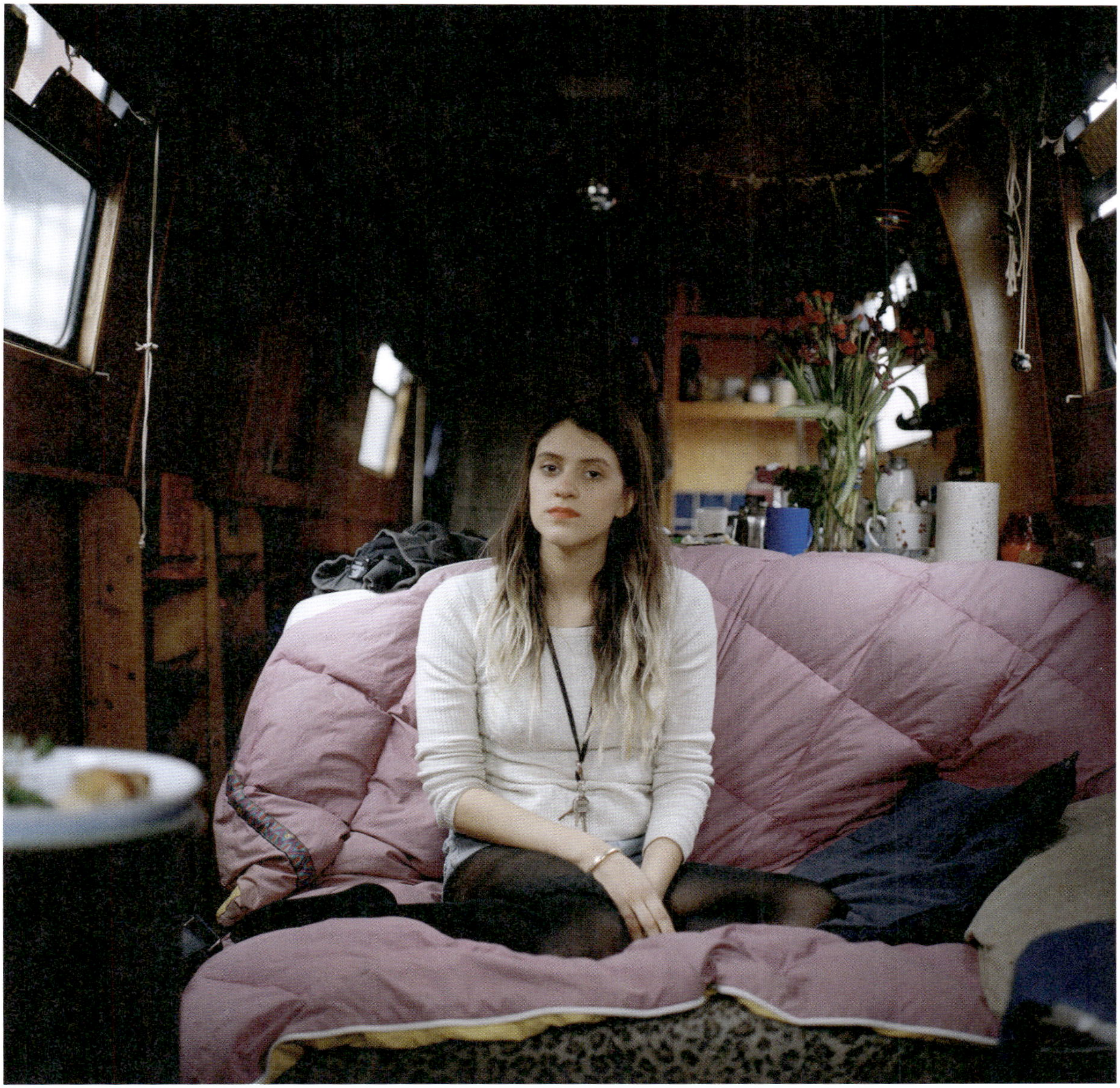

 Mio, Hertford Union Canal, March 2014 Carl Bigmore

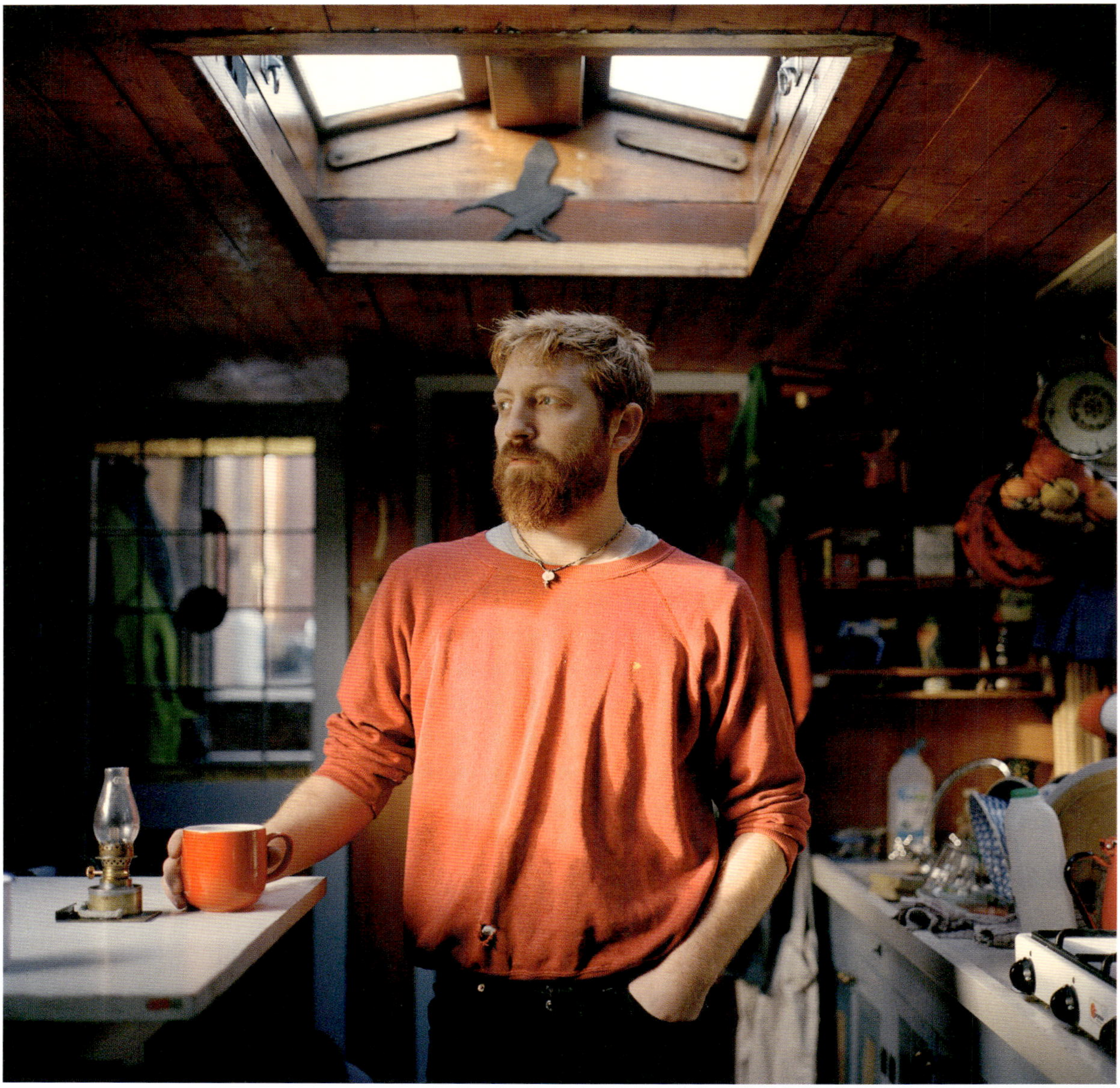

Josh, Regent's Canal, February 2014

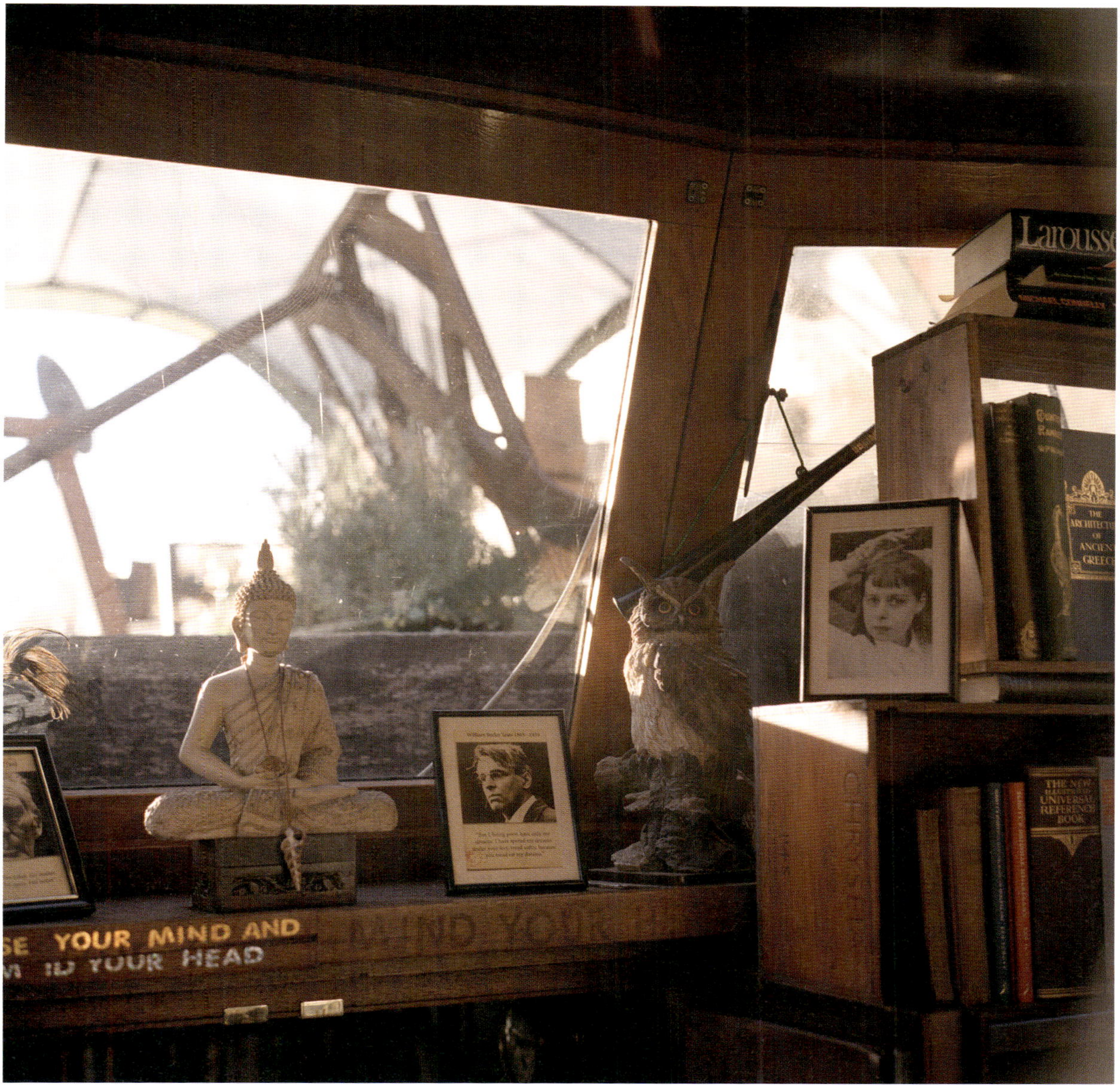

A detail onboard the 'Word On The Water'
bookshop barge, Regent's Canal, November 2015

Carl Bigmore

Barbican Residents

A rare peek inside the iconic
Brutalist estate to see the
creativity of its residents
and the tasteful interiors
of their apartments.

Anton Rodriguez

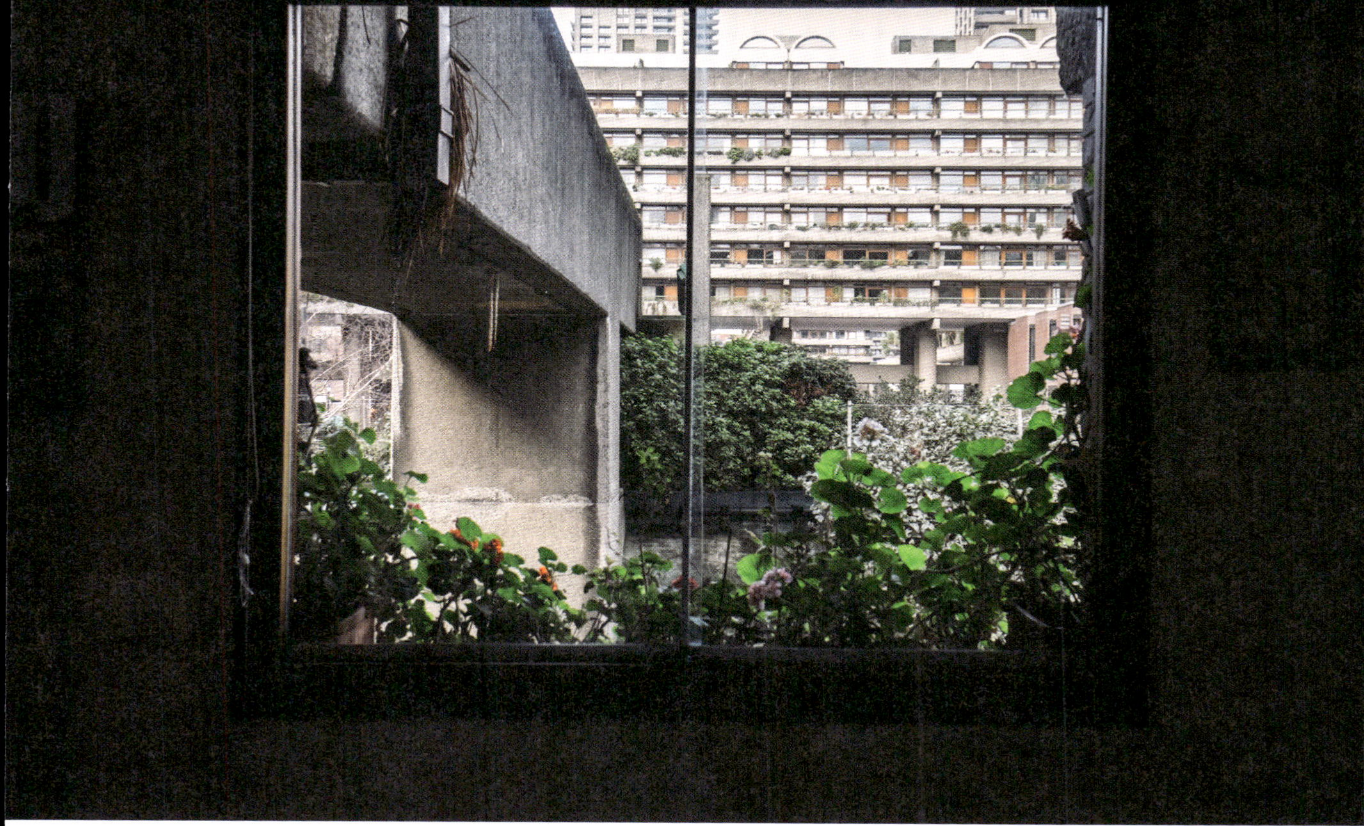

In 2003, the Barbican estate was named Britain's "ugliest" building. An austere, functional form in murky grey-brown hues, it certainly isn't to everyone's tastes. And yet the people who live there are positively fanatical. "We just fell in love with it," says Liverpool-born photographer Anton Rodriguez, who moved to the estate five years ago. "It's hard to think about living anywhere else in London."

Designed in the 1950s after the area was severely bombed in the war, the Barbican is a concrete medley of high-rises, seven-story blocks and raised walkways. It has become a very expensive address – as much of London has – but at the heart this was a utopian project, intended to provide affordable, imaginatively designed urban housing for young professionals. Rodriguez praises "the space and the light, every flat has floor-to-ceiling windows", lush communal gardens and lakes, the proximity to the arts complex, as well as the ease of life – post delivered to your door, rubbish collected, underfloor heating. "They thought of everything," he enthuses.

Barbican Residents, first a blog, then a book, was born of "being a nosy neighbour", he admits. "You'd walk down the corridor, someone would open their door to go in or out and you'd have a look as you go past." When he posted a call for participants on Barbican Chat, the online forum for estate residents, responses poured in. Formerly a fashion photographer, this was the first time that Rodriguez had shot interiors, although it's something he's specialised in since. "I'd go to see the resident, chat to them for about 45 minutes and then say, 'Do what you usually do, have a cup of tea or make a coffee, and I'll go around and take photos of the flat.' It was very organic."

Other photography projects – notably David Heathcote's *Barbican: Penthouse Over the City* or Alan Ainsworth's *The Barbican: Architecture and Light* – have drawn attention to the Barbican's Brutalist exterior but Rodriguez is the first to lure us inside, to peep at the people and appraise their taste in decor. It's fascinating to observe the variety across his crisp, breezy pictures. The 2,000 flats share certain design features: white walls, magnificent windows and, if you're lucky, an original 1960s kitchen with a famous Barbican sink, but they fall into some 110 different types, from studios to duplexes and penthouses. "There's sort of a hierarchy so you can start off small, get a bigger place and then, if you get rich, you can progress to a tower," says Rodriguez.

Is there a Barbican 'type'? "Most people featured in the book are involved in the creative industries," he says, citing architects, photographers and designers. "And you have to appreciate Brutalist architecture to live here because otherwise you're going to be pretty unhappy." Despite soaring prices, Rodriguez discovered "a diverse culture, a real mix of different classes living together". He adds, "The Barbican is a book cover, you don't know what you're going to get until you open it up."

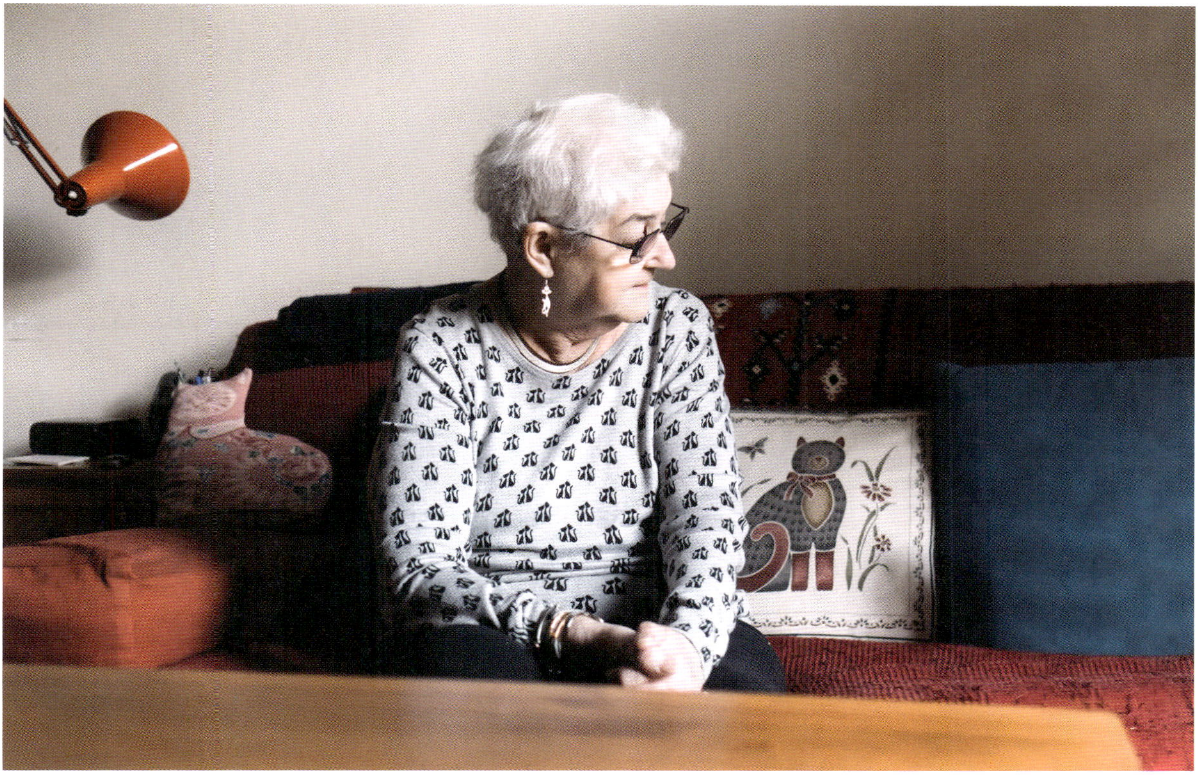

Previous: Kate, Type 121 – Lakeside View, 2015
Above: Kate, Type 121, 2015

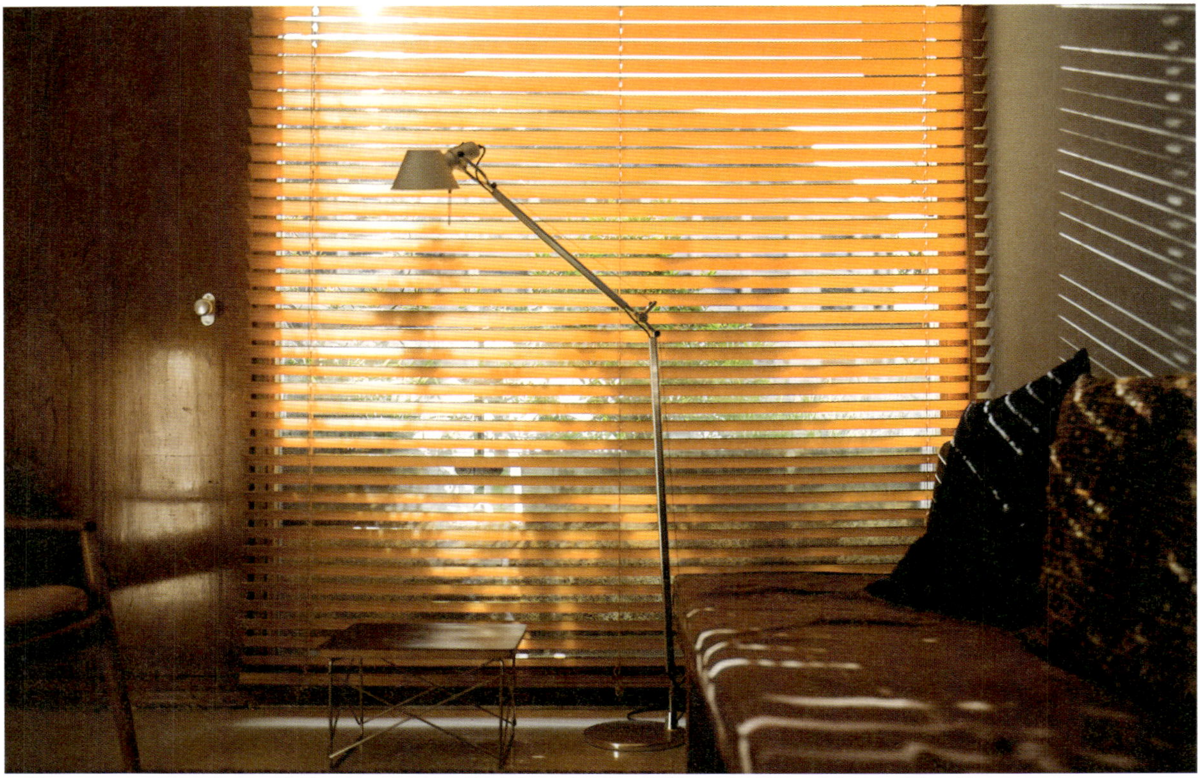

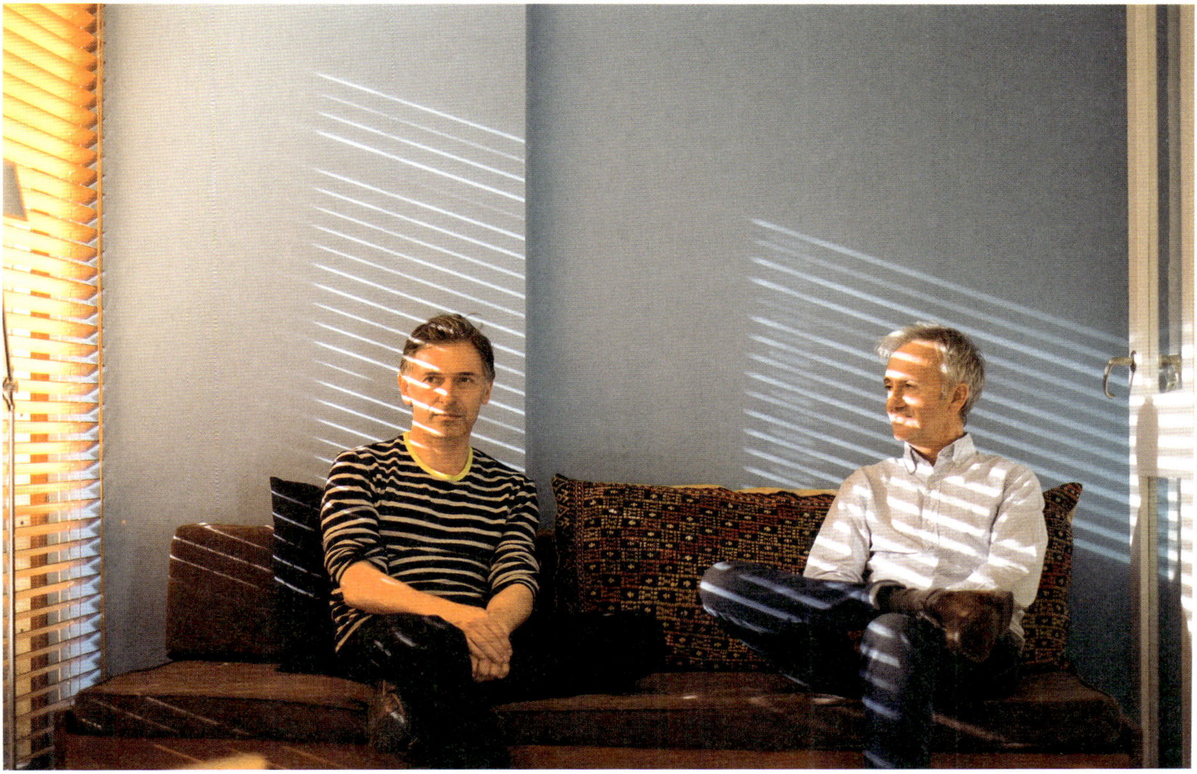

Mark & David, Type 31– One Bedroom, 2015

Anton Rodriguez

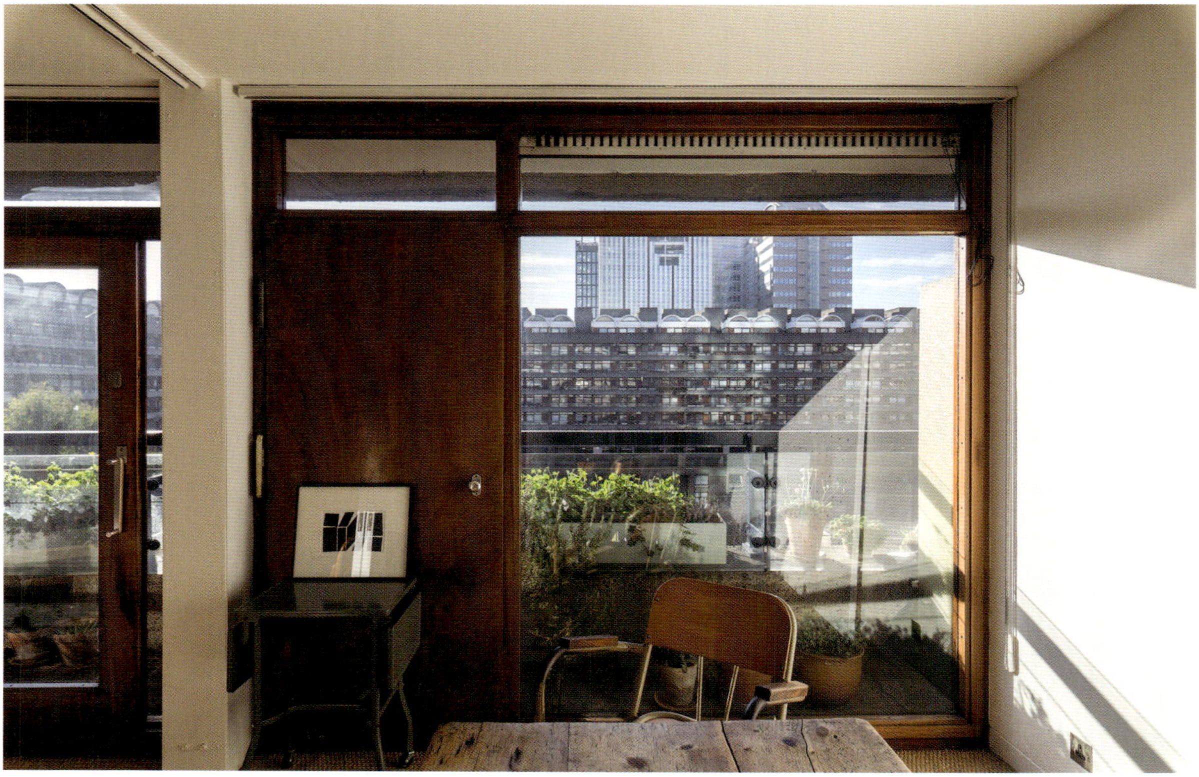

Matt, Type 20 – Living Area, 2016

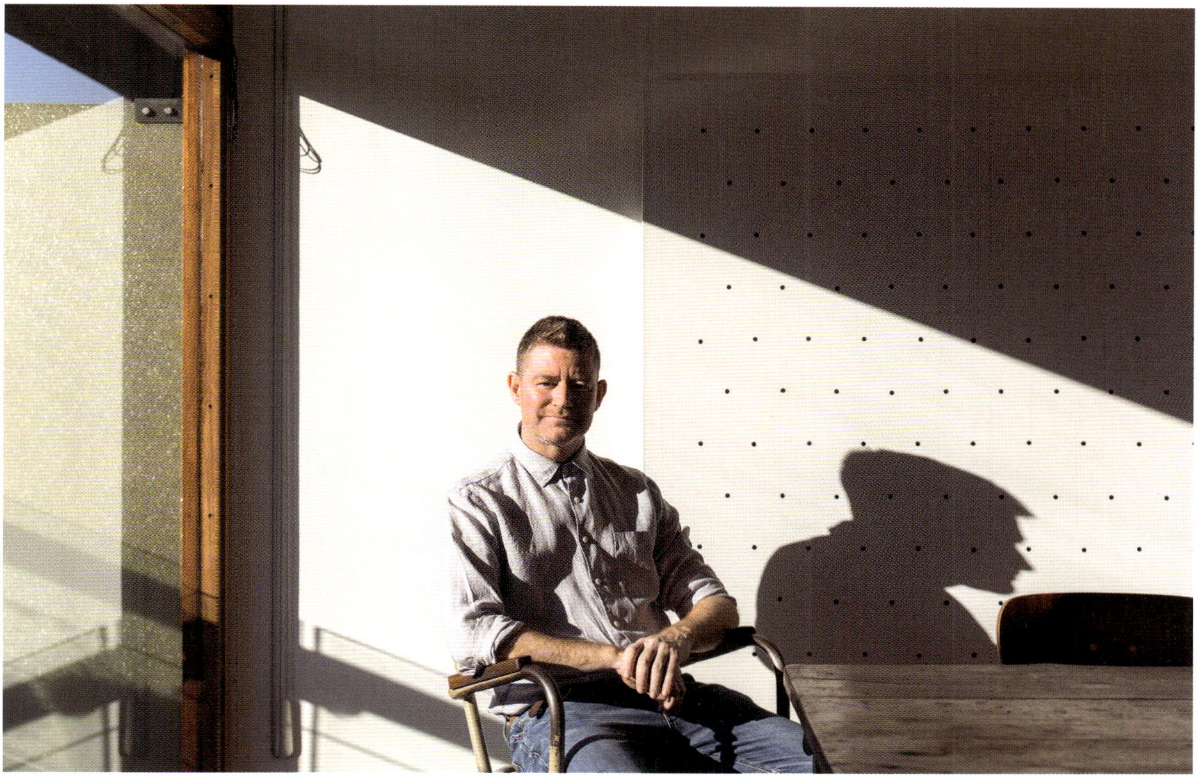

Matt, Type 20, 2016

Anton Rodriguez

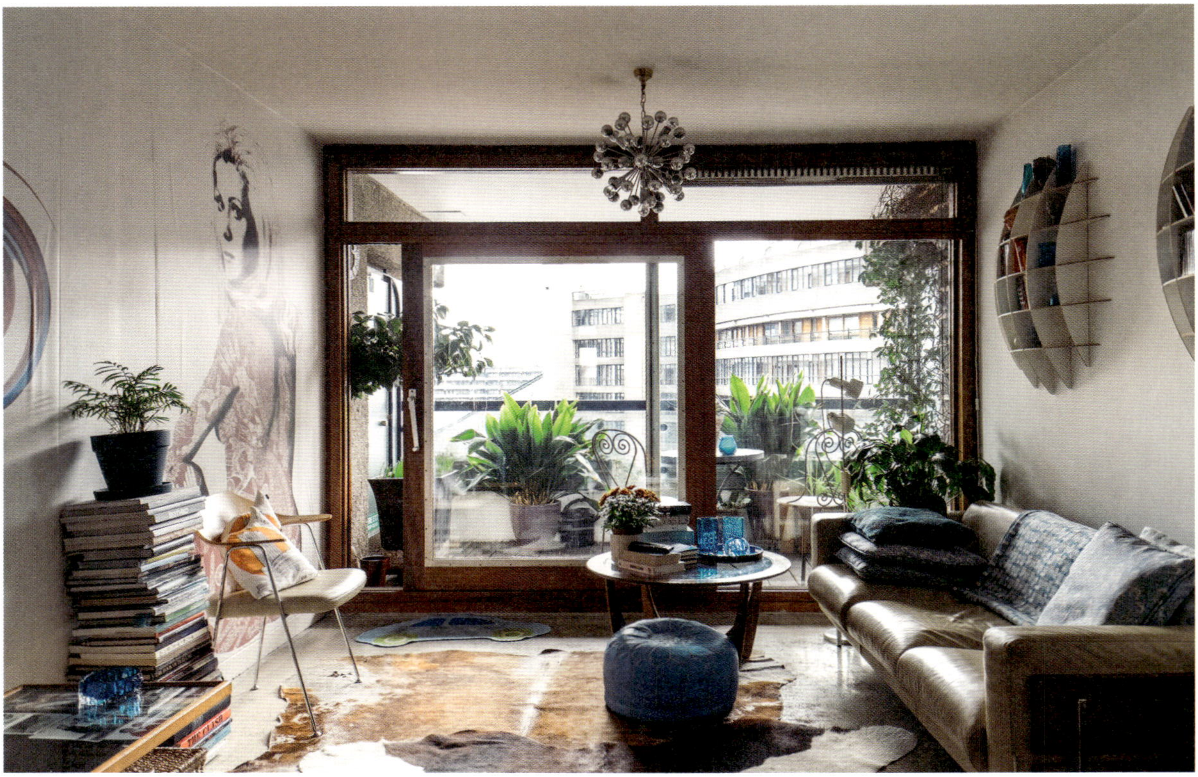

Wendy, Type M2A – Duplex, Living Room, 2015

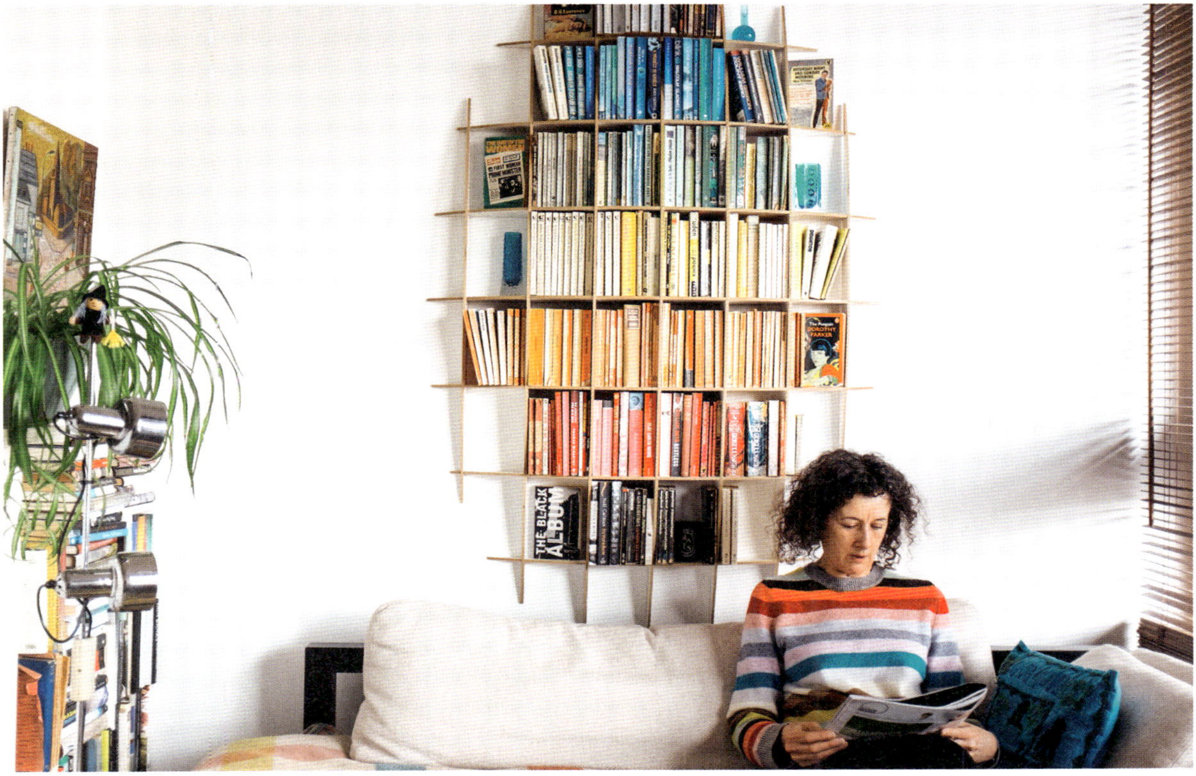

Wendy, Type M2A – Duplex, Dining Area, 2015

Anton Rodriguez

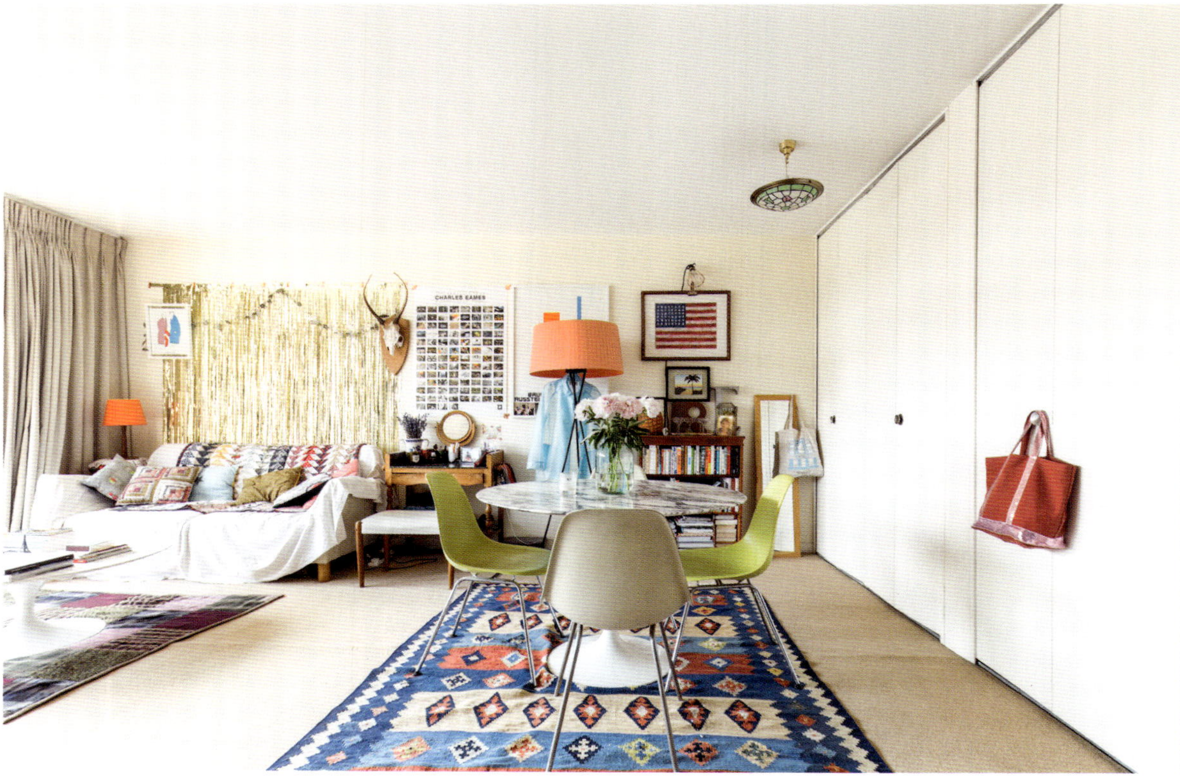

Caroline, Type F2A – Studio Flat, Living Area, 2015

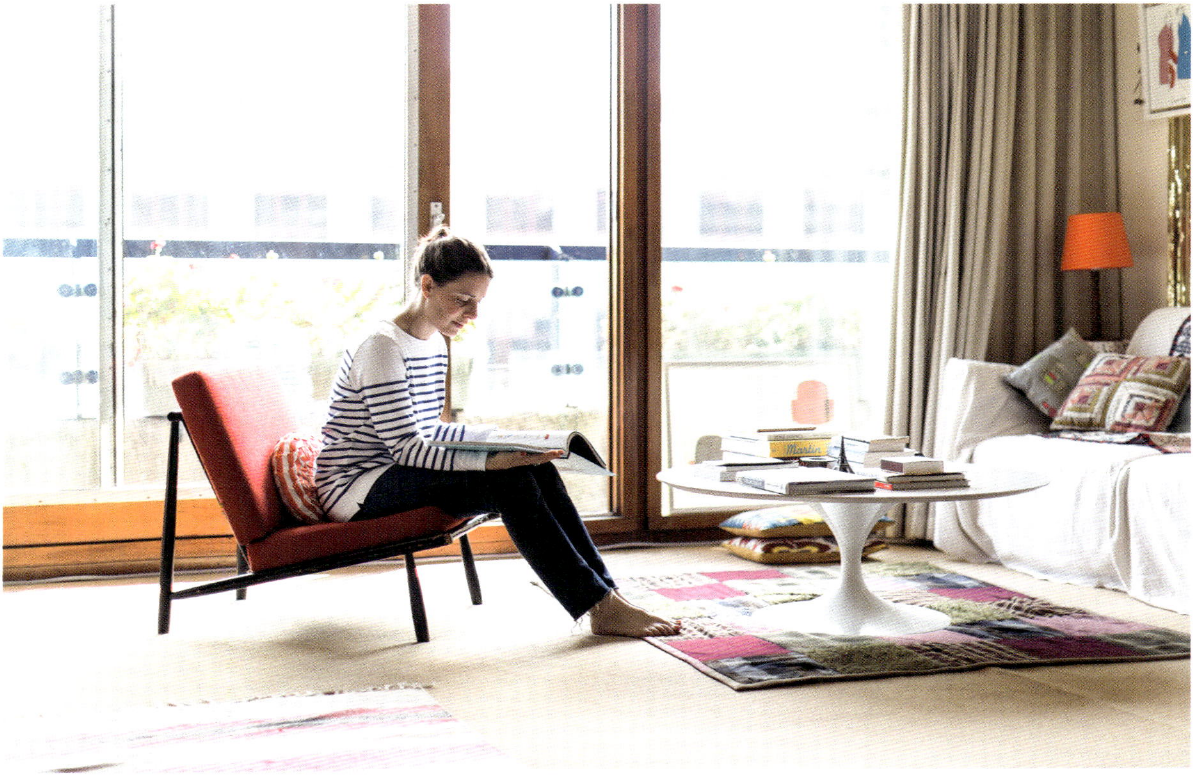

Caroline, Type F2A – Studio Flat, 2015

Anton Rodriguez

Last Stop

Random bus journeys around London provide a new perspective on the city and its intriguing scenes.

George Georgiou

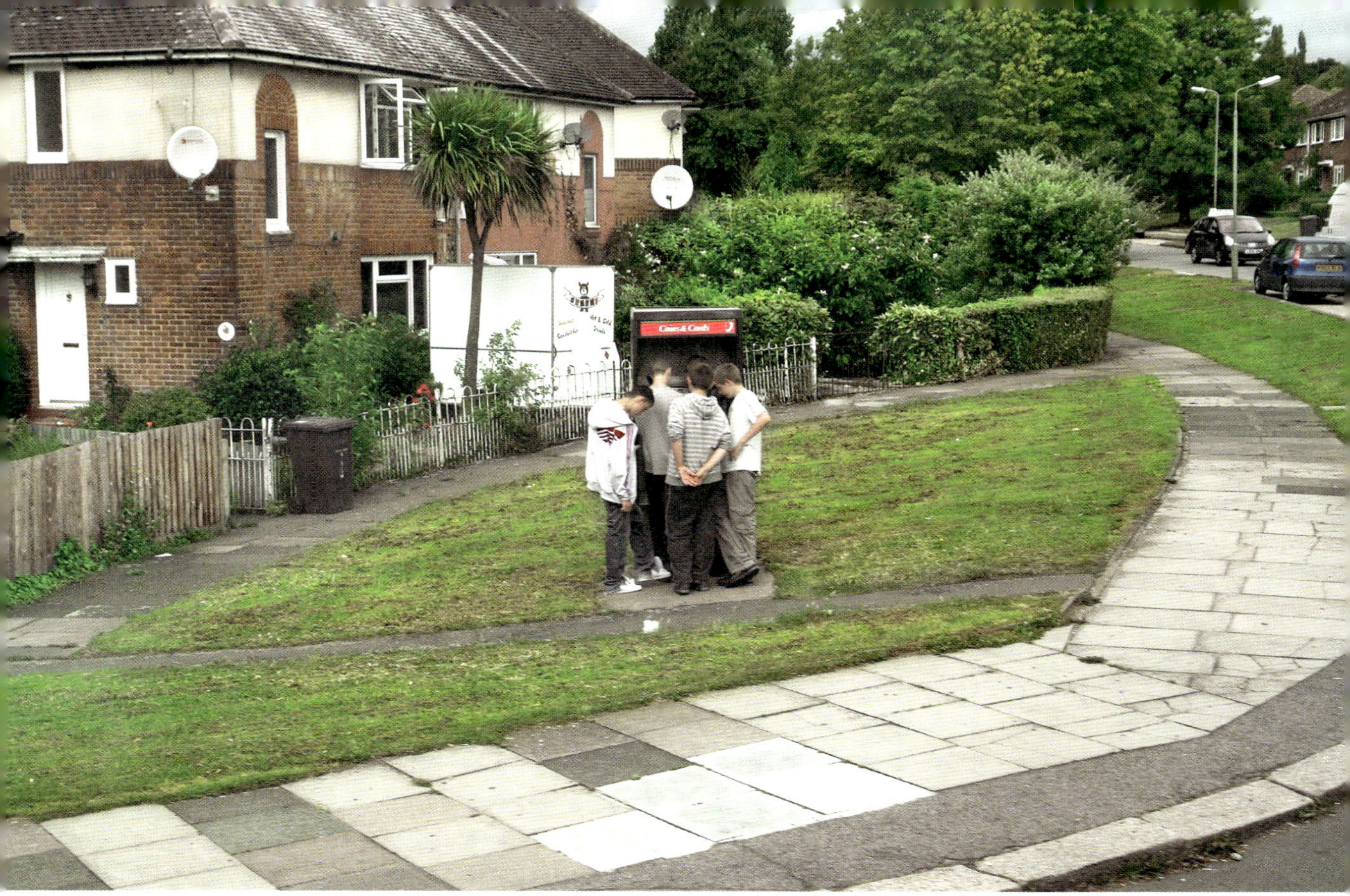
Coins & Cards

As a teenager in 1970s North London, George Georgiou used to play a game with his friends. They'd jump on a bus at random and see where it went. Jump off, jump on another, and so on, an exercise in the kind of adventure that only urban life can offer. Little did he know that years later these youthful japes would be a blueprint for *Last Stop*, a series of sometimes haunting, always suggestive photographs, shot through the windows of London buses.

"Mini movie scenes", as he aptly refers to them, the encounters we see in Georgiou's pictures have a way of lodging themselves in your head and sparking question after question. What's that elderly lady asking those two young men? Are those girls being arrested or are they reporting a crime? And if so, what? Is that couple husband and wife or are they complete strangers? "You see some kind of encounter but you're not really sure what's going on," the photographer explains. "So you make up a story."

When Georgiou began the series he'd just returned to London after 10 years living and working abroad in Serbia, Greece and Turkey. The project was a way to reacquaint himself with a city he knew well but that had changed since he left in 1999. "I wanted the challenge of being on a bus where I could only photograph what was in front of me," says Georgiou, who would spend stints of three or four days at a time working on the project. Any less and it wasn't worth it, any longer and it would have been exhausting. "You had to be so focused all the time. Things move quickly and if the bus jerks, you've lost it."

On the upper deck he worked like a landscape photographer, capturing London's glorious, mismatched cityscapes as they unrolled before him. "If you go on any high street they almost look identical. With the same shops, you miss the architecture behind them – a building that's 200 years old next to one that's post-war." On the lower deck, shooting at street level, he was sometimes inches from his subjects. But Georgiou's approach was markedly different from that of a street photographer. "I'm interested in the street as a political playground rather than quirky moments or visual puns," says Georgiou. *Last Stop* is about community and identity. "It's about moving through the city, how we perceive the city. It's set in London but it applies to any city."

The title refers to London as a destination for migrants. In recent years many photographers have, in many different ways, represented refugees' journeys to Europe in the hope of a new life – Daniel Castro Garcia's *Foreigner* used intimate portraits and testimonies to personalise the migrant experience and Richard Mosse shot *Incoming* with a heat-sensitive military camera to make the viewer think about their alienation from this experience. In *Last Stop,* Georgiou shows us where these migrants hope to end up but it is possibly not the promised land they imagine; London is shown to be a sprawling, shouty, messy city but one that somehow functions. "I wanted to share the difficulty of the city but also to celebrate it – how people co-exist together, not necessarily mixing with each other all the time but sharing space," he says. "It's incredible." Nowhere is this more obvious than aboard a London bus.

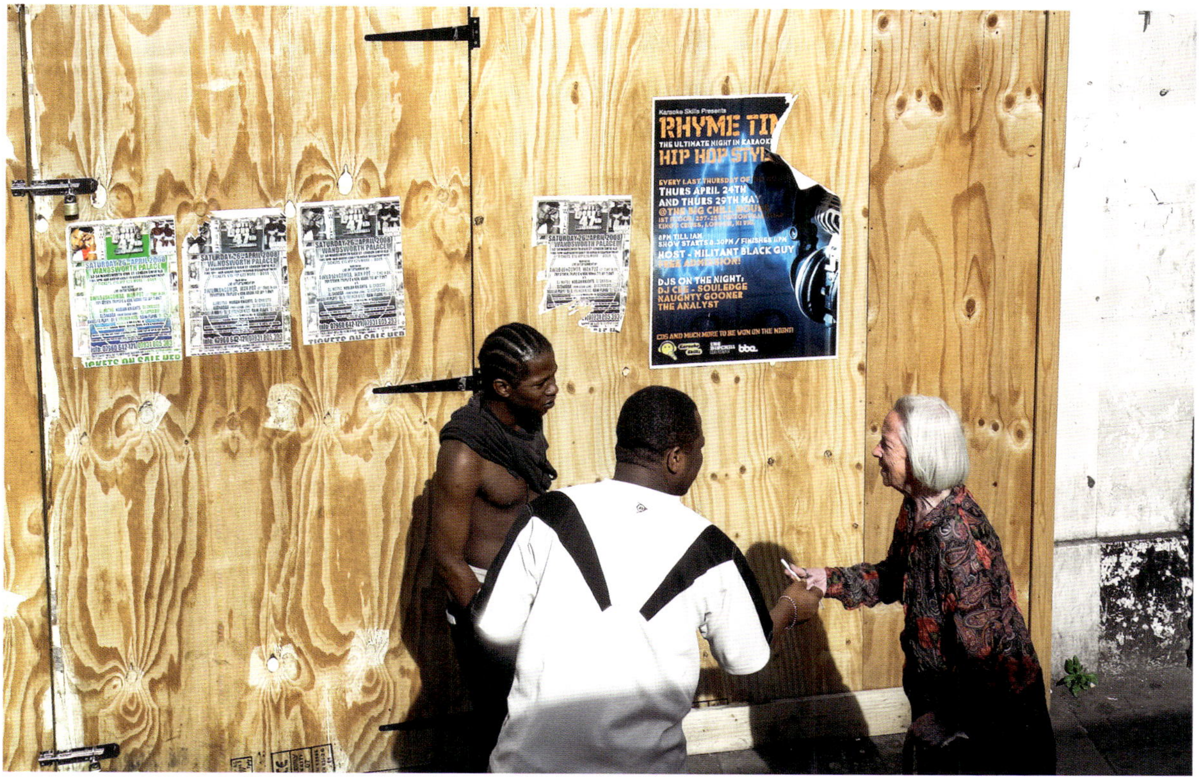

Previous: Bus 221, Edgware to Turnpike Lane, 2008–10
Above: Bus 63, Blackfriars to Honor Oak, 2008–10

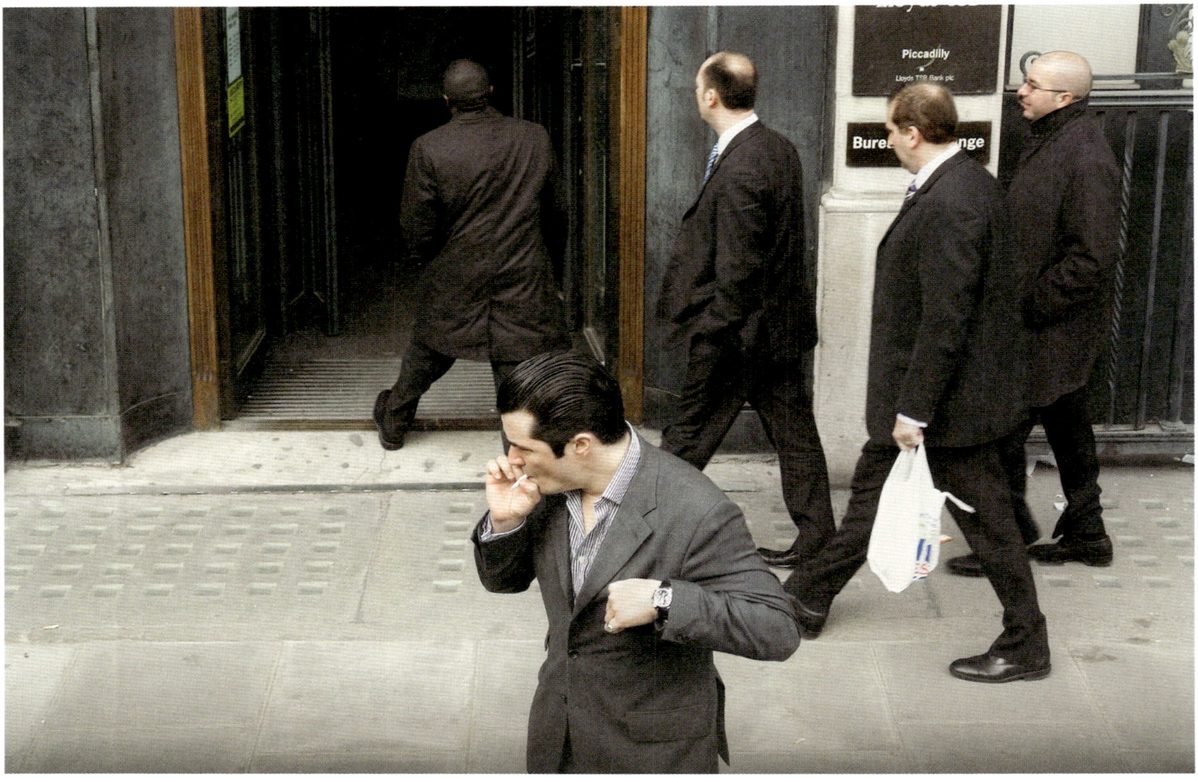

Bus 19, Piccadilly to Finsbury Park, 2008–10

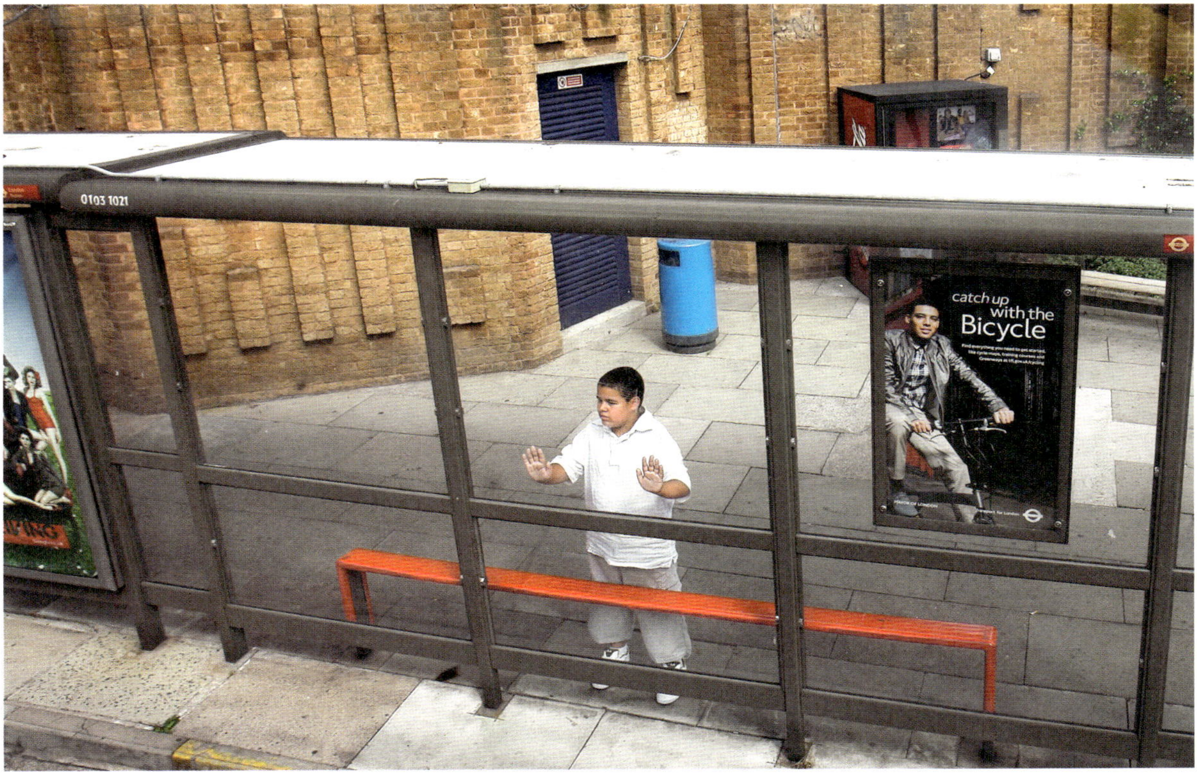

Bus 266, Brent Cross to Acton Central, 2008–10
Overleaf: Bus 377, Oakwood to Enfield Town, 2008–10

George Georgiou

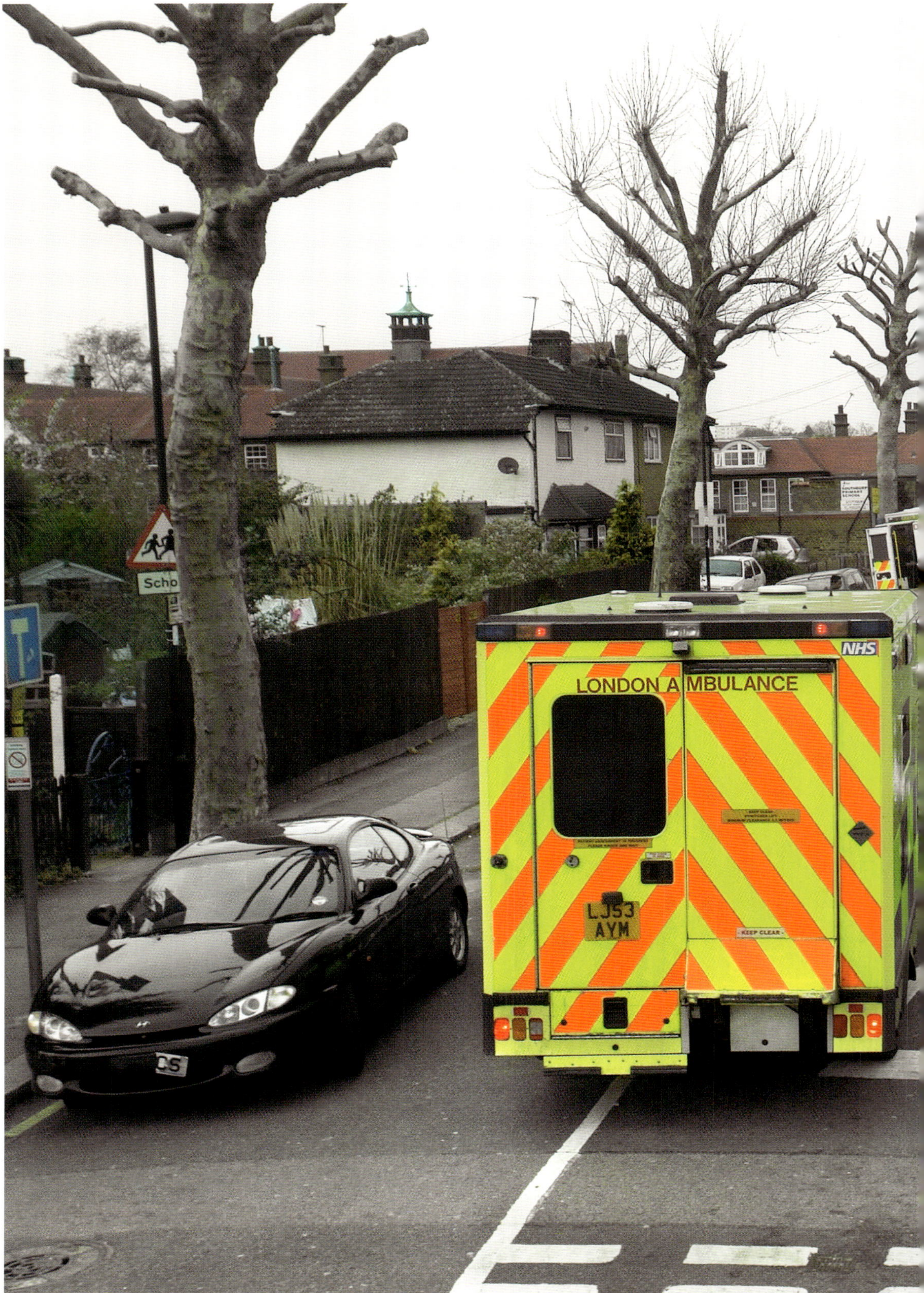

LONDON AMBULANCE
NHS
LJ53 AYM
KEEP CLEAR

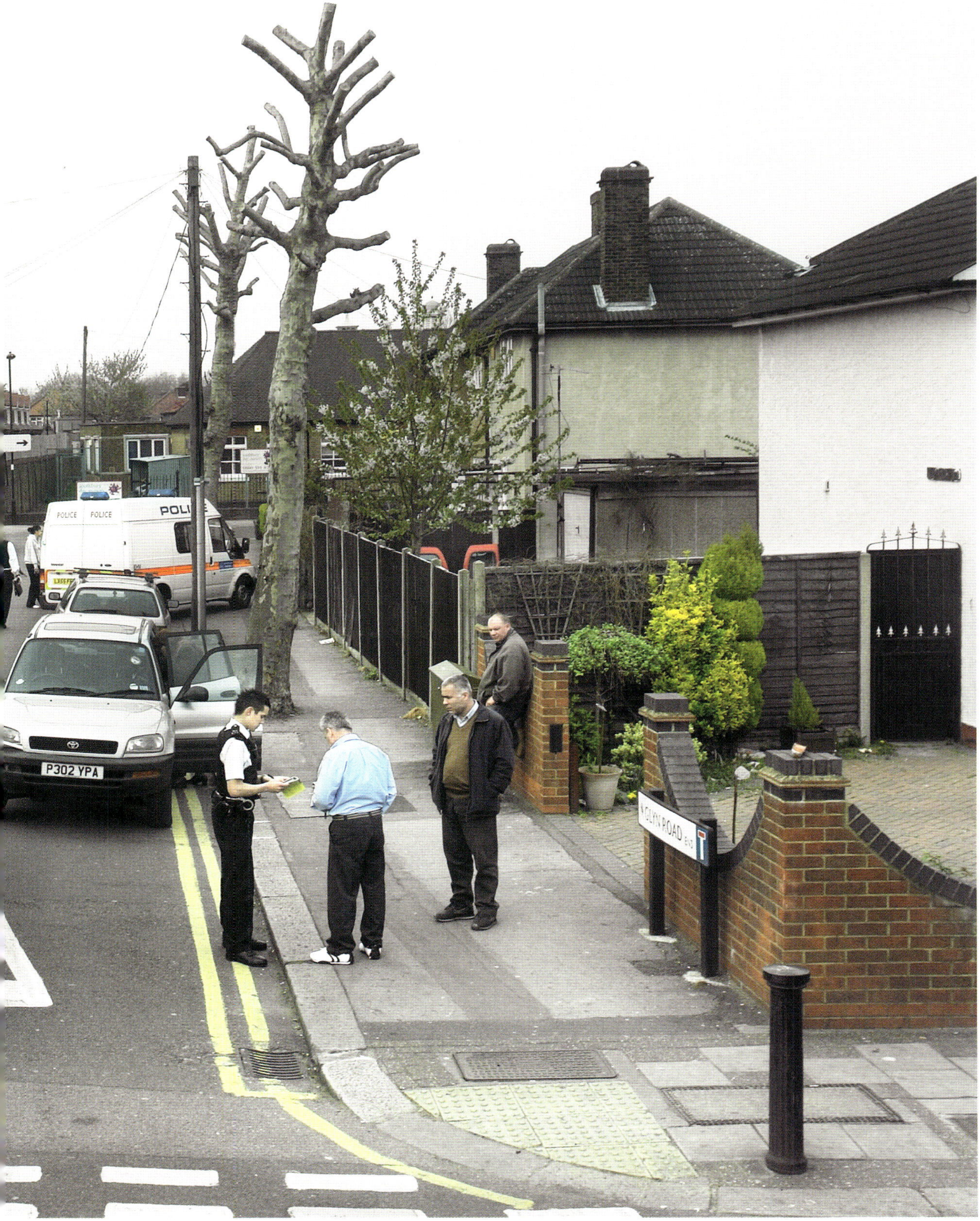
POLICE POLICE
POLI
P302 YPA
ROAD

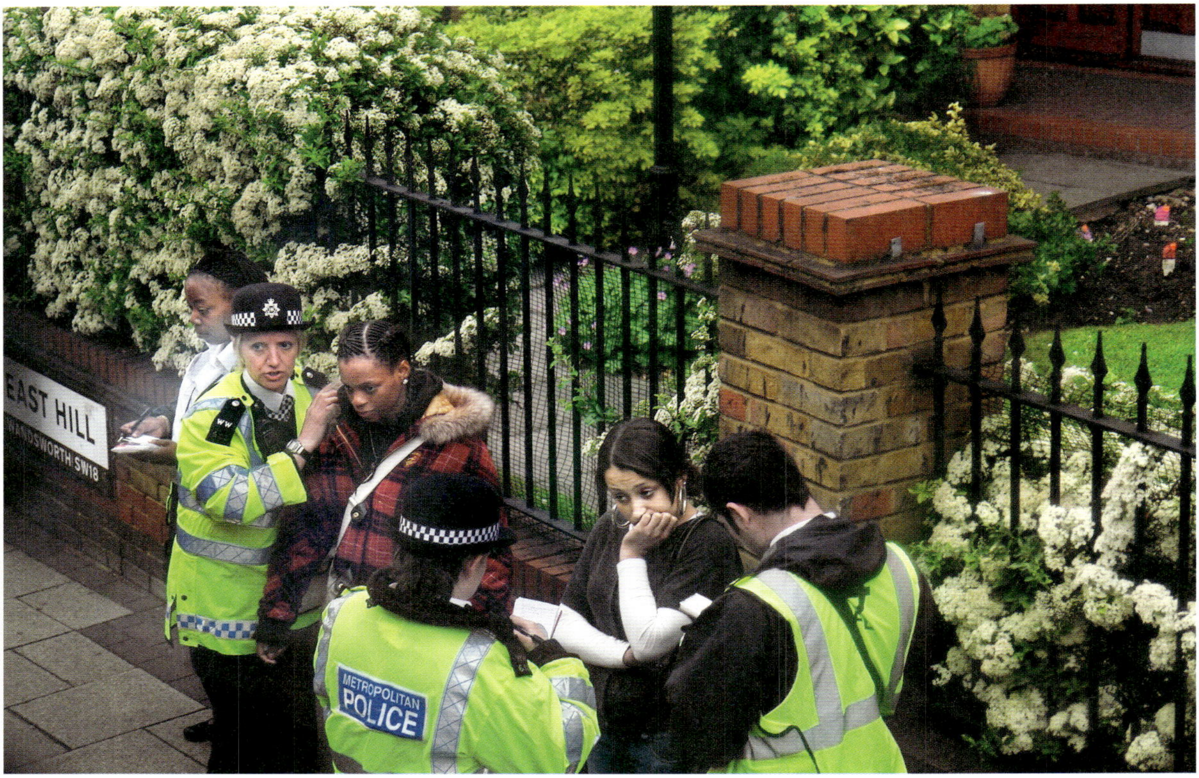
EAST HILL
WANDSWORTH SW18
METROPOLITAN
POLICE

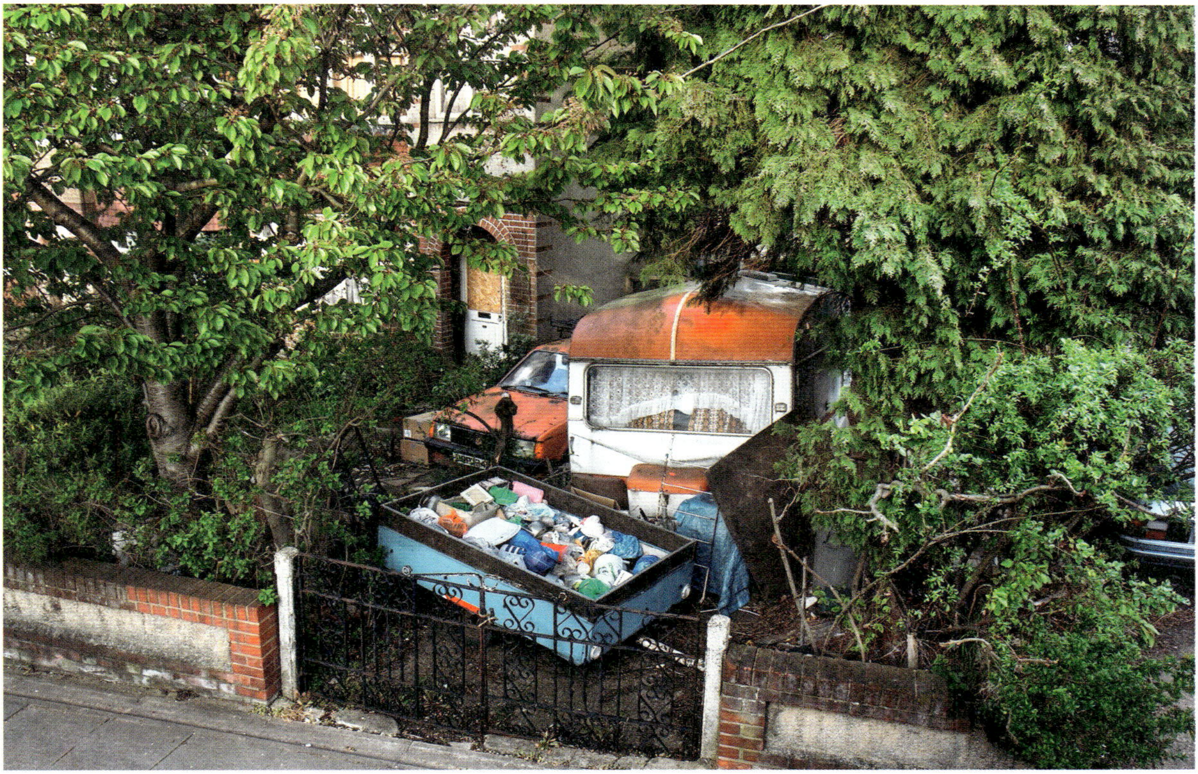

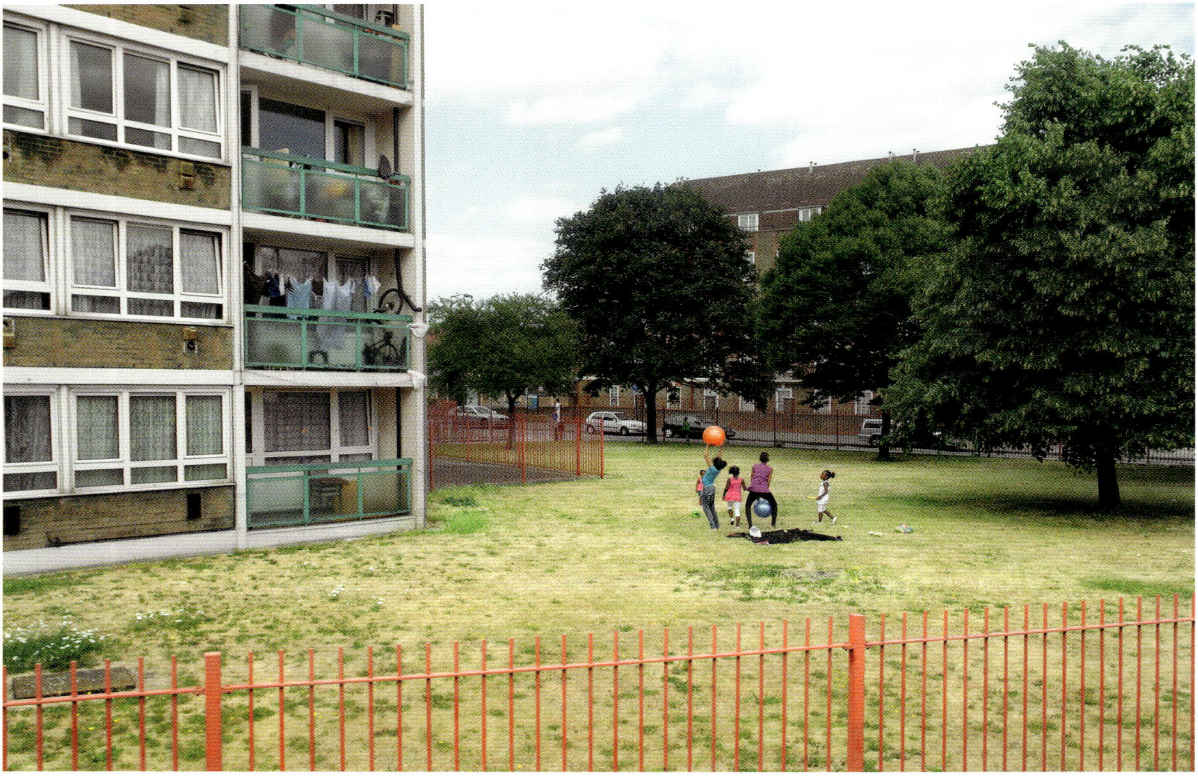

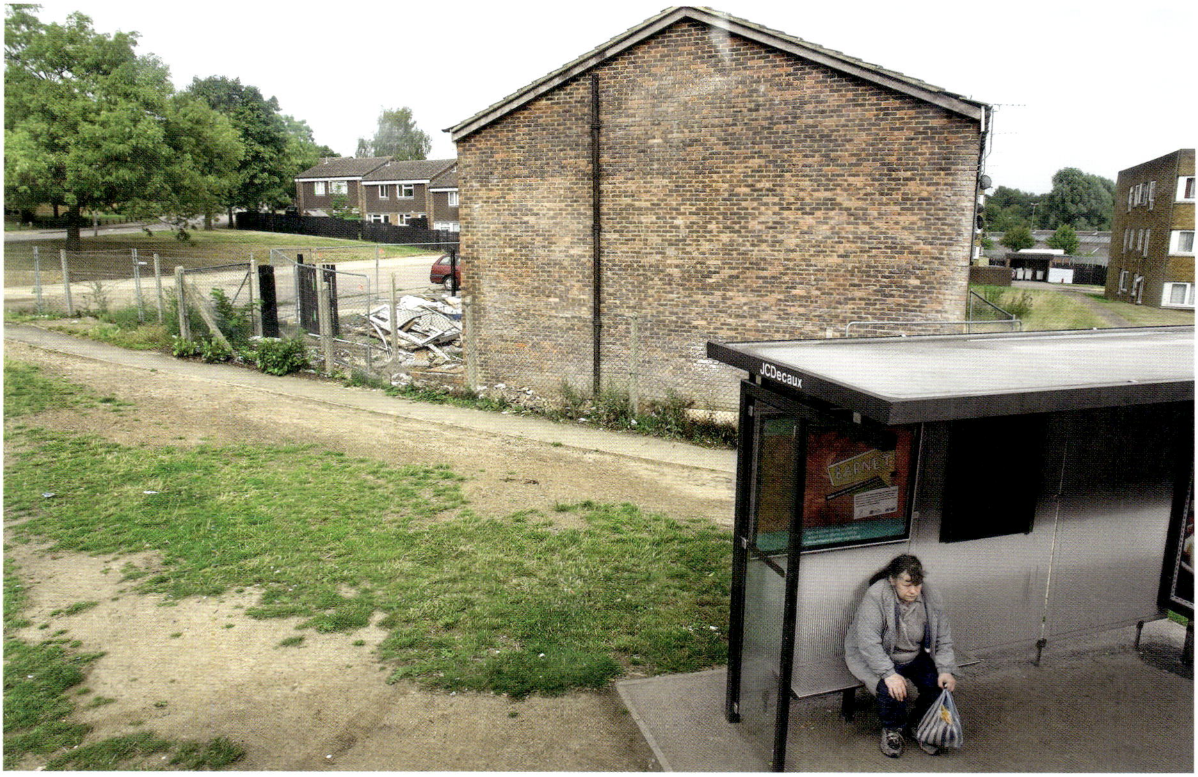
JCDecaux

Harrodsburg

Brazen street portraits expose the exaggerated style of super-rich shoppers around Kensington and Chelsea.

Dougie Wallace

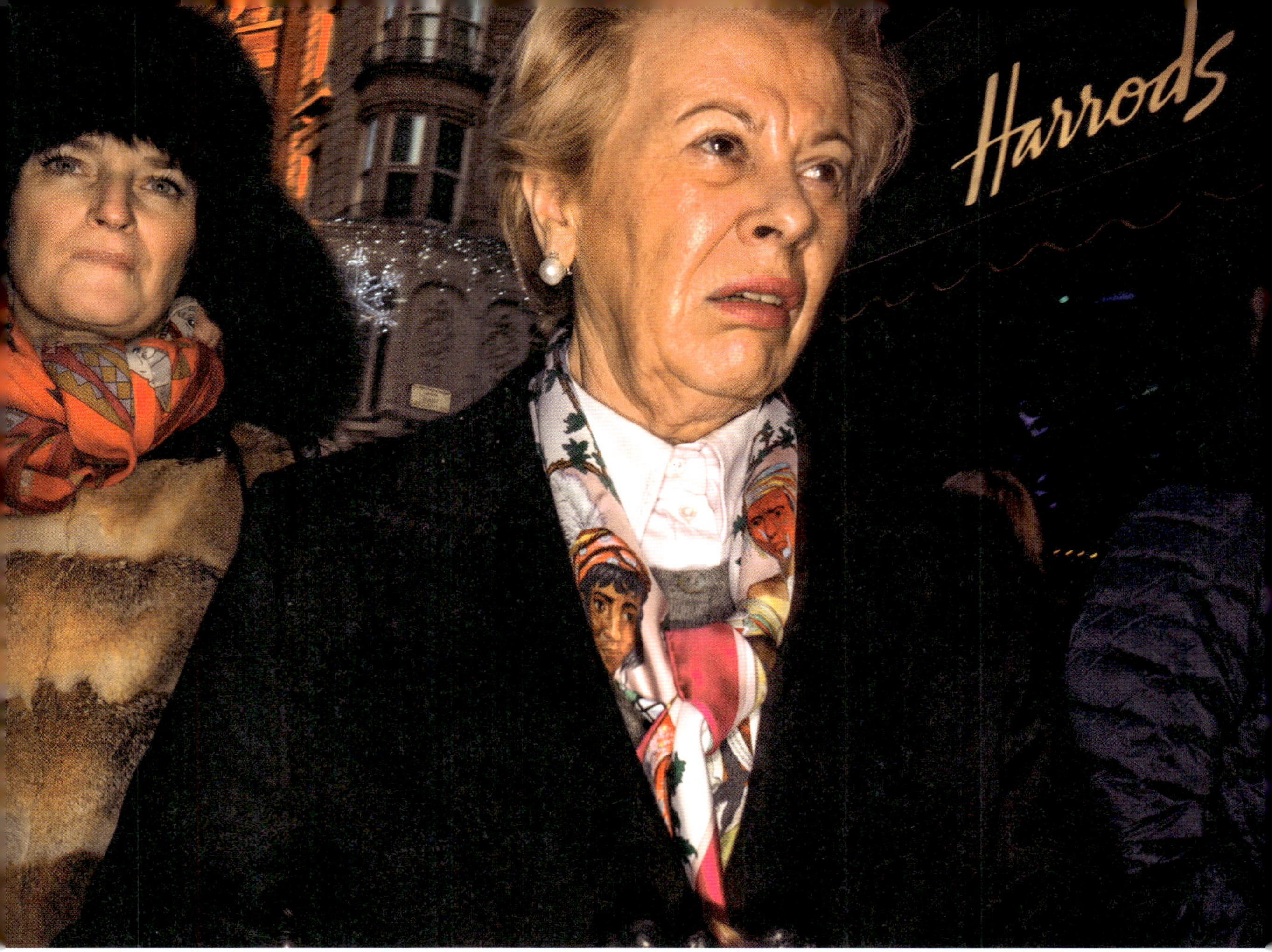
Harrods

In the unforgiving glare of Dougie Wallace's flash, there's nowhere to hide. "Look, she's been pulled back, it's the hands that give it away," he says, indicating one of the subjects from his series *Harrodsburg*. The woman is typical of the fantastically wealthy types who grace these gilded pavements – an international jet set of Old English sloanes in tweed, perma-tanned Americans and blinged up Middle Eastern women on shopping trips.

Wallace began shooting in "the playground of the super rich" – or "Harrodsburg" as he describes this section of Kensington and Chelsea – in 2013, making 70 trips over two and a half years. He'd read that men in the Royal Borough can be expected to live 30 years longer than those in some parts of his hometown of Glasgow. First came *The Age of Wealth*, portraits of people in both areas shot through buses or cars, which make for disturbing comparison. But after he'd finished that project his photographic "safari" of London's rich continued.

Hunting down subjects was intense work – physically and psychologically. Wallace ducks and weaves like a boxer. "You just have to go in hard, get rid of all the consequences in your head, they're just pollutants," he says. "I know exactly what I'm looking for. It's the style, what they're wearing." When he moves in for the kill, it's quick and close range. As he shoots, Wallace might surprise his subject with a quip: "You're beautiful!" "Is that a Mercedes?" This confrontational approach finds him in the street photography tradition of ballsy, in-your-face New Yorkers like Garry Winogrand and Bruce Gilden. Their unsuspecting subjects, like Wallace's, often seem to stare directly into the lens, eyeing the photographer with suspicion.

Wallace joined the army at 18, did a degree in sport, and then bought and sold campervans for a living before taking a course in photojournalism 12 years ago. Since then he's lent his bright and bolshie style to projects on wasted Shoreditch hipsters, boozed-up hens and stags in Blackpool, and Mumbai's taxi drivers. But there's a notable difference between those projects and this – his relationship with his subjects is more critical. Though he insists he's no activist, Wallace was aware throughout of the growing wealth inequalities that shape his adopted home and that affected his approach to the project. "It wasn't the easiest thing to shoot," he says. "In Blackpool I could have a laugh with them. [Shooting *Harrodsburg*] did start getting to me a bit by the end. I knew when I was finished."

With their caked-on make-up, coiffed hair and surgically enhanced lips, the people of *Harrodsburg* are clearly image conscious. They want to be looked at – just not like this. In some pictures they try to hide behind designer sunglasses or shopping bags. Wallace's approach might be brutal but, he says, it's "an antidote to the poverty porn you see on the telly". A kind of visual comeuppance.

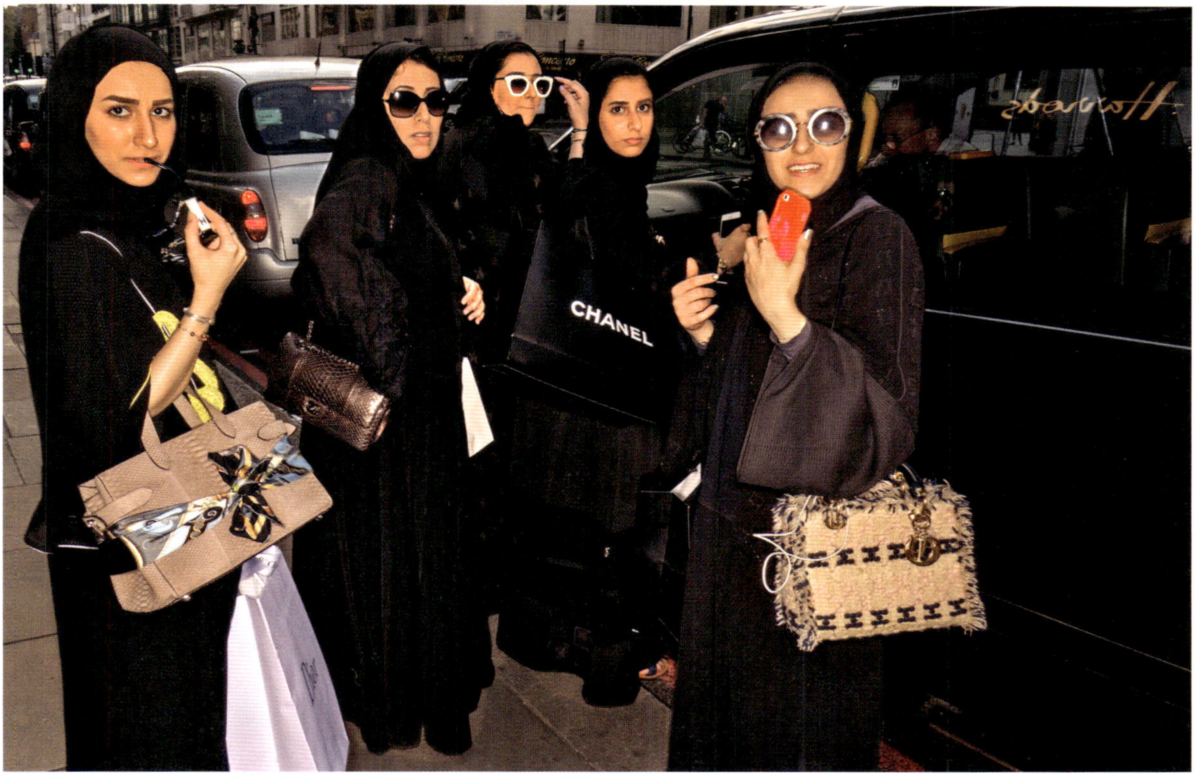

Previous and above: Harrodsburg, London, 2015–16

Dougie Wallace

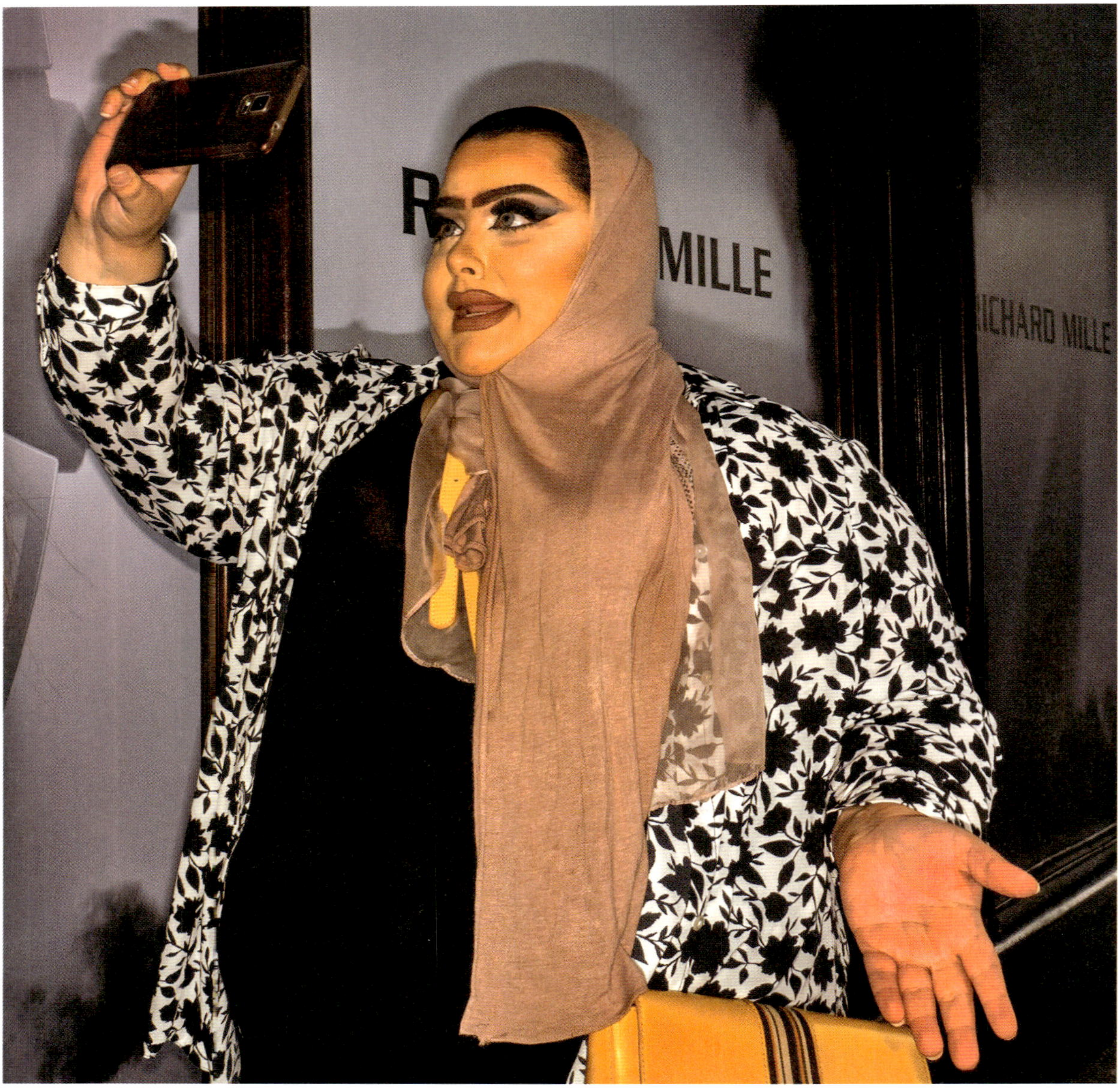

Harrodsburg, London, 2015–16

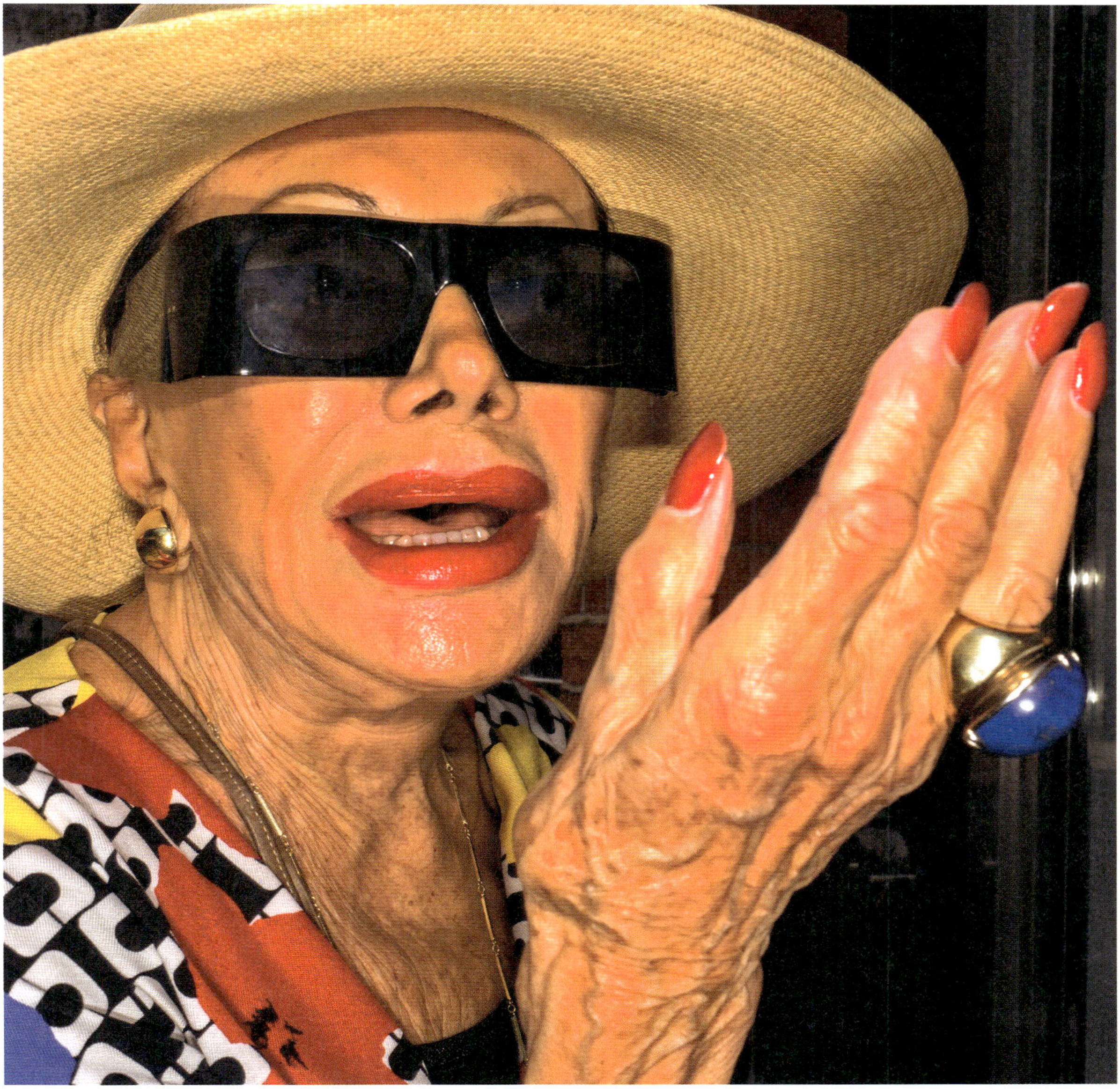

 Harrodsburg, London, 2015–16 Dougie Wallace

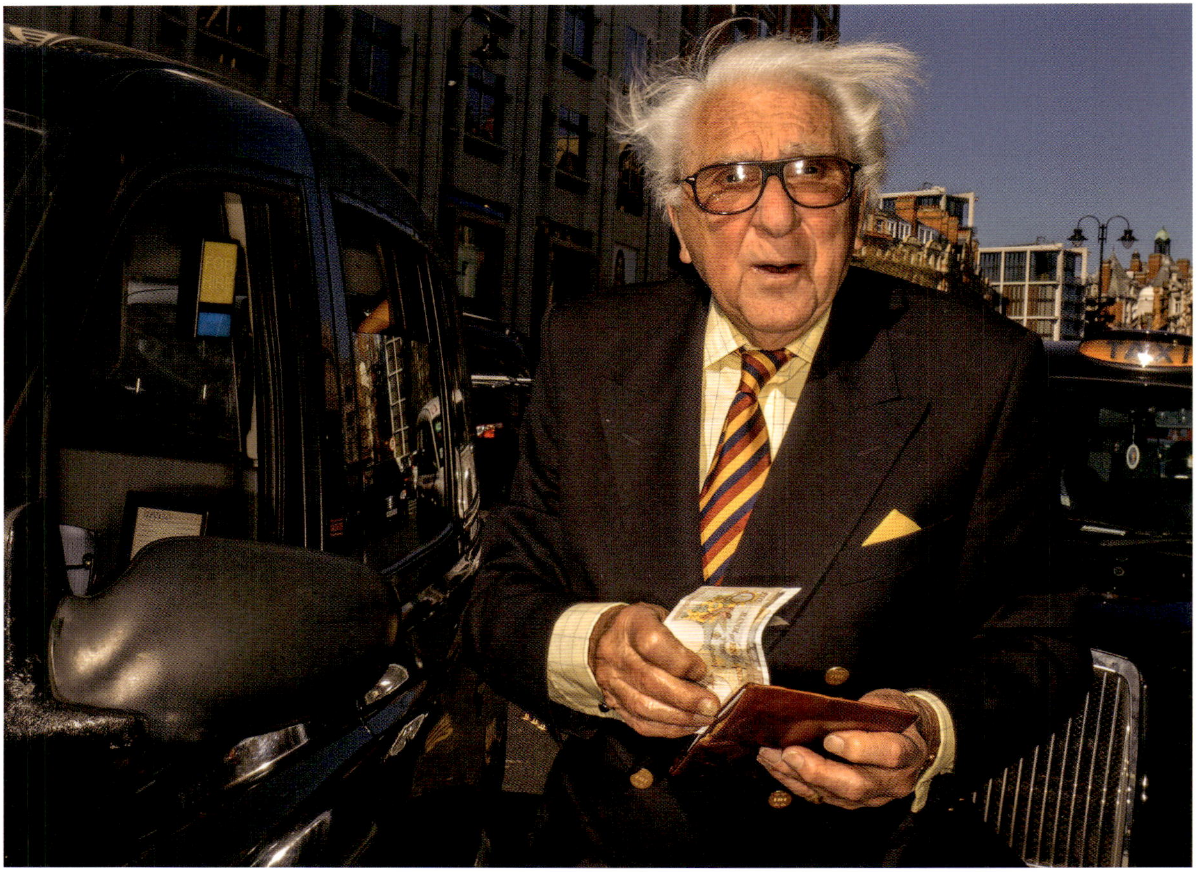

Harrodsburg, London, 2015–16

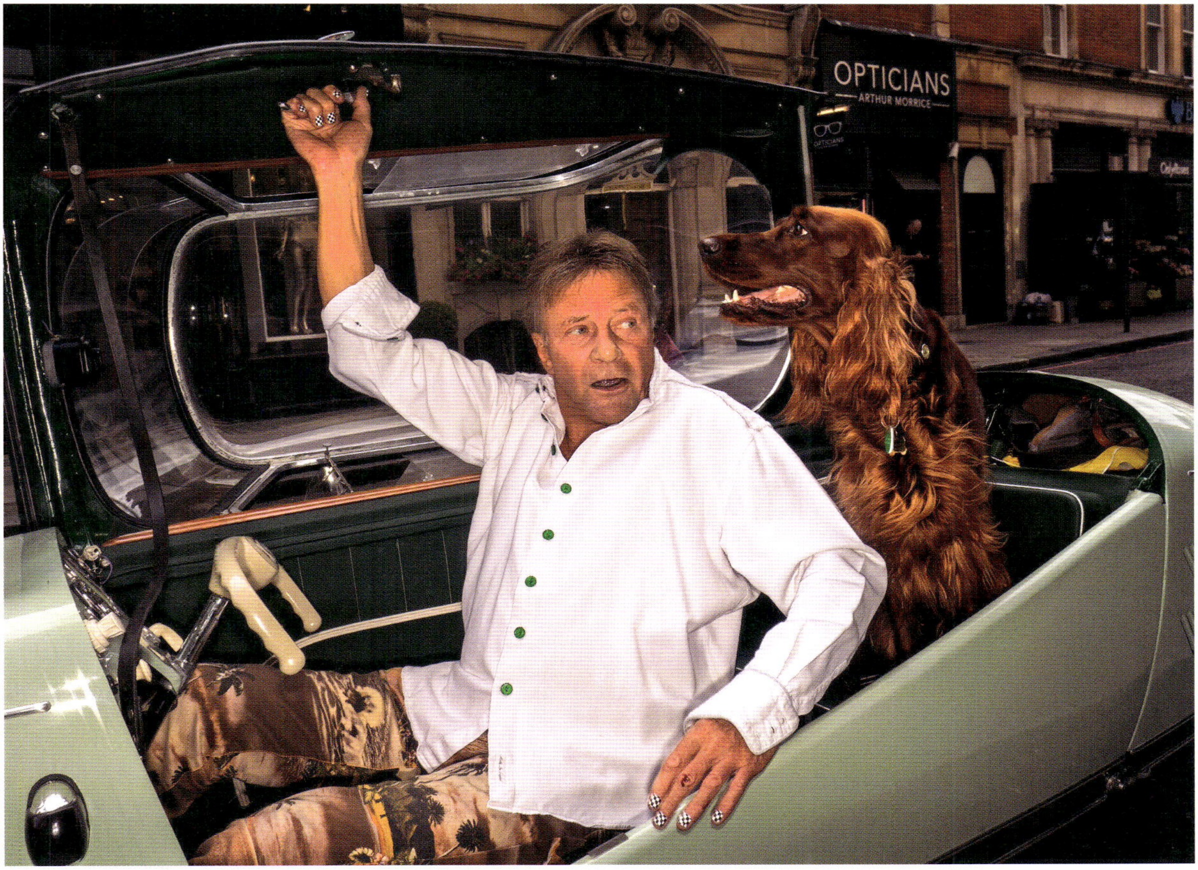

Above and overleaf: Harrodsburg, London, 2015–16

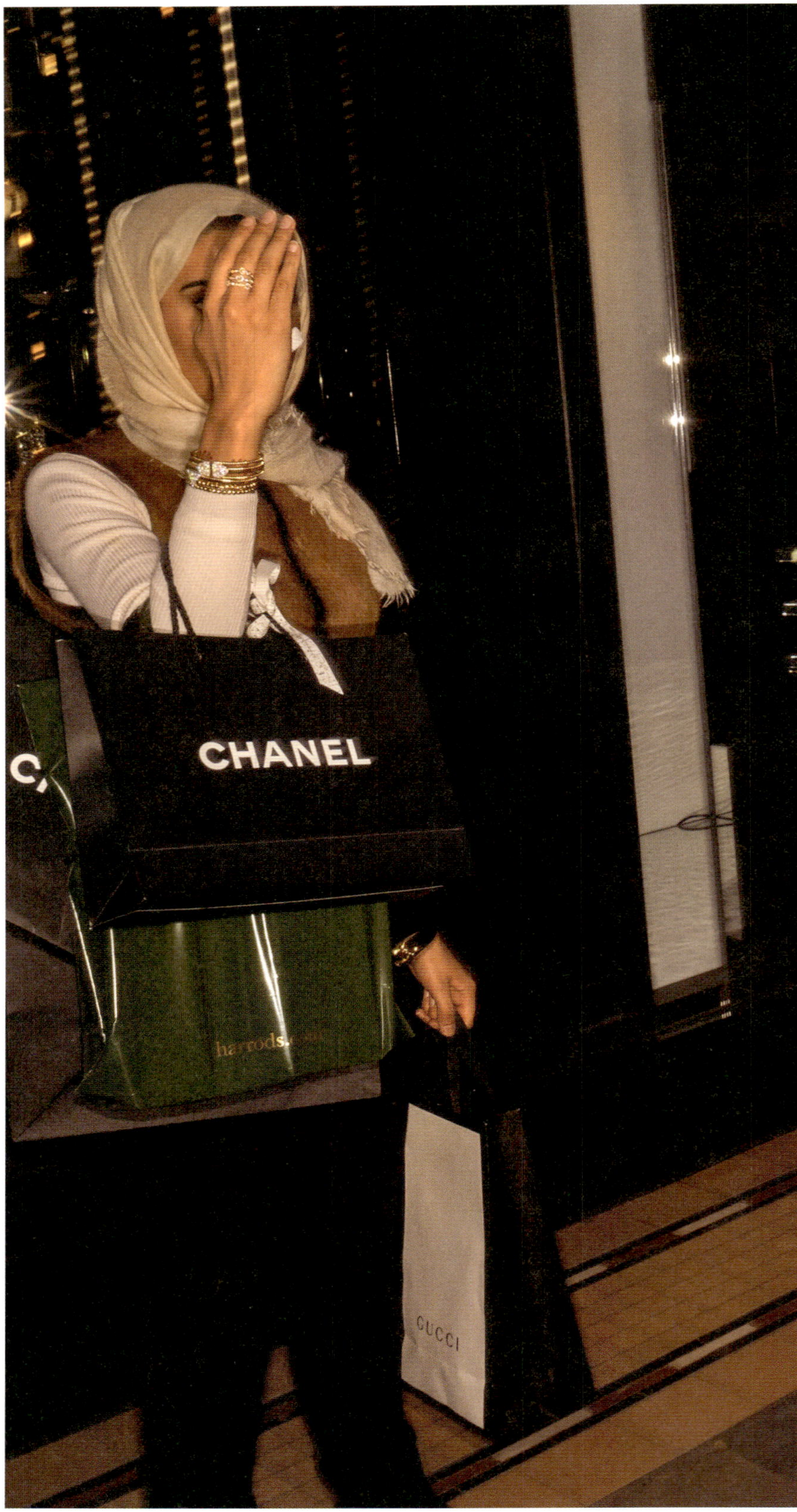
CHANEL
GUCCI

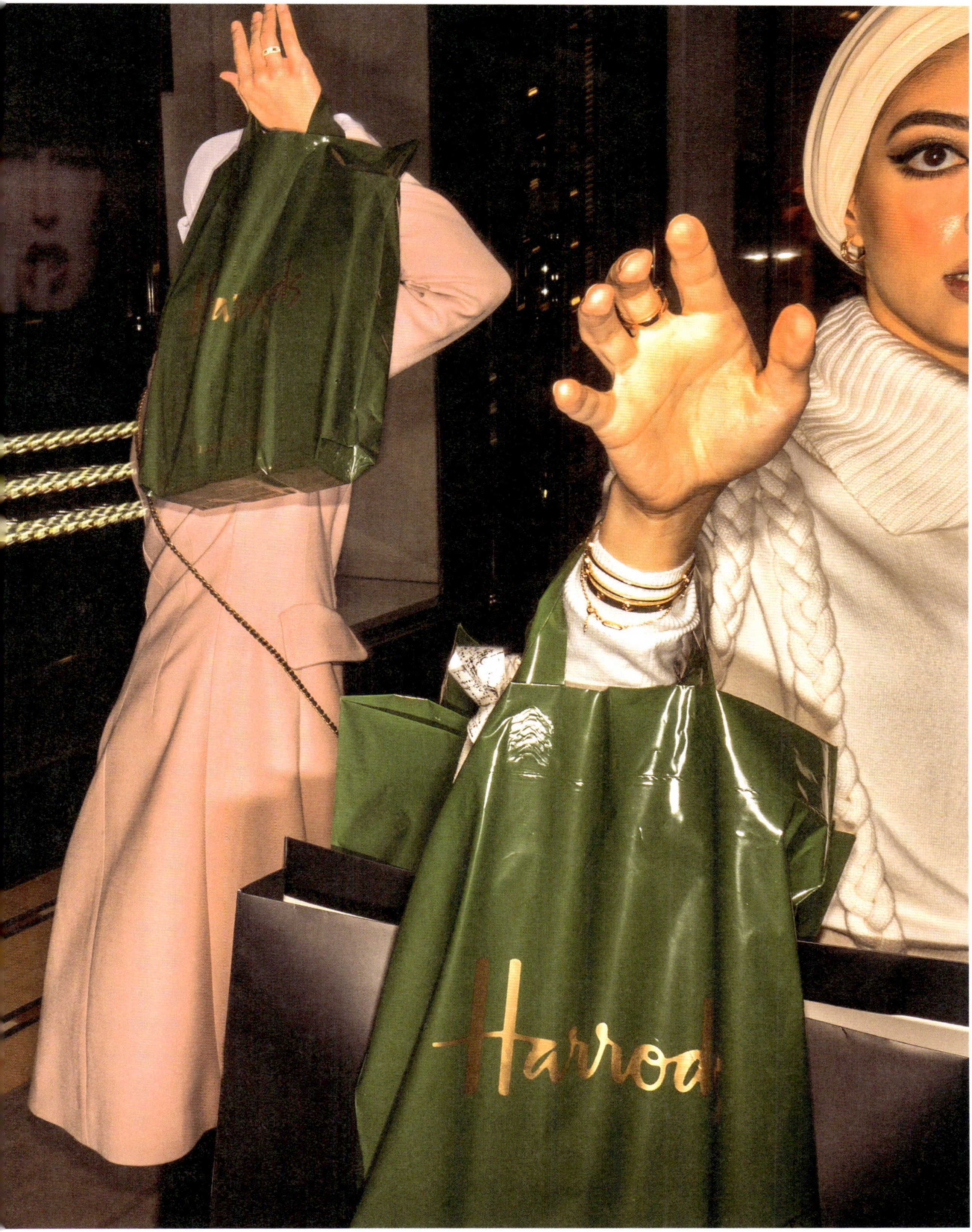
Harrod

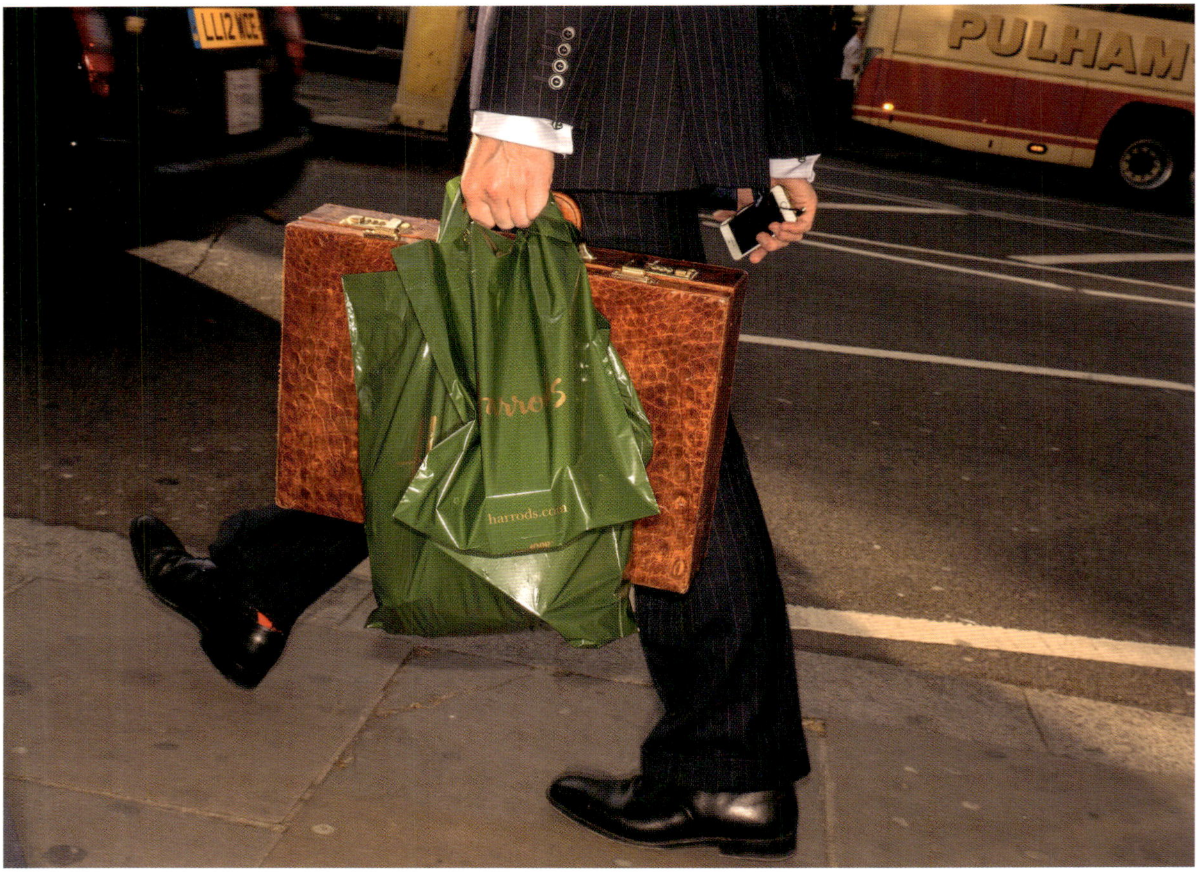

Harrodsburg, London, 2015–16

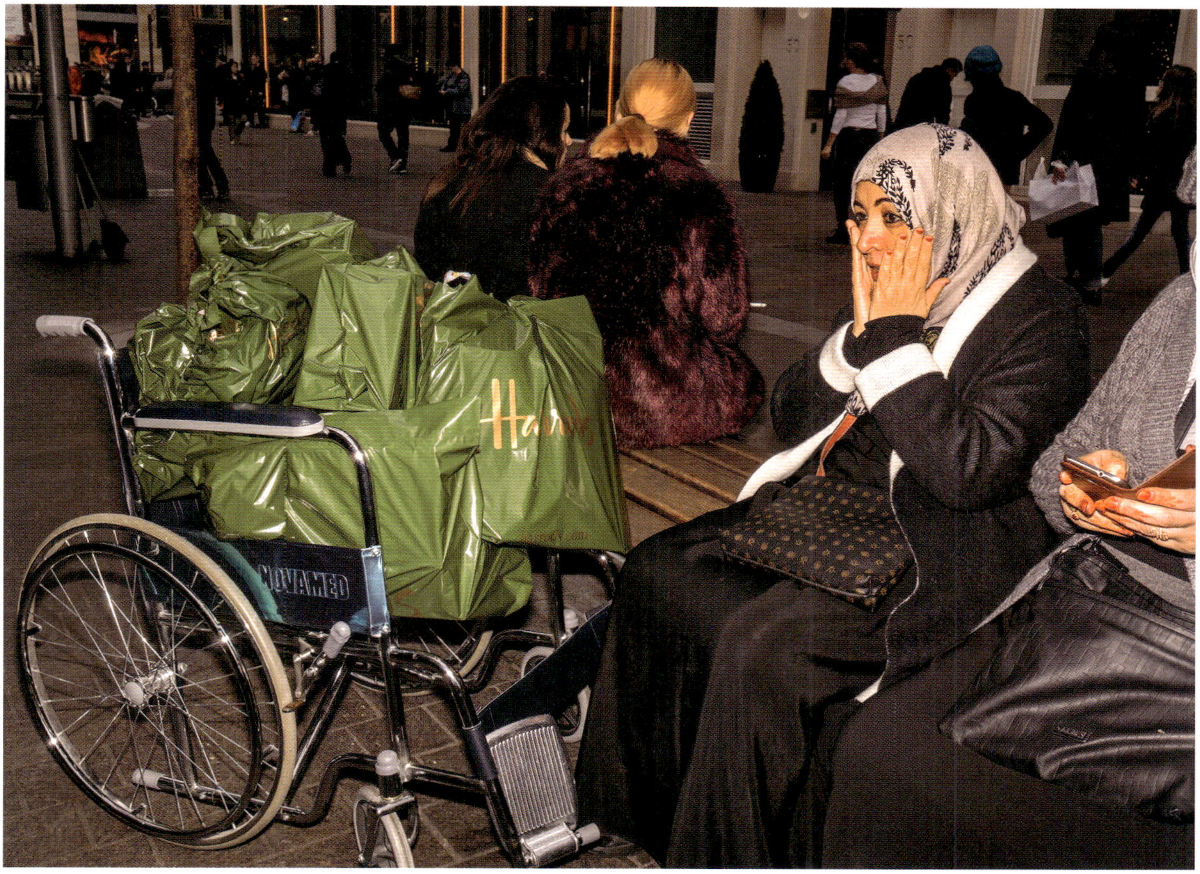

Harrodsburg, London, 2015–16

Dougie Wallace

Purim in Stamford Hill

For one day a year, London's Hasidic community takes to the streets in a revelrous carnival of costumes.

Stephen Leslie

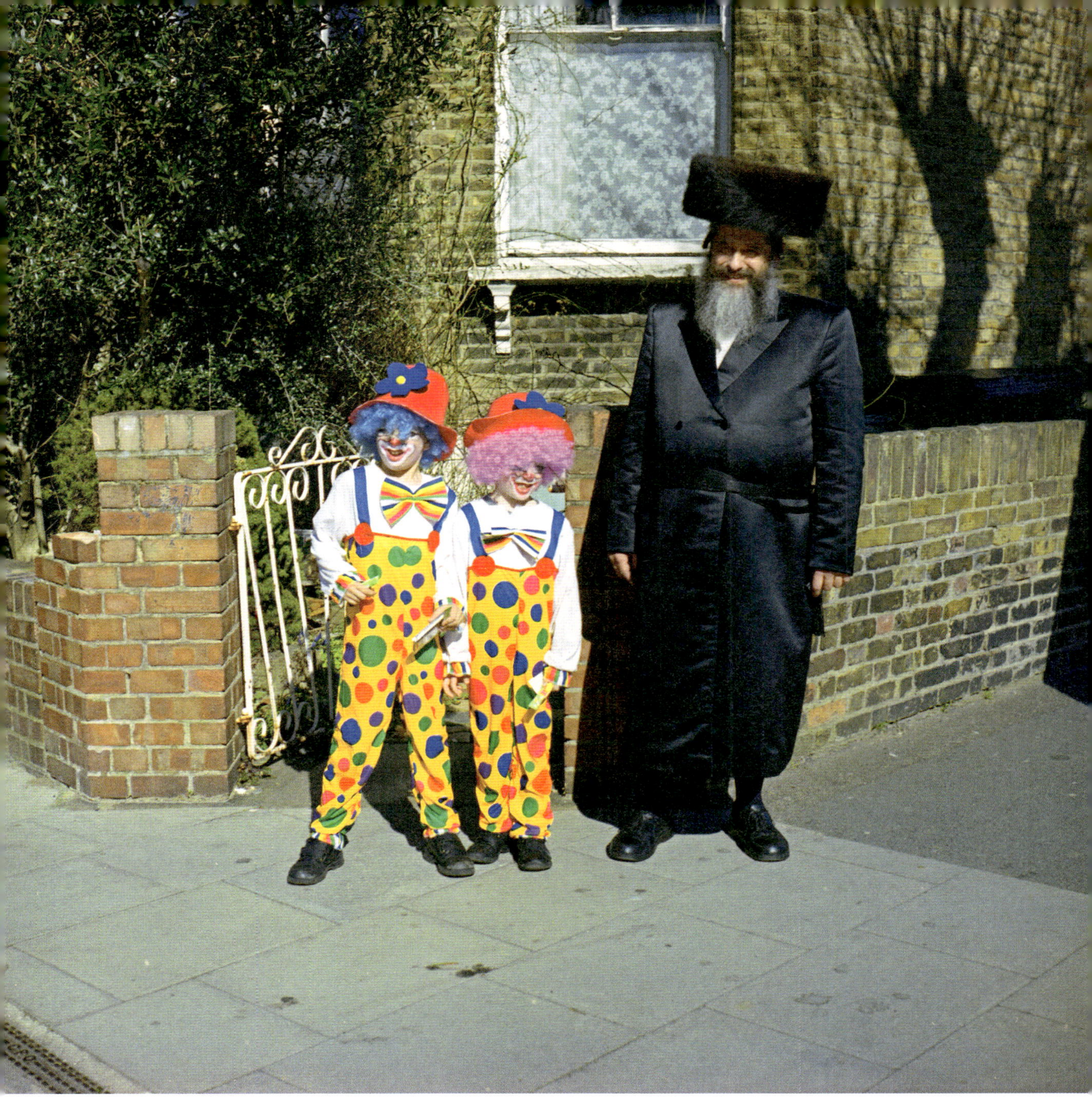

On a normal day, Stamford Hill is a pretty sedate place. This patch of North East London is home to Britain's largest Haredi Orthodox Jewish community, peopled by bearded men in long black coats and fur hats, and women modestly dressed in a spectrum of grey, beige and navy. At Purim, it's a whole different story. The atmosphere is pure carnival. Clown-wigged kids mingle with mini policemen, Little Bo Peeps, fluffy bears, peacocks and pizzas. When night arrives so do the large groups of young men to sway and sing in the street, their usual sober attire swapped for Superman suits with comedy six-packs.

"Everyone is out celebrating, they're drawing attention to themselves in a way which they usually never do," says street photographer and film director Stephen Leslie, who has captured the annual Jewish festival every year for the past five. Purim, which takes place in late February or early March, marks the story of how the Jews narrowly avoided being killed by an ancient Persian politician named Haman. It's a jolly occasion when it's obligatory to stuff your face, swap gifts, donate to charity and – for men at least – to get mightily tipsy. "The atmosphere is just amazing," adds Leslie. "Completely bananas."

Leslie sees familiar faces in different costumes each year and they greet him like an old friend. When he mentions that he too is Jewish, though secular, they swap numbers and invite him into their homes. This year he was adopted by a particularly boisterous young man called Avi. "He was so drunk – dressed as Hello Kitty – and he just took me around, took me to this rabbi's house, started dancing, got a huge staff and balanced it on his chin while lying on the floor, it was incredible."

For a street photographer, the project offers thematic clarity along with an apparently endless source of remarkable material. "With street photography, there's no plan, no formula, there's nothing predictable about it at all," says Leslie. "It's nice having a day when you know that there's going to be lots of stuff going on but equally you don't know what you're going to get." All the same, each year he heads out riddled with "an immense amount of anxiety" about whether he's going to get everything he's after, armed with a different combination of 35mm film cameras and a medium-format twin-lens reflex from the 1970s – just in case.

Since he started the series, he's noticed changes. More photographers on the same beat, for a start. "You can't have something this productive and photogenic without other people cropping up – but that's fine, there's enough for everyone," he says. This year, alongside the classic costumes, there was a gaggle of men dressed as Donald Trump, a sign of "the outside, commercial world infiltrating", Leslie suggests, and maybe an increasing Americanisation of the festivities. And as in the rest of London, smart flats have started to pop up alongside older, shabbier buildings.

But there's also an enduring overtone to the day. "In the Jewish calendar there's a festival virtually every month – it's meant to give you a sense of belonging and home, wherever you are. That's what Purim does with bells on – literally," Leslie says. "This is something that's been celebrated for thousands of years and I'm just seeing a small fraction of it. I'm aware that I'm trying to record something that's going to go on endlessly. In 50, 100, 200 years' time, there's always going to be Purim." We can only imagine what the costumes will be like then.

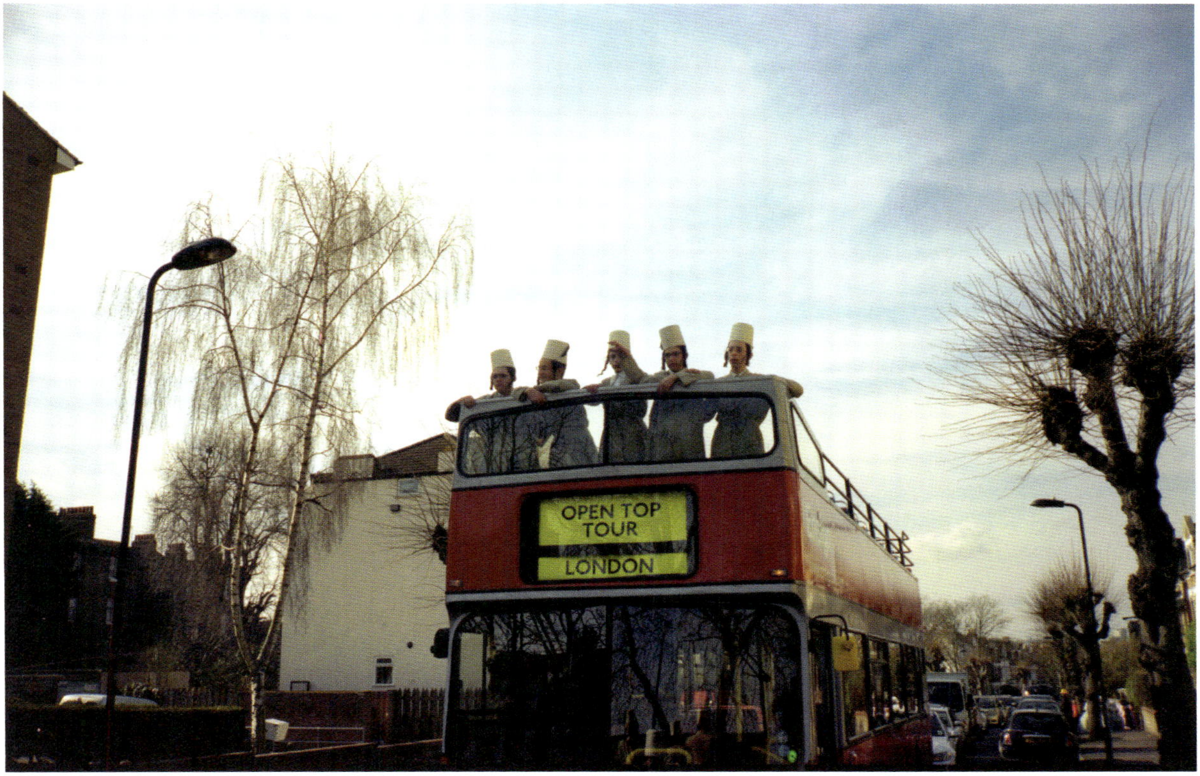

Previous: Two Clowns, Stamford Hill, 2014
Above: Open Top Tour, Stamford Hill, 2015

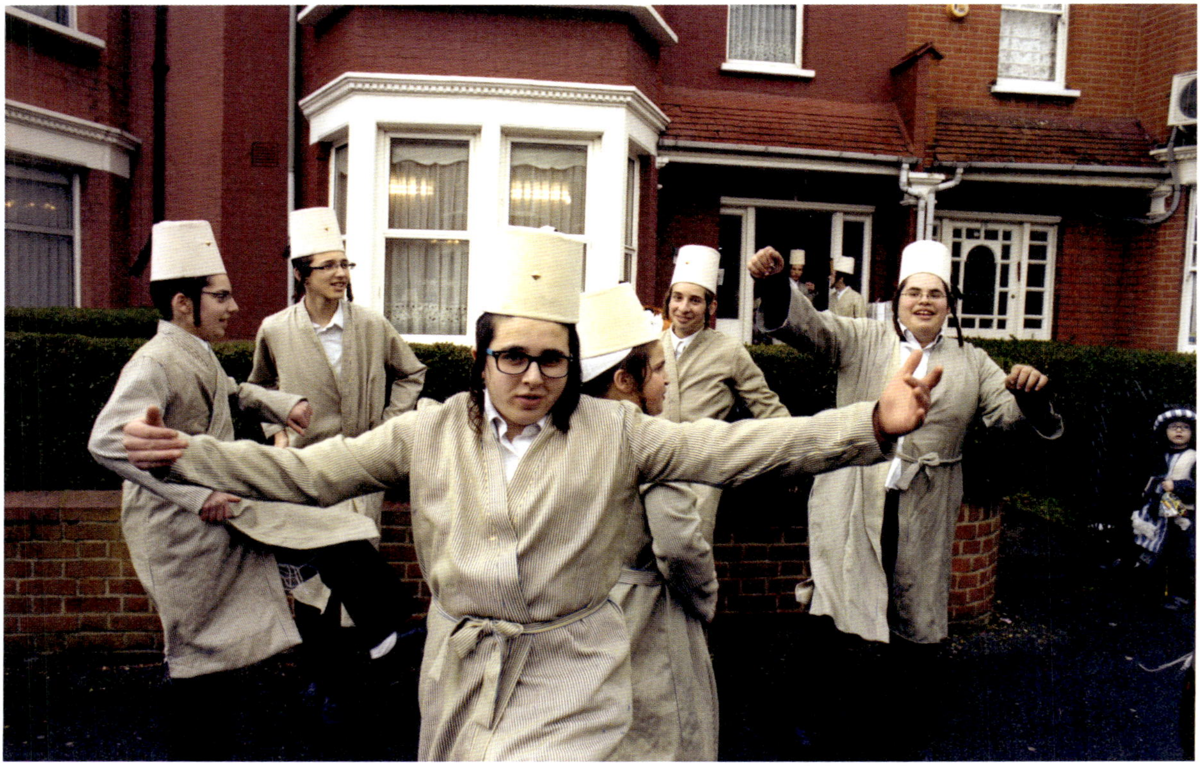

Street Dancers, Stamford Hill, 2016

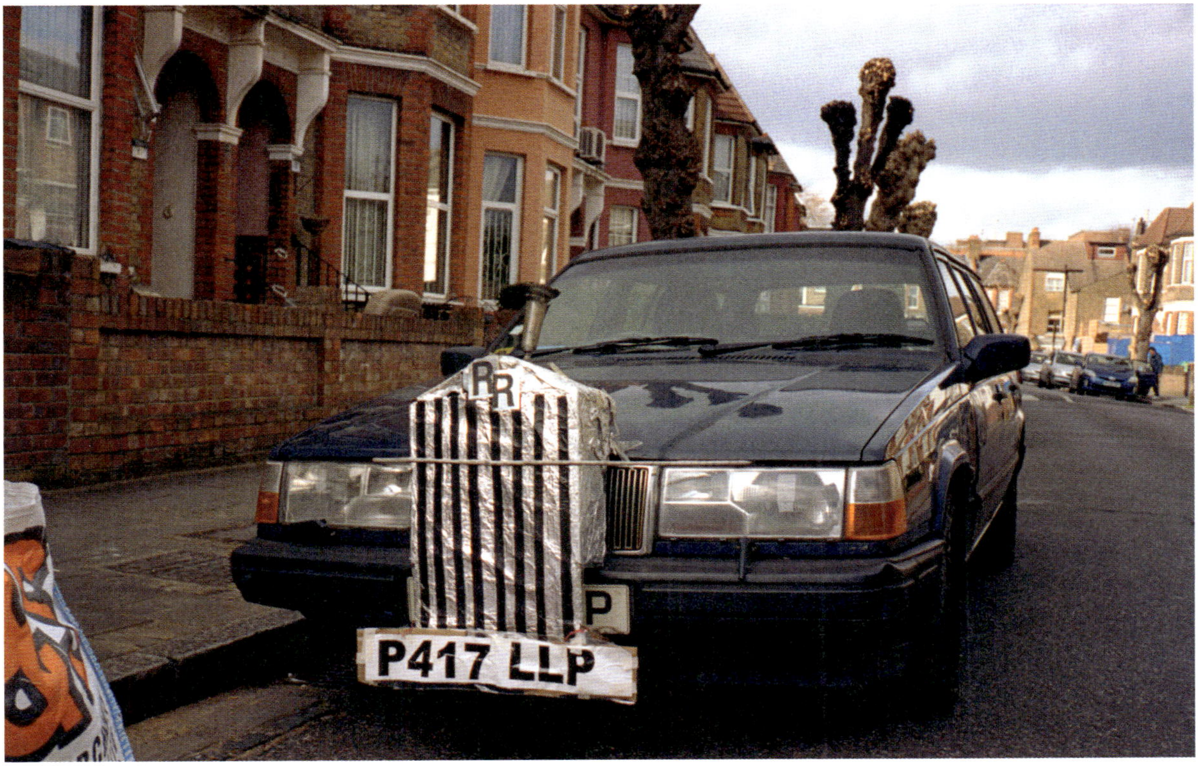

 Fake Rolls Royce, Stamford Hill, 2015 Stephen Leslie

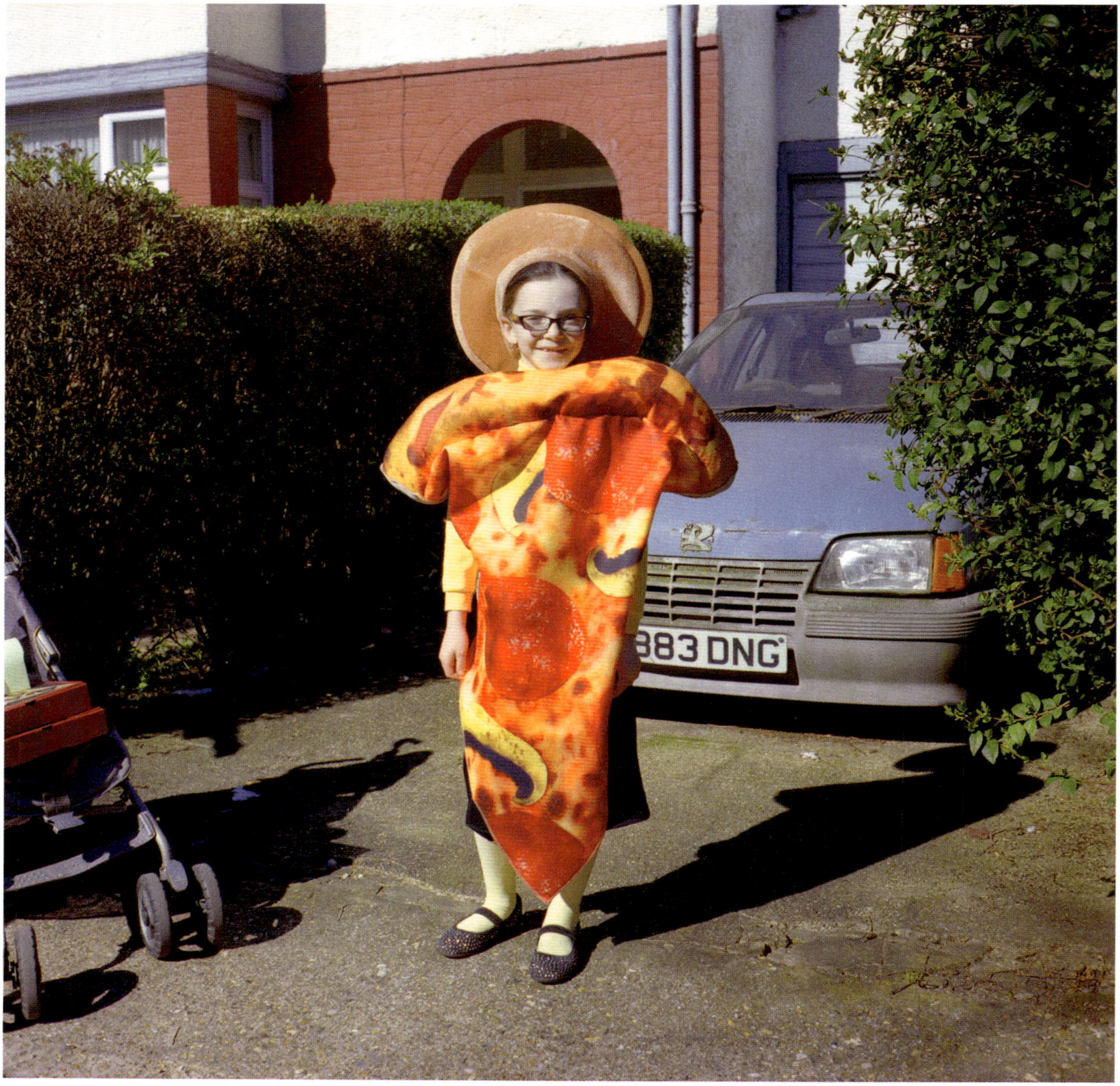

Pizza Slice Girl, Stamford Hill, 2014

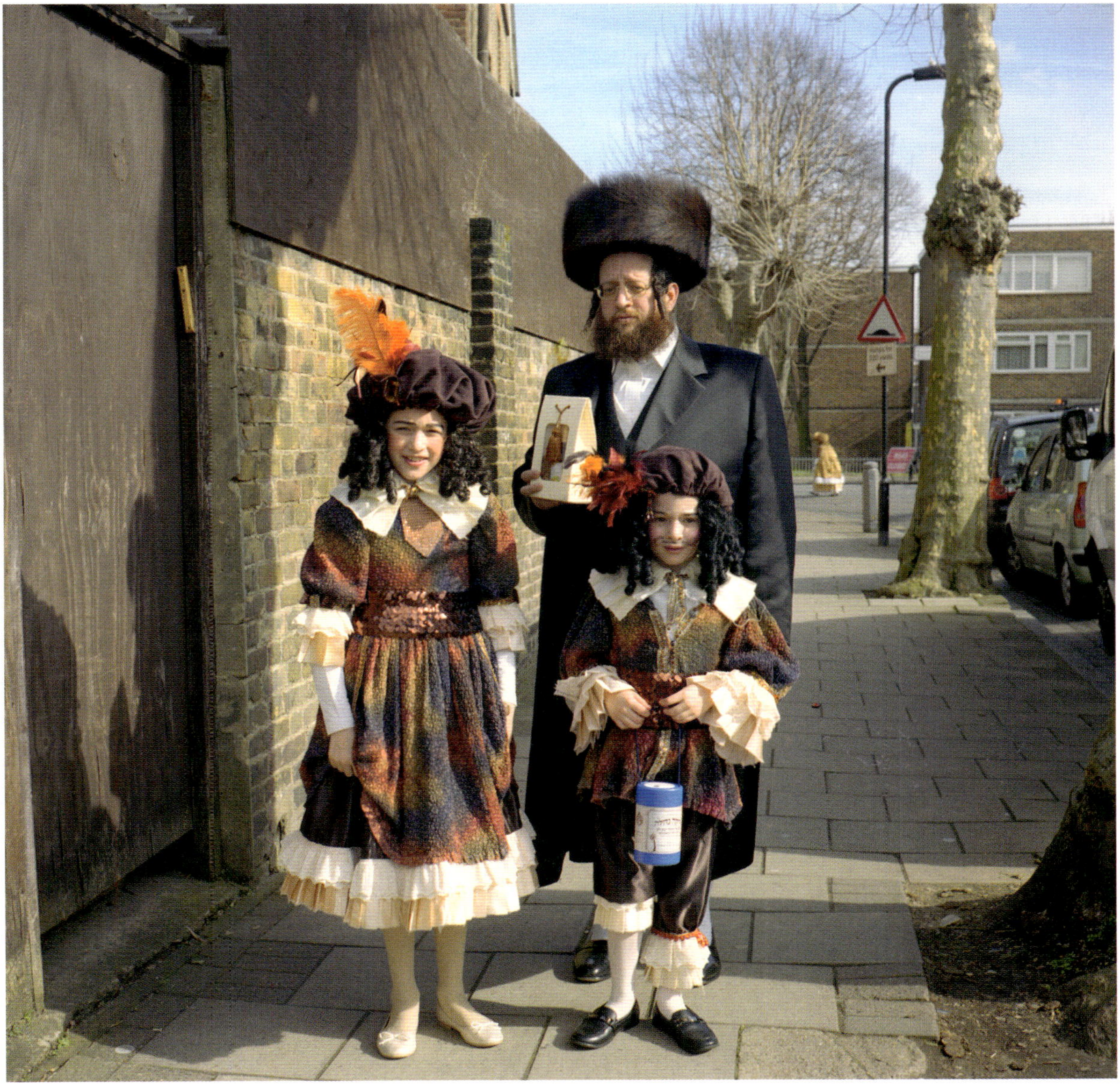

Two Cavaliers, Stamford Hill, 2015

Stephen Leslie

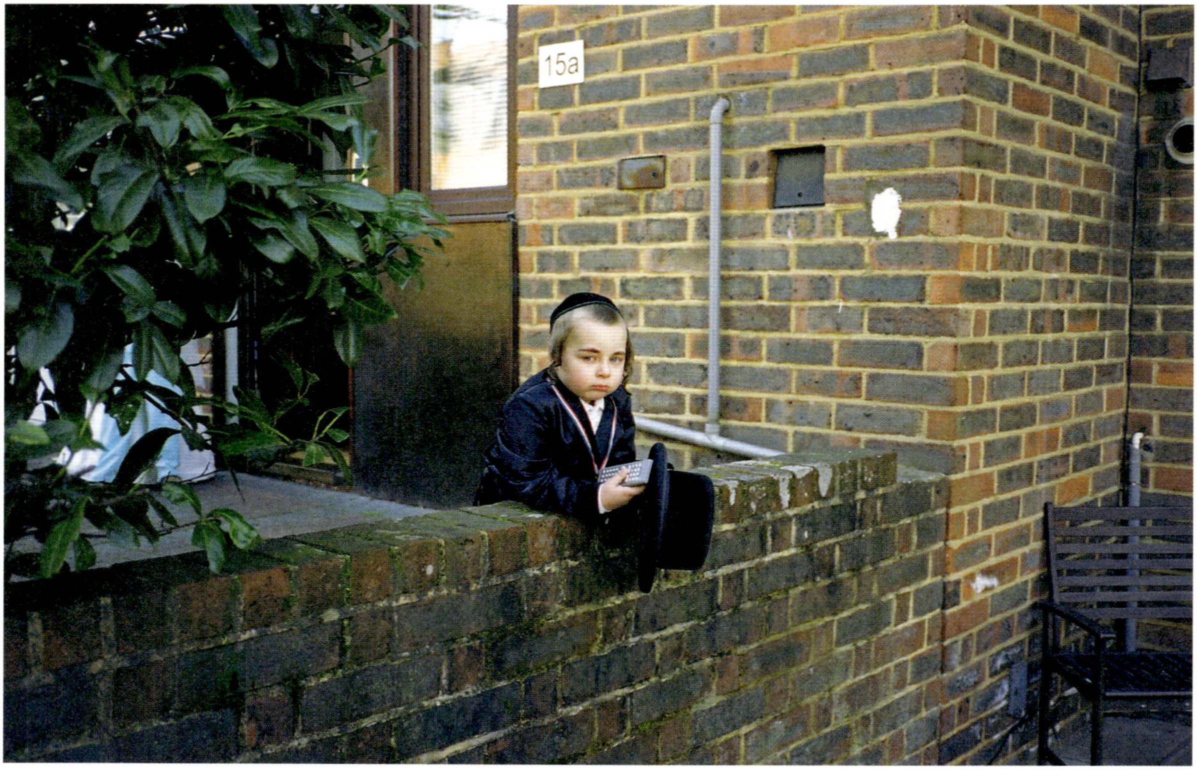

Boy with Remote Control and Hat, Stamford Hill, 2015

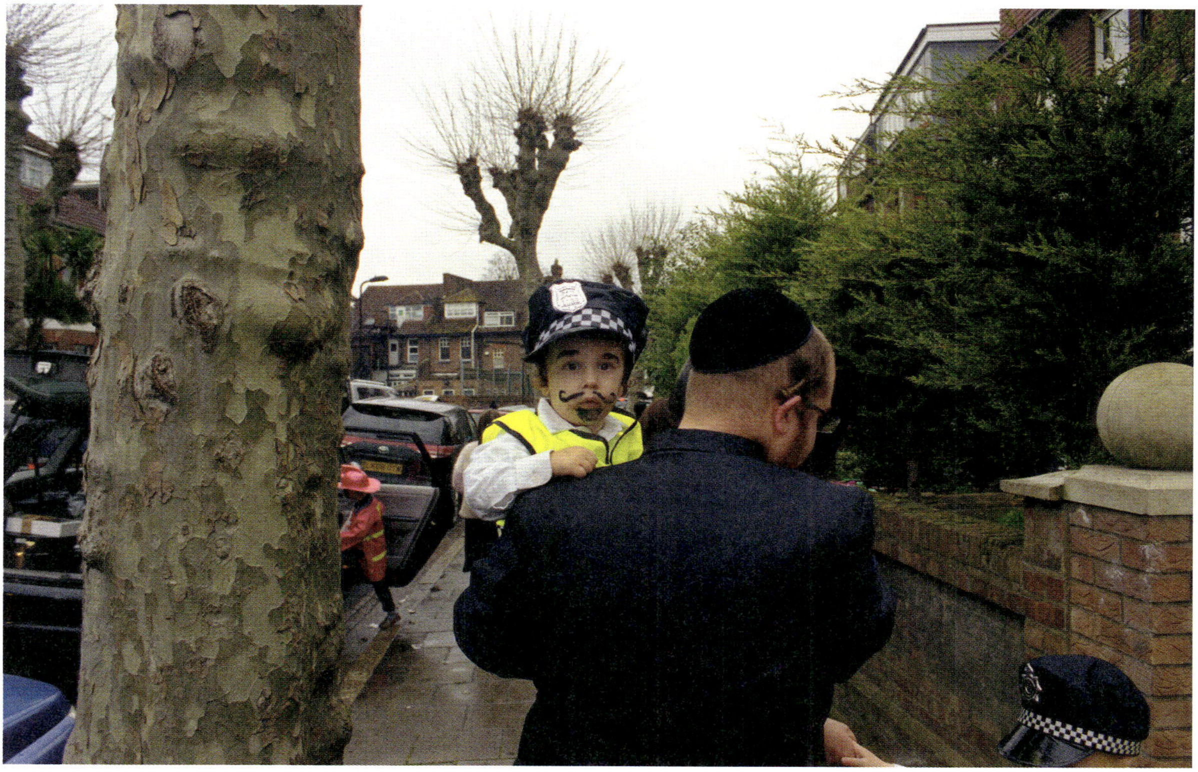

Busted by a Traffic Cop, Stamford Hill, 2017

Stephen Leslie

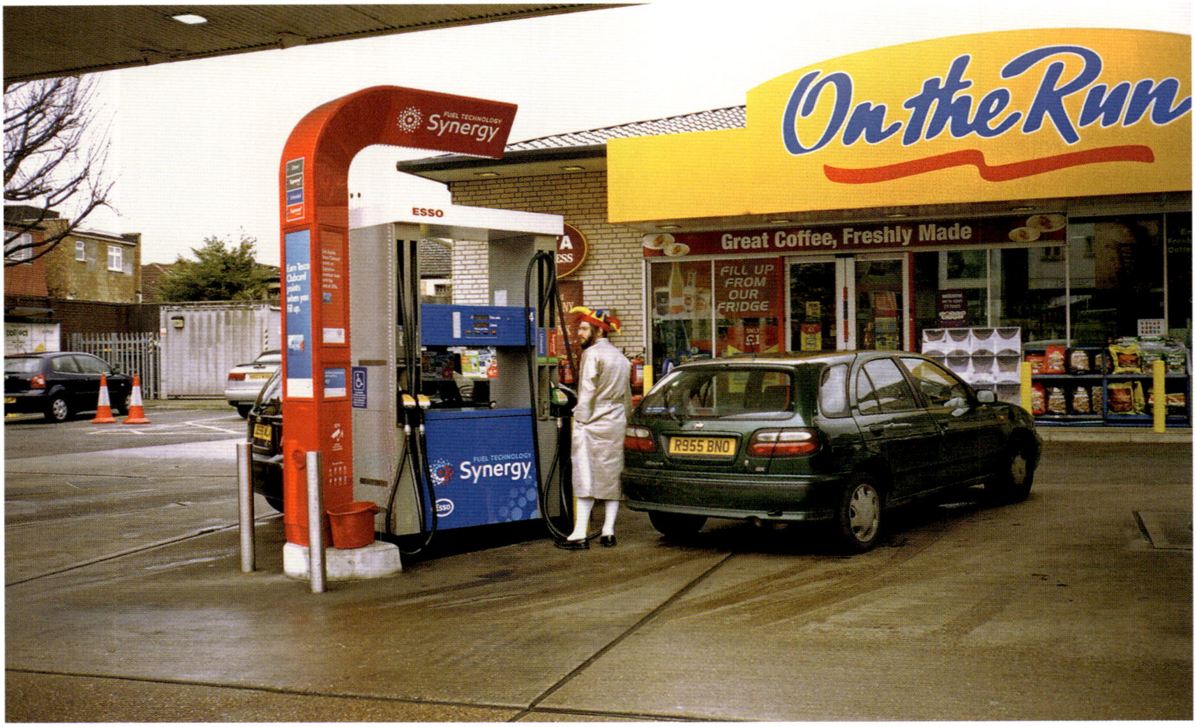

Petrol Stop, Stamford Hill, 2016

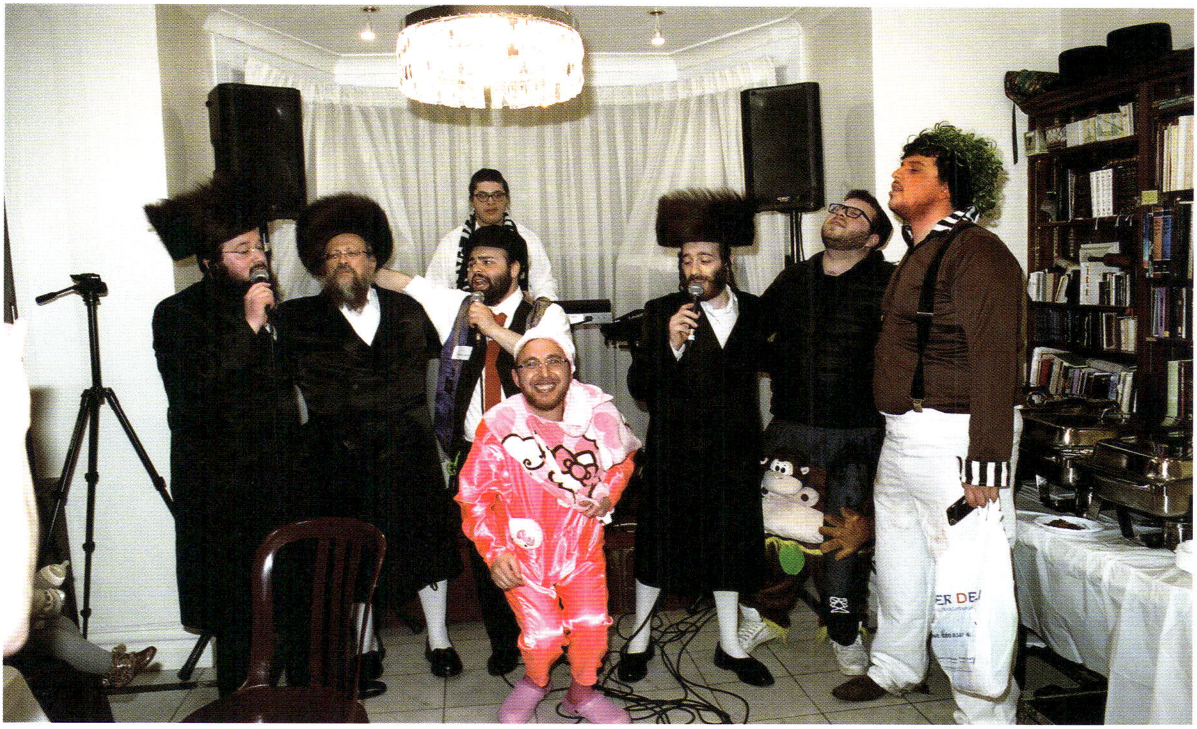

Hello “Gitty” and Friends, Stamford Hill, 2007

Stephen Leslie

Eternal London

Contemporary London is barely recognisable in these atmospheric, ominous black-and-white shots, reminiscent of 40s film noir.

Giacomo Brunelli

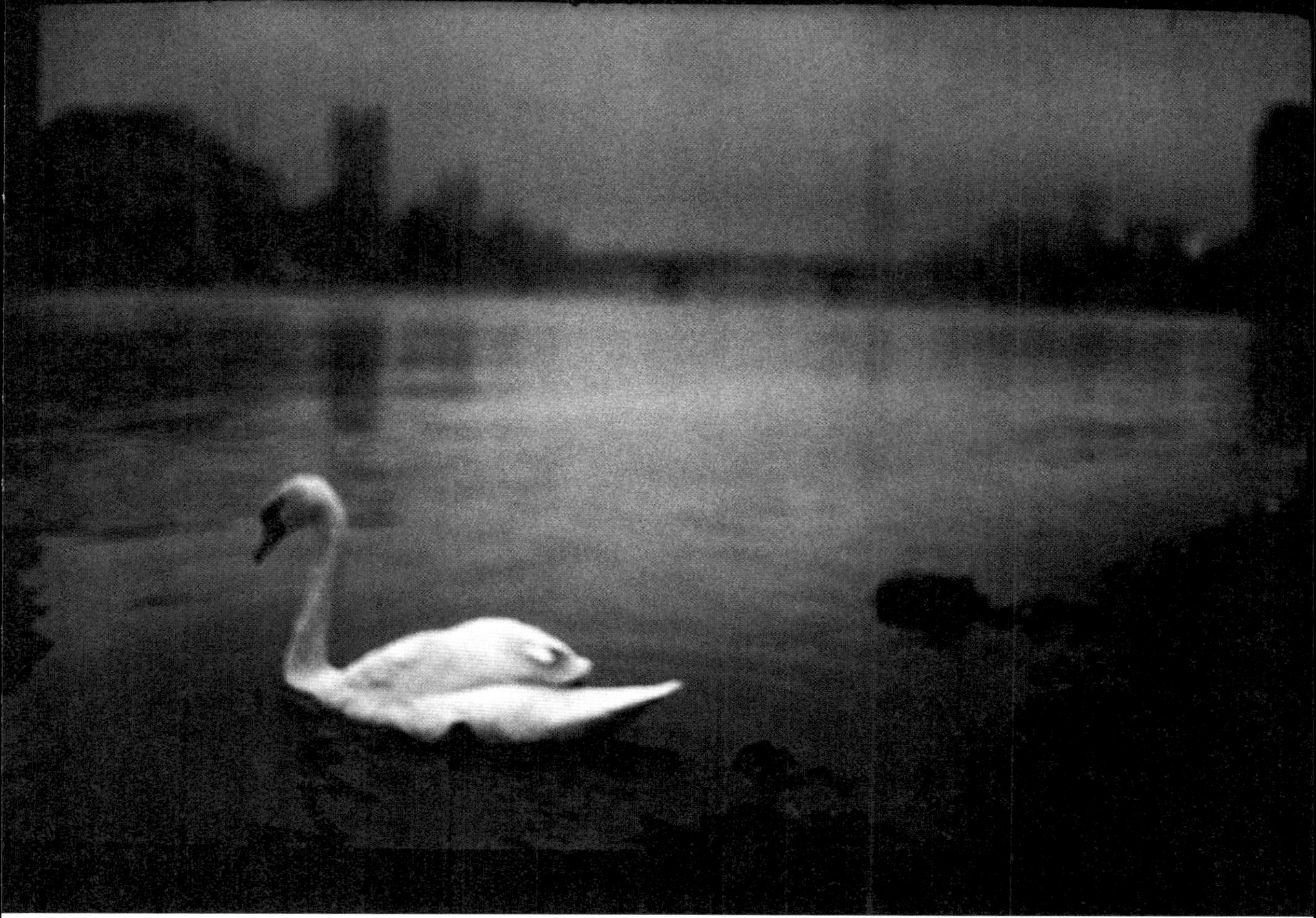

You'd be forgiven for thinking that the photographs that make up Giacomo Brunelli's *Eternal London* were taken in the 1940s or 50s. In these moody black-and-white portraits of silhouetted figures, smudgy dark shadows conspire with flashes of light, tilted frames and low angles to produce a sinister, film noirish tone. In fact, the series was commissioned in 2011 by The Photographers' Gallery. Their brief was to take the stark vision of Brunelli's previous series, *The Animals*, and apply it to a new subject: London.

At first unsure how to approach the project, it was only when Brunelli took a picture of the back of a policeman's head 20 days into it that he finally hit on a method. Big Ben was faintly visible in the background, a ghostly clue to the city's identity. After that breakthrough, he would get up early each day, grab his camera – an old 1962 Miranda Sensomat 35mm – and head to an obvious landmark like Tower Bridge. From there he would spend the day ambling for miles around Central London in search of these moments.

"I wanted London to be recognisable – the starting point was the background and then I'd find the subject," he explained. Brunelli would notice something interesting about someone – a raincoat, a hat or an umbrella, say – and then follow them "like a character in a spy story". Because he was looking down into the viewfinder of his camera, which he held at waist height, it wasn't obvious to others what he was doing. When the perfect light would eventually pass overhead, he would shoot two, maybe three frames and the loud clatter of his shutter would give him away.

Suddenly, remembers Brunelli, "they're not spontaneous anymore, they become tense, they become my actors, they're not the way they were when I saw them. It's fascinating the way people react to your presence when you have a camera." Not everyone was pleased about having their picture taken unawares. One particularly irate woman on Tower Bridge turned around and demanded to know why he was stalking her. "As my subjects are not recognisable I don't think I'm doing anything wrong," says Brunelli, whose standard response is to walk away. "It's very hard to explain."

If the technique has creepy undertones, it could be because it reminds us guilty viewers what photography is really about – a desire to look at others – while simultaneously thwarting that voyeurism by hiding the subjects' faces from us. Instead we get their feet or their hunched backs and must fill in the rest ourselves. "A face can tell a lot," says Brunelli. "I wanted to create an idea of timelessness... I feel most at ease when there's nothing contemporary in the frame." Just as cars, fashion and road signs do, faces reveal the present. Their absence only adds to the 1940s thriller feel that makes *Eternal London* such a strange and striking representation of the city today.

Previous: Untitled (Swan, Thames), 2012
Above: Untitled (Man, Trafalgar Square), 2013

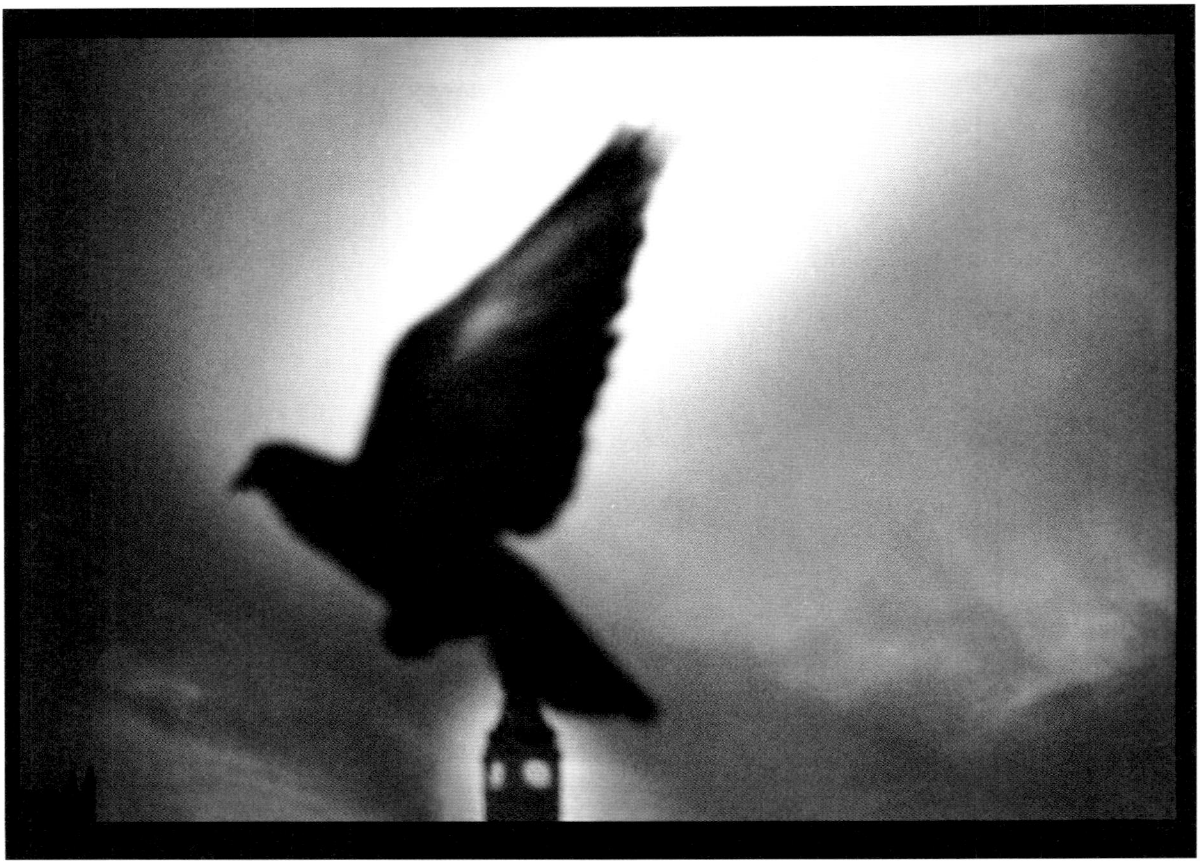

Untitled (Pigeon, Big Ben), 2013

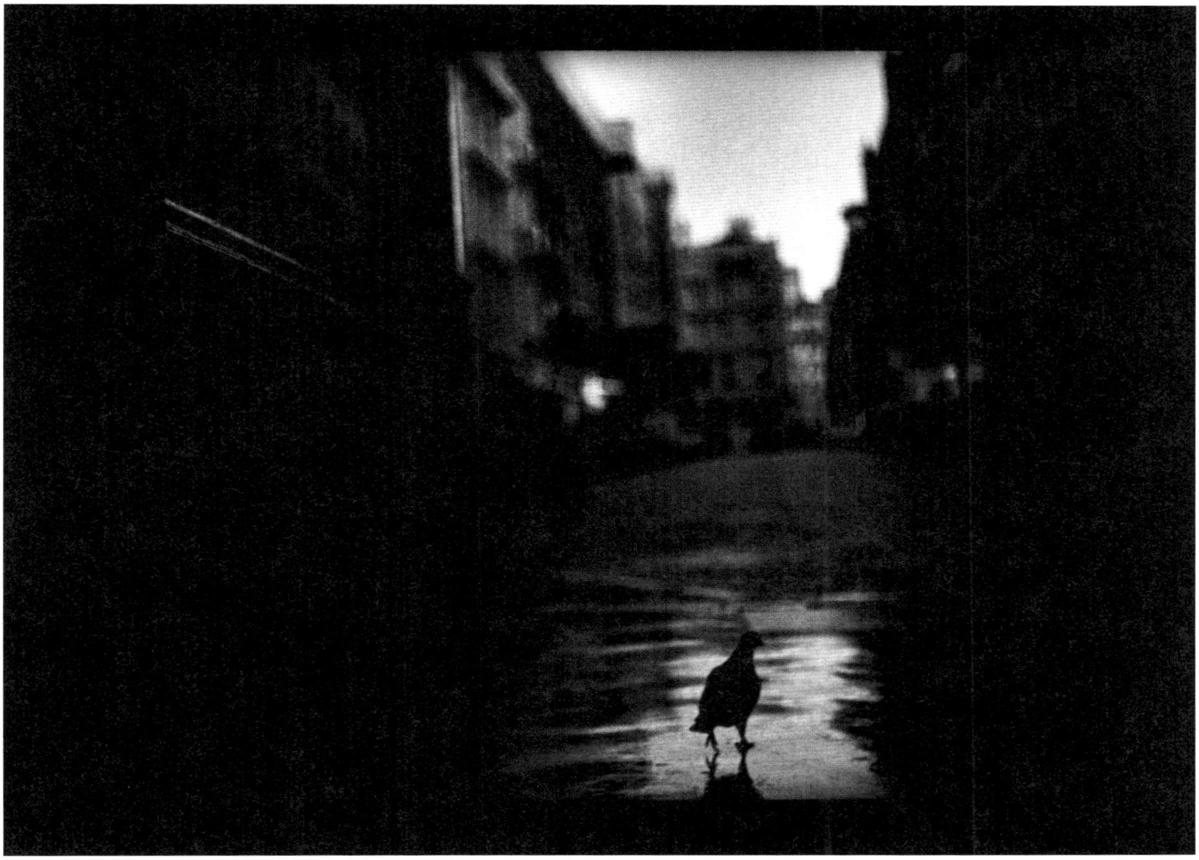

 Untitled (Pigeon, Covent Garden), 2013 Giacomo Brunelli

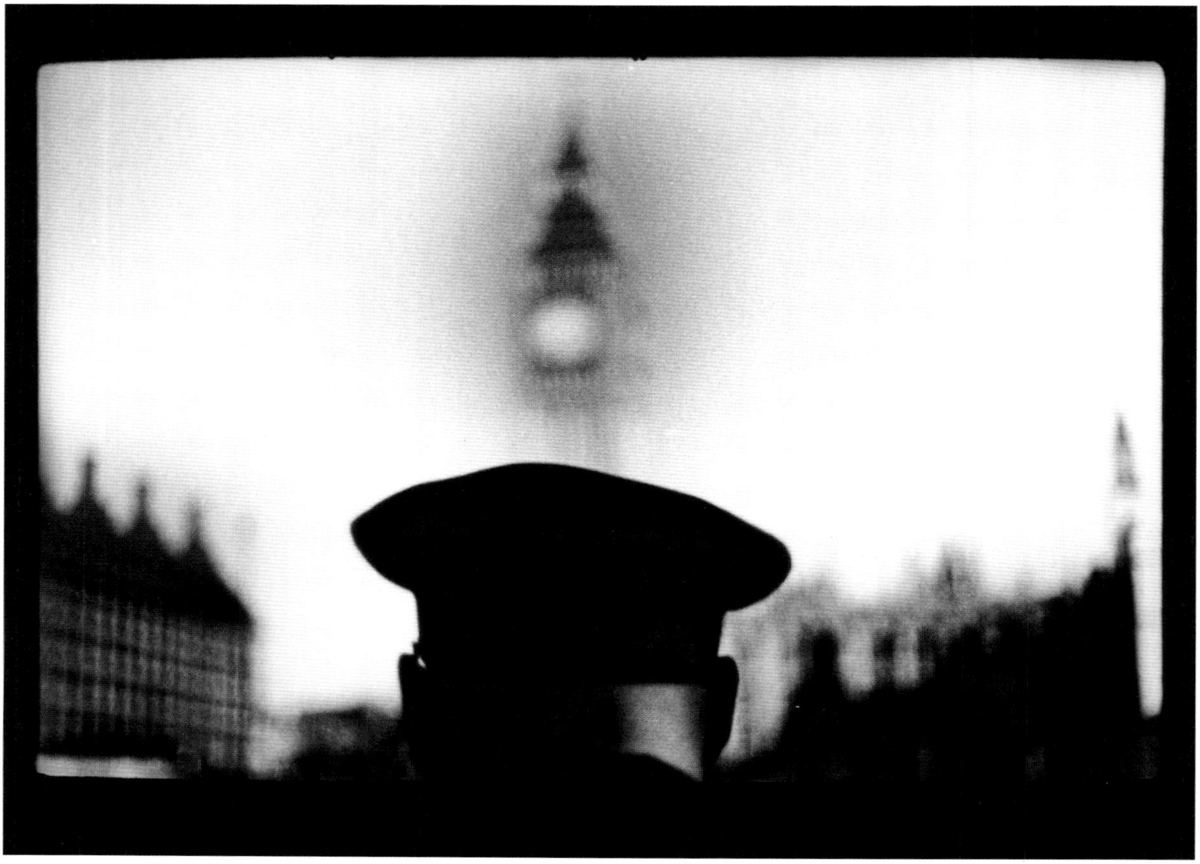

Untitled (Policeman, Big Ben), 2012

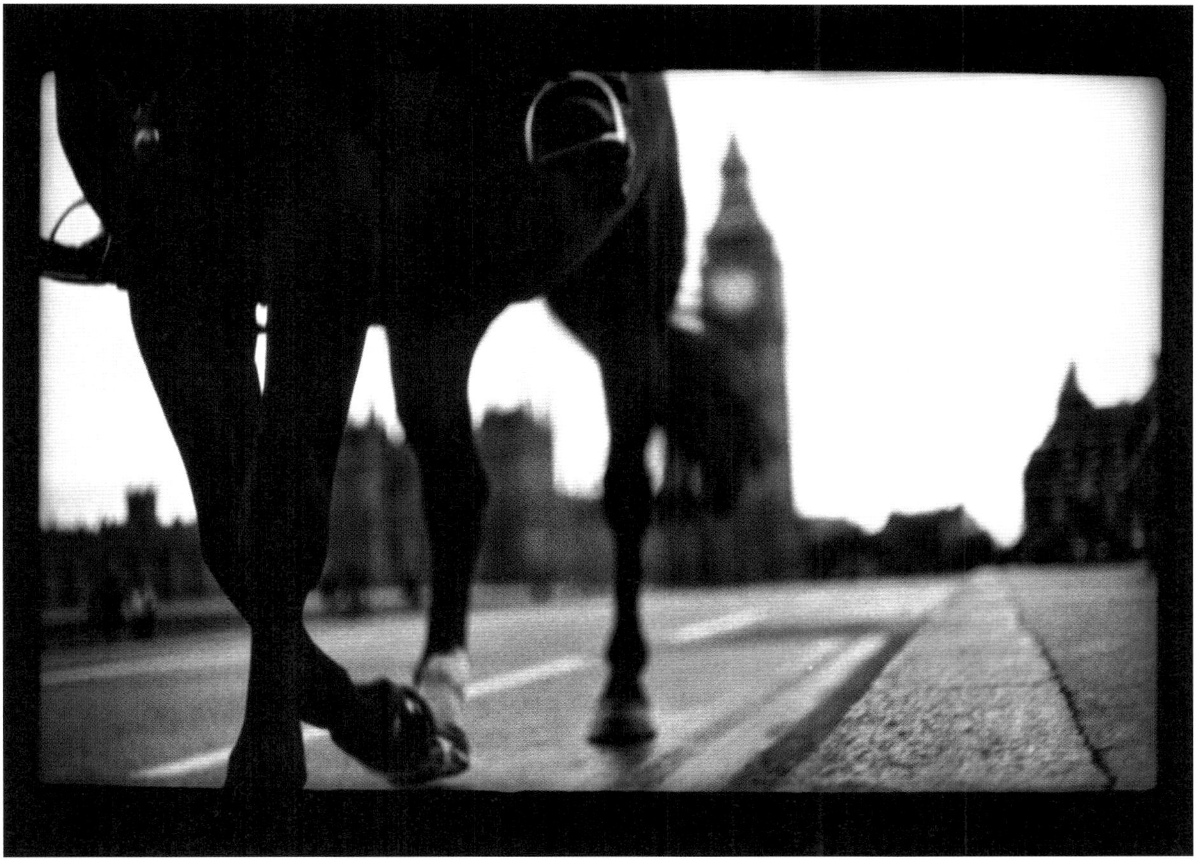

 Untitled (Horse, Westminster Bridge), 2012 Giacomo Brunelli

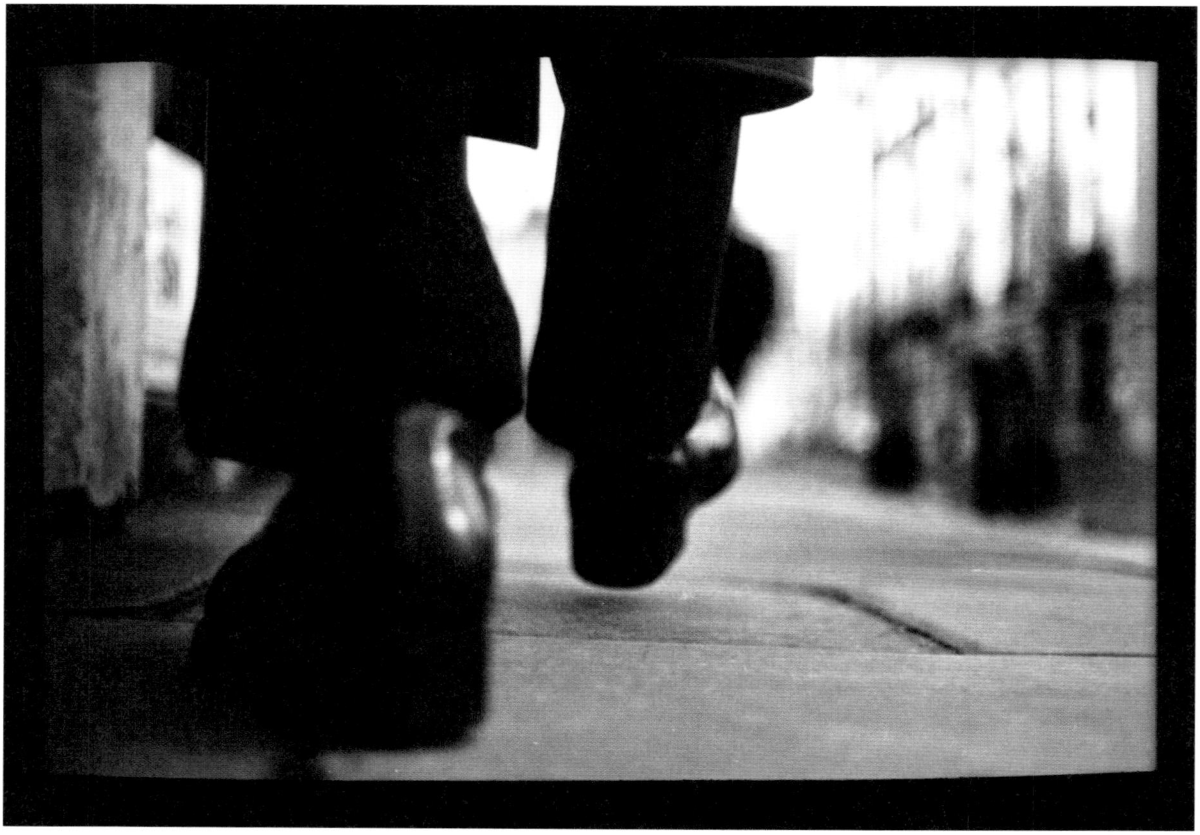

Untitled (Queen's Guardman, St. James's Palace), 2013

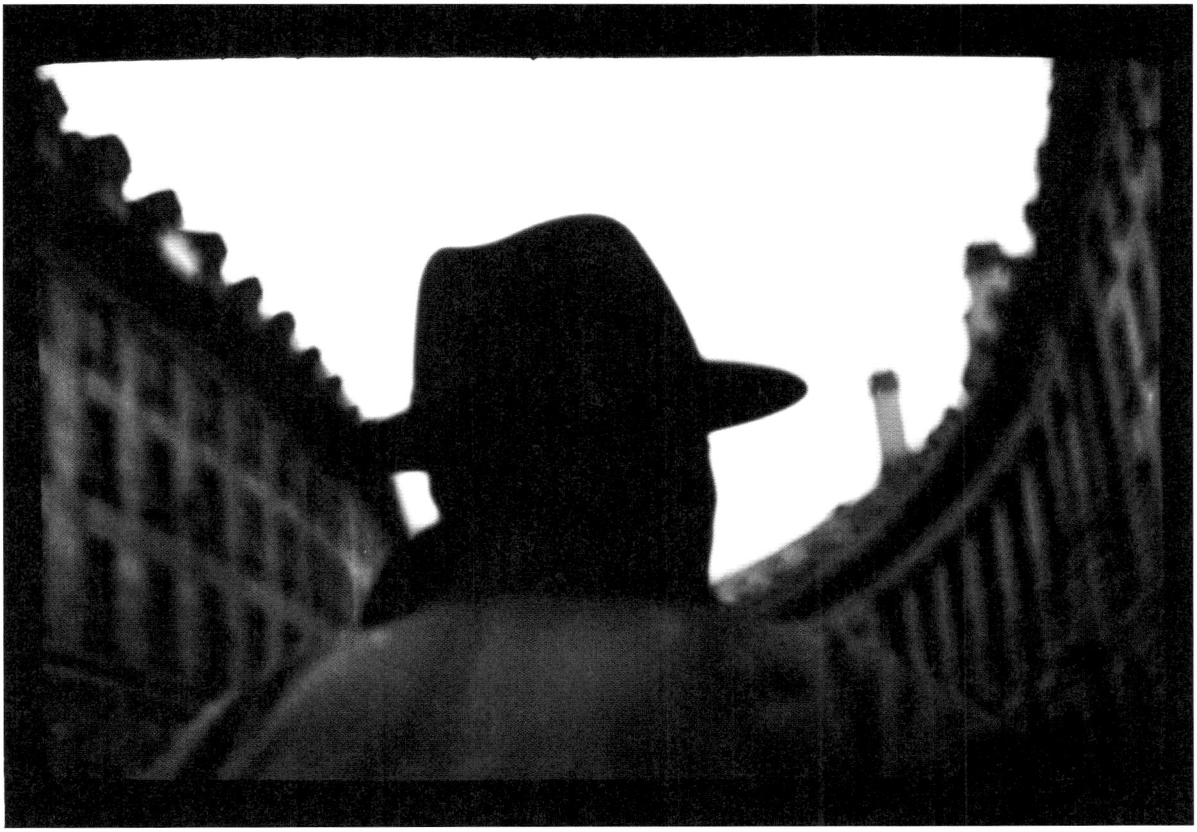

Untitled (Man, Regent Street), 2012

Giacomo Brunelli

On the Night Bus

Melancholic, painterly portraits
of weary commuters, shot through
steamed up bus windows as they
make the journey home.

Nick Turpin

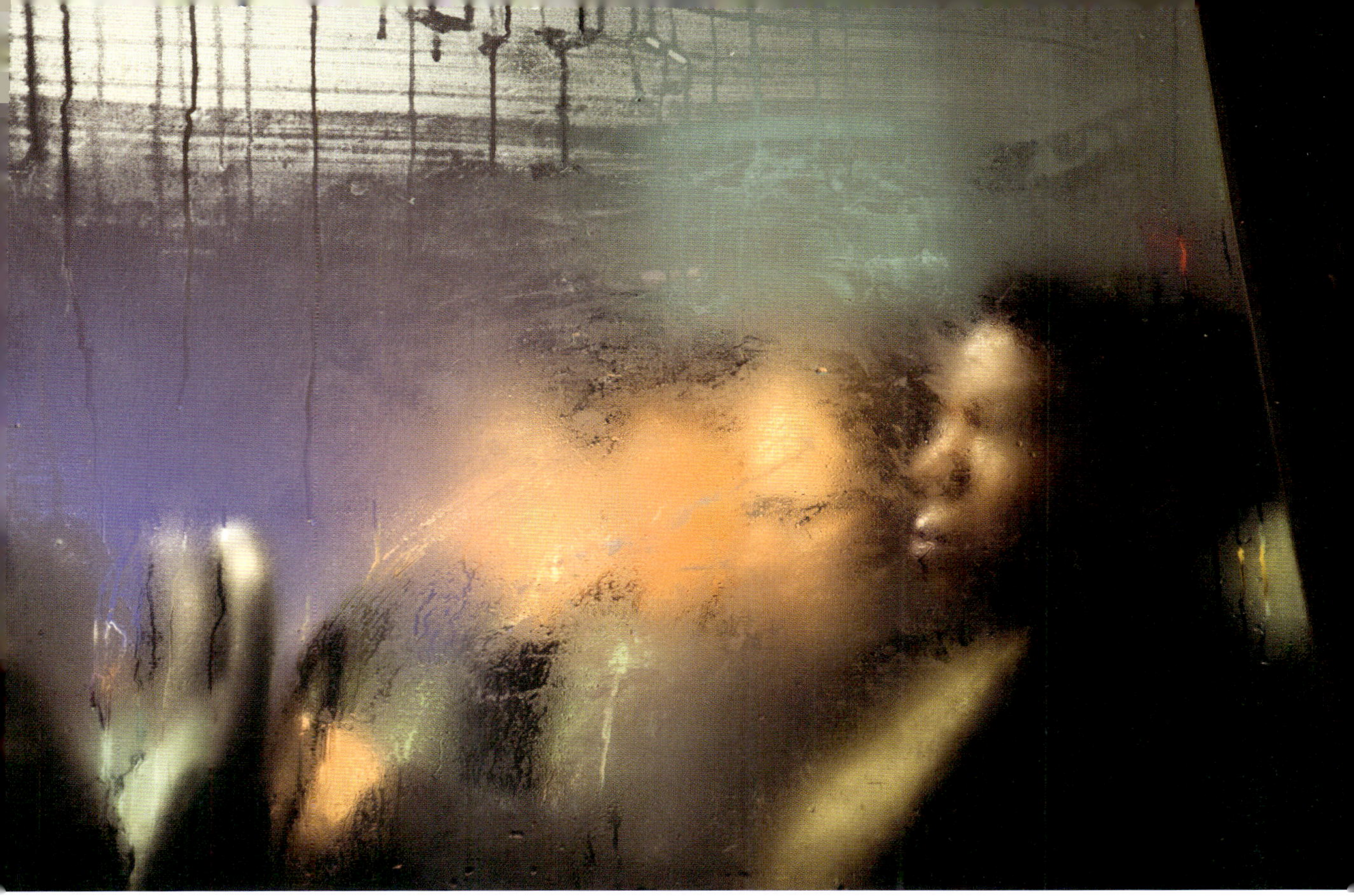

Shattered after a gruelling day at work, they slump against windows steamy with condensation. Some snooze, some check their phones or read books. Others just sit in a daze. Nick Turpin's pictures capture exactly what it feels like to be a London commuter crammed into a rush hour bus home. "In a city of 9 million people you're unlikely to meet anyone you know [on the bus]," he says. "You can be yourself." There's a poignant charm to the painterly colours that recalls the work of New York photographer Saul Leiter – his pictures also find transcendent moments in the urban grind.

Looking at these quiet portraits, you feel incredibly near to their subjects. In fact, Turpin shot the series through a long lens. Over three winters between 2013 and 2015, he returned whenever he could to the same spot – a raised platform by Elephant and Castle shopping centre. From there he could see straight into the top decks of the buses coming from the city and going out towards South London. But as it was dark outside and light inside the bus, his unwitting sitters couldn't see him. That was crucial. "As soon as there's a relationship between you and them, you lose the candid gaze and it changes the meaning of the photograph," he says. "Even if you haven't spoken to them, they're still reacting to your presence."

Turpin started as a staff photographer at *The Independent* but in the last 20 years has become one of Britain's best-known street photographers and founder of the international photography collective iN-PUBLiC. "An observer" is how Turpin sees himself. "On the streets you're watching other people, their gestures, their conversations, how they interact, what they might do next, and the concentration is so great that you forget yourself – I really like that feeling."

And yet in some ways *On the Night Bus* subverts the conventions of classic street photography, which generally gets close to its subjects and is "about having a complete implied narrative in the single frame," says Turpin. Exemplified by American Alex Webb, most street photographers today tend to use a 35mm lens, which mimics the way the eye sees, and a shallow depth of field so that all the contents of the frame are in focus. "Everything is as important as everything, everything has a relationship with everything else – it's all competing for your attention," Turpin explains. "In street photography, all you have is the rectangle and the shutter button. You're not lighting things, you're not staging things, you're not using equipment to make the picture special."

The simplicity and difficulty of that approach still appeals to Turpin but now he believes that "the message is more important. You need to adapt your technique in order to say what you want to say." And the message here? "I'm asking whether modern life in cities is all it's cooked up to be," he says. "Just to buy or rent a property in London is so difficult for most people." London can be hard and *On the Night Bus* shows life here for what it is: a tug of war between struggle and relief.

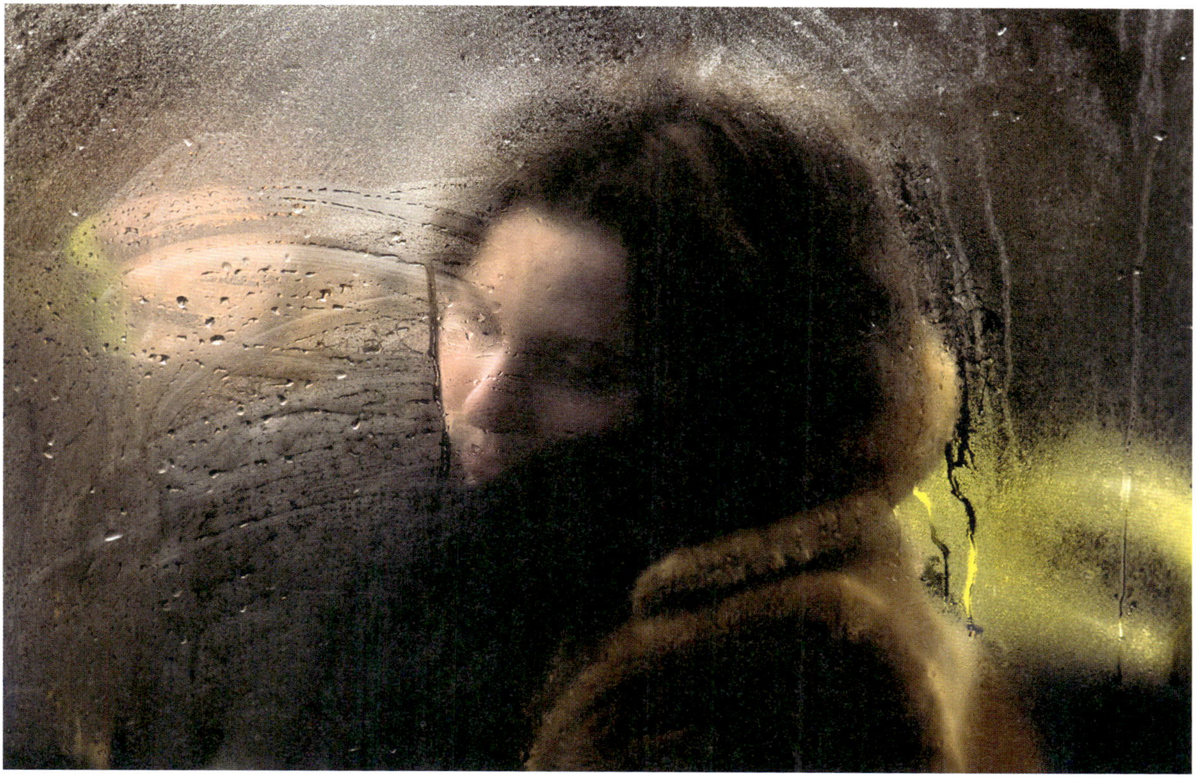

Previous: #27, London, 2014–16
Above: #36, London, 2014–16

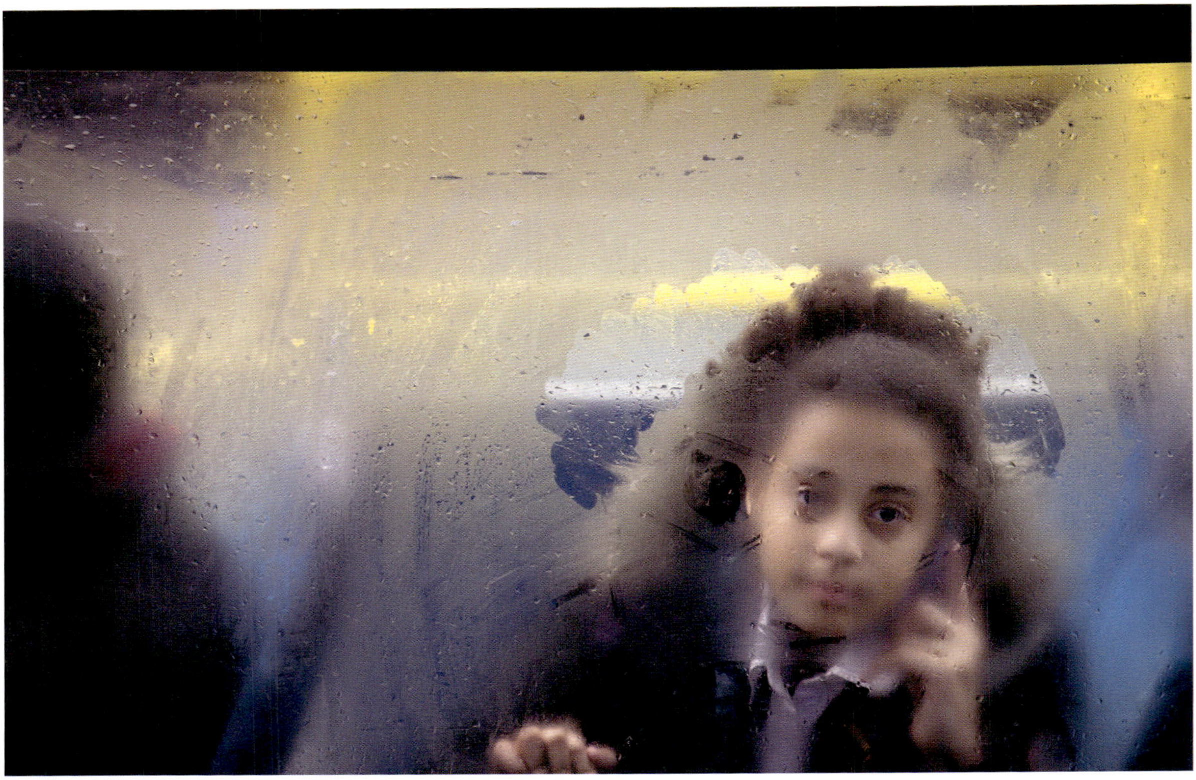

#10, London, 2014–16

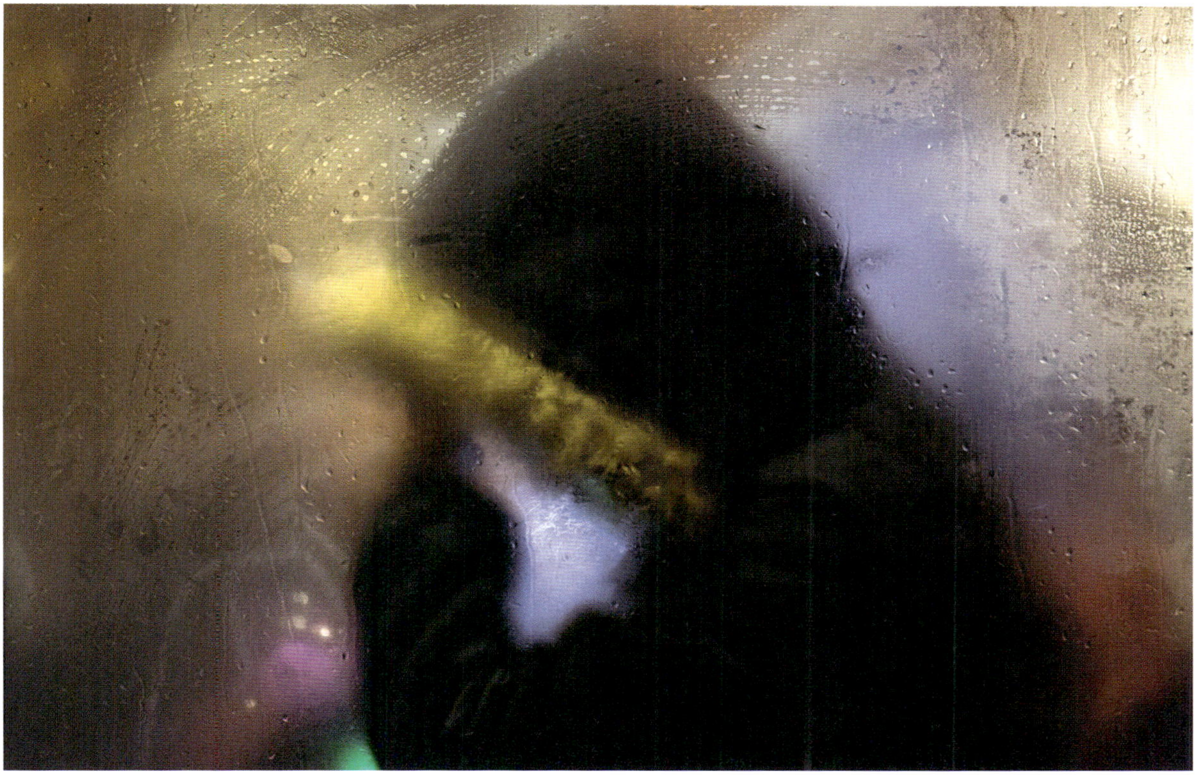

#32, London, 2014–16
Overleaf: #29, London, 2014–16

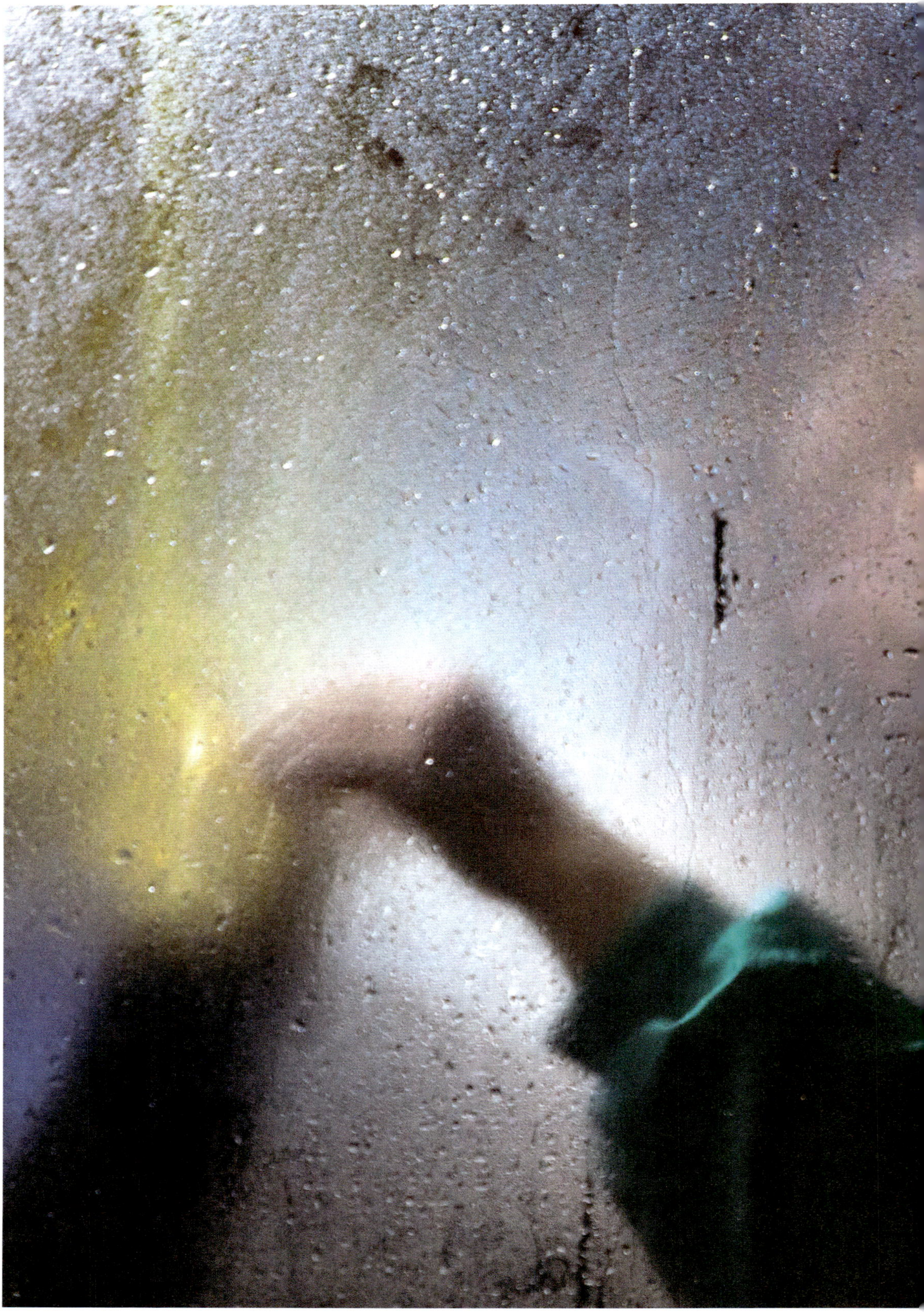

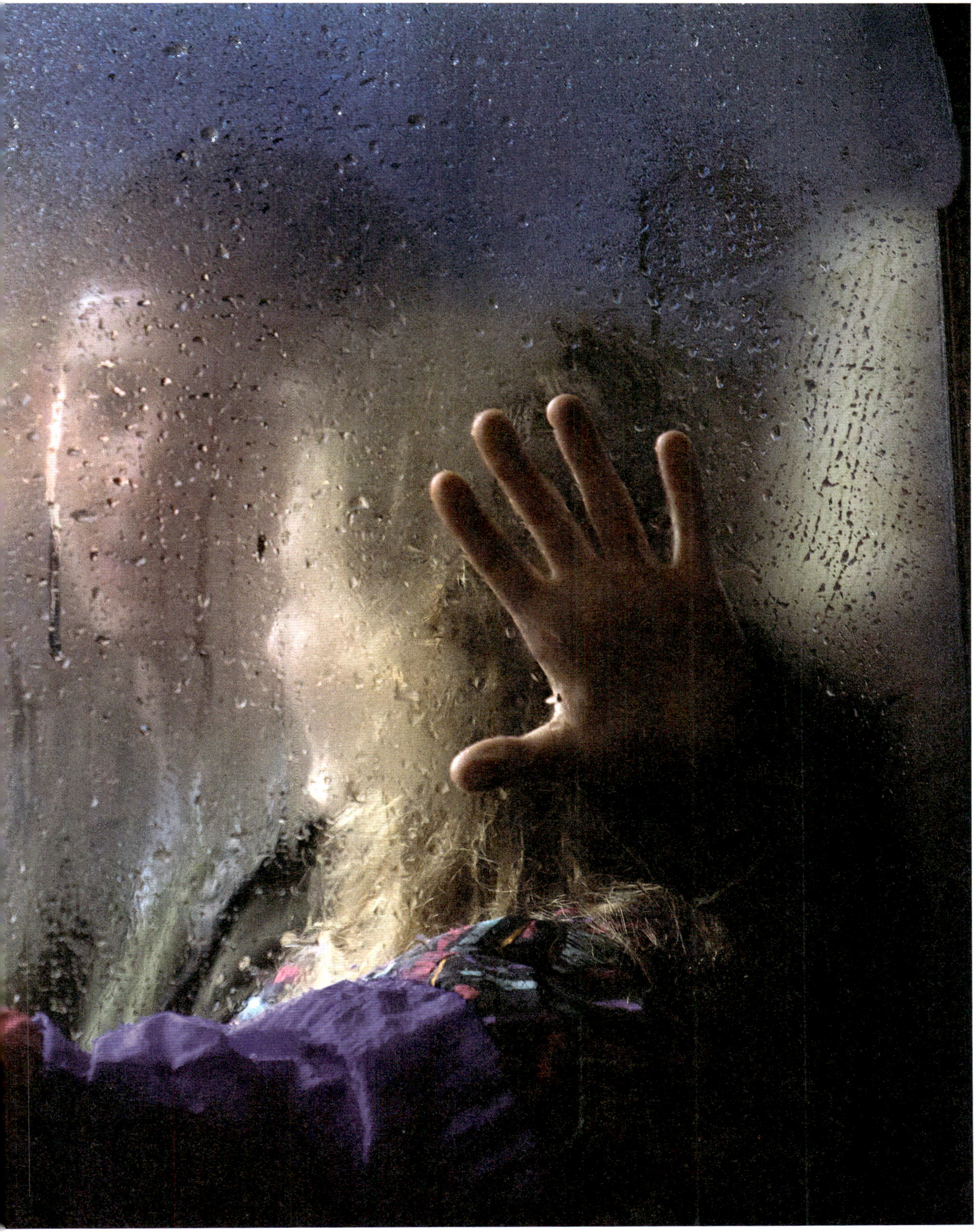

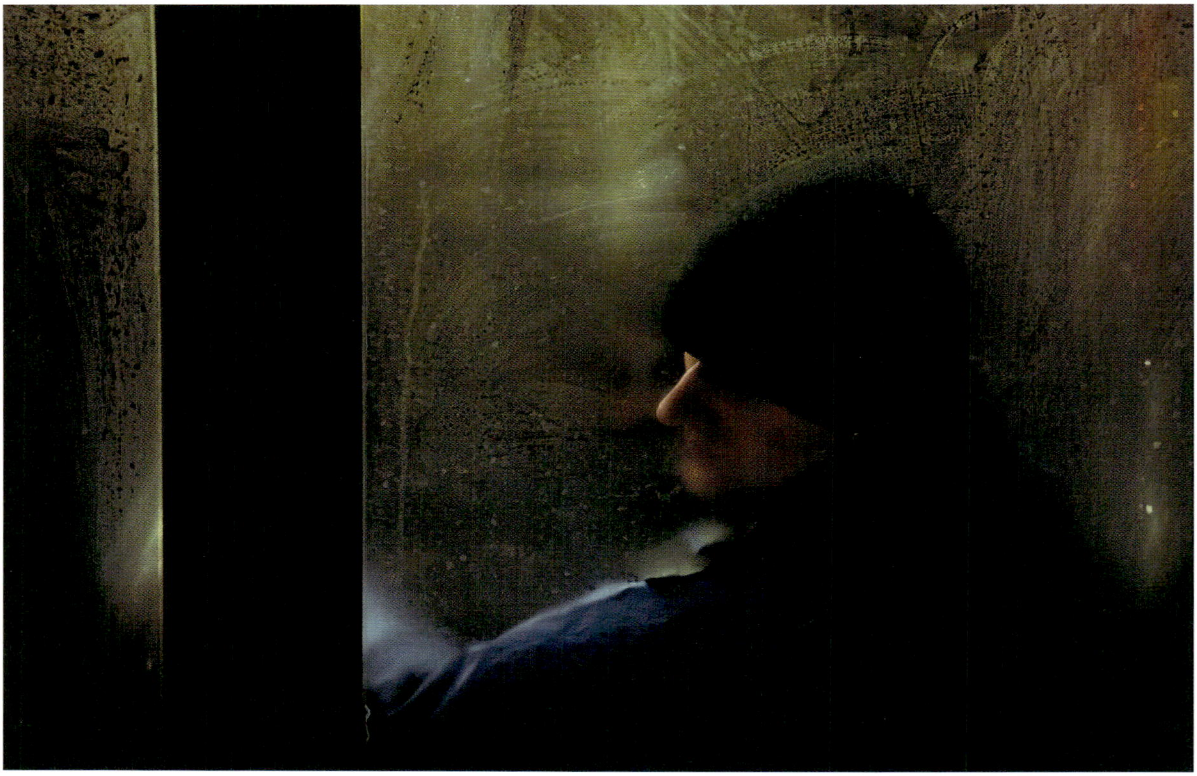

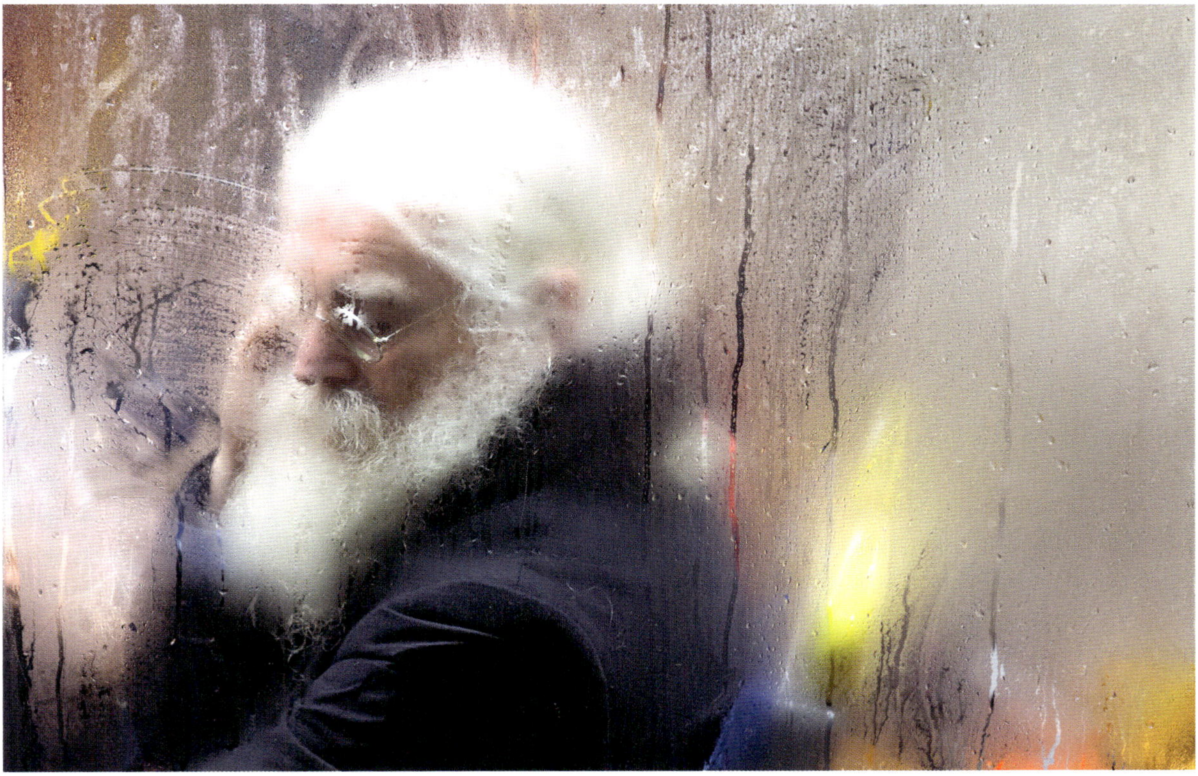

#28, London, 2014–16

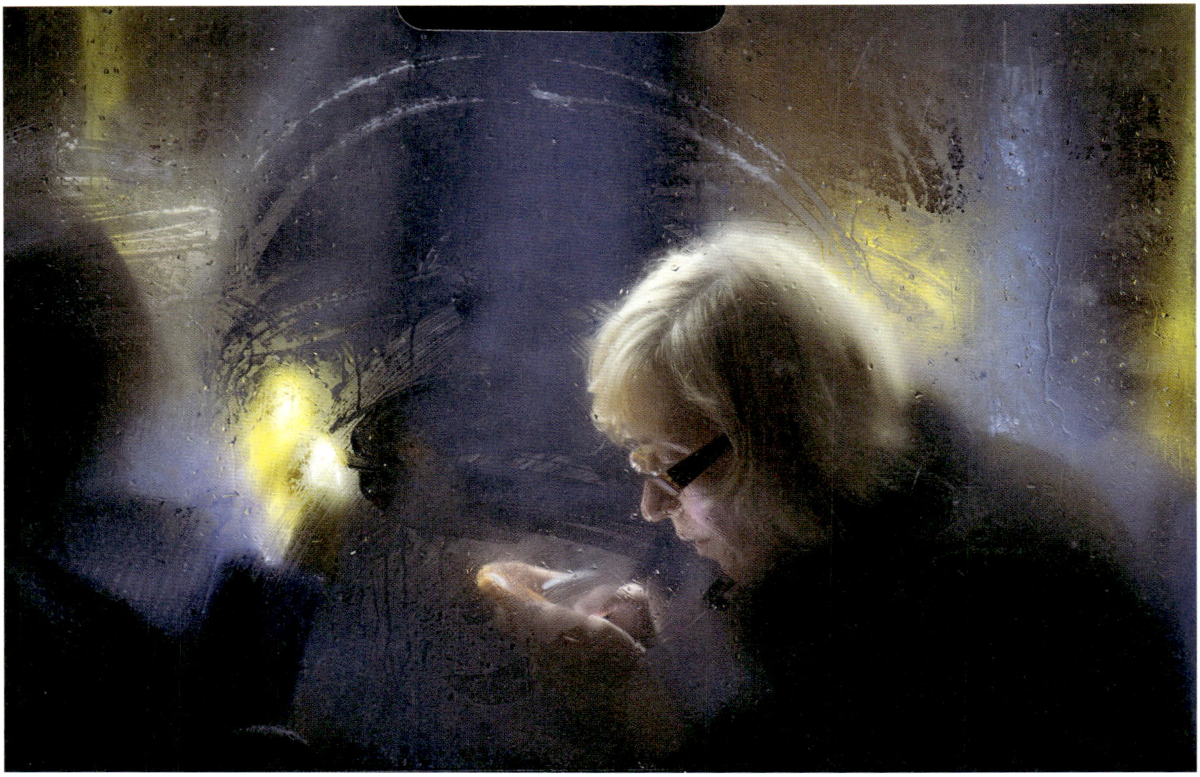

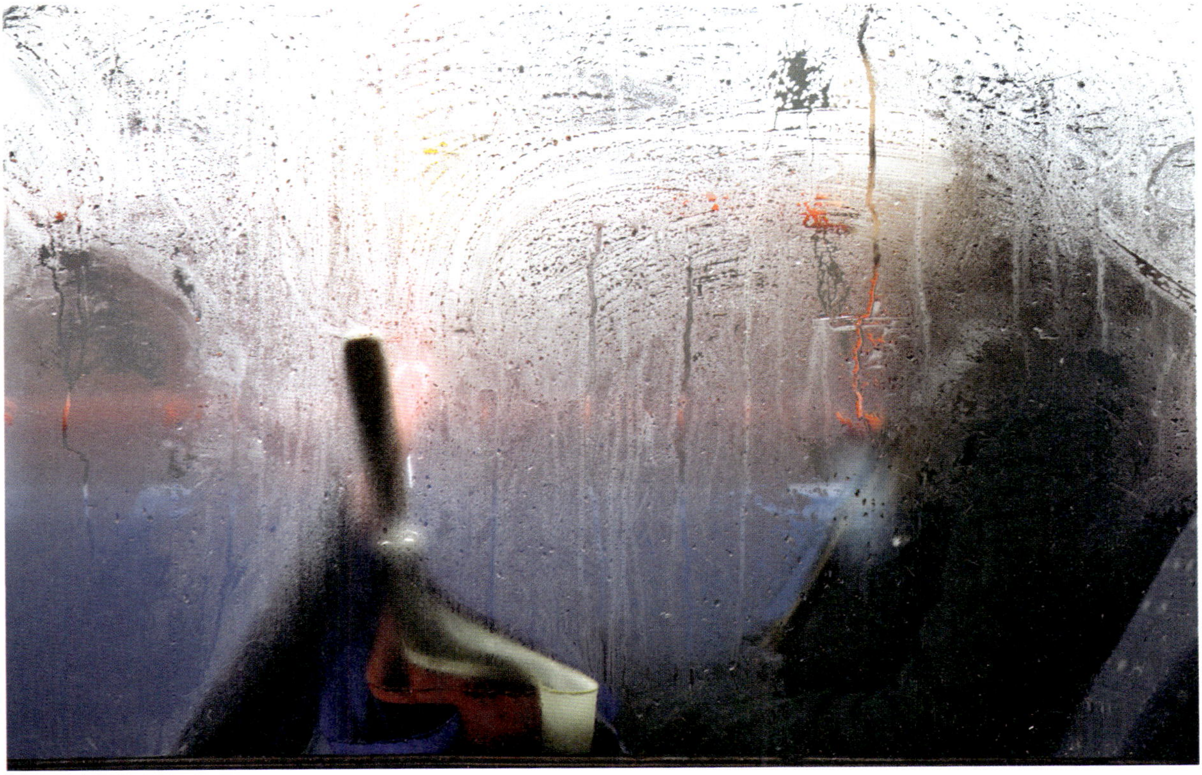

#12, London, 2014–16

Nick Turpin

Dalston Anatomy

Precarious sculptures, powdered paint and photographic portraits mingle in this vivid celebration of a street market on the edge of change.

Lorenzo Vitturi

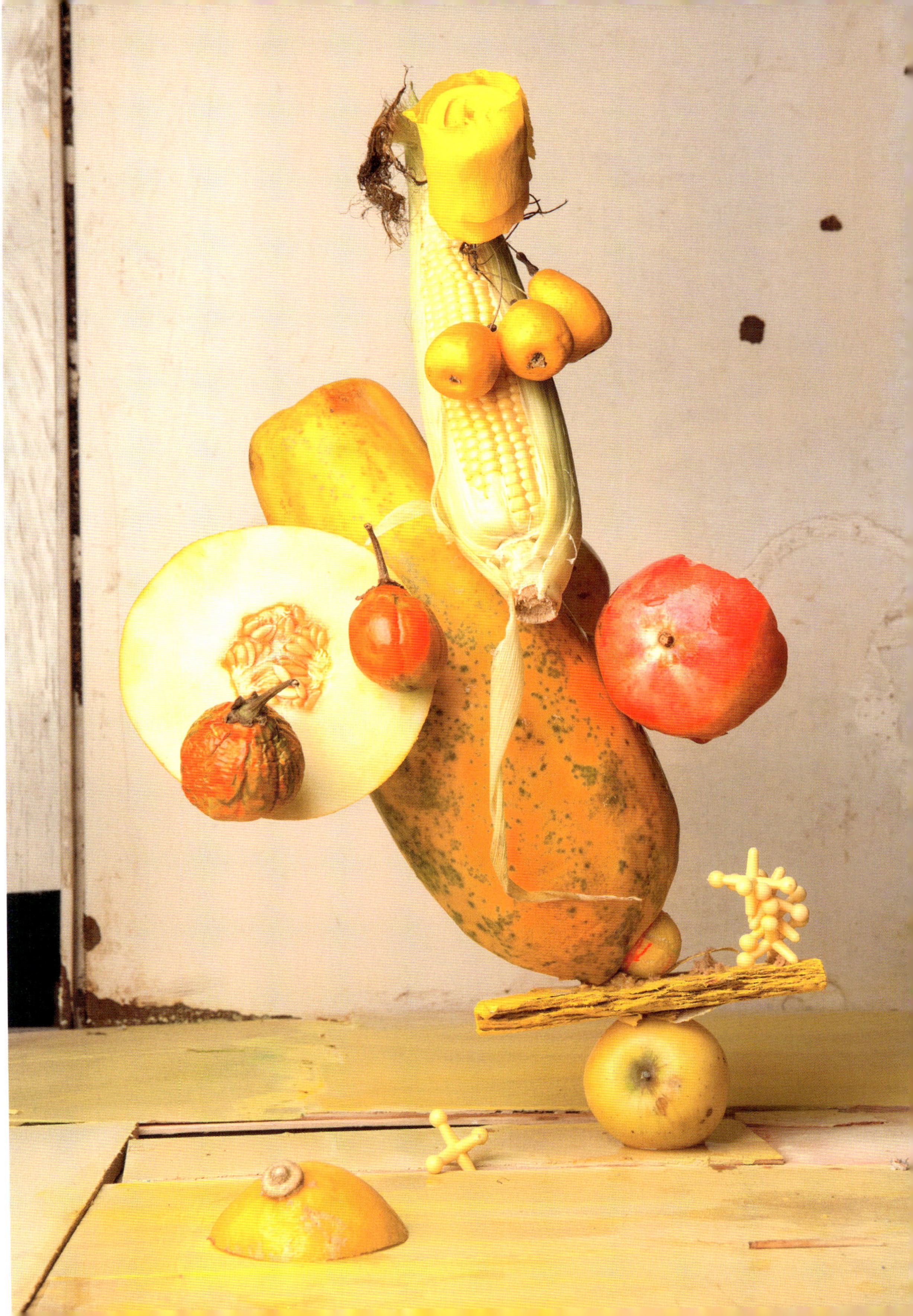

When Lorenzo Vitturi arrives in a new city, the first place he heads is the local street market. It's there, he says, that you can really "discover the soul of a place". *Dalston Anatomy* is Vitturi's tribute to Ridley Road Market in Dalston, a neighbourhood the Italian-born photographer fell in love with when he moved there. He describes the market as "an explosion of energy, life, different materials, different textures, everything coming together in this unstoppable mix". Mirroring this in making the series, Vitturi (often literally) grabbed elements off the streets and combined them in thrilling new ways through photography and sculpture. A Ridley Road remix.

Before *Dalston Anatomy*, the former film set painter was working in high-pressured advertising and editorial photography. Life had "a harsh rhythm". The time had come to take a break from the commercial work, so he rented a small studio in Dalston to focus on his own creative pursuits. Every day for the next eight years he would collect objects from the surrounding area and take them back to his studio where he'd transform them into surreal sculptures.

In advertising, an image took weeks of meticulous preparation but this time Vitturi didn't do a single sketch. Instead he followed "the shape, the colour, the form, my aesthetic interest". A head in a portrait he'd shot in the morning might lead to the curve of a guava in the late afternoon or the bright pink of a woman's top might reappear in a flower the next day. Some of the colourful materials he'd gleaned from the streets were, he realised, debris from the redevelopment taking place as a wealthier cohort moved in. "The market became a metaphor. It represents a daily cycle of creation and destruction," says Vitturi. "I wanted to make these beautiful sculptures that were attractive but also precarious." Delicately balanced, alive with colour, even as the rot sets in, they are a nod to both the makeshift nature of the market and the uncertain future faced by Dalston's longer-term residents as property developers circle.

The sculptures owe something to art history. In the attention they pay to everyday objects, they continue a thread that begins with Renaissance still life painting – considered shocking at the time for their naturalism and runs through Marcel Duchamp's readymades, artworks created from objects he'd found (most famously a urinal). Since 19th century pioneer Henry Fox Talbot, photographers have made sculptures their subjects. But echoing the approach of Swiss artists Fischli & Weiss, Vitturi creates sculptures in order to photograph them. Along with contemporaries like Darren Harvey-Regan, he's part of a wave of photographers questioning where the medium begins and ends. Before publishing it as a photobook, Vitturi first showed *Dalston Anatomy* at the market itself – not just on the walls but in the form of a stall, which he ran according to market hours, taking his preoccupation with locality to the extreme.

Another victim of rising rents, Vitturi no longer has a studio in Dalston but the impact of this small locality on his artistic career has been transformative. "I discovered so much about Western Africa – Nigeria, Ghana, all those communities – on the streets of Dalston," he says. "I'd never been to Africa [before this]." Eventually that was rectified. Off the back of *Dalston Anatomy* he was invited by the African Artists' Foundation to do a residency in Lagos, where he completed his latest project, a book entitled *Money Must be Made*. And where do you think he went when he landed? Balogun Market, of course.

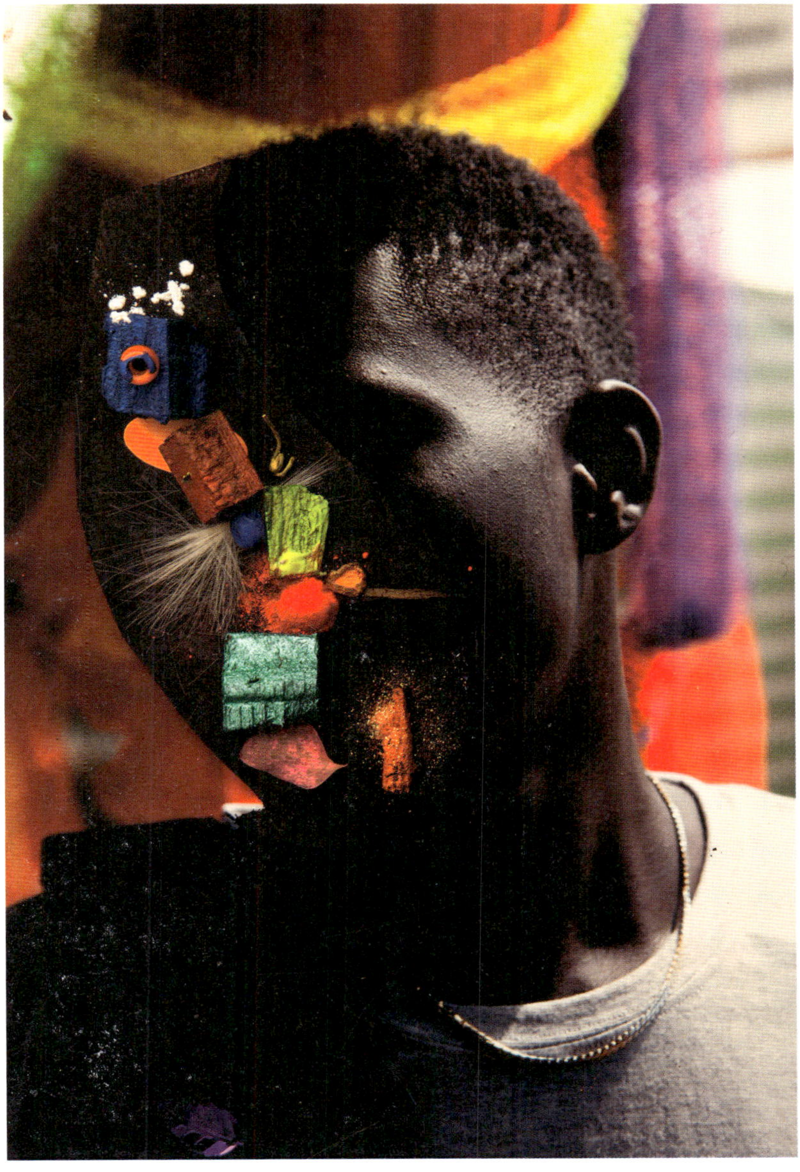

Previous: Yellow #1, London, 2013
Above: Multicolor #1, London, 2013

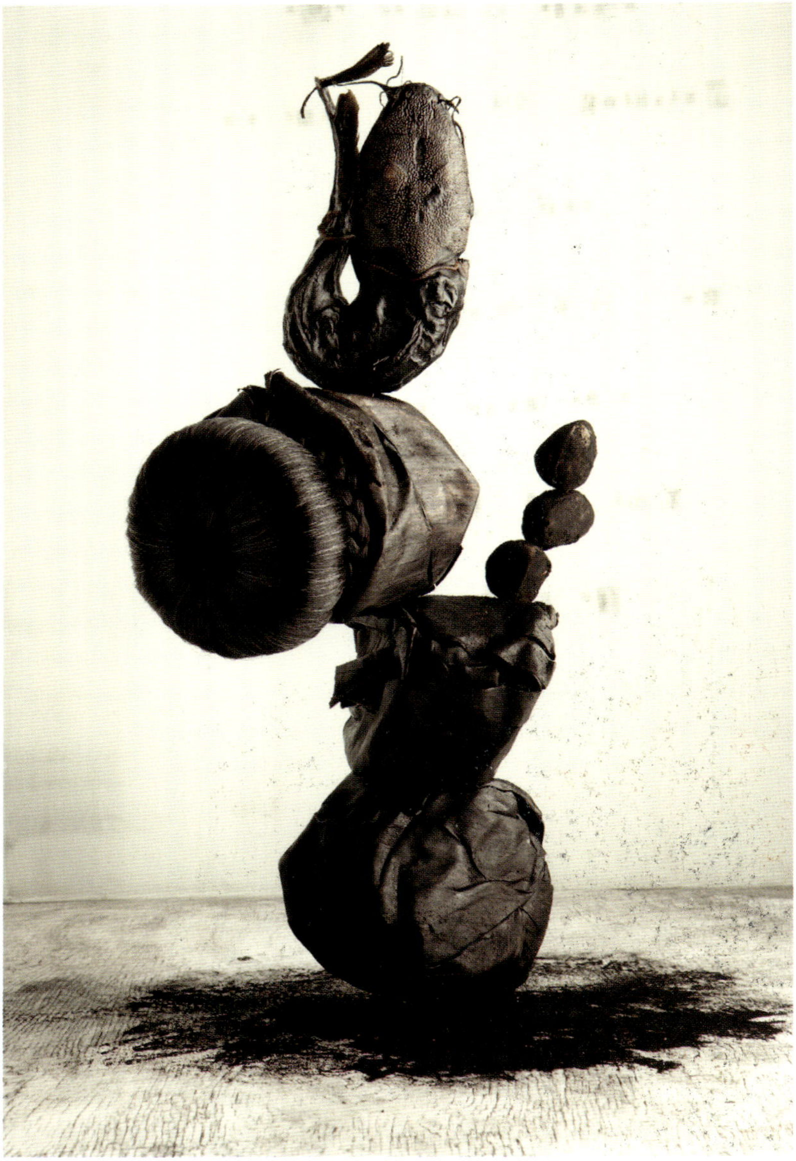

Black #1 & 2, London, 2013

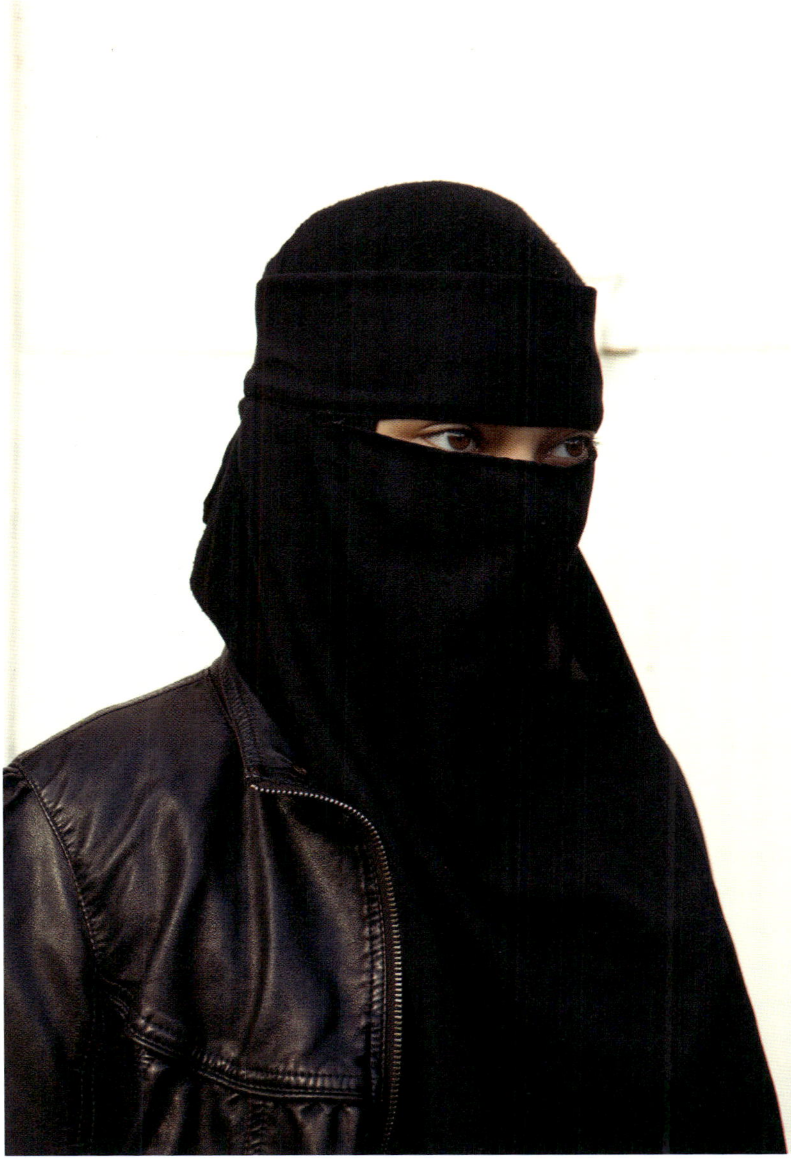

 Black #1 & 2, London, 2013

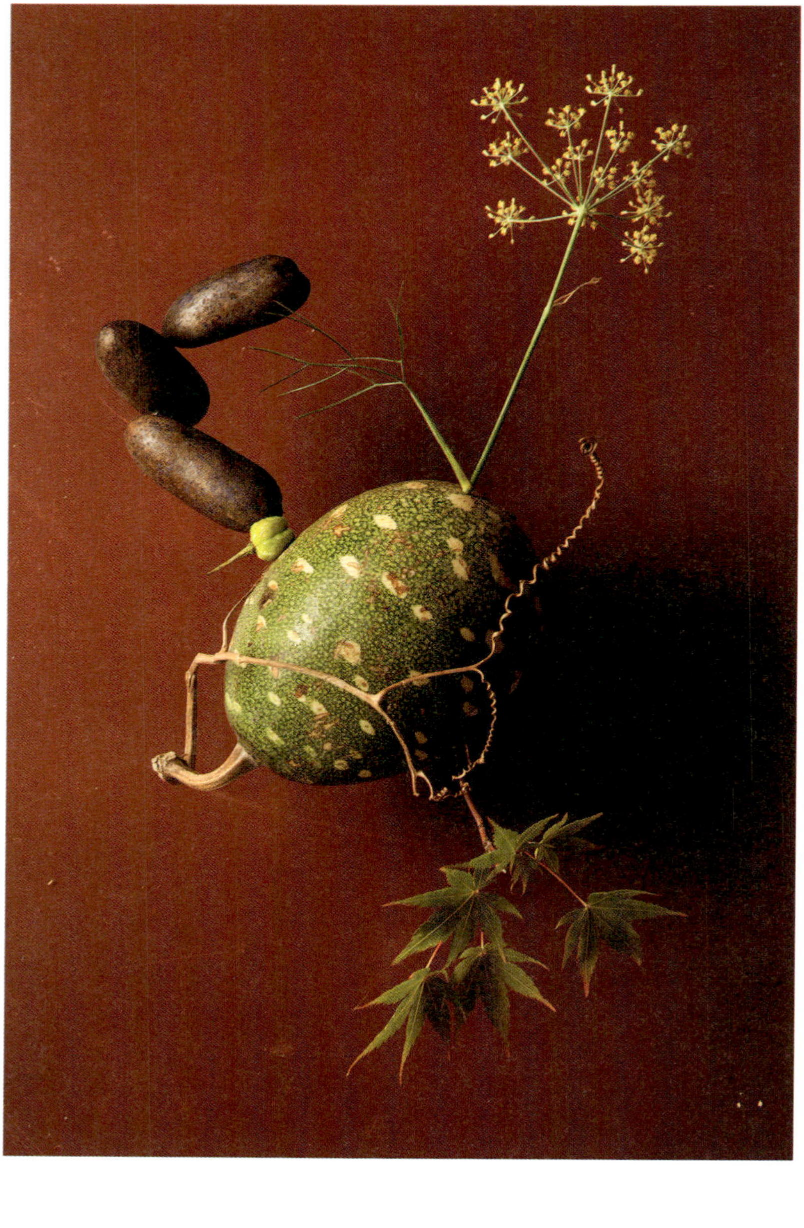

Fawn #1 & 2, London, 2013

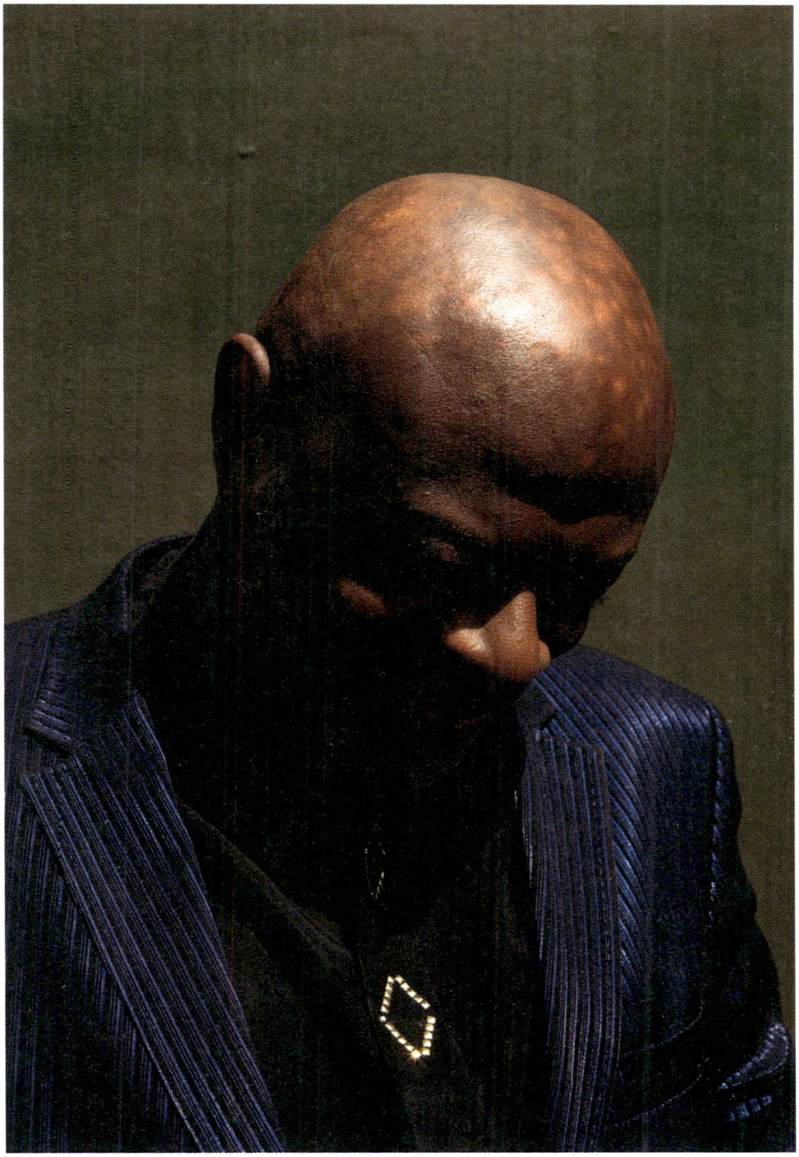

Fawn #1 & 2, London, 2013

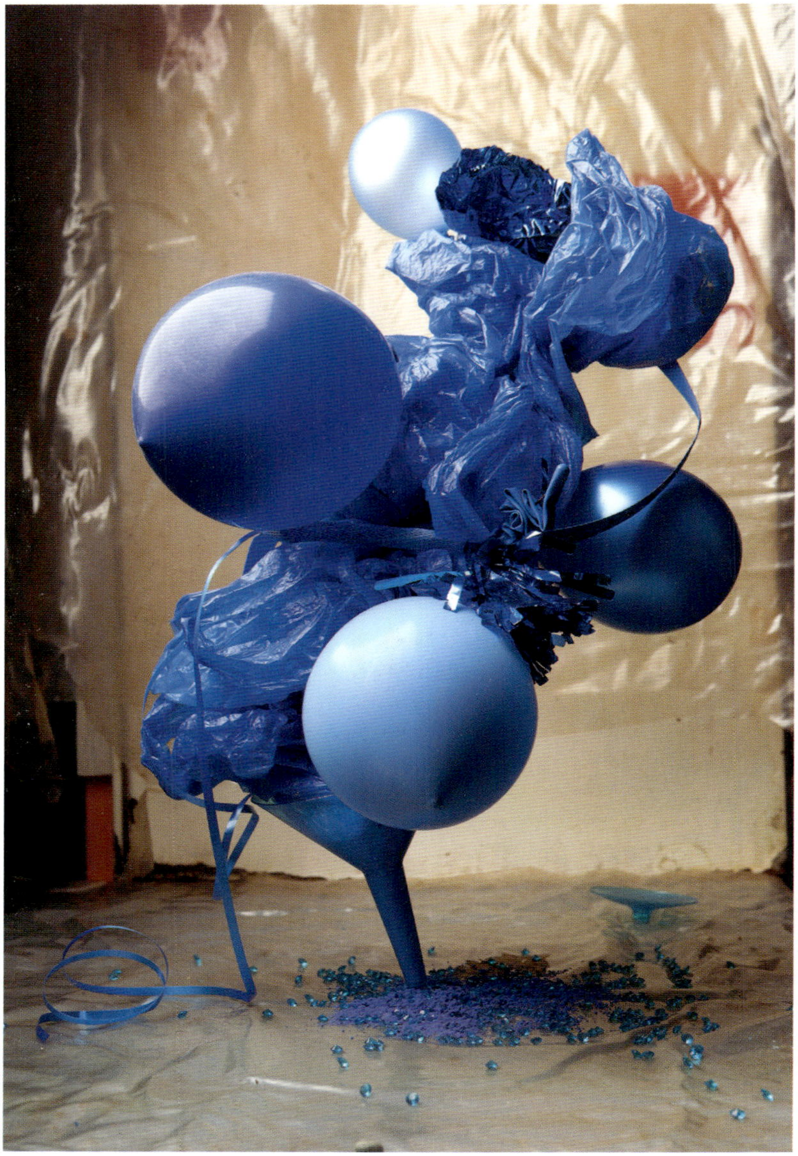

Plastic Blue #1 & 2, London, 2013

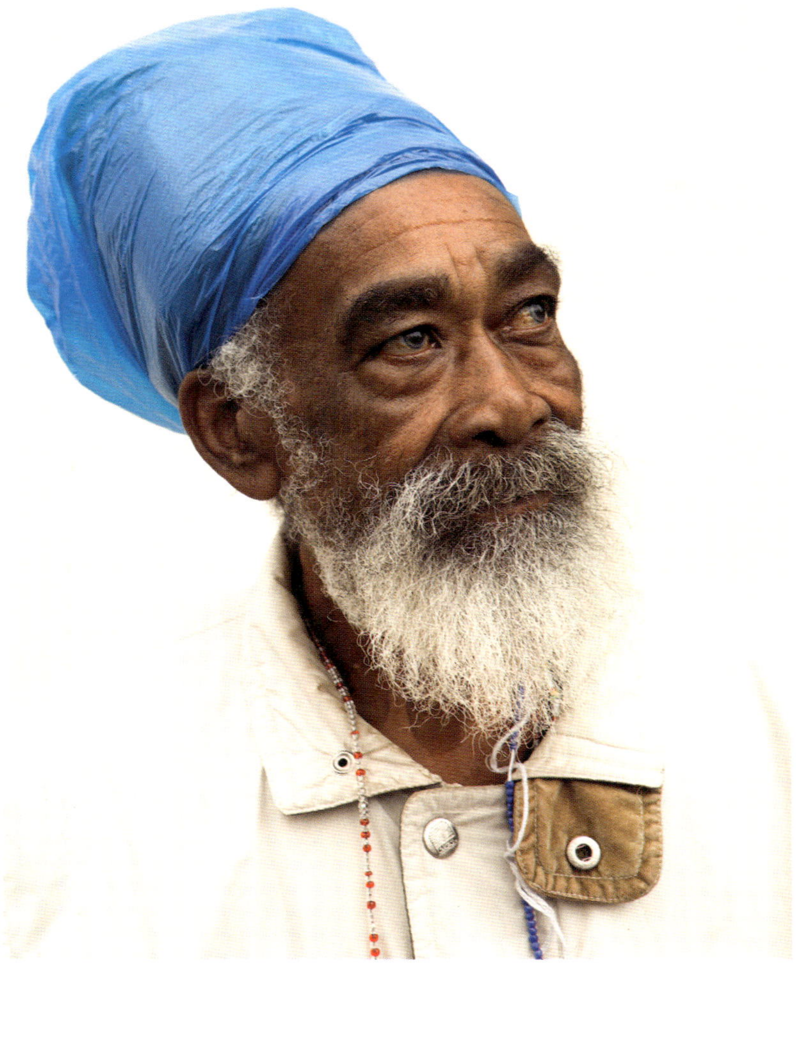

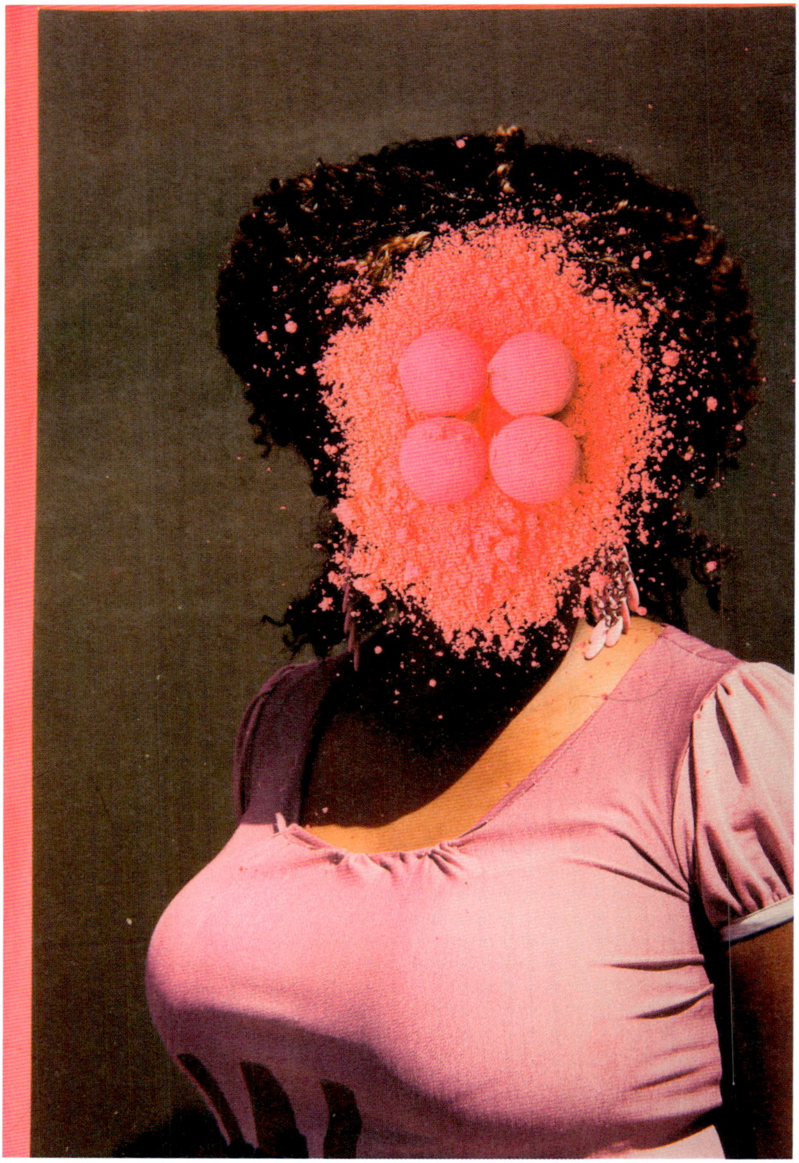

Pink #1 & 2, London, 2013

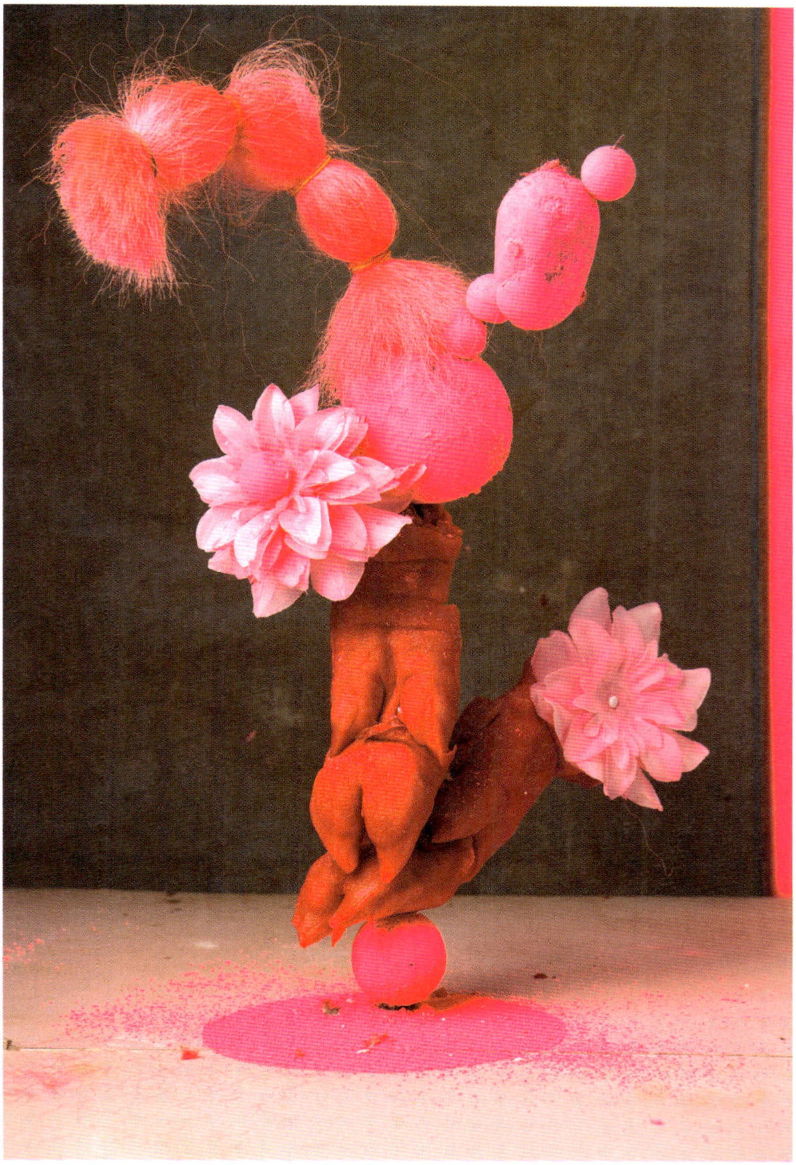

Pink #1 & 2, London, 2013

Olympic Structures

Unconventional views of Olympic architecture, immaculate and empty, captured just a fortnight before London 2012 began.

Janie Airey

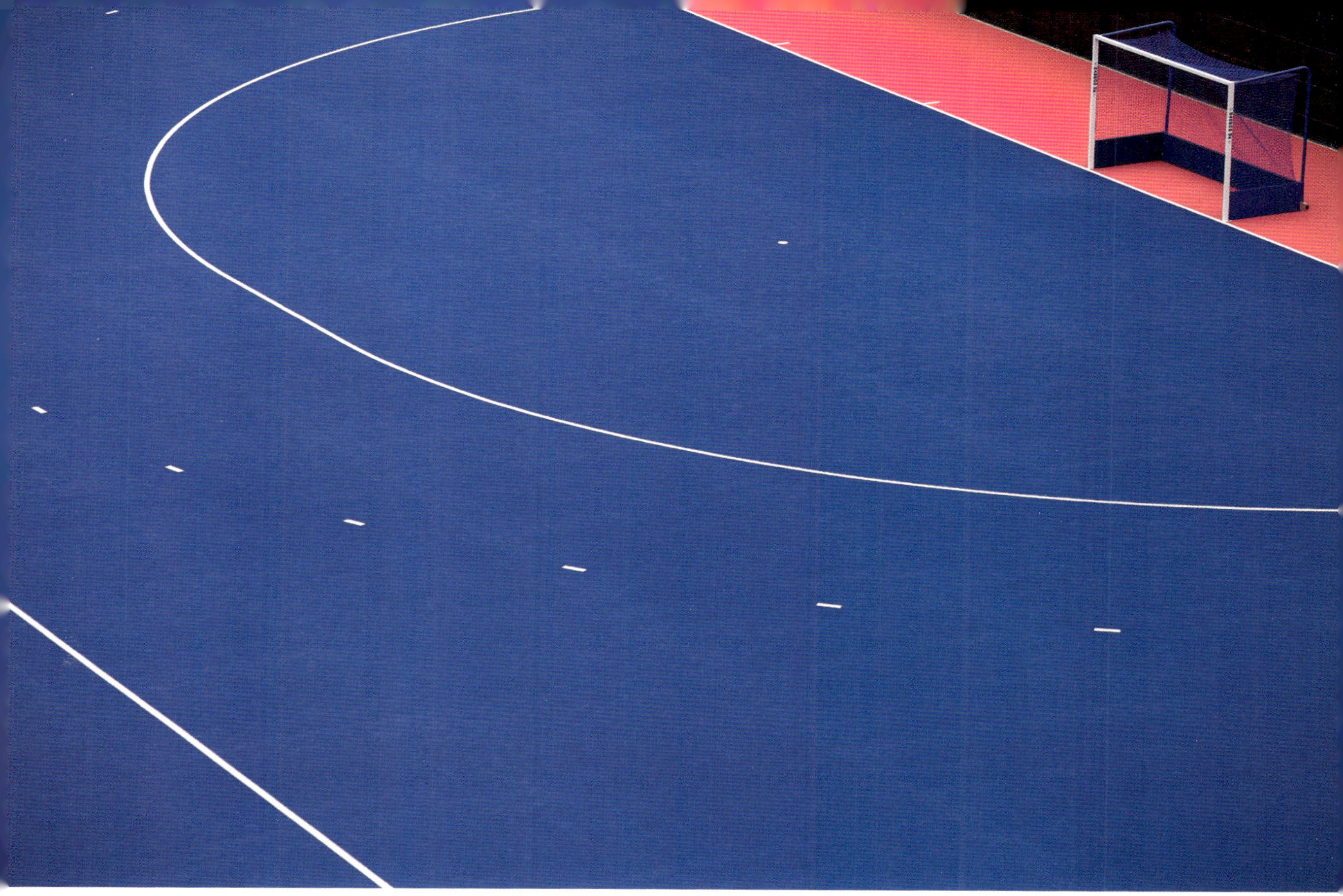

London's Olympic buildings will never look as pristine as they did they when Janie Airey shot them. A fortnight before the Games opened in summer 2012, so new that some spaces were still under construction, there were still barriers here and there. Plastic covered seats in the velodrome. Apart from the odd workman adding finishing touches and a chaperone from the Olympic Delivery Authority, Airey was in the unique position of being free to wander alone around spaces designed to hold thousands. "You're in this big, majestic space where there's supposed to be the roar of the crowd, a buzz," she says. "And there's nothing."

It wasn't just the flawless buildings that made this a novel commission for Airey. A lifestyle and corporate photographer for 15 years, she had never really photographed architecture before. For a first gig, the commission was ideal. "I was allowed to do pretty much what I wanted," she recalls. "There was no pressure to fulfil a particular brief, you just had to make it look good." Bold, graphic, two-dimensional almost to the point of abstraction, her pictures show characterful details shot from nimble angles. One moment we're staring up at the concrete diving boards in Zaha Hadid's Aquatics Centre, the next gazing down to the bright blue floor of the hockey pitch below.

Architectural photography has traditionally stuck to certain conventions. "Shoot the whole building, straighten the edges and shoot it when the light's nice – that's what's expected," Airey explains. Even as contemporary architectural photographers such as Iwan Baan adopt a looser style, most continue work in a similar way: slowly, using a tripod-mounted camera and lenses that shift and tilt to capture the building in perfect perspective. Not Airey. "I lie down, I climb up a ladder, I don't stand and look for an hour and then press the button, I fly around. I'm used to shooting people and they have a short attention span." She shot the Hopkins Architects-designed velodrome while horizontal on the freshly lain, sweet-scented maple floor. "I thought, I'm never going to do this again and unless you fall off your bicycle, you're never going to see it from that perspective." Hers is "an instinctive response to a pure environment".

It's become trendy for photographers to shoot urban decay. Critics accuse them of exploitation but viewers can't get enough of the kind of crumbling architecture we see in French duo Yves Marchand and Romain Meffre's series on Detroit. Snappers flock to Chernobyl to document the eerie abandoned amusement parks that remain there, while photographic blogs such as *Derelict London* anticipate our post-apocalyptic future. The sleek, clean elegance of *Olympic Structures* is the antithesis of "ruin porn", as it's been dubbed – it shows empty buildings full of hope, before they've been ravaged by time.

Airey has been back twice to the Aquatics Centre. On the first occasion, a Michael Phelps race during the Olympic Games, she was "so wrapped in the atmosphere and the people and the noise" that she barely noticed the buildings. But a swim there three years later, as a paying member of the public, gave her a new appreciation of the space and its legacy. "It's like being in the belly of a whale, it's amazing," she says. "If you go to Barcelona or to Rio now you see they've just left everything, falling to bits. People have gone back and photographed the derelict sites. Here, it's been designed to work after the event. They really did think that through." Good for London, but less so for fans of ruin porn. That interior shot of a resplendently dilapidated Aquatics Centre will have to wait.

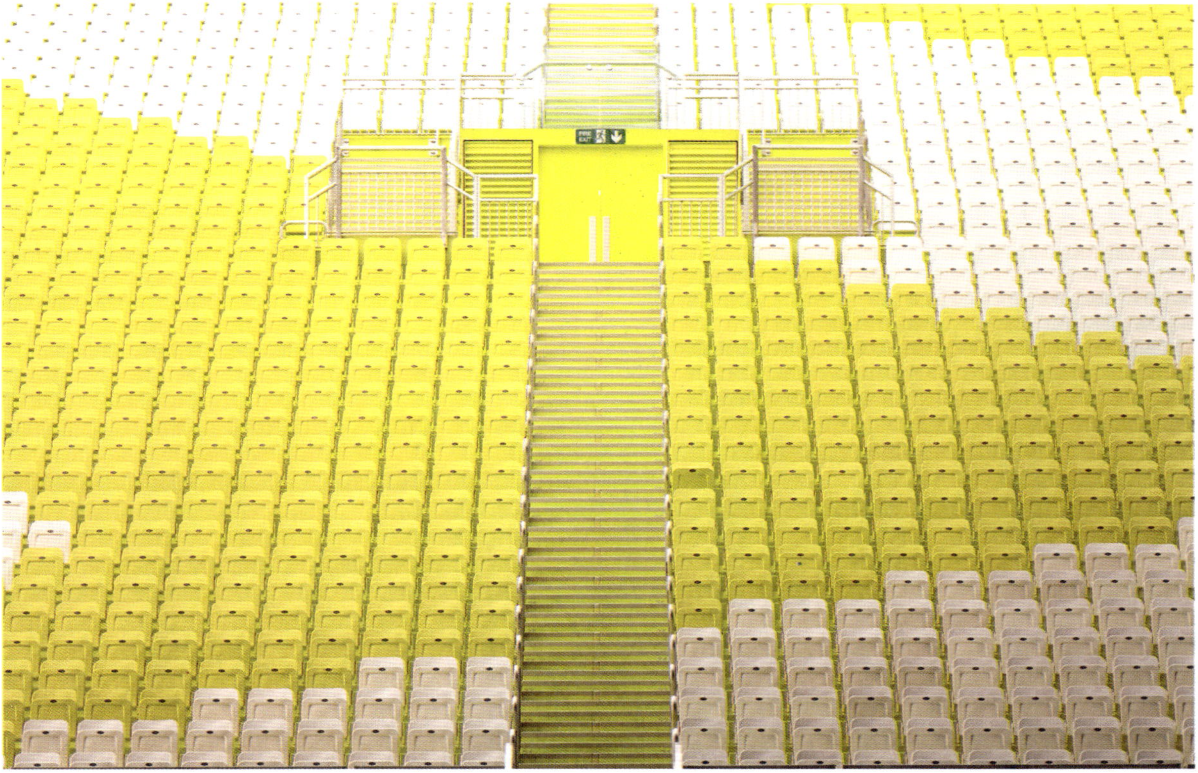

Previous: Hockey Centre by Stanton Williams, London Olympic Park, Stratford, 2012
Above: Aquatics 2 by Zaha Hadid, London Olympic Park, Stratford, 2012

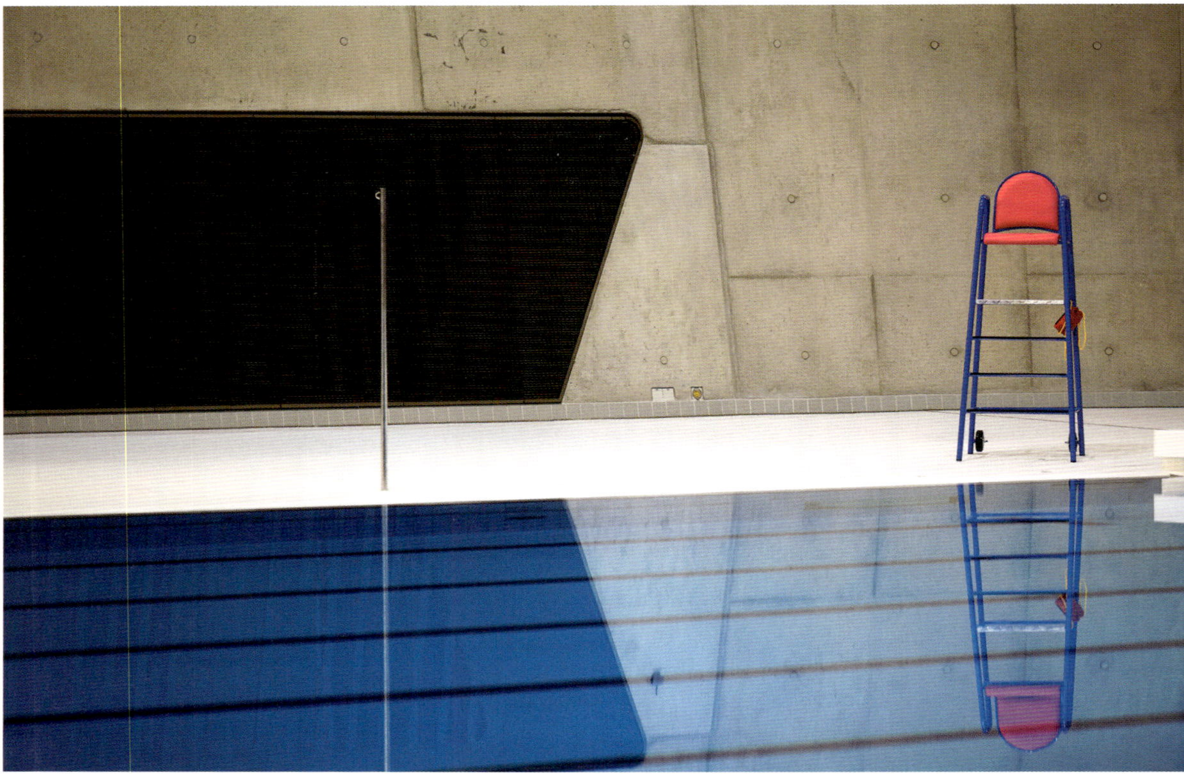

Aquatics 4 by Zaha Hadid, London
Olympic Park, Stratford, 2012

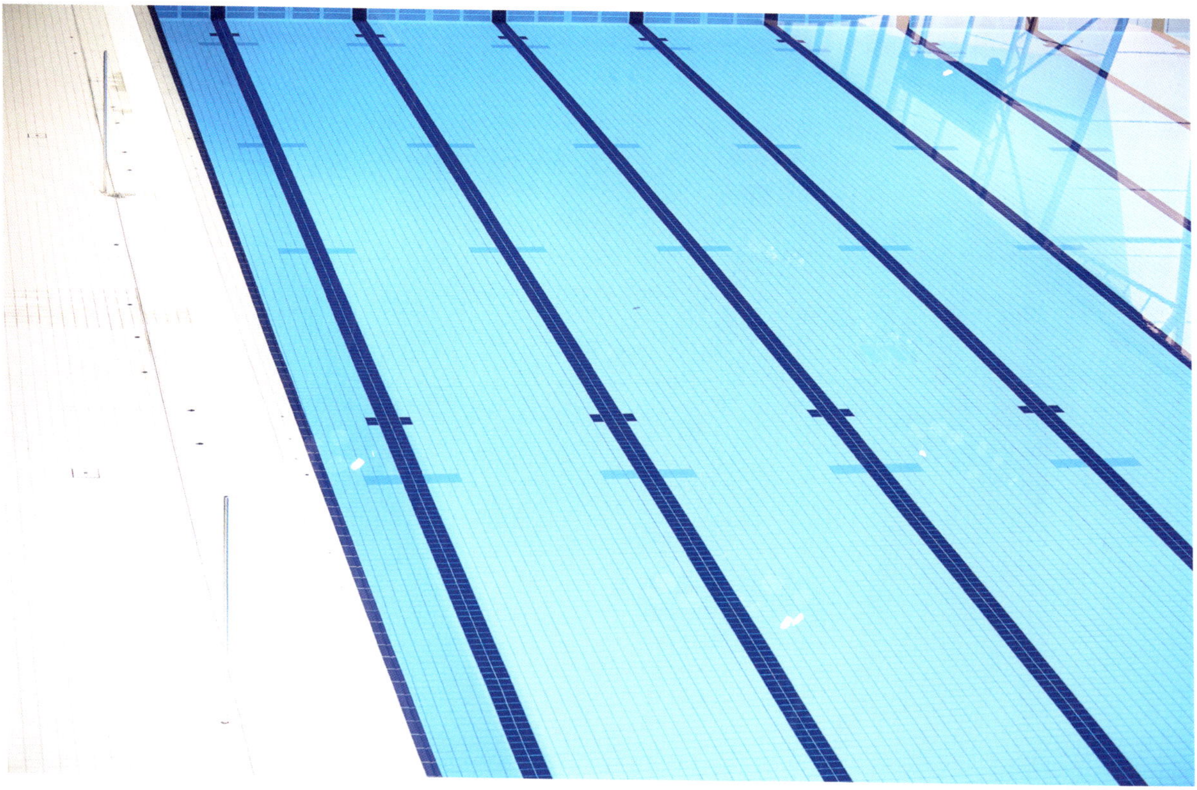

Aquatics 1 by Zaha Hadid, London Olympic Park, Stratford, 2012

Overleaf: Velodrome 1 by Hopkins Architects, London Olympic Park, Stratford, 2012

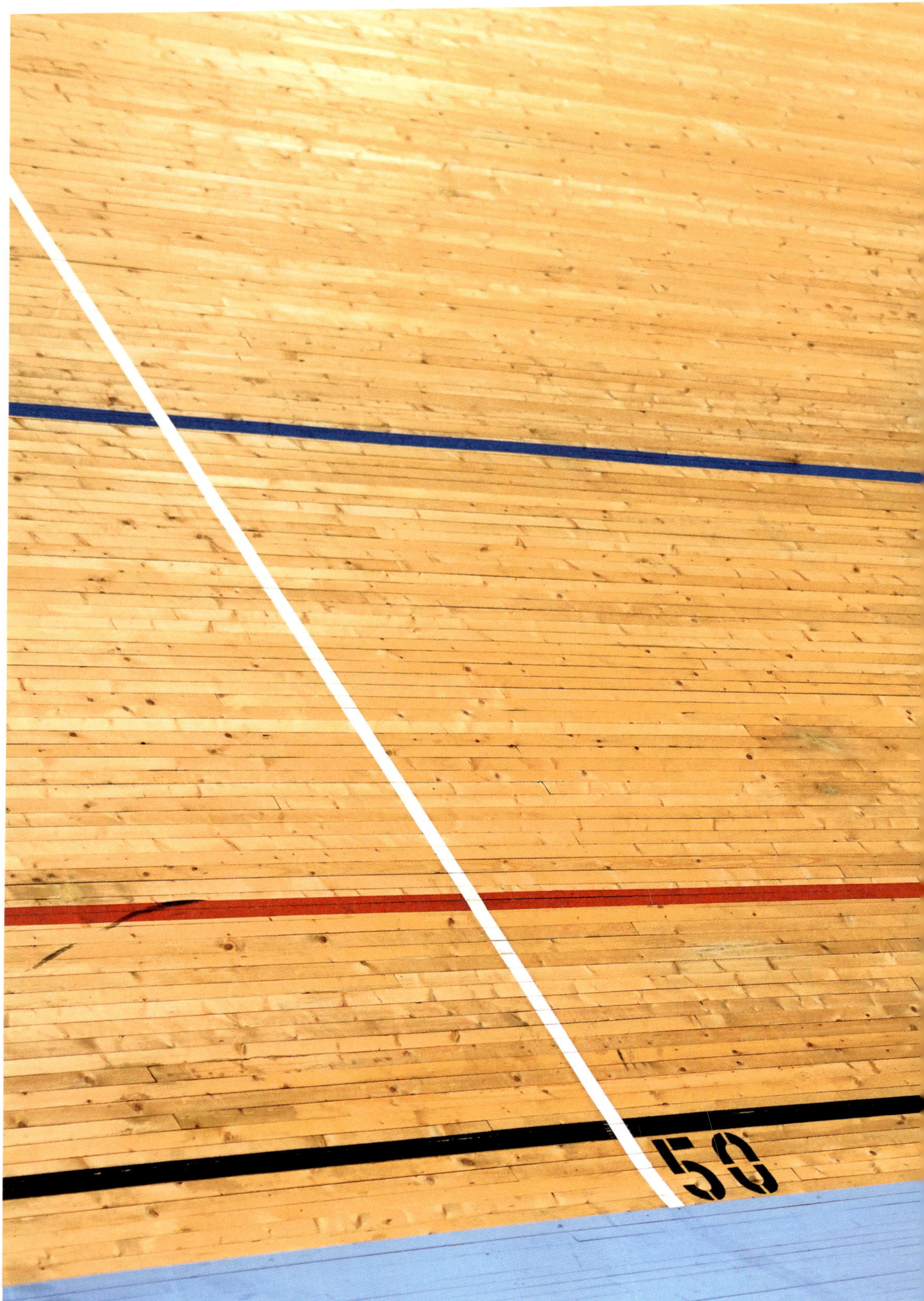
50

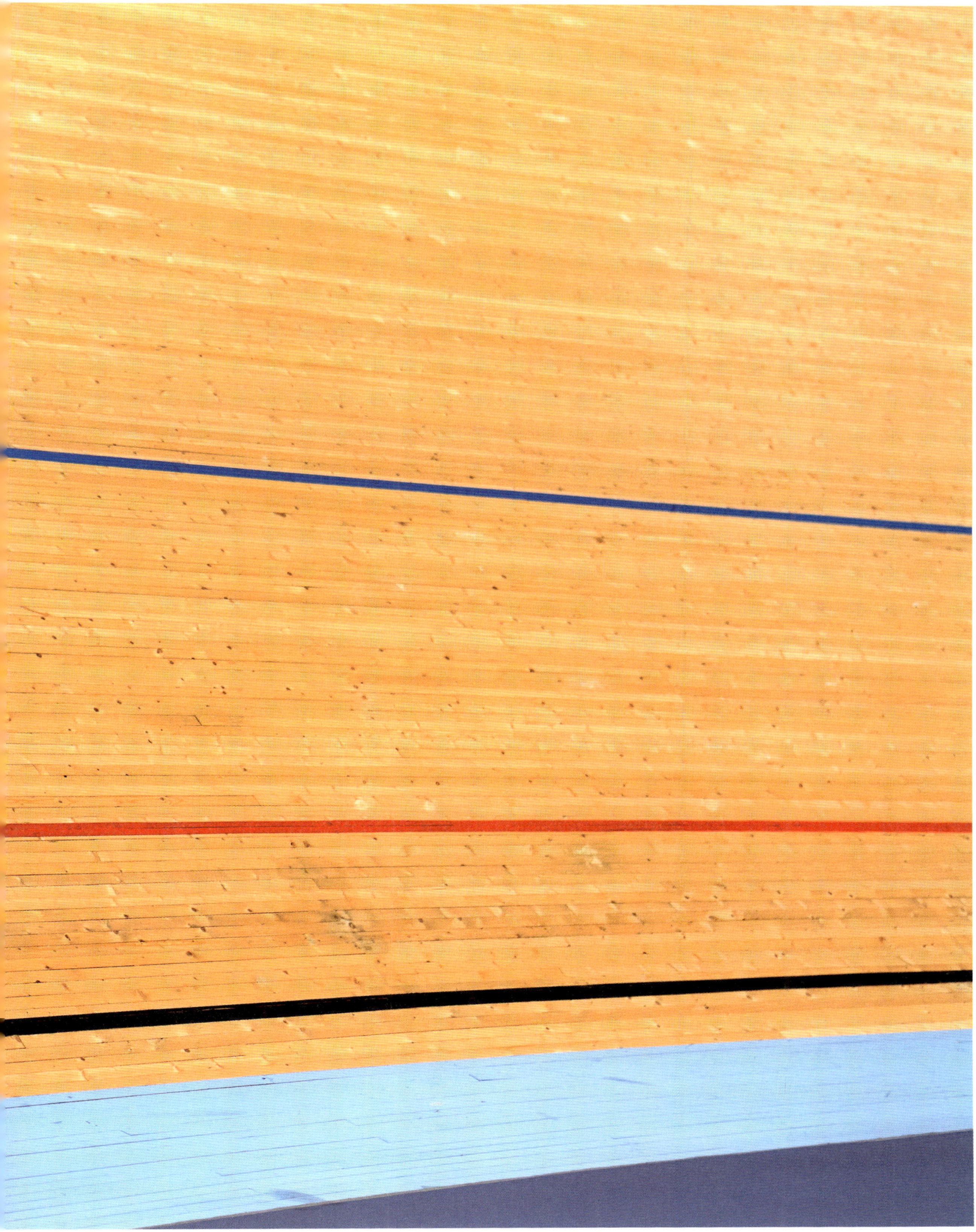

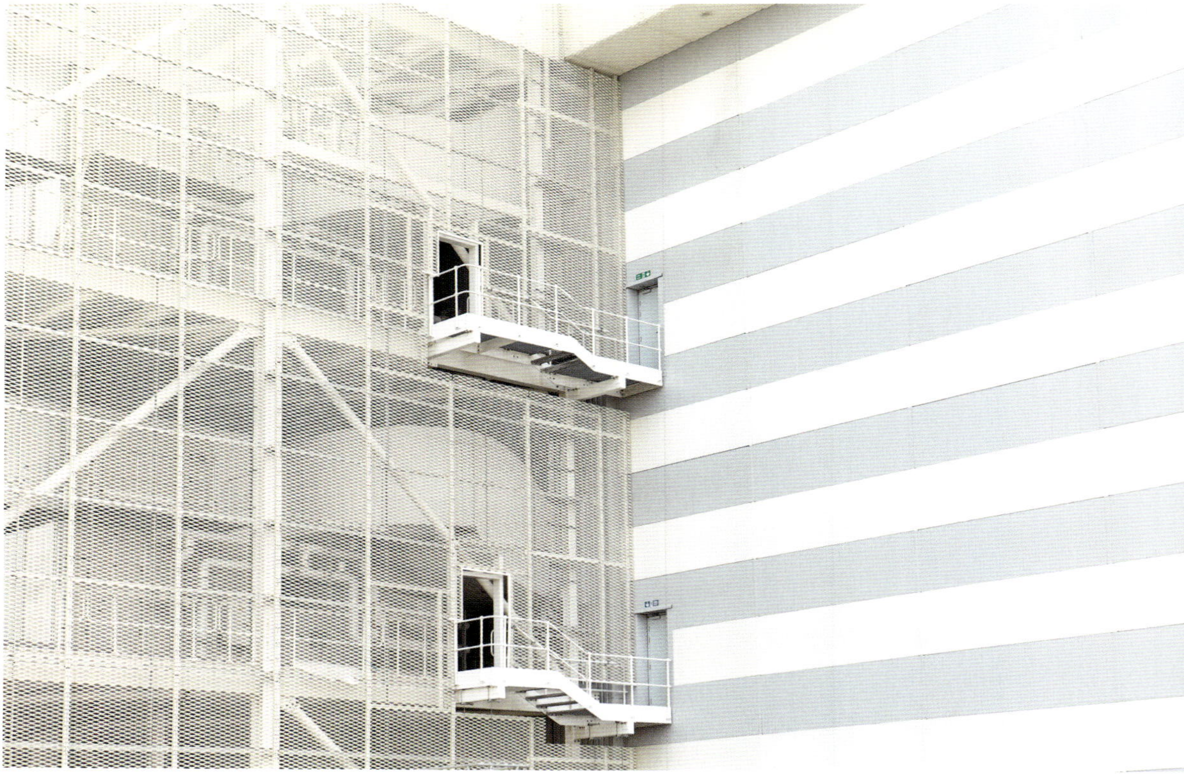

Media Centre by Allies & Morrison,
London Olympic Park, Stratford, 2012

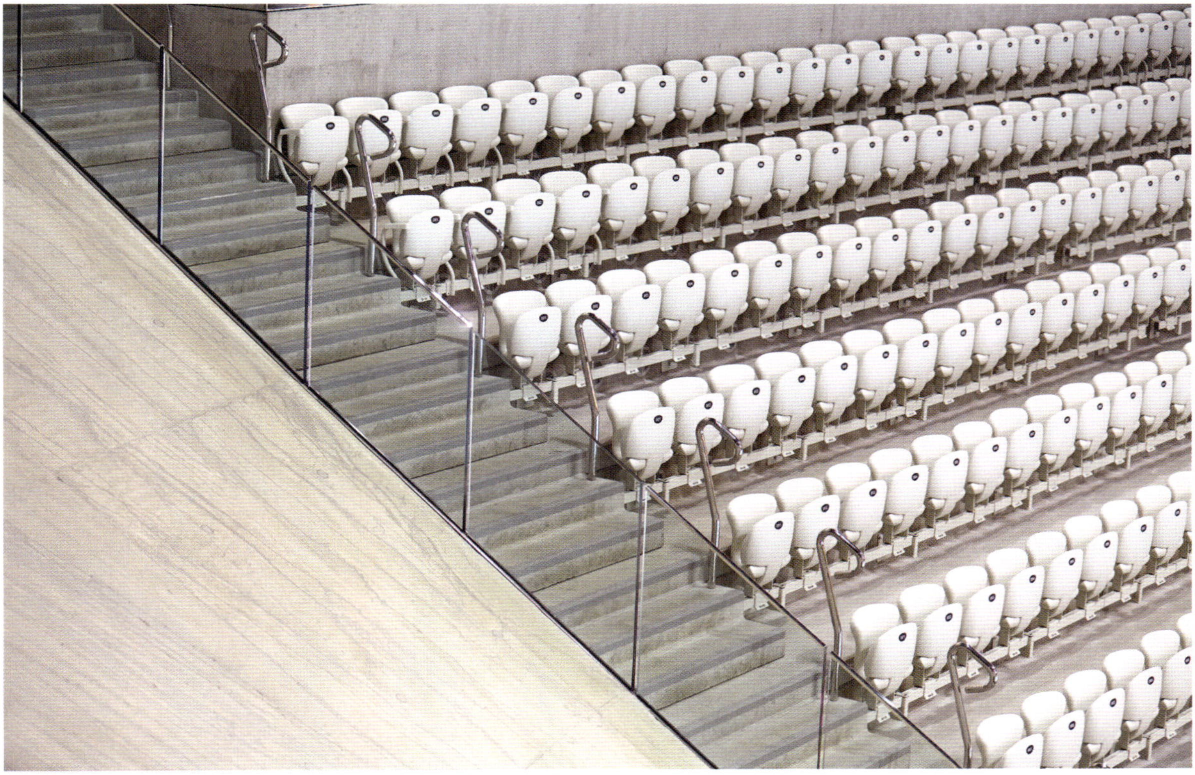

Aquatics 5 by Zaha Hadid, London Olympic Park, Stratford, 2012

Janie Airey

Urbis

Lowry-inspired photographs
find a quiet solitude among the
frantic flow of City commuters.

Mark Sanders

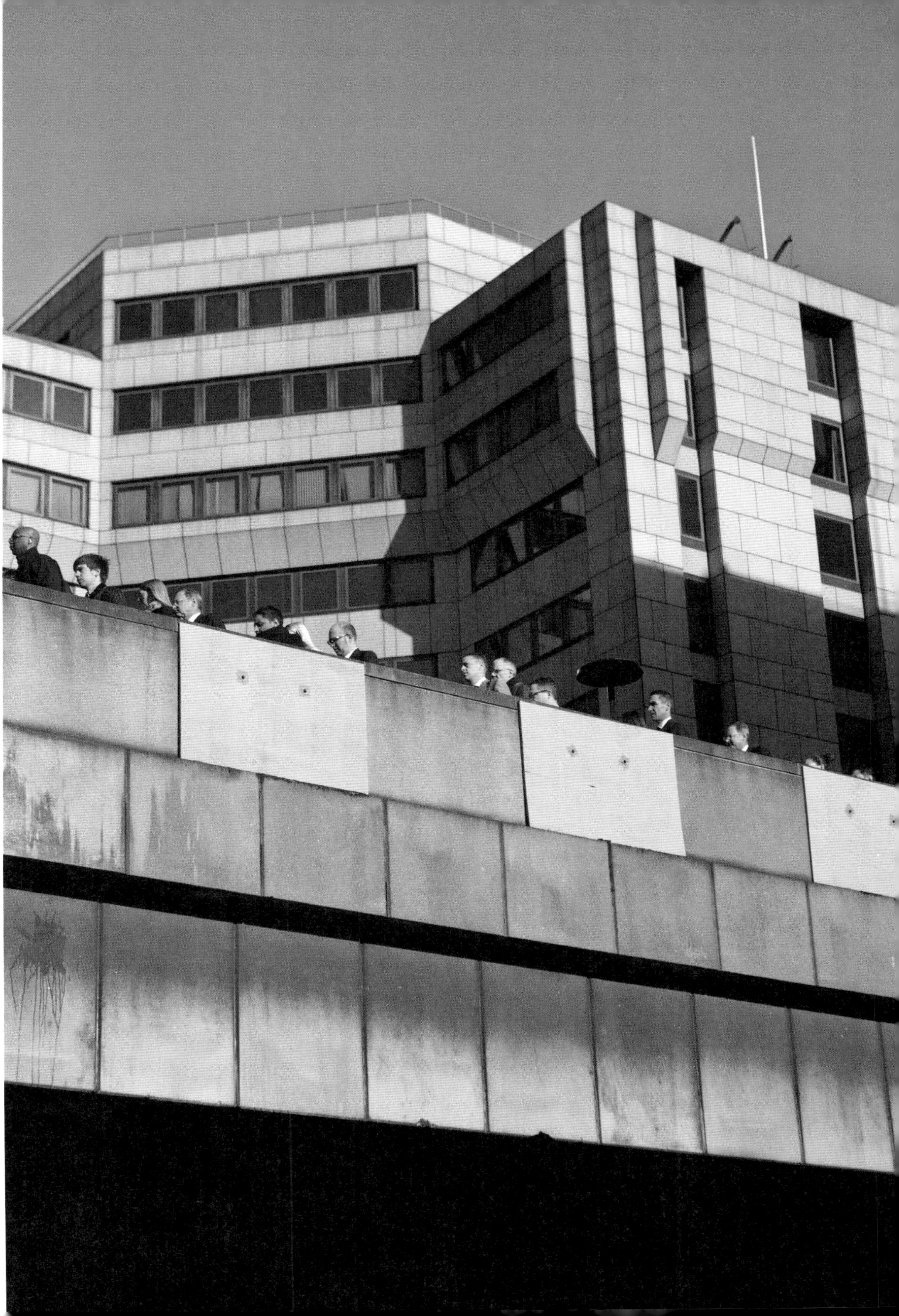

Standing on London Bridge one morning in 2014, the frantic stream of besuited men and women rushing to work in the City flowing around him, photographer Mark Sanders spotted what would become a defining picture of his series, *Urbis*. "The painter L. S. Lowry sprang to mind: everyone looking exactly the same, heads down, like stick figures, as they're walking across the frame from right to left, upright to start with and, by the end, quite bent over."

It took some time before the picture in his mind was matched by his camera. "I kept going back, it became a bit of an obsession to go out in the early morning and see these people," he says, having spent the better part of a year studying them. On the journey to nailing that elusive shot came many others: portraits of people clutching notebooks, reading the paper, absorbed in iPads or simply staring, headphones on, surrounded by the spectacular yet forbidding architecture of the City.

Sanders was struck by how "plugged in" they all were. "Everyone is so focused. In the whole time I was shooting it I think one person noticed me. I wanted to shoot the buildings, too, because I felt like no-one was looking at them." His background as a fashion and lifestyle photographer for clients such as Monocle, Mr Porter and Hardy Amies brought certain preconceptions about the workers he would see on the bridge. "I thought it was going to be lots of people looking really sharp in their suits, with nice briefcases." Instead, he found them with ties undone, hanging loose around their necks, "everyone was wearing their trainers, they've got utility rucksacks on".

What we're seeing here are workers not yet in role. Like athletes walking from the changing room out onto the track, they're inhabiting an in-between space, not private, not public, where they're psyching up for the race but still belong to themselves. This contrasts with other depictions of the Square Mile as a site for work and play such as the 1988 series *Work Stations* by Anna Fox. With their moustaches and pinstriped shirts, Fox's subjects exemplify the image of City boys (as they mostly were) as a brash breed, over-confident, super competitive. Those in *Urbis* seem introverted, muted, sombre, even – perhaps a sign of their changing status in a post-crash world.

The tranquillity that runs through these pictures is at odds, Sanders admits, with how hectic it is to be in the commuter crush. "If you go towards the station you've got everyone coming towards you, you feel like you're going against this weight and nobody's stopping for you or getting out your way, it's quite aggressive." Sometimes Sanders, who has never had a desk job, would put down his camera and soak up the ambience. "I didn't want to live it all through the lens, I wanted to observe as well, to try to get a feeling for myself of what it must be like to work in the City," he says, adding, "Because nobody noticed me and nobody interacted with me, at times it felt very lonely." Nonetheless, there's a wistful elegance to Urbis that turns the everyday grind of commuting into something almost noble.

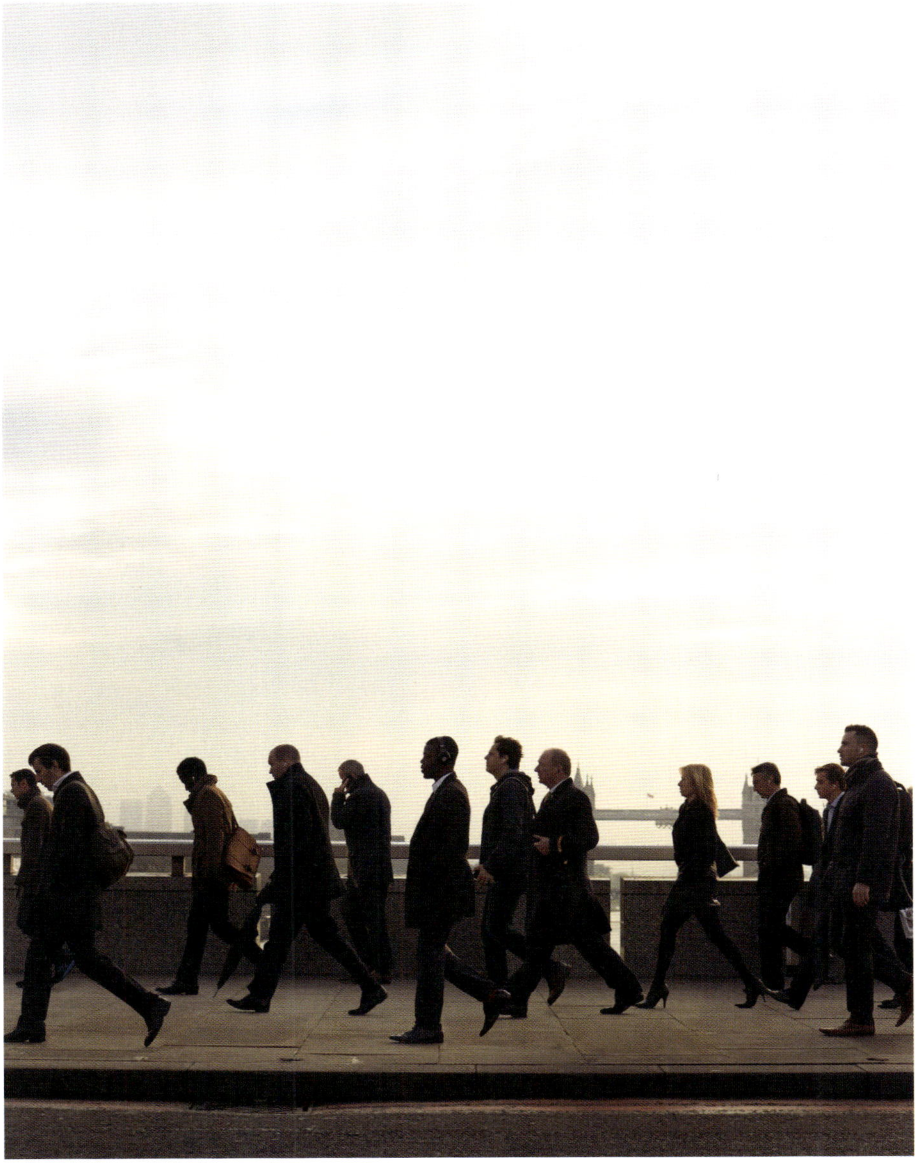

Previous and above: Urbis, London, 2015

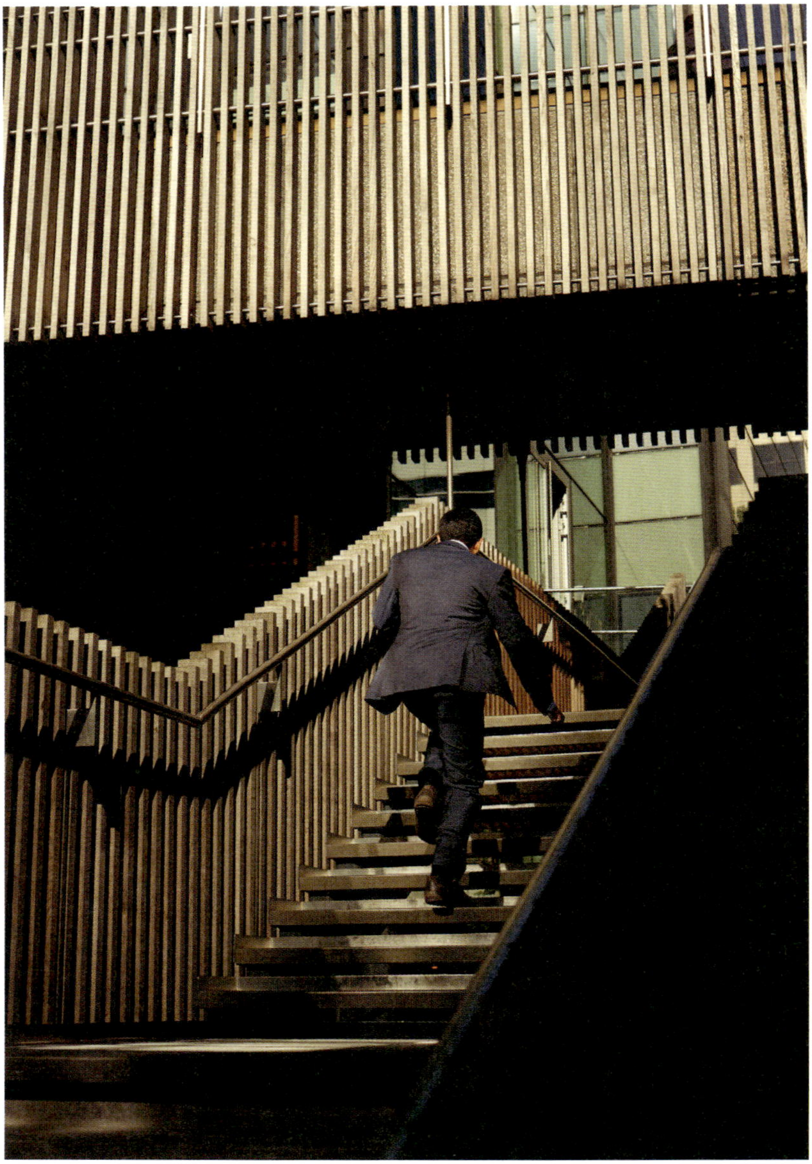

Urbis, London, 2015

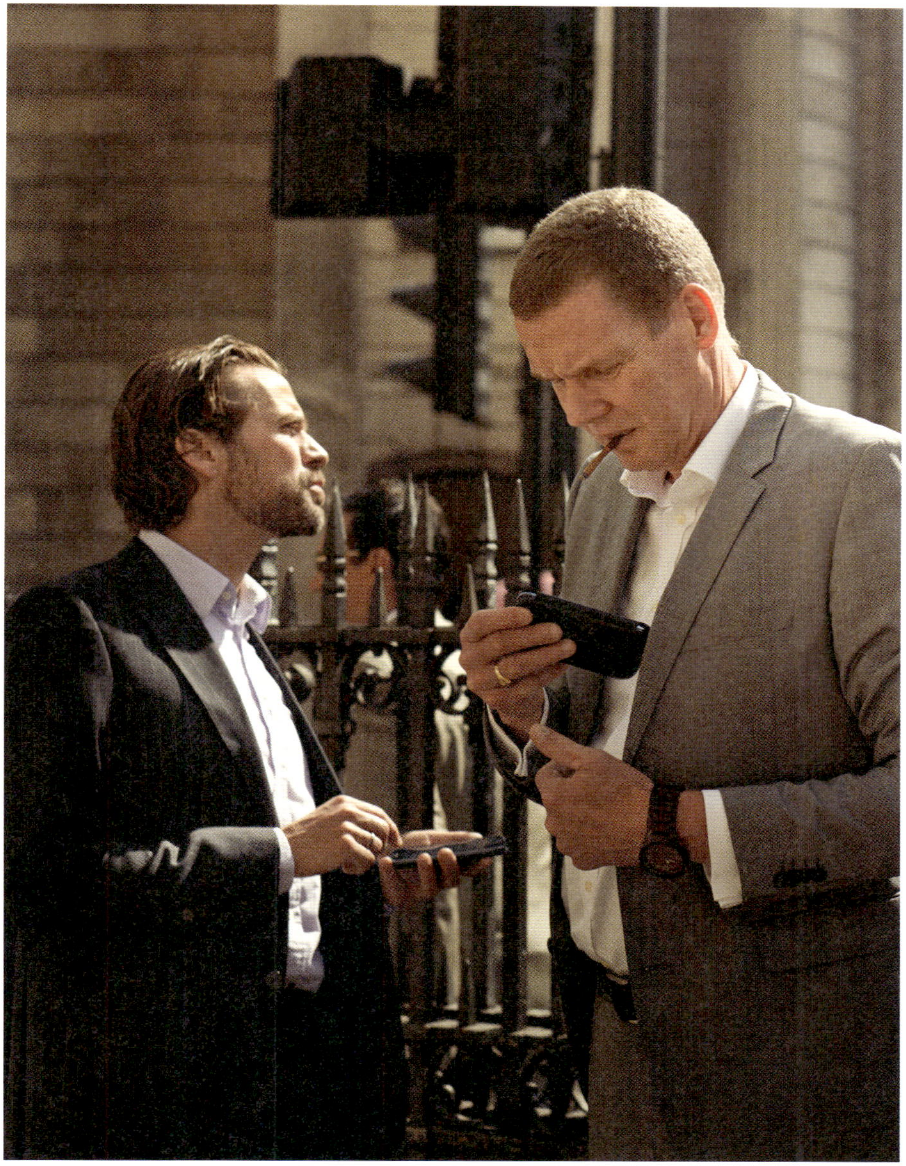

Urbis, London, 2015

Mark Sanders

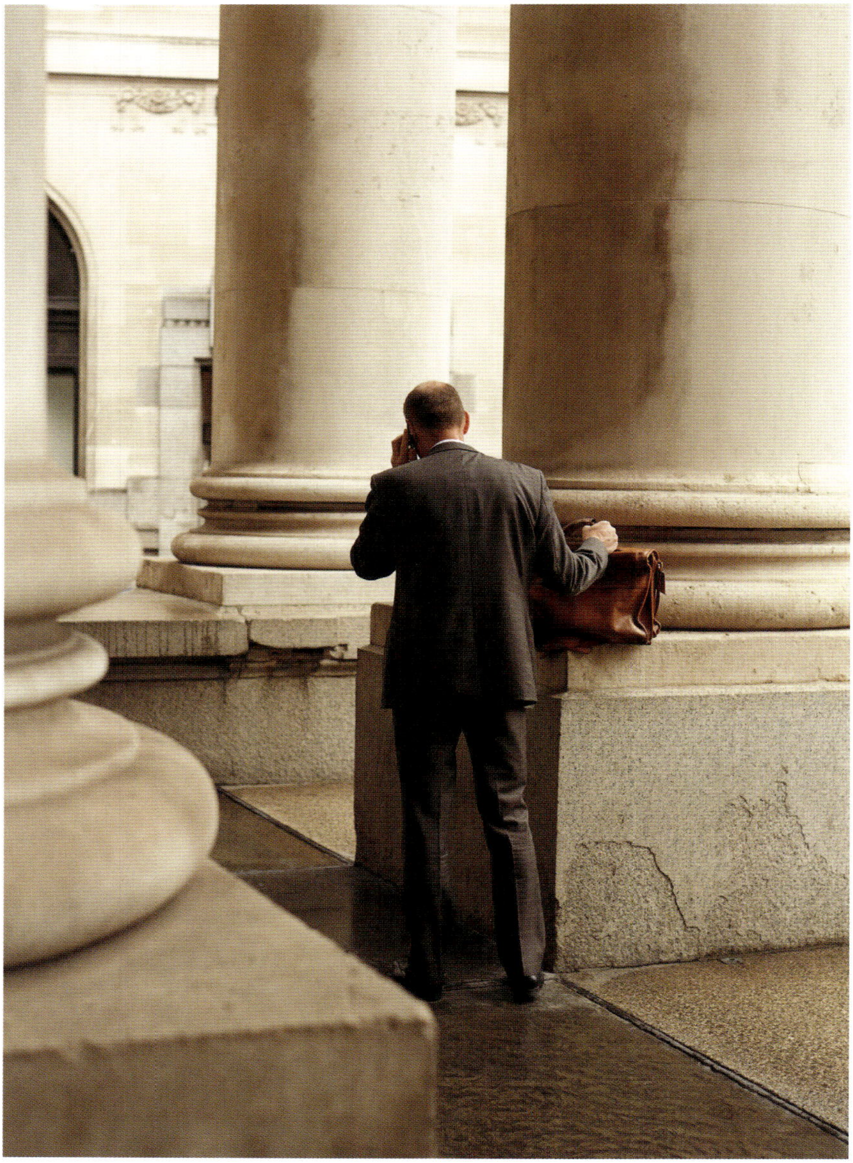

Urbis, London, 2015

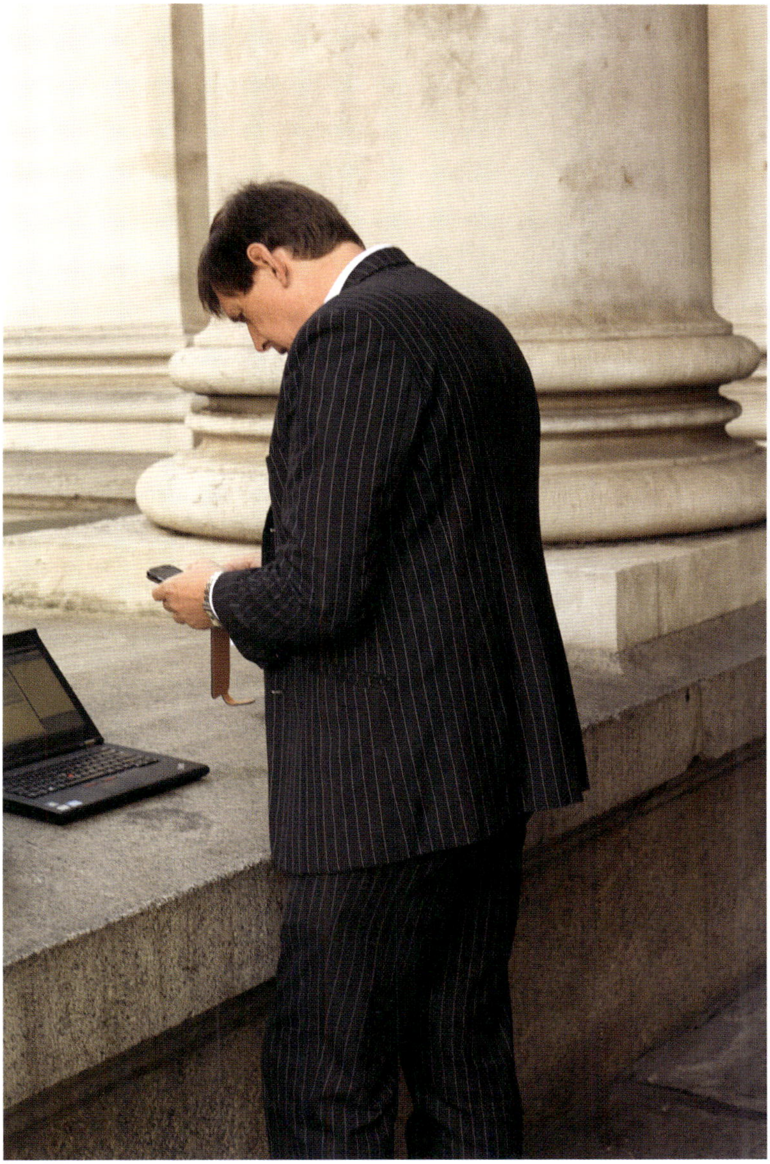

 Urbis, London, 2015 Mark Sanders

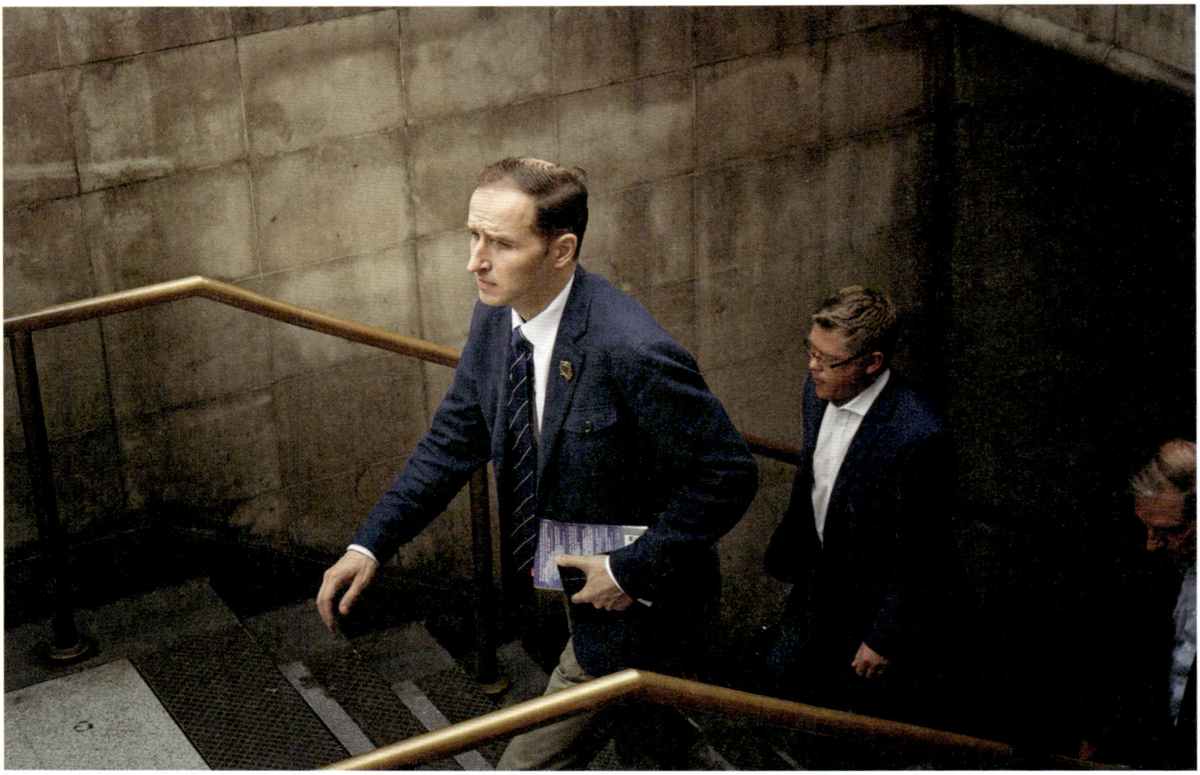

Urbis, London, 2015

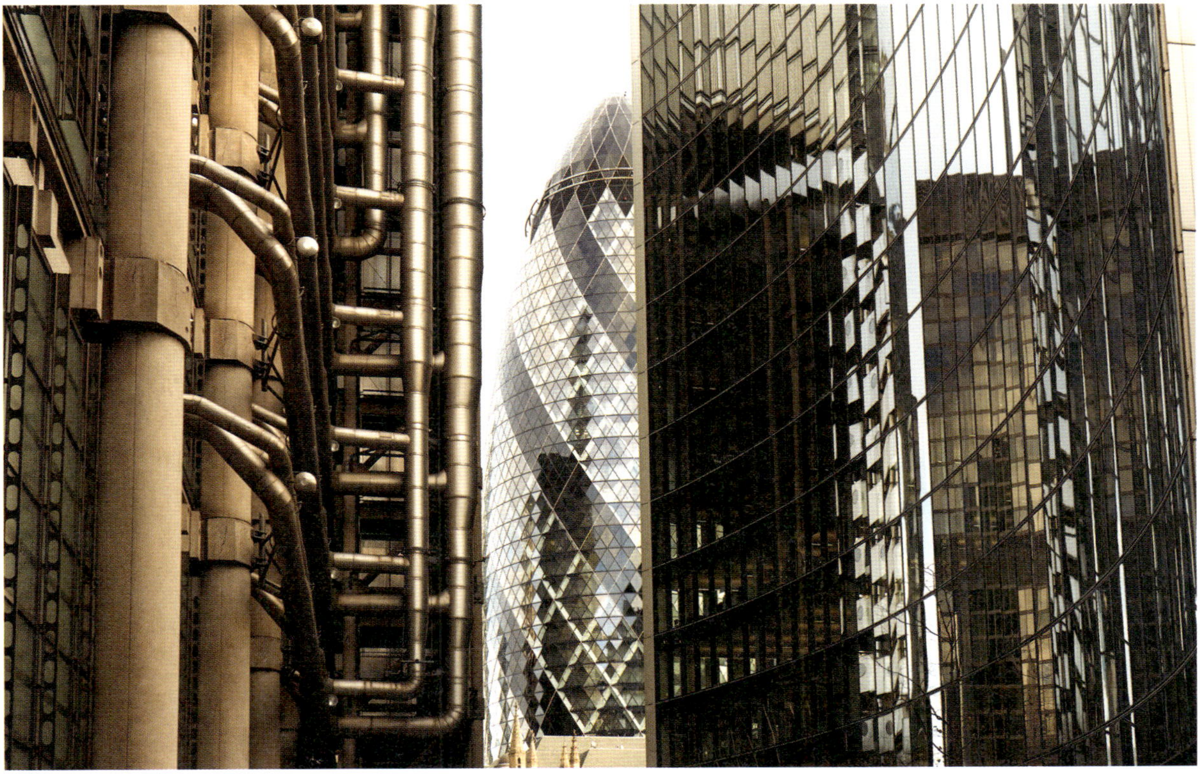

Urbis, London, 2015

Mark Sanders

Metropole

Vertiginous multiple exposures mimic the confusion the photographer experiences when looking up at London's rapidly changing skyline.

Lewis Bush

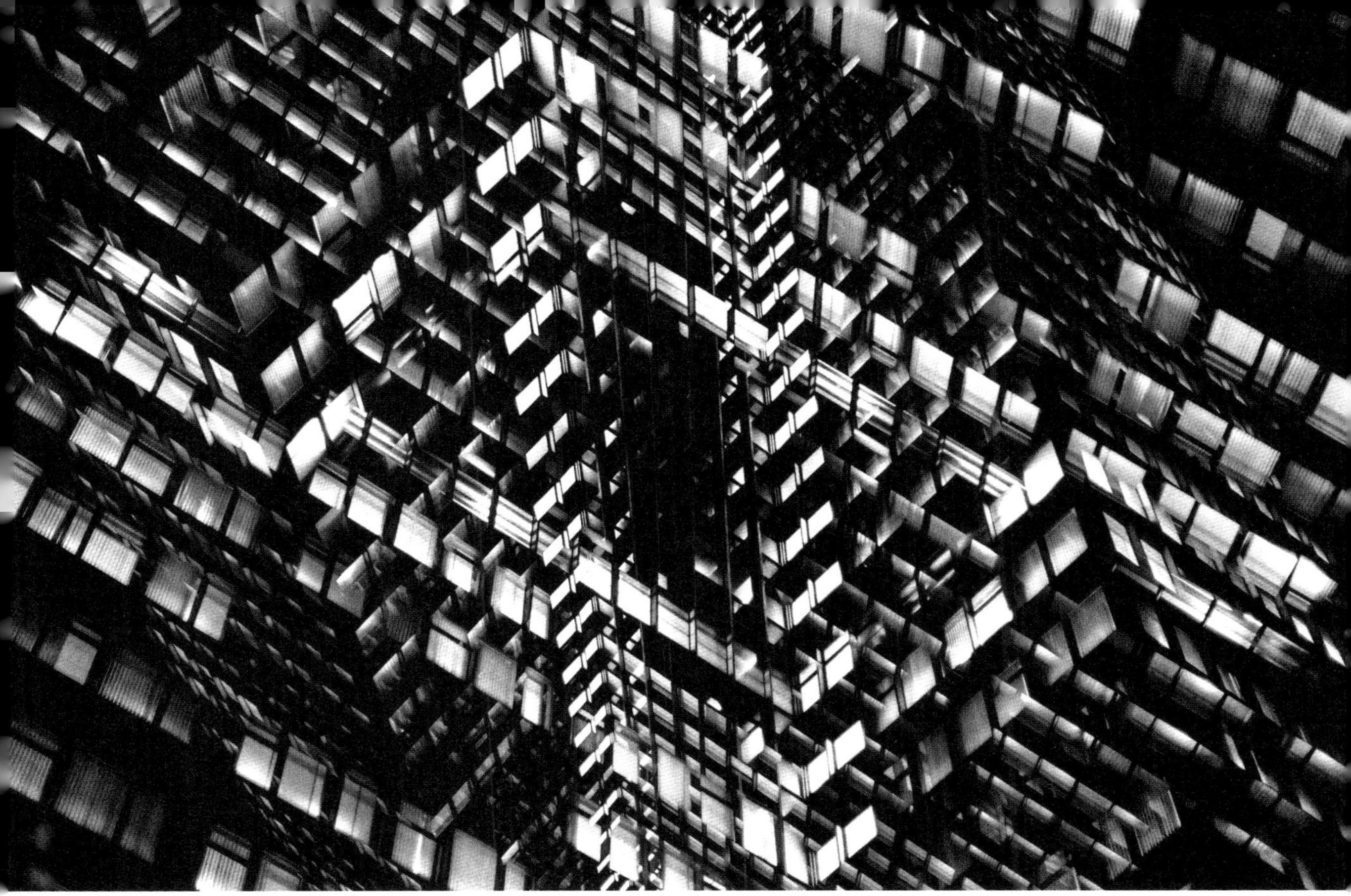

Looking at Lewis Bush's photographs of London skyscrapers is an unsettling experience. You can make out buildings but you can't tell where they begin or where they end. They're shot in high-contrast black and white, with multiple images layered one on top of the other, intensifying and distorting the more you look. Like a painting by the Vorticist artist Wyndham Lewis or the Magic Eye pictures so popular in the 1990s, they suck you in, spit you out and leave you giddy.

And this is exactly how Bush wants you to feel. It's how he, a lifelong Londoner, now feels when he strolls the once-familiar city streets. "Increasingly, I find London a disorientating place," he says. "If I haven't been to an area for six months it's not uncommon that I'll go there and the landmarks I previously used have been knocked down and replaced."

When the Shell Centre, the oldest edifice to feature in *Metropole*, was built in the 1960s it was the highest tower in London, a herald of the upward building frenzy that began in the 1980s and continues today. "The city used to be low-lying and historically didn't have buildings over five stories. Since then it's been transformed into a city in the image of New York or Shanghai", all swanky office blocks and high-rise luxury flats, inaccessible and unaffordable to most Londoners.

It's not the first time that Bush has turned his lens on London. For a previous project, *Camera Obscured*, he used a homemade pinhole camera to document sites where photographers are banned (or at least strongly discouraged) and his recent series *City of Dust* expands on *Metropole*'s themes of what London's febrile redevelopment has cost the city.

Bush shot *Metropole* in 2014 during dark, winter walks around the Square Mile, Blackfriars, Nine Elms and Elephant and Castle. The pictures are digital double exposures – a modern twist on a technique favoured by photographers since the medium's invention. Victorians like William H. Mumler used it to add fake ghosts to their pictures, a practice known as 'spirit photography', while in the 20th century Boris Mikhailov merged snaps of everyday grind in the Soviet Union with nude portraits to imbue them with a sense of dreamy yearning.

Here, the double exposures don't immediately register – and the result is menacing. Some pictures recall lonely stretches of outer space more than bustling London, others echo shots in Hitchcock's *Vertigo*. Bush was heavily inspired by cinema – both by experimental documentaries such as Dziga Vertov's *Man With A Movie Camera* and Paul Strand's *Manhattan*, as well as dystopian movies, from Fritz Lang's *Metropolis* to Ridley Scott's *Blade Runner*. "I'm interested in science fiction and horror, because even though superficially a fantasy, it's often about something that's occurring at the time," he says.

The Shell Centre has long since been surpassed as London's tallest building. Today that title goes to the Shard, which more than any other tower symbolises the cash-driven, visually aggressive skyline development *Metropole* rallies against. "These buildings are sold as spectacles that we should all enjoy," says Bush. "Renzo Piano once described the Shard as a gift to Londoners. The thing about a gift is that if you don't want it, you can return it." And, in a way, that's exactly what *Metropole* does.

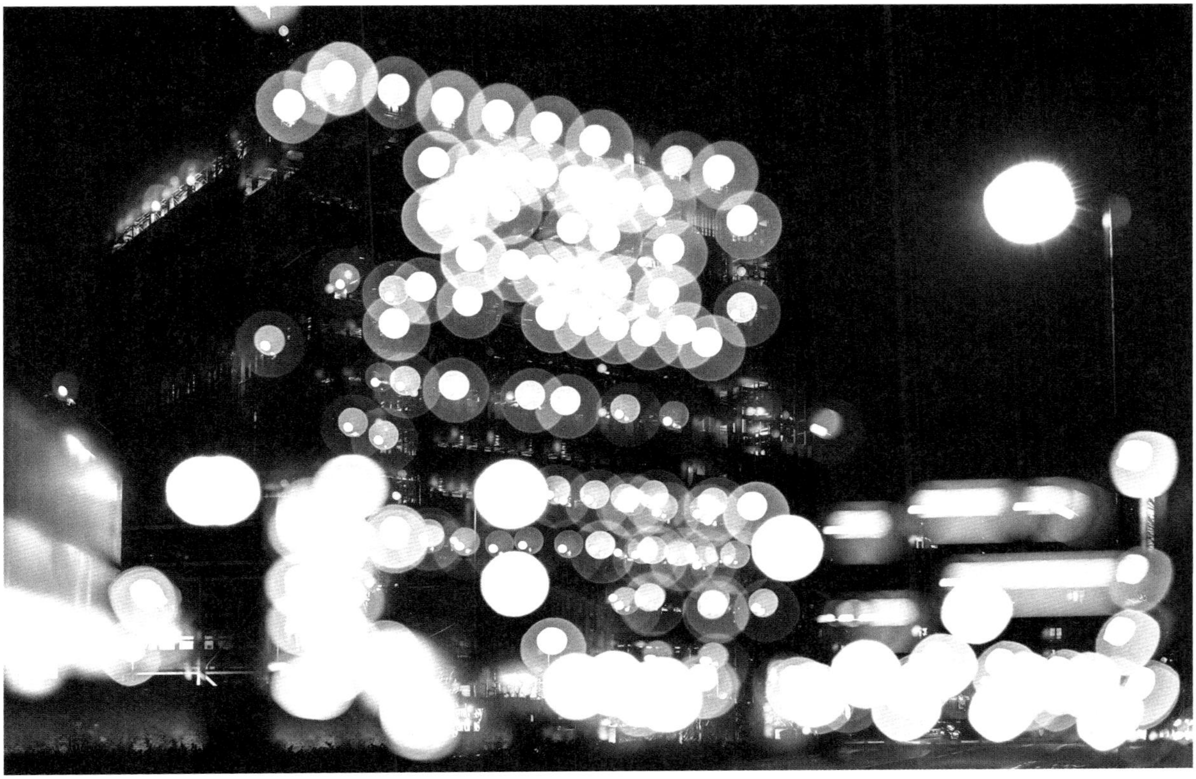

Previous: Euston, London, 2014
Above: Albert, London, 2015

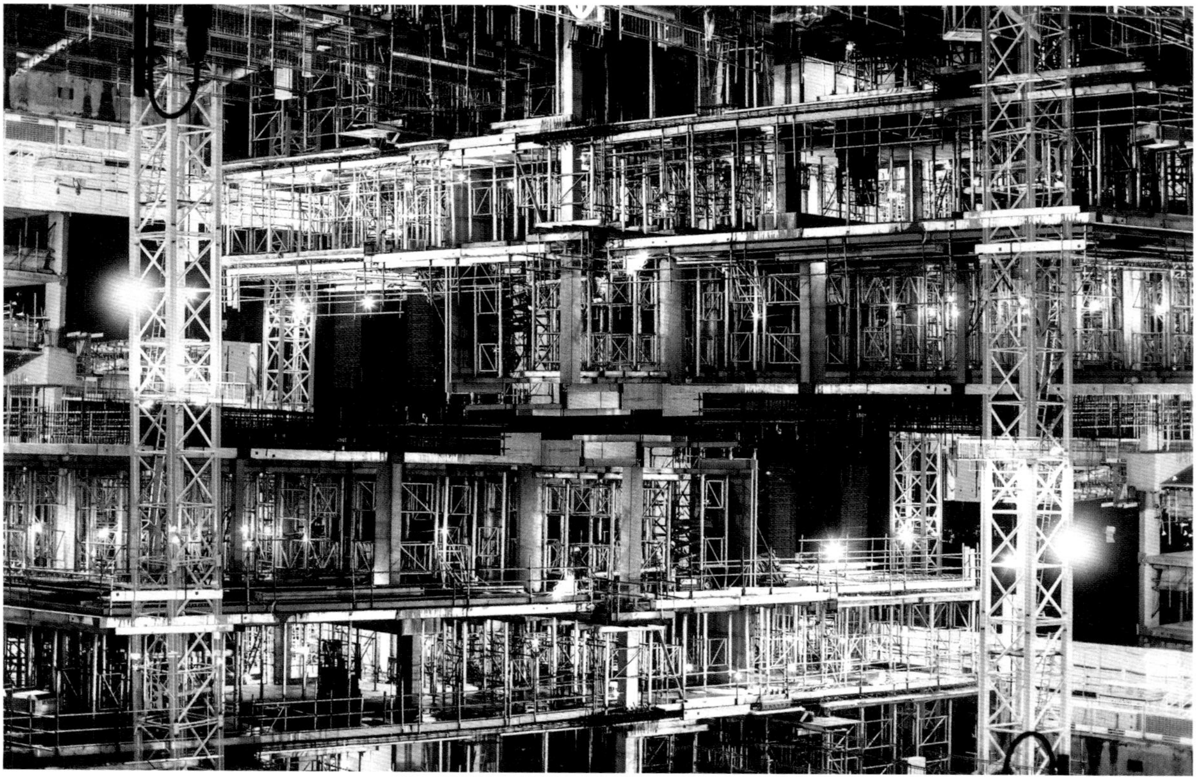

Elephant, London, 2014

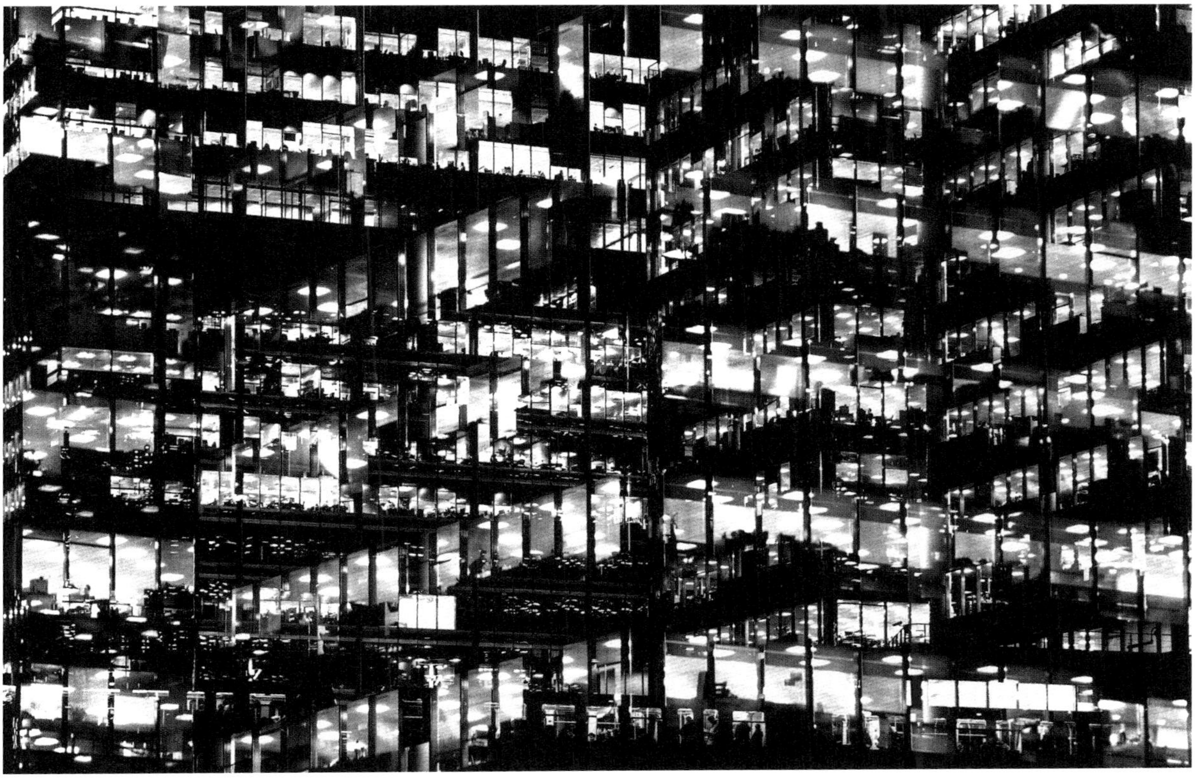

Cabot, London, 2015
Overleaf: Thomas, London, 2015

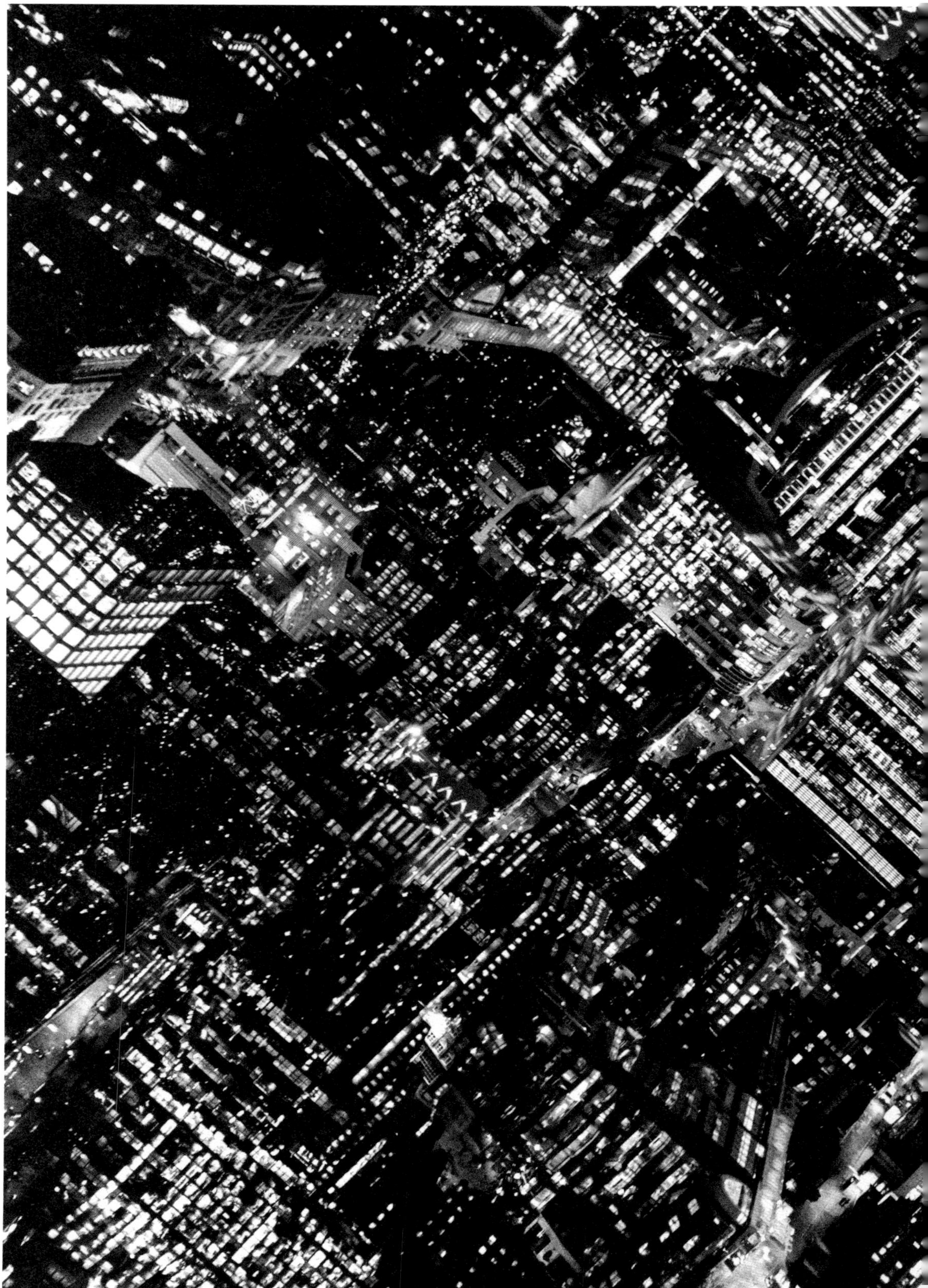

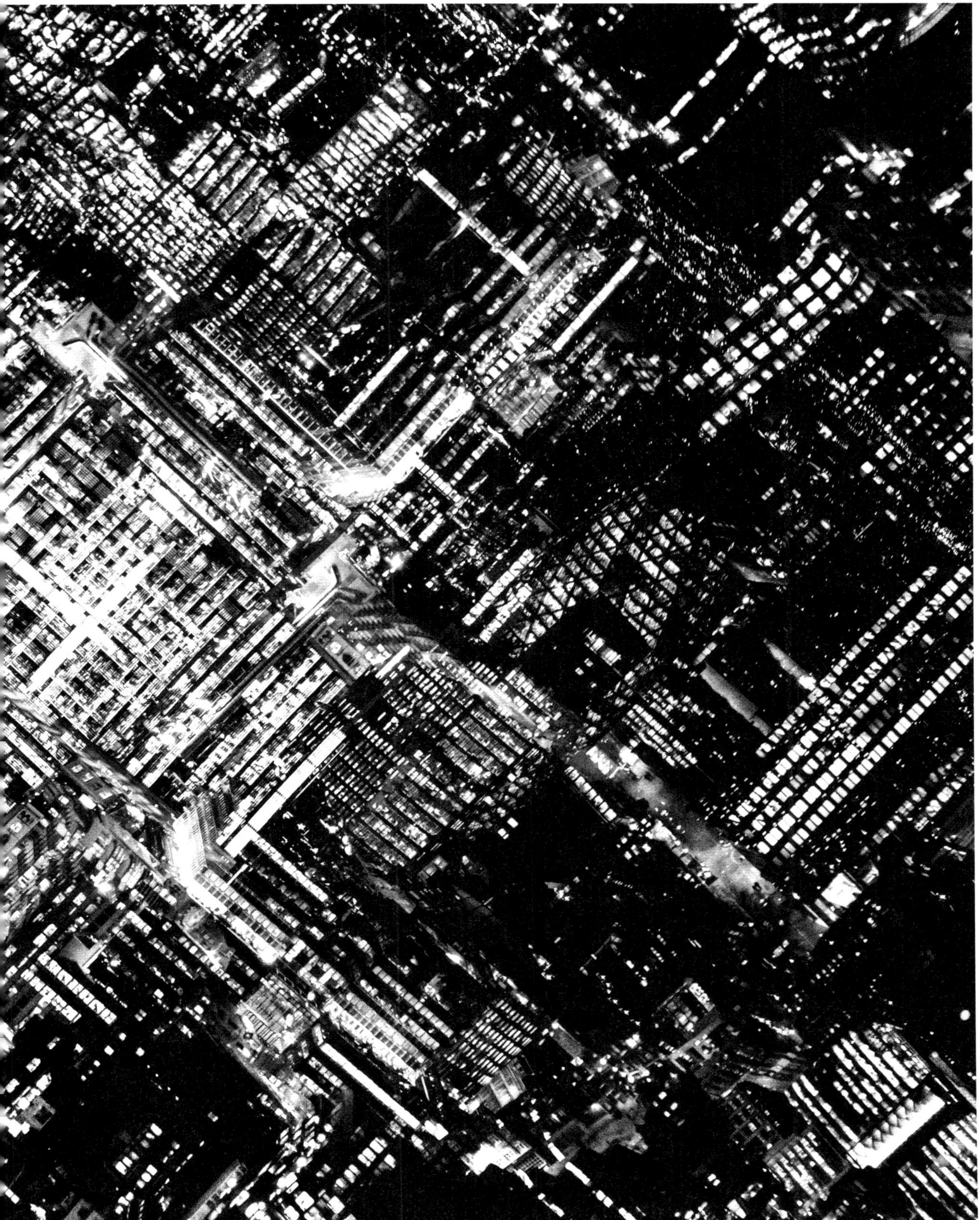

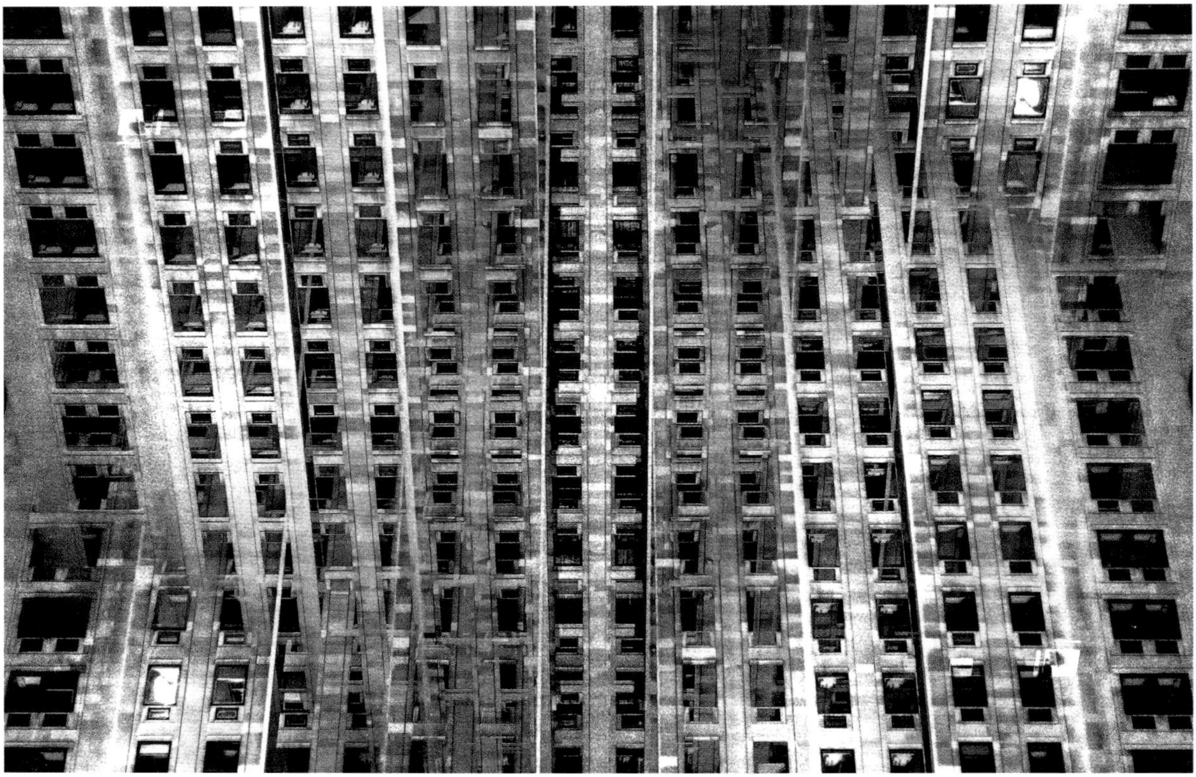

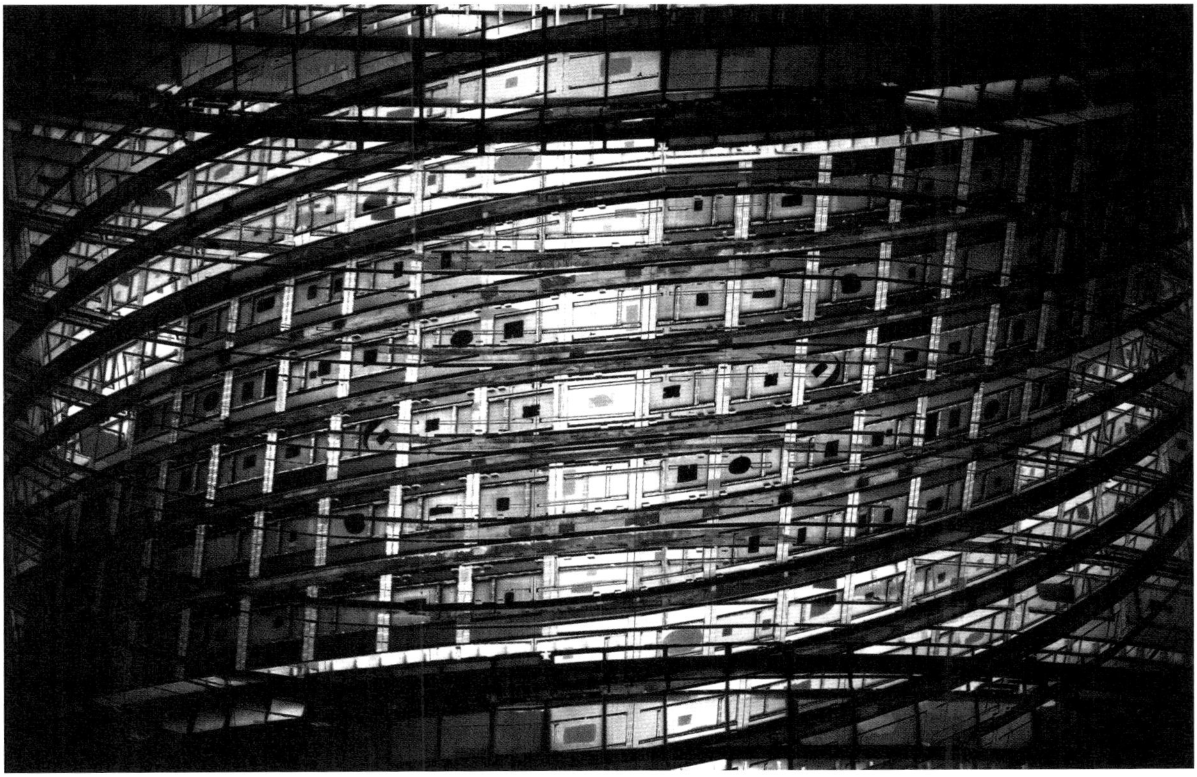

Lambeth, London, 2014

Lewis Bush

Under London

Peeling back the city's skin to explore
the hidden histories unearthed
by archaeologists working on the
Crossrail development.

Simon Norfolk

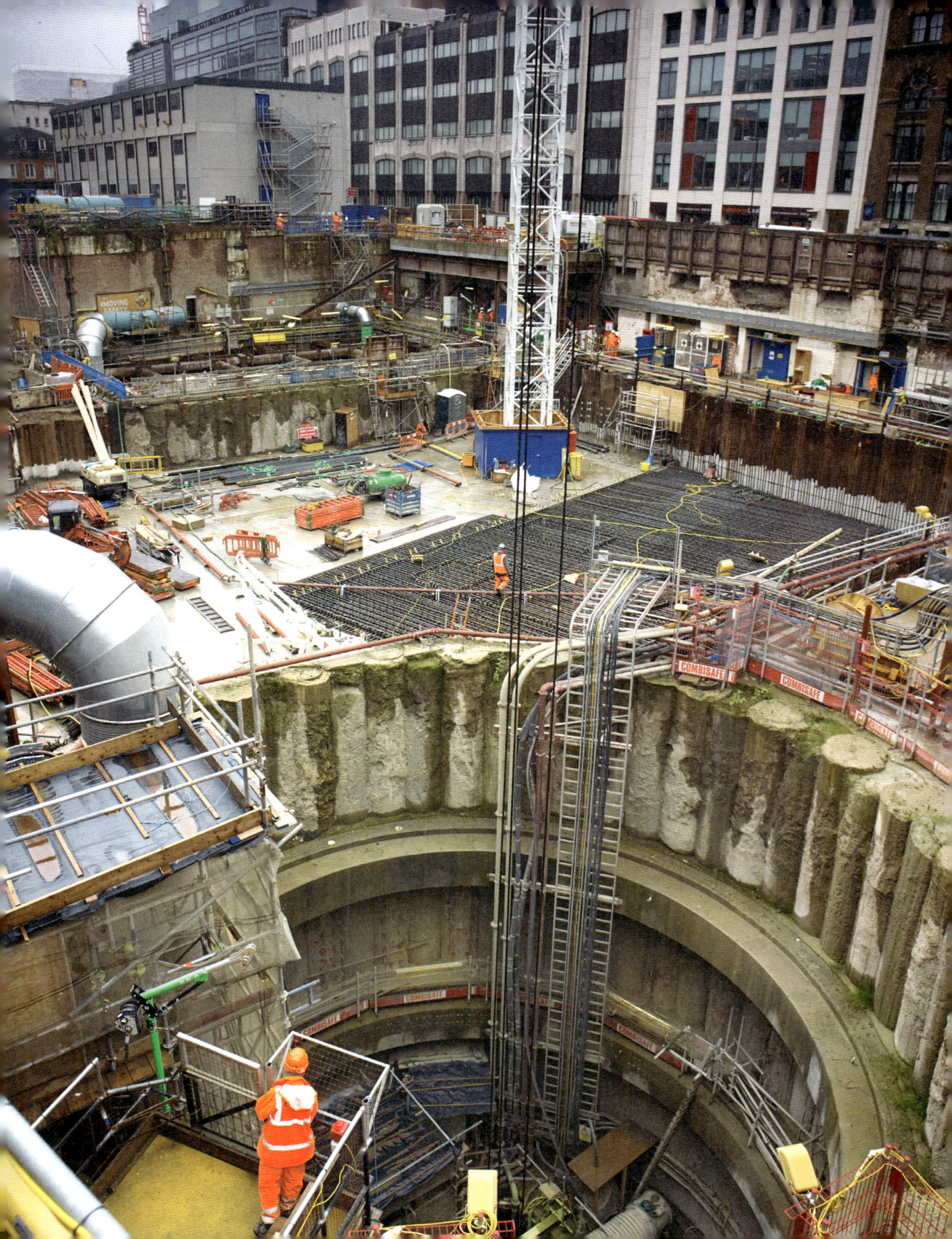
COMBISAFE

"I've always been more of an archaeologist than a photographer," says Simon Norfolk. It seems like a surprising comment from someone acclaimed for stirring photographic studies of landscapes that have seen conflict. But for the past 10 years the Lagos-born, London-based photographer has also shot archaeological sites for *National Geographic*, a role that's taken him everywhere from Guatemala's Mayan ruins to Afghanistan's Buddhist temples and, closer to home, London's Crossrail.

On completion, the Crossrail line will run for 73 miles through London and into the Home Counties. By law, development projects in London must include an archaeological element because the city has been in the same location for thousands of years so workers are bound to find something of note. "Normally you'd dig down and find some Tudor stuff, then you'd dig further and find some Roman stuff," Norfolk explains. "But with Crossrail they were digging in North Woolwich, in Paddington, in Central London, in the City – the layers of London's history all being poked about with at the same time."

Shot over a year, *Under London* has two strands. The first is a series of documentary photographs of the tunnels being constructed. The second is more artistic. Inspired by the Crossrail finds, Norfolk sourced objects already in the Museum of London archive to represent each period revealed by the dig, and photographed them in relevant locations. The idea was to show "an arc in the history of London", illustrated by Roman-era skulls through to a souvenir china plate dating from Queen Victoria's reign, taking in Anglo Saxon axes and a Shakespearean cannonball along the way. In one picture we see an ethereal blue perfume bottle against a background of contemporary skyscrapers. It is 12th-century, probably Syrian, and proof, says Norfolk, that there were Muslim traders living in London back then.

Although the archive is a gold mine of artefacts, there were limitations on what Norfolk could choose – nothing too big, too small or too valuable. For ethical reasons he could only photograph human remains in the position they were found, and to shoot in locations such as Buckingham Palace required permission. "There was no spontaneity whatsoever," says Norfolk. The council needed to know in advance the exact spot for each shot and the relationship between foreground and background.

The under-construction shots also brought logistical hoops to jump through: hard hats, special training courses – even drug tests. But what he found was a breathtaking feat of human ingenuity. "When I was in the tunnels I had the impression that these are the new streets of London. Crossrail is the new pavement," says Norfolk. "As spaces I loved them. The size, the volume, the depth when you're looking up through shafts, down tunnels that are half a mile long, it's very impressive."

Crossrail is "the trigger", says Norfolk, but beyond this his pictures speak to the singularity of London as a historical site. They're a reminder that to see wonder we don't always need to look up but sometimes down. Buried not far beneath our feet are thousands of years of culture, trade, life and death. The continuity with his other work couldn't be clearer. As he puts it: "It's not destroyed buildings in Afghanistan – but all those ideas about history are there. Empires rising and falling, and leaving their detritus, another layer on another layer."

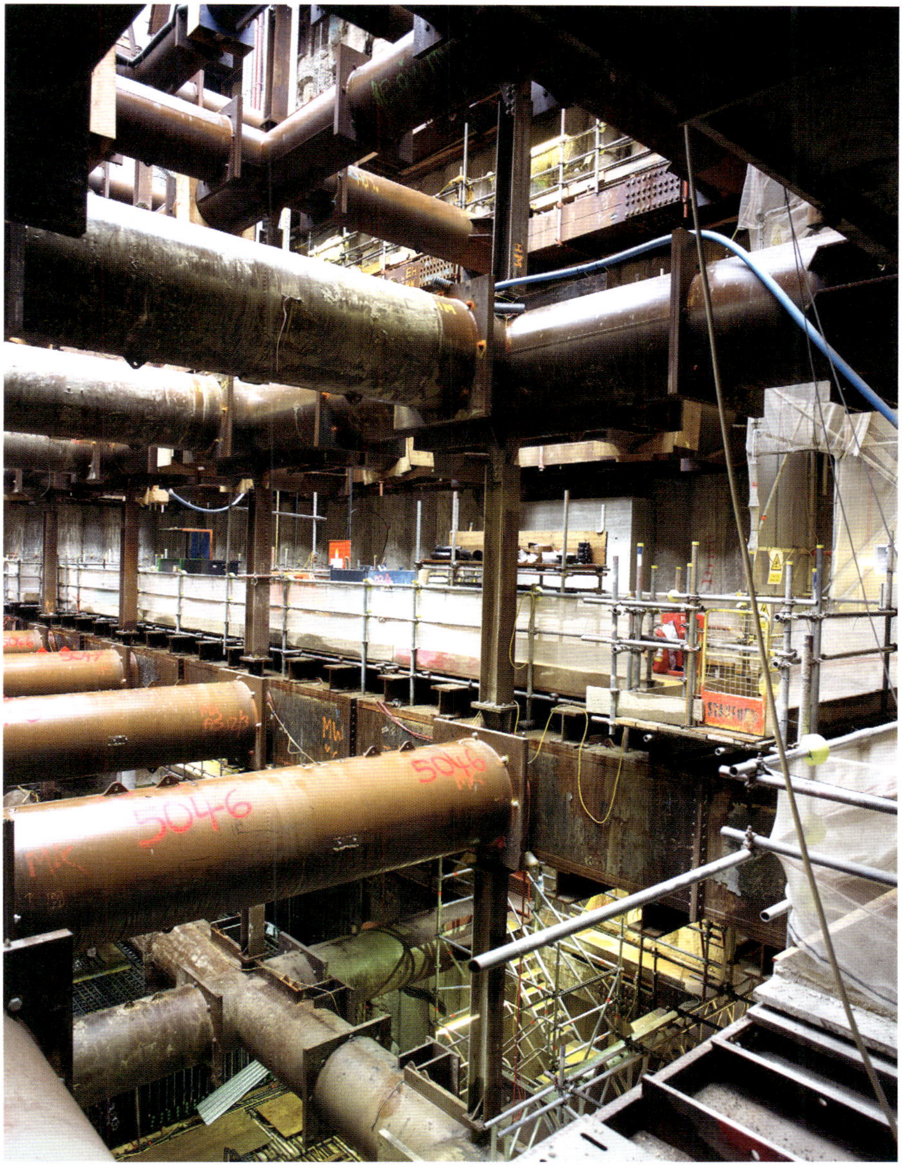

Previous and above: Crossrail construction at Farringdon, 2015

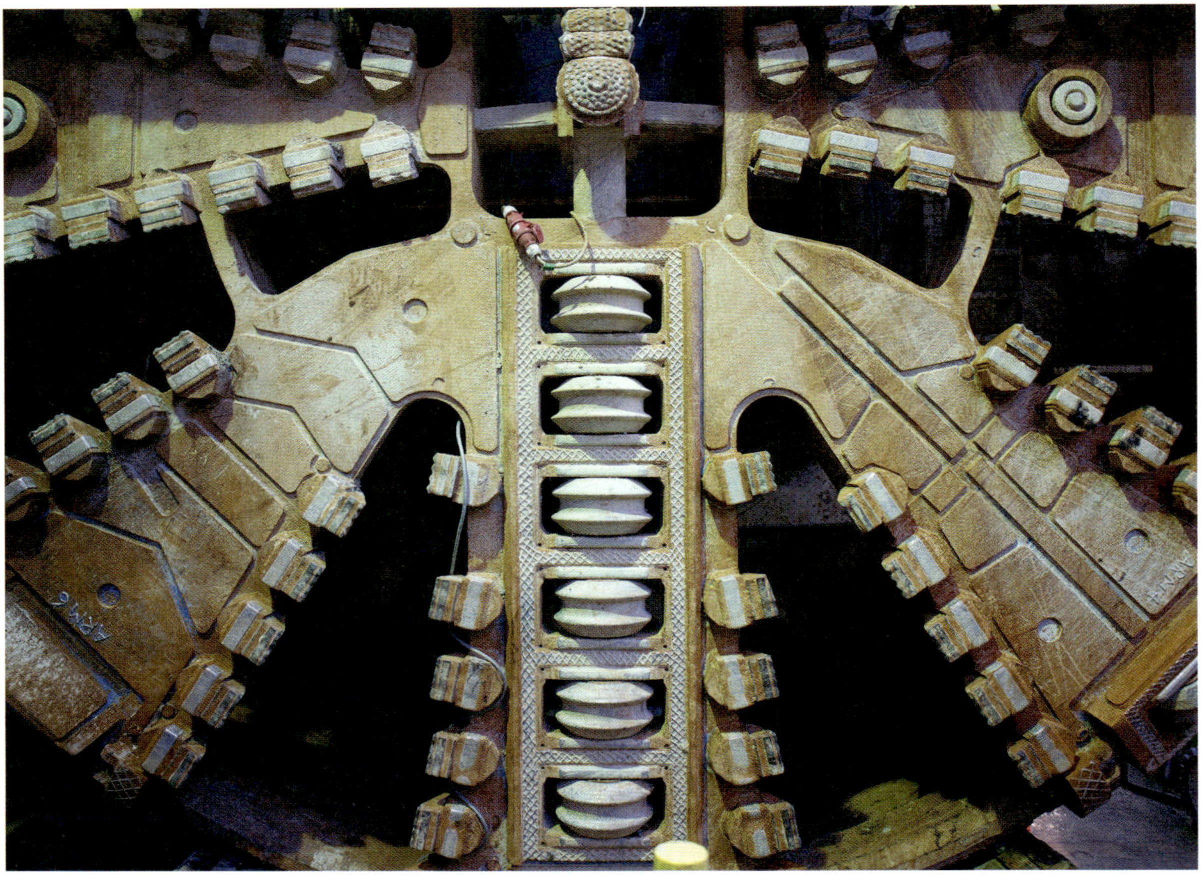

Tunnel boring machine 'Mary' at the North Woolwich portal, 2015

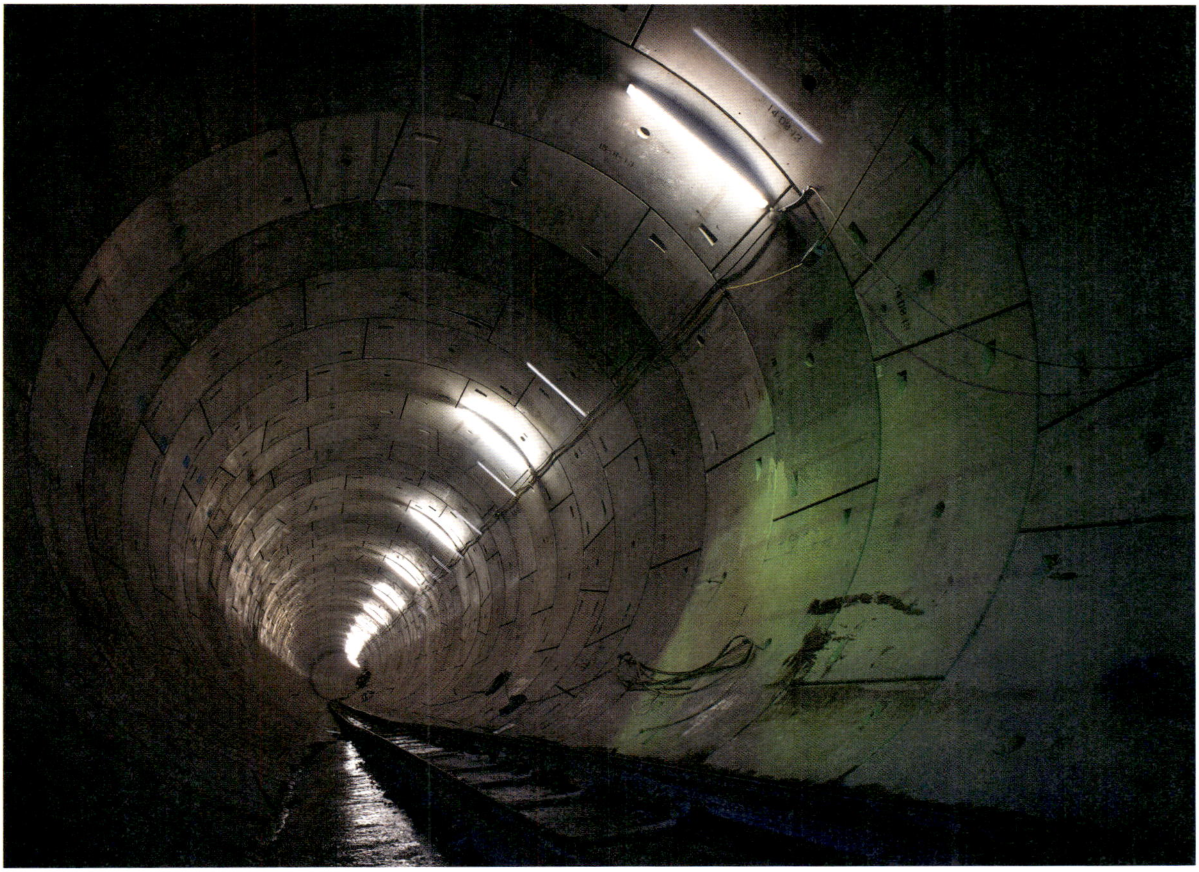

Tunnel boring machine 'Mary' at the North Woolwich portal, 2015
Overleaf: Crossrail tunnels being constructed at Stepney Green, 2015

Simon Norfolk

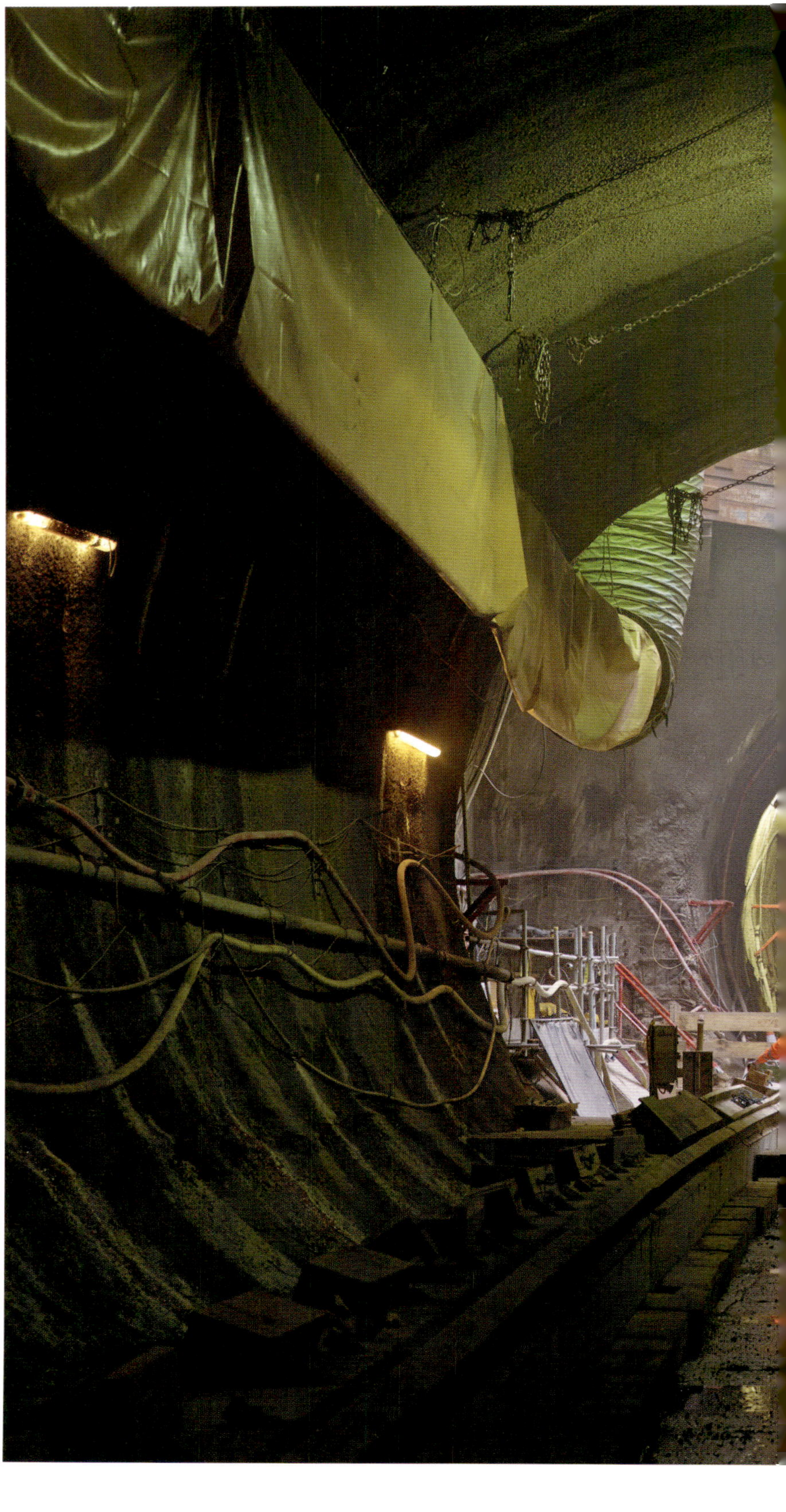

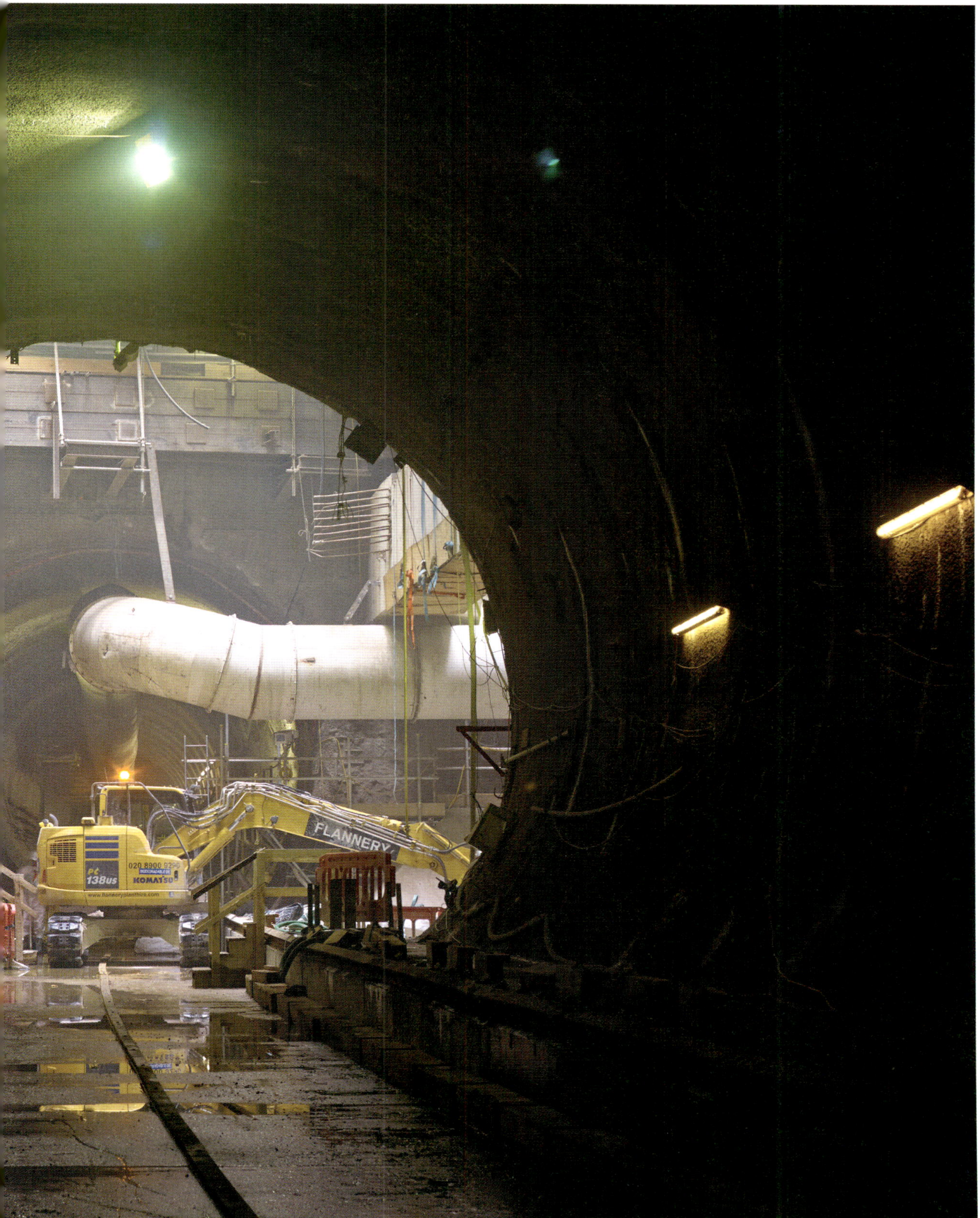
FLANNERY
PC 138us
020 8900 9290
KOMATSU
www.flanneryplanthire.com

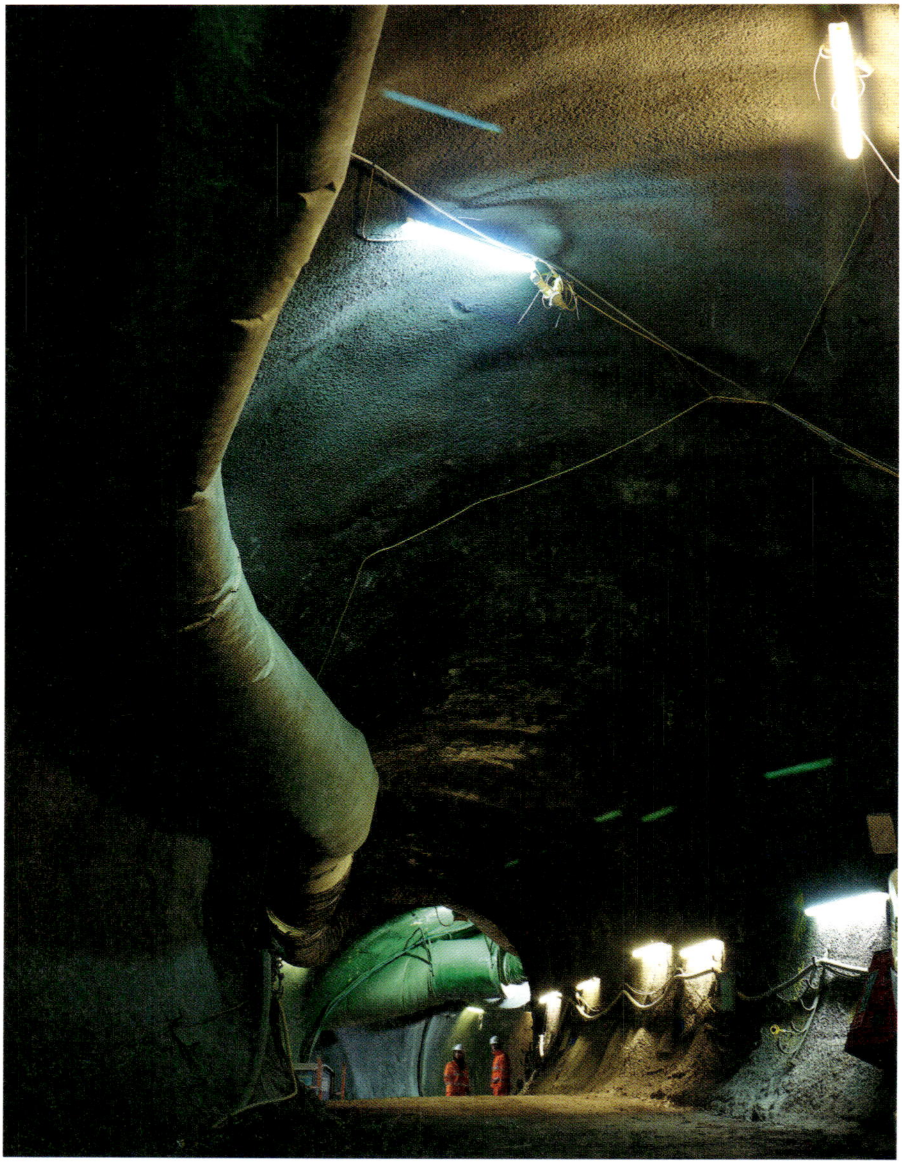

 Crossrail's underground tunnels beneath the City of London, 2015

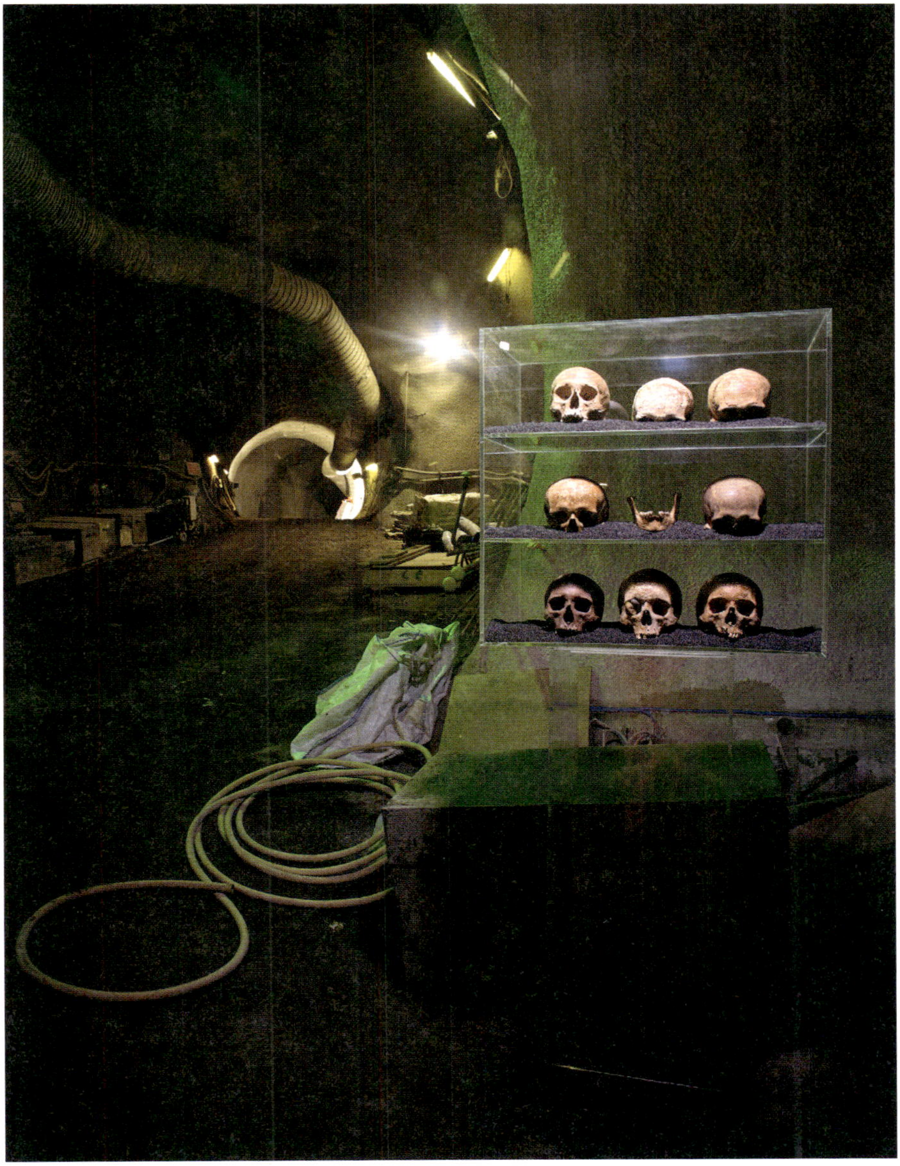

Roman-era skulls, between Moorgate
and Liverpool Street stations, 2015

Simon Norfolk

London: A Modern Project

One photographer's nocturnal rambles around 90s London uncover the soulful beauty of apparently mundane spaces.

Rut Blees Luxemburg

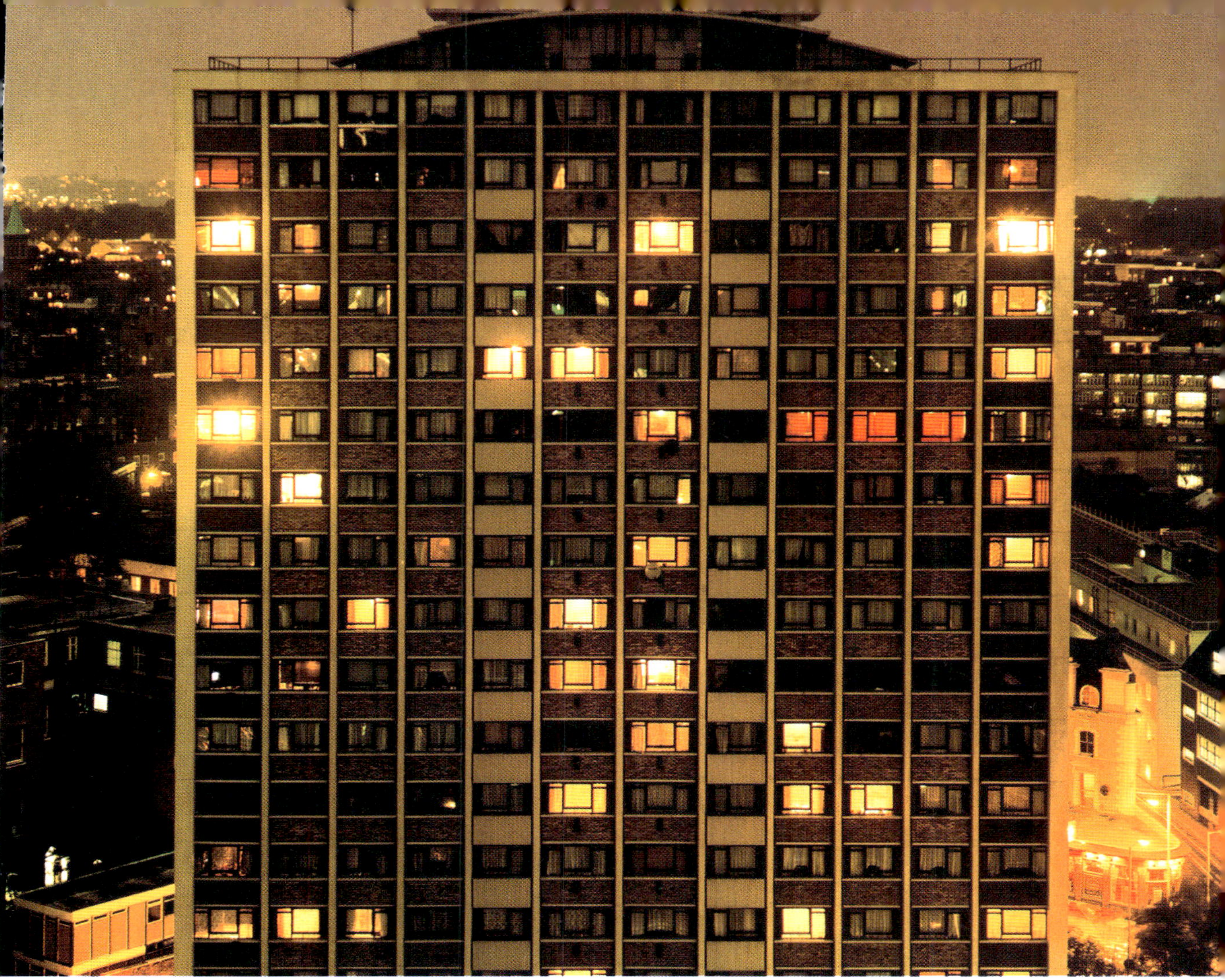

"I still get that rush of adrenalin," Rut Blees Luxemburg says as she looks at 'Vertiginous Exhilaration', her favourite image from *London: A Modern Project*. She took the perspective-bending picture by hanging her camera over the 16th-floor balcony of a high-rise on Old Street. Back then, in the early 90s, "London was a very different place", a place where you could roam around at night holding a conspicuous large-format camera, sneak up council tower blocks and into corporate tennis courts without a second's pause. "It was much easier to navigate the city, to get access to places then – I don't think this would be possible now."

Originally from rural Germany, Blees Luxemburg was in London studying for an MA in Photography at Westminster University when, captivated by the "dynamic and excitement" of the city, she began to photograph its urban landscape. Her strategy was intuitive, responsive, she says, a quest "to find the pulsing core of London". And she found it in unlikely places – the Westway motorway, run-down estates "dismissed as places of social deprivation, unrest". Shot in shades of rusty red, yellow and green, these areas take on a hallucinatory beauty. Even the dirt shimmers. "I'm interested in the residue of life, the things you're not meant to see," says Blees Luxemburg. "That patina is comforting. If it was all clean and perfect it would be repellent, whereas this lets you inhabit the image."

Due to long exposure times of between 7 and 10 minutes, no figures are perceptible in the frame. During that time, though, people came and went, turned the lights in their flats on and off, parked their cars, drove away. You can see evidence of this human activity in the streams of light that appear almost like scratches, scars on the road. "You never knew what you were going to get – there's an element of suspense, of chance," says Blees Luxemburg. But this isn't the chance of the street photographer who throws him or herself into the crowd in search of what Henri Cartier-Bresson described as "decisive moments", when everything comes together in perfect harmony in the frame. We're not looking at an instant, we're looking at a period of time compressed.

The legacies of this series have been many – not least that it gave Blees Luxemburg a preoccupation with London itself. Her work has been infused with the city ever since – from her personal self-initiated series *Liebeslied* and *London Dust*, to commissions such as *Silver Forest*, a 7×30m photographic installation on the facade of Westminster City Hall. Since being published as a book in 1997, pictures from *London: A Modern Project* have appeared in exhibitions, books, under a bridge in Shoreditch, and, famously, on album covers for The Streets and Bloc Party.

"That made a real impact," says Blees Luxemburg, pleased that The Streets' poster campaign across London and other cities meant that her photography reached new audiences. "It was great to see it become a public artwork." Because in the end that's what Blees Luxemburg's work is all about: what counts as public space and what's lost when that space is no longer shared. "In London, civic space has been eroded as it becomes commercial space or gated communities. For me, these were spaces of freedom," she says, "of poetic immersion and love."

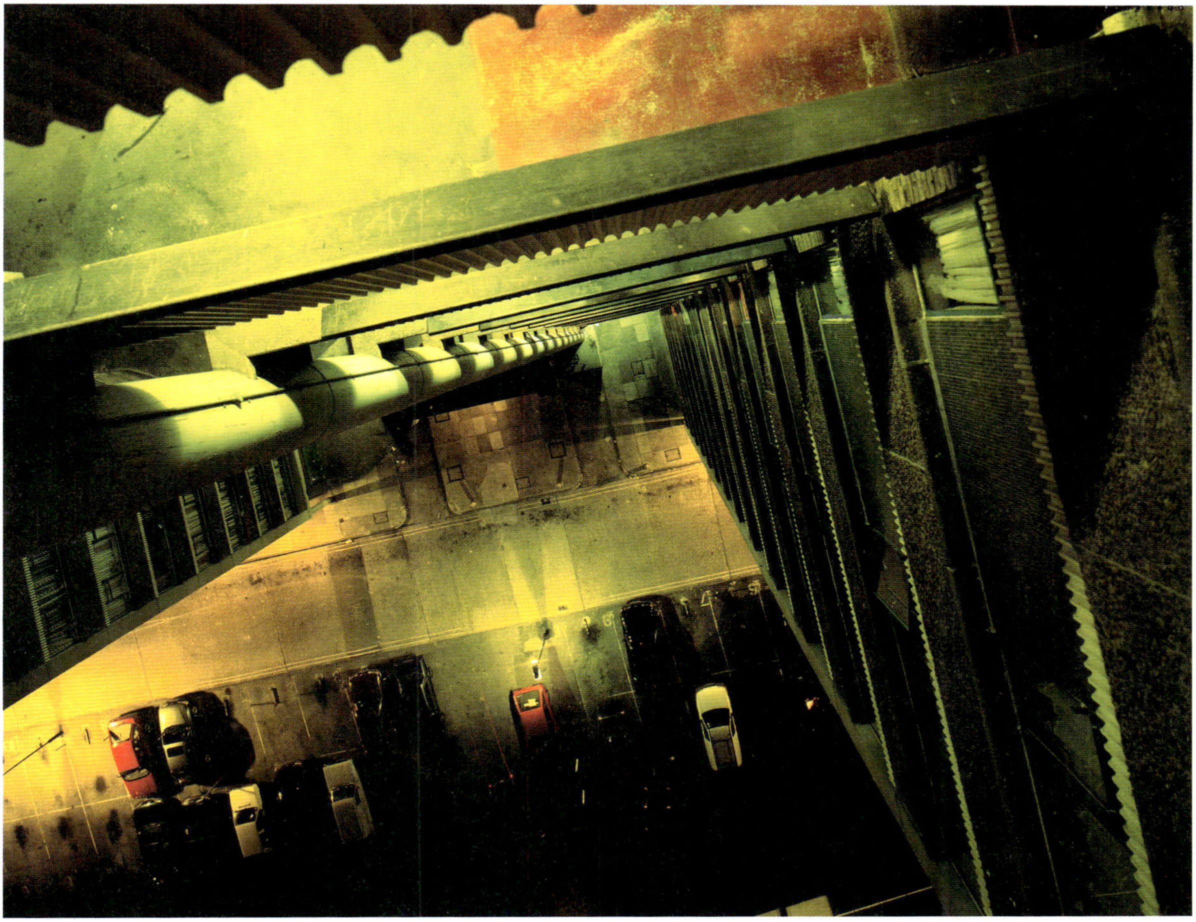

Previous: London – A Modern Project, London, 1995
Above: Vertiginous Exhilaration, London, 1995
Overleaf: A Modern Project, London, 1996

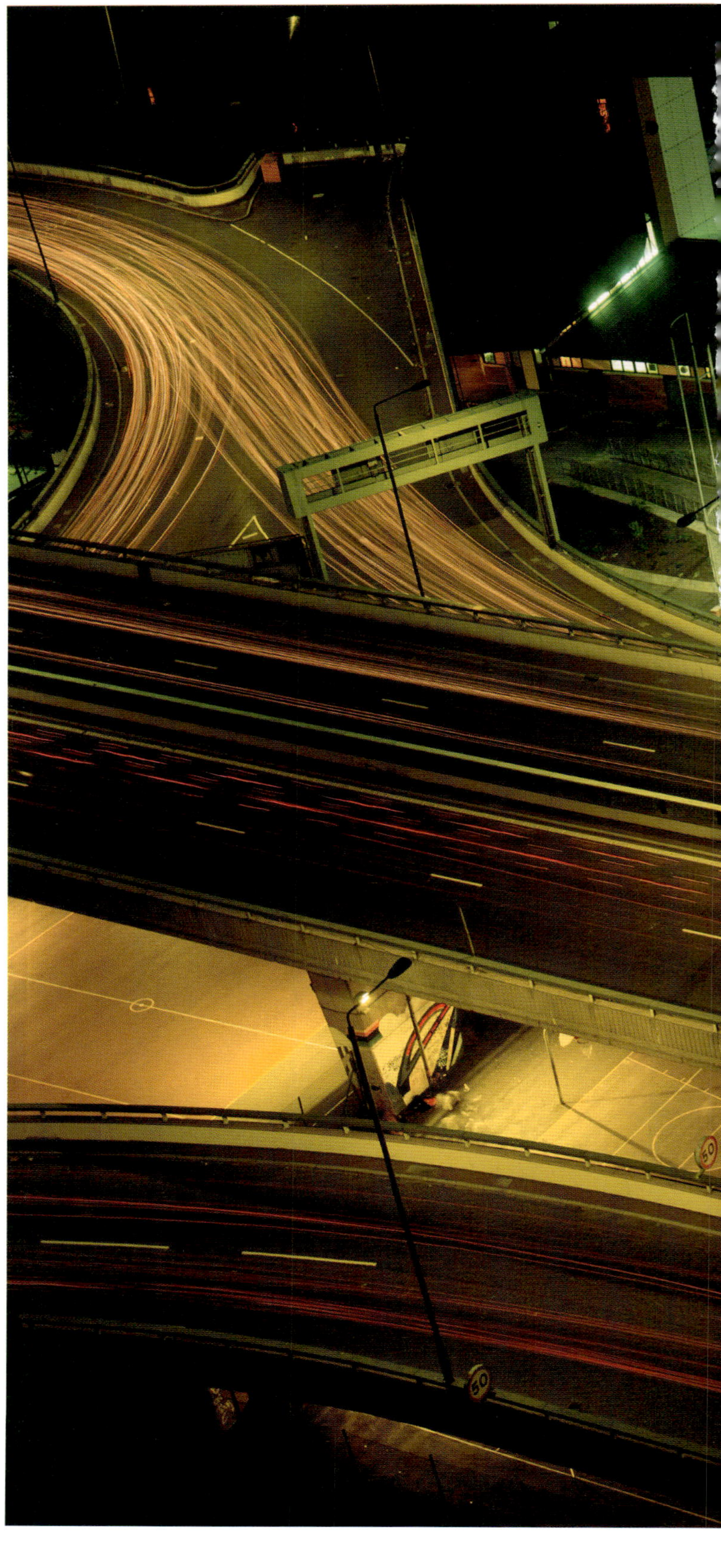
50
50

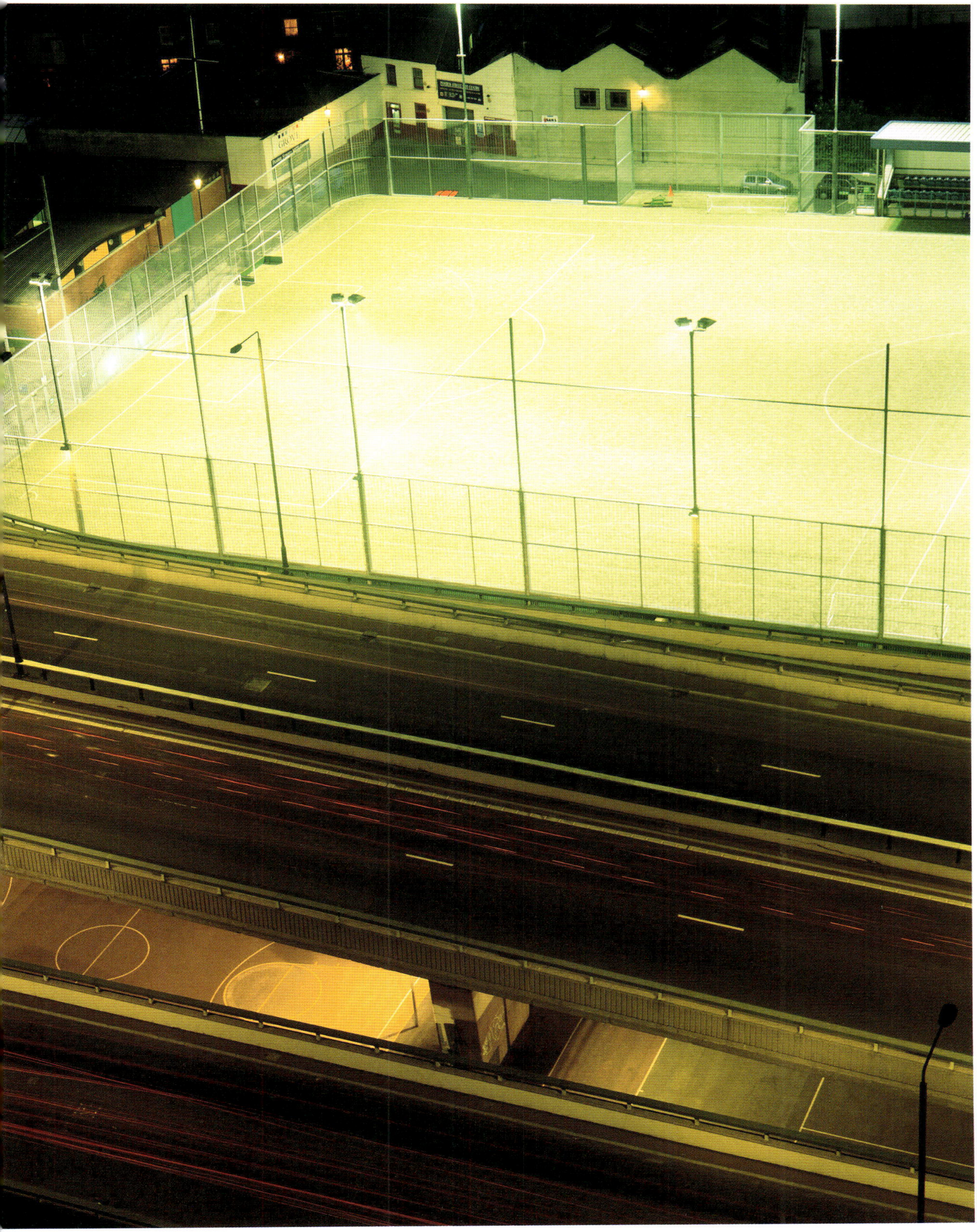

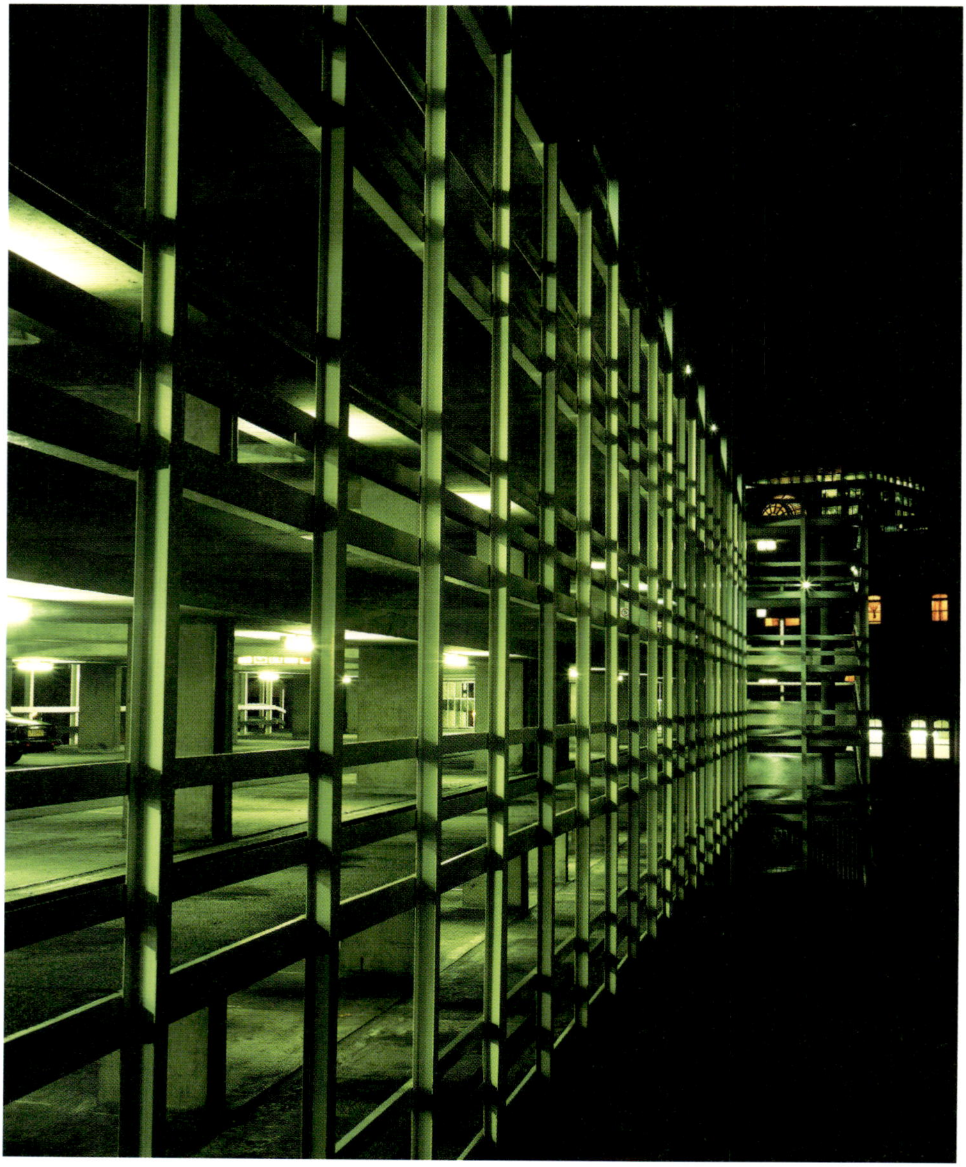

Parkhaus I, London, 1996

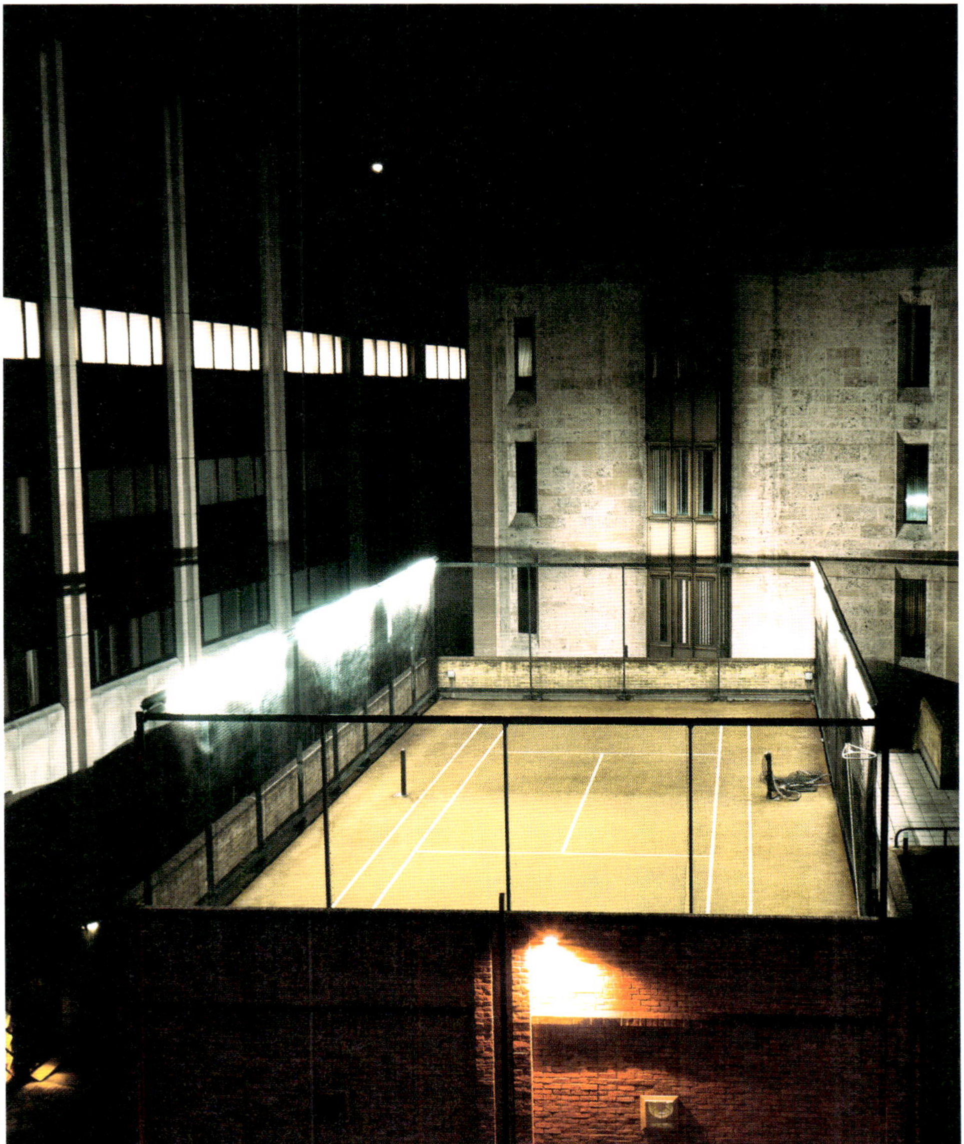

Corporate Leisure, London, 1997

Overleaf: Mount Pleasant, London, 1997

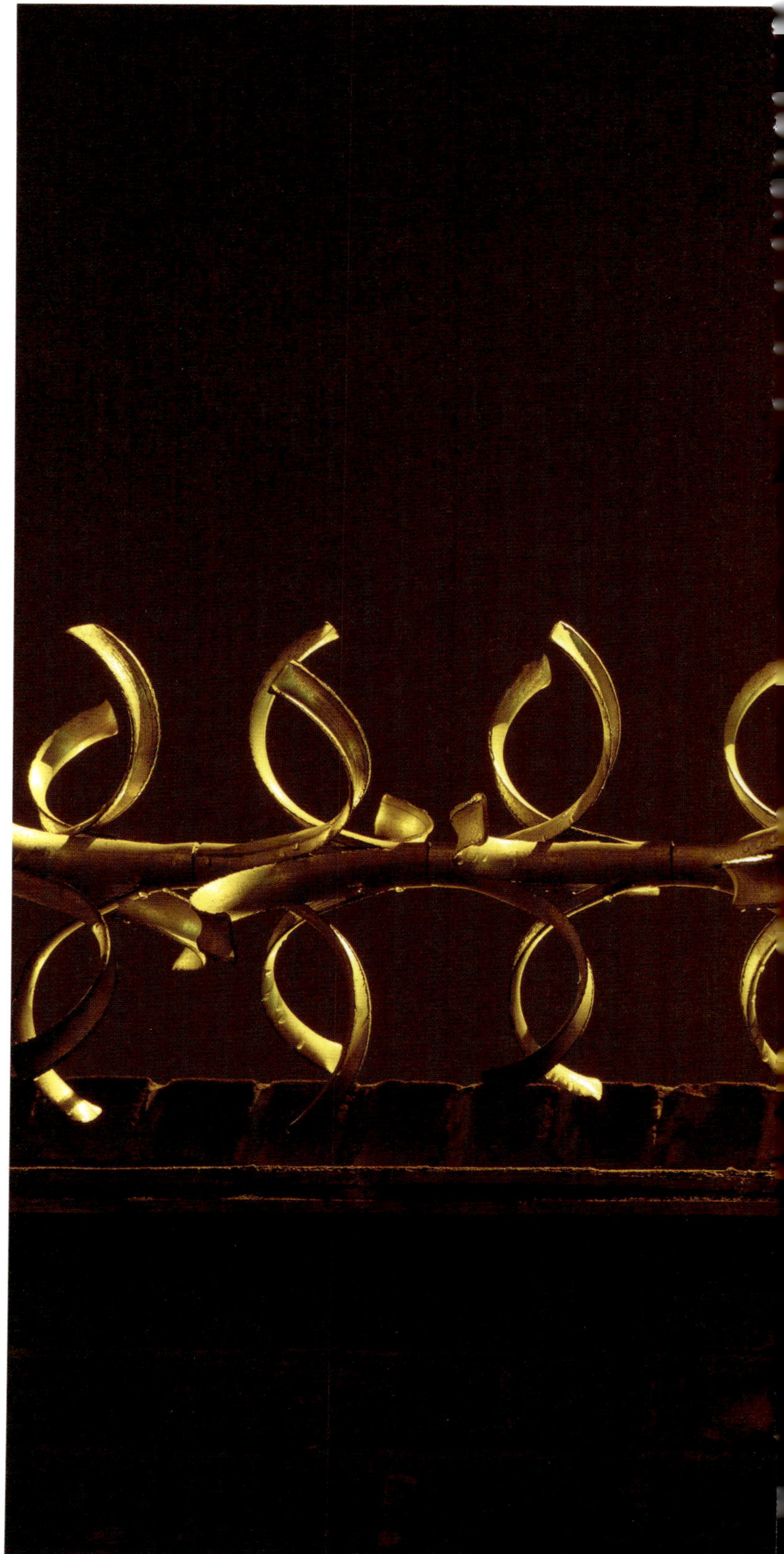

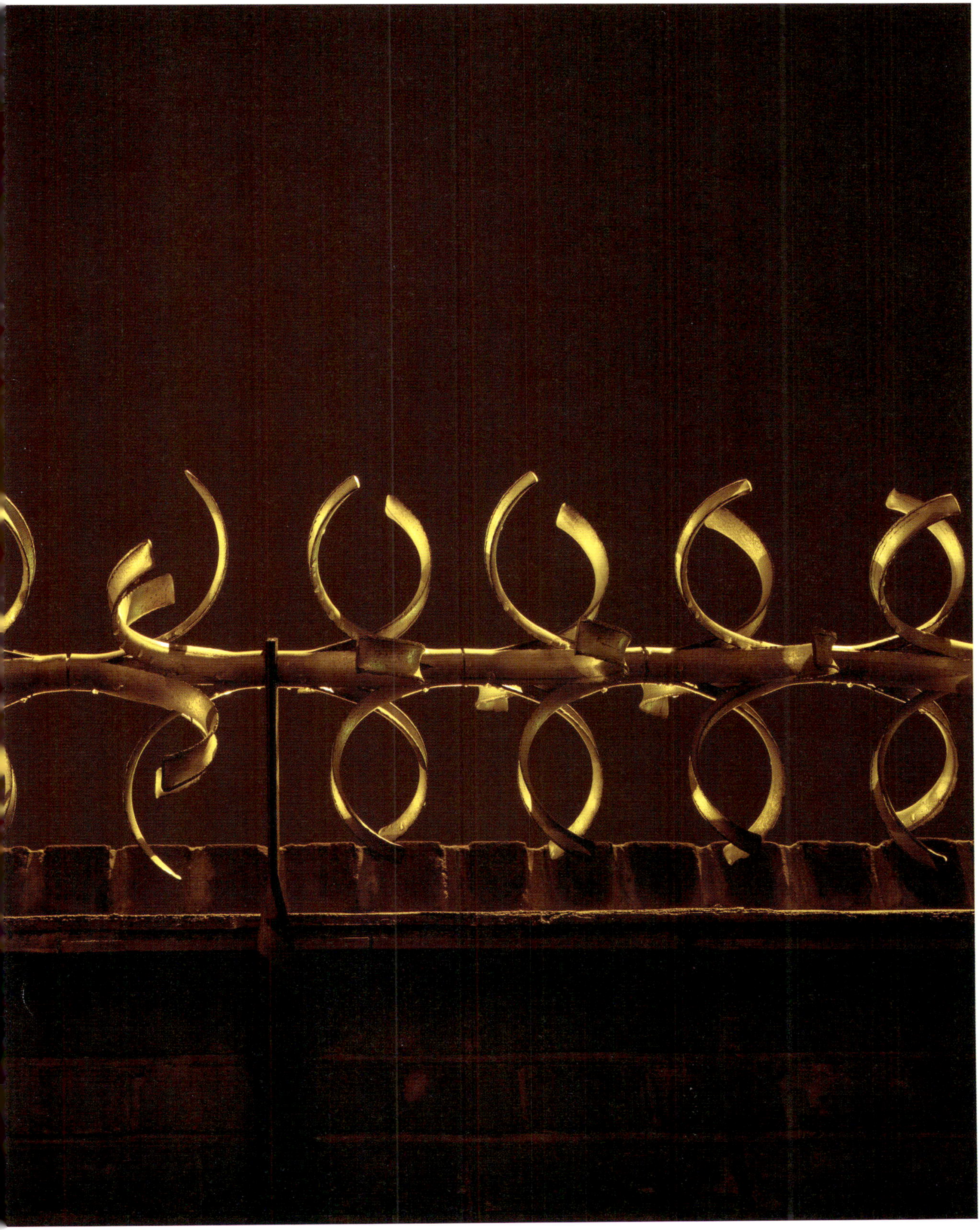

Unseen London
First Edition

Copyediting by Kate Solomon
Design and sequence by Hoxton Mini Press with A Practice for Everyday Life
Special thanks to Gemma Fletcher and Jamie Allen Shaw for creative consultations

Cover: *On the Night Bus*, #12, London, 2014–16 by Nick Turpin
Back cover: *All That Life Can Afford*, Regent Street, 2004–16 by Matt Stuart
Images on p.8 courtesy Getty Images
Image on p.10 © Estate of Roger Mayne/Museum of London
Image on p.11 © Tracey Emin. All rights reserved, DACS/Artimage 2017, courtesy White Cube
Image on p.17: *Sketch*, Untitled, British Museum, 02.11.15 by David Vintiner
Images for Dougie Wallace and Simon Norfolk courtesy INSTITUTE
Images for Thom and Beth Atkinson courtesy Hwæt Books

A CIP catalogue record for this book is available from the British Library.

ISBN 978-1-910566-24-4

First published in the United Kingdom in 2017 by Hoxton Mini Press.

Printed and bound by: Livonia Print, Latvia

To order books, collector's editions and signed prints please go to:
hoxtonminipress.com

MIX
Paper from responsible sources
FSC www.fsc.org FSC® C002795